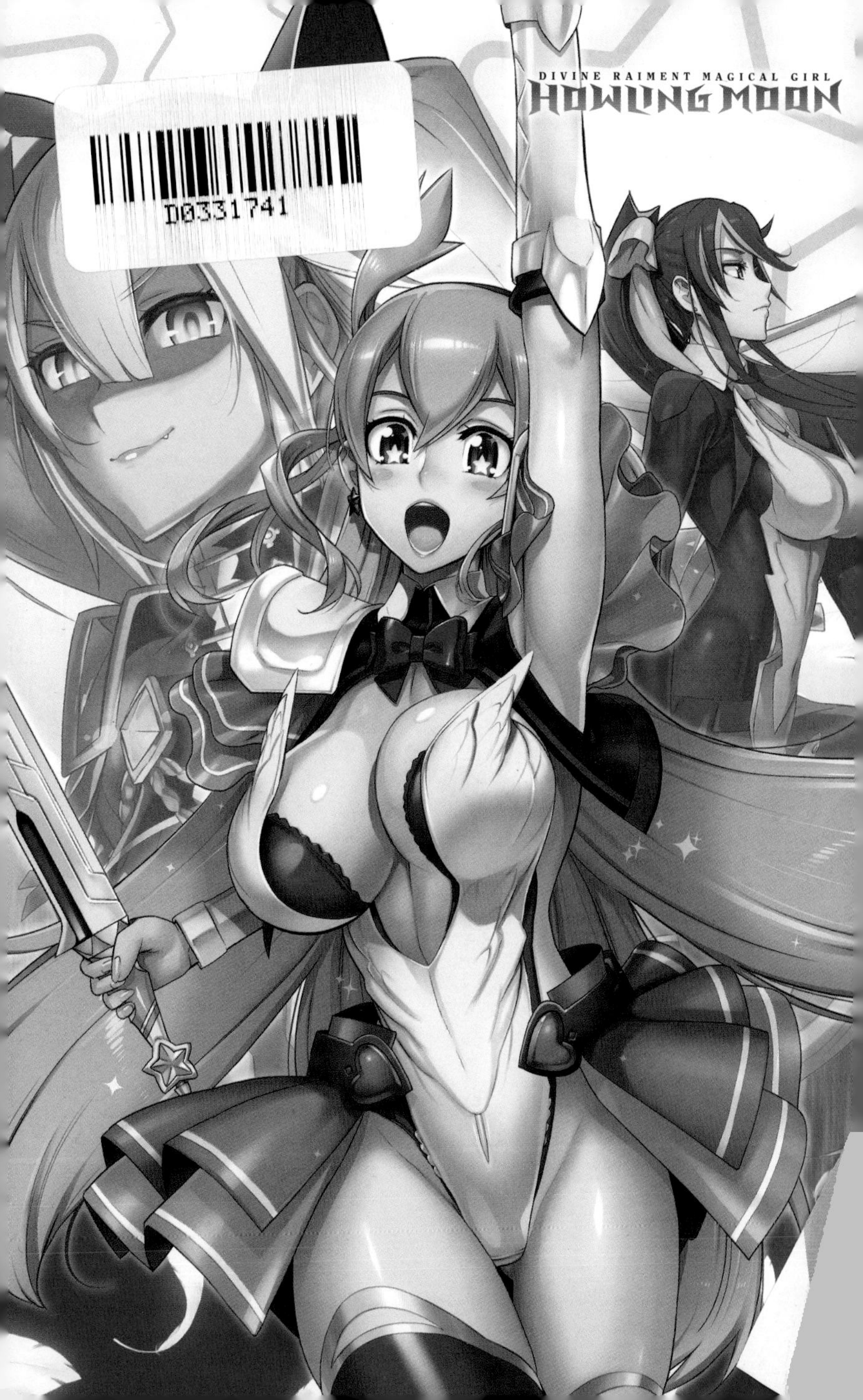
DIVINE RAIMENT MAGICAL GIRL
HOWLING MOON

DIVINE RAIMENT MAGICAL GIRL
HOWLING MOON

CONTENTS

DIVINE RAIMENT MAGICAL GIRL
HOWLING MOON

Story: **KENJI SAITO** Art: **SHOUJI SATO**

2

Translation: **KO RANSOM**   Lettering: **ANTHONY QUINTESSENZA**

Volume

SHINSO MAHOSHOJO HOWLING MOON Volume 2
© Kenji Saito 2019 © Shouji Sato 2019
First published in Japan in 2019 by KADOKAWA CORPORATION, Tokyo.
English translation rights arranged with KADOKAWA CORPORATION, Tokyo through
TUTTLE-MORI AGENCY, INC., Tokyo.

English translation © 2020 by Yen Press, LLC

Yen Press
150 West 30th Street, 19th Floor
New York, NY 10001

Visit us at yenpress.com
facebook.com/yenpress
twitter.com/yenpress
yenpress.tumblr.com
instagram.com/yenpress

First Yen Press Edition: May 2020
Yen Press is an imprint of Yen Press, LLC.
The Yen Press name and logo are trademarks of Yen Press, LLC.

The publisher is not responsible for websites (or their content) that are not owned by the publisher.

Library of Congress Control Number: 2019935204

ISBNs: 978-1-9753-1075-2 (paperback)
978-1-9753-1074-5 (ebook)

10 9 8 7 6 5 4 3 2 1

WOR

Printed in the United States of America

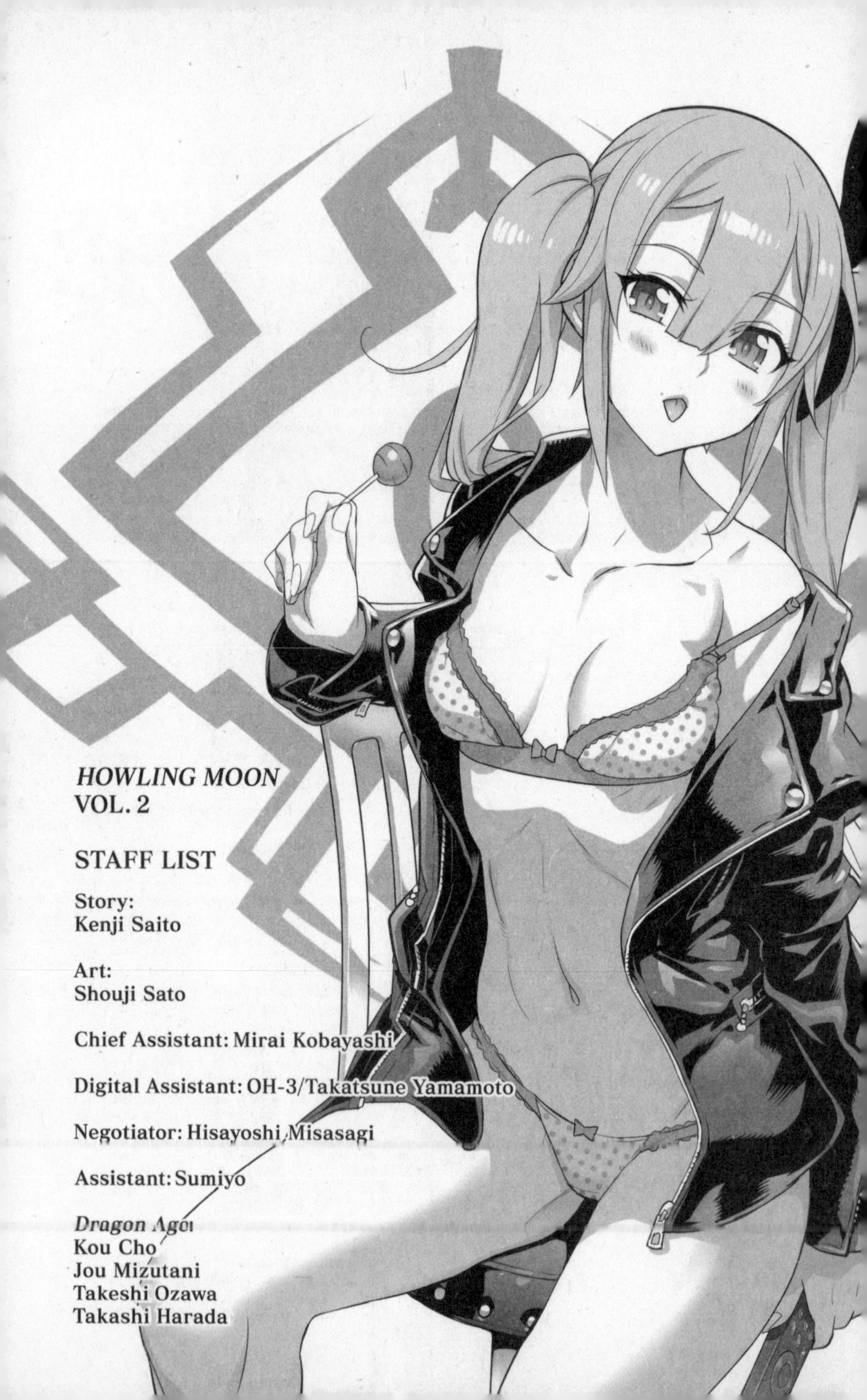

HOWLING MOON
VOL. 2

STAFF LIST

Story:
Kenji Saito

Art:
Shouji Sato

Chief Assistant: Mirai Kobayashi

Digital Assistant: OH-3/Takatsune Yamamoto

Negotiator: Hisayoshi Misasagi

Assistant: Sumiyo

Dragon Age
Kou Cho
Jou Mizutani
Takeshi Ozawa
Takashi Harada

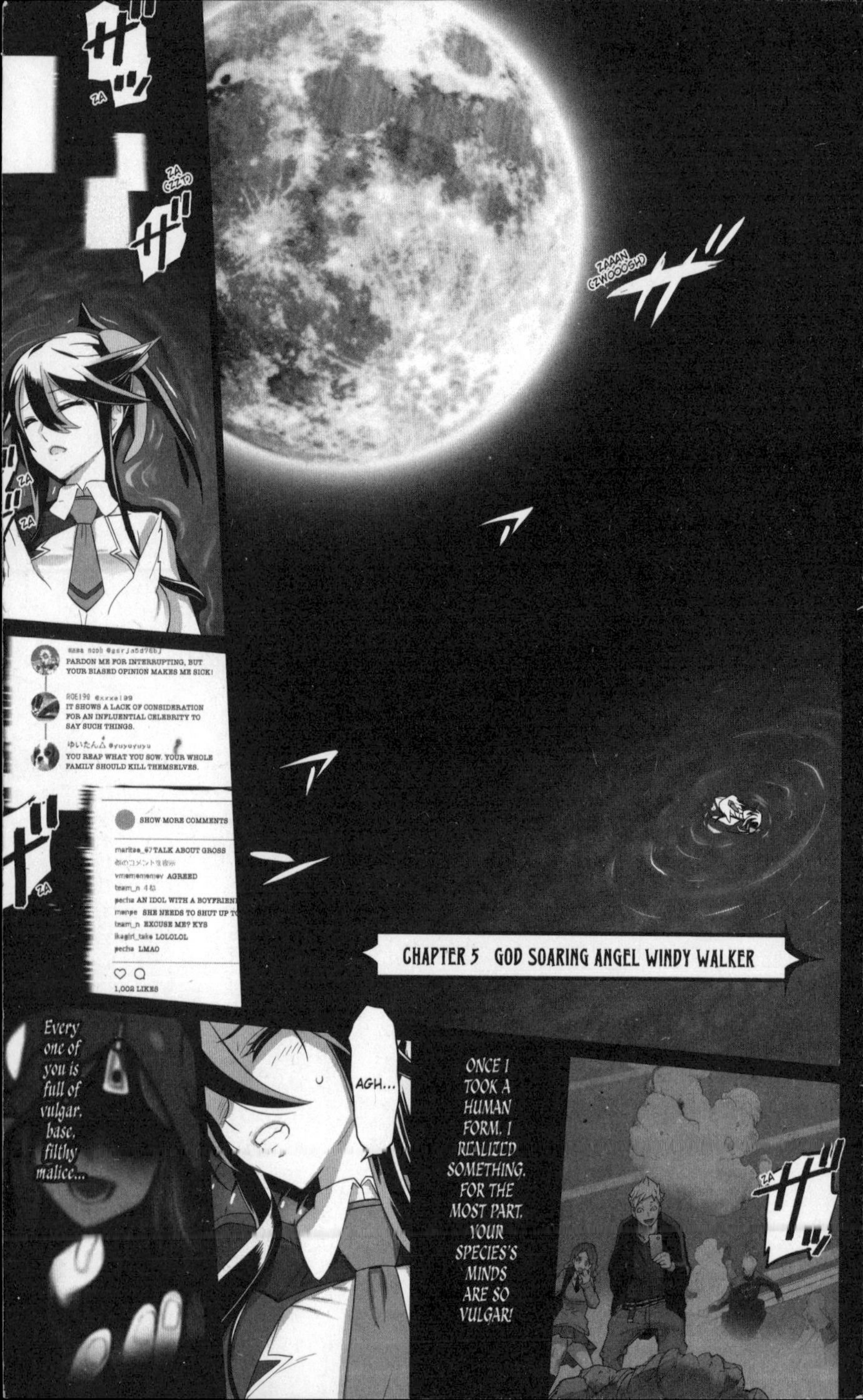
ZAAAN (ZWOOOSH)
ZA
ZA (ZZZT)
ZA
ZA
PARDON ME FOR INTERRUPTING, BUT YOUR BIASED OPINION MAKES ME SICK!
ROE199
IT SHOWS A LACK OF CONSIDERATION FOR AN INFLUENTIAL CELEBRITY TO SAY SUCH THINGS.
ゆいたん
YOU REAP WHAT YOU SOW. YOUR WHOLE FAMILY SHOULD KILL THEMSELVES.
ZA
SHOW MORE COMMENTS
TALK ABOUT GROSS
AGREED
AN IDOL WITH A BOYFRIEN
SHE NEEDS TO SHUT UP T
team_n EXCUSE ME? KYS
LOLOLOL
pecha LMAO
1,002 LIKES
CHAPTER 5 GOD SOARING ANGEL WINDY WALKER
ZA
ONCE I TOOK A HUMAN FORM, I REALIZED SOMETHING. FOR THE MOST PART, YOUR SPECIES'S MINDS ARE SO VULGAR!
AGH...
Every one of you is full of vulgar, base, filthy malice...

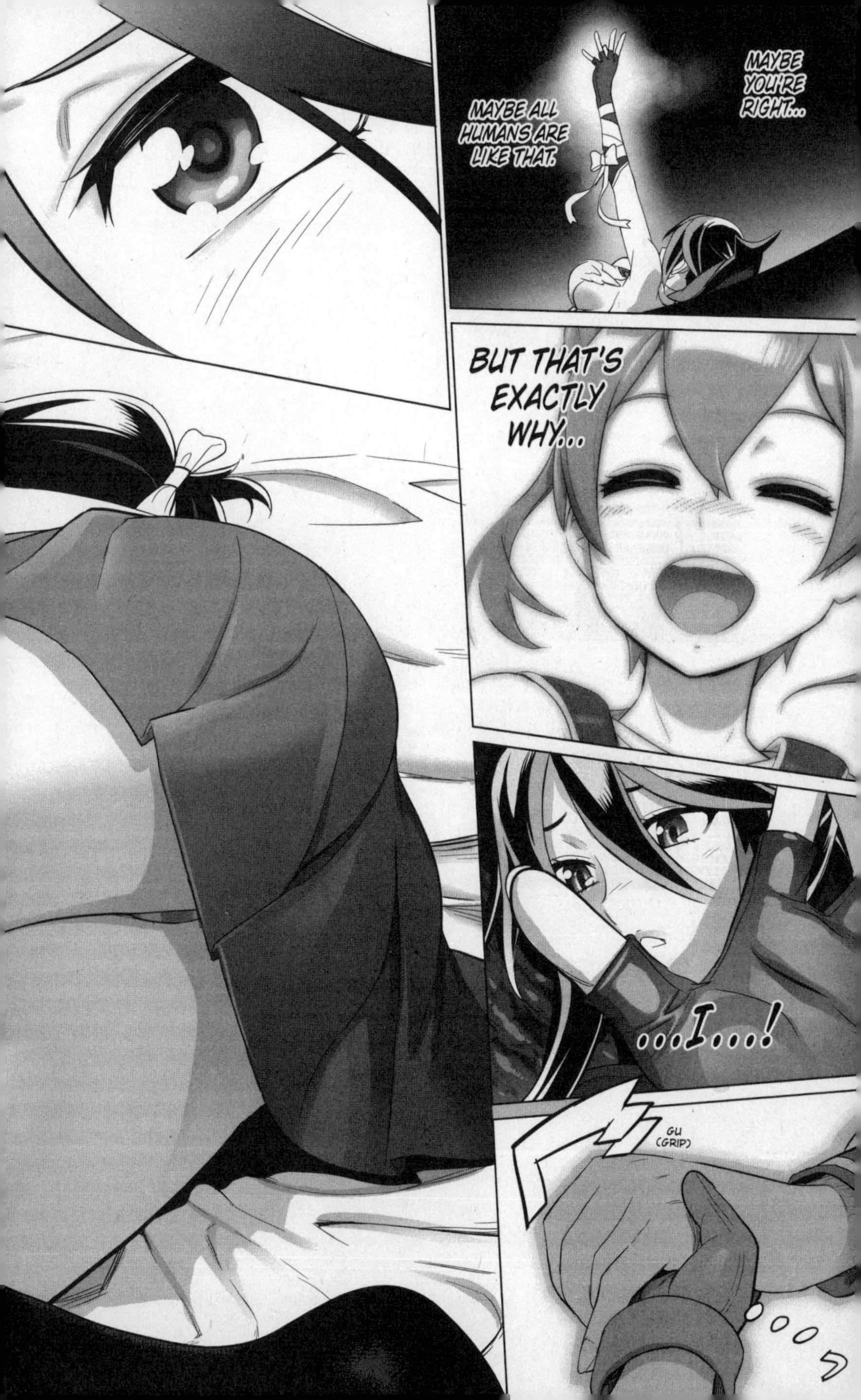
MAYBE YOU'RE RIGHT...
MAYBE ALL HUMANS ARE LIKE THAT.
BUT THAT'S EXACTLY WHY...
...I...!
GU (GRIP)

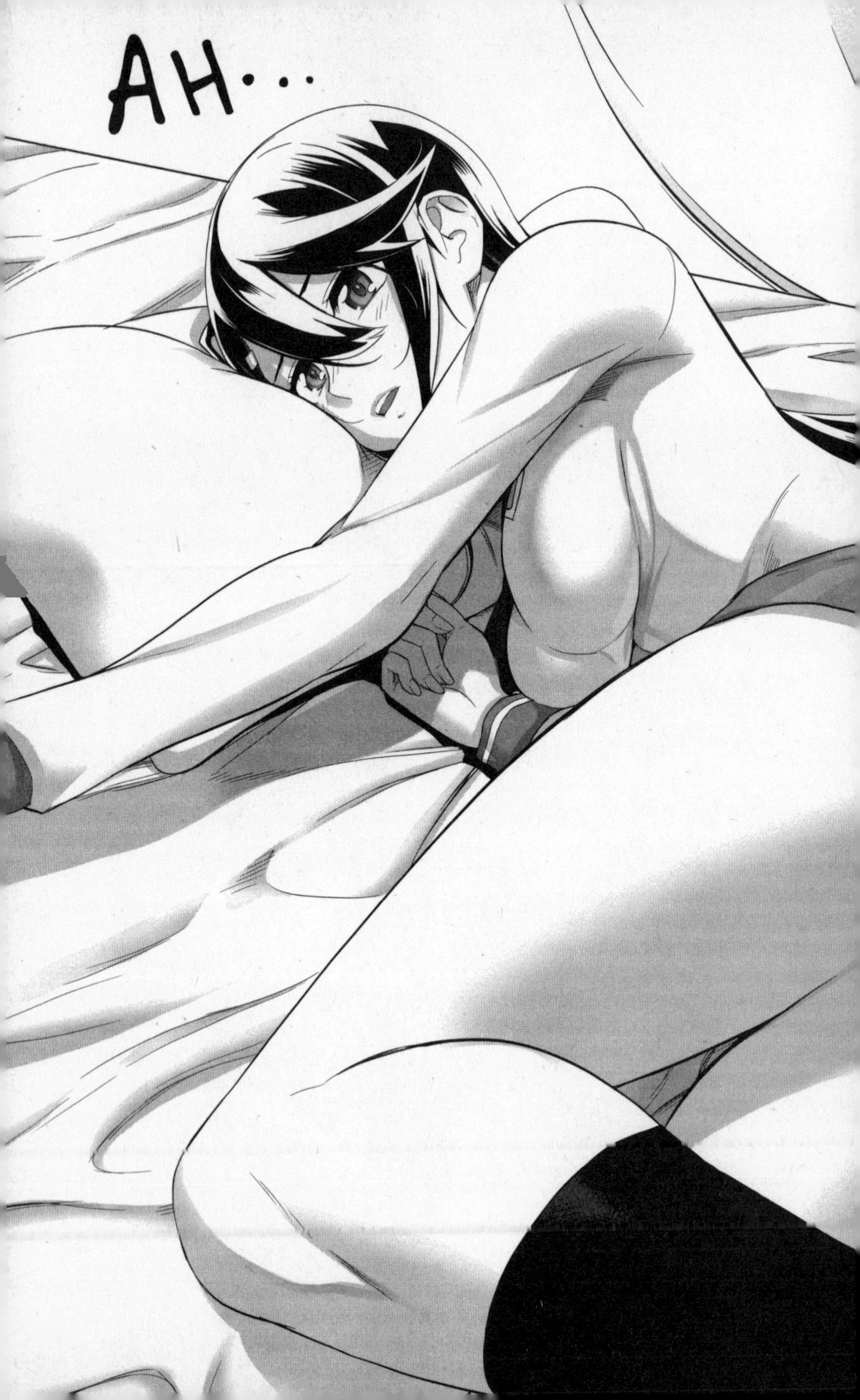
AH...

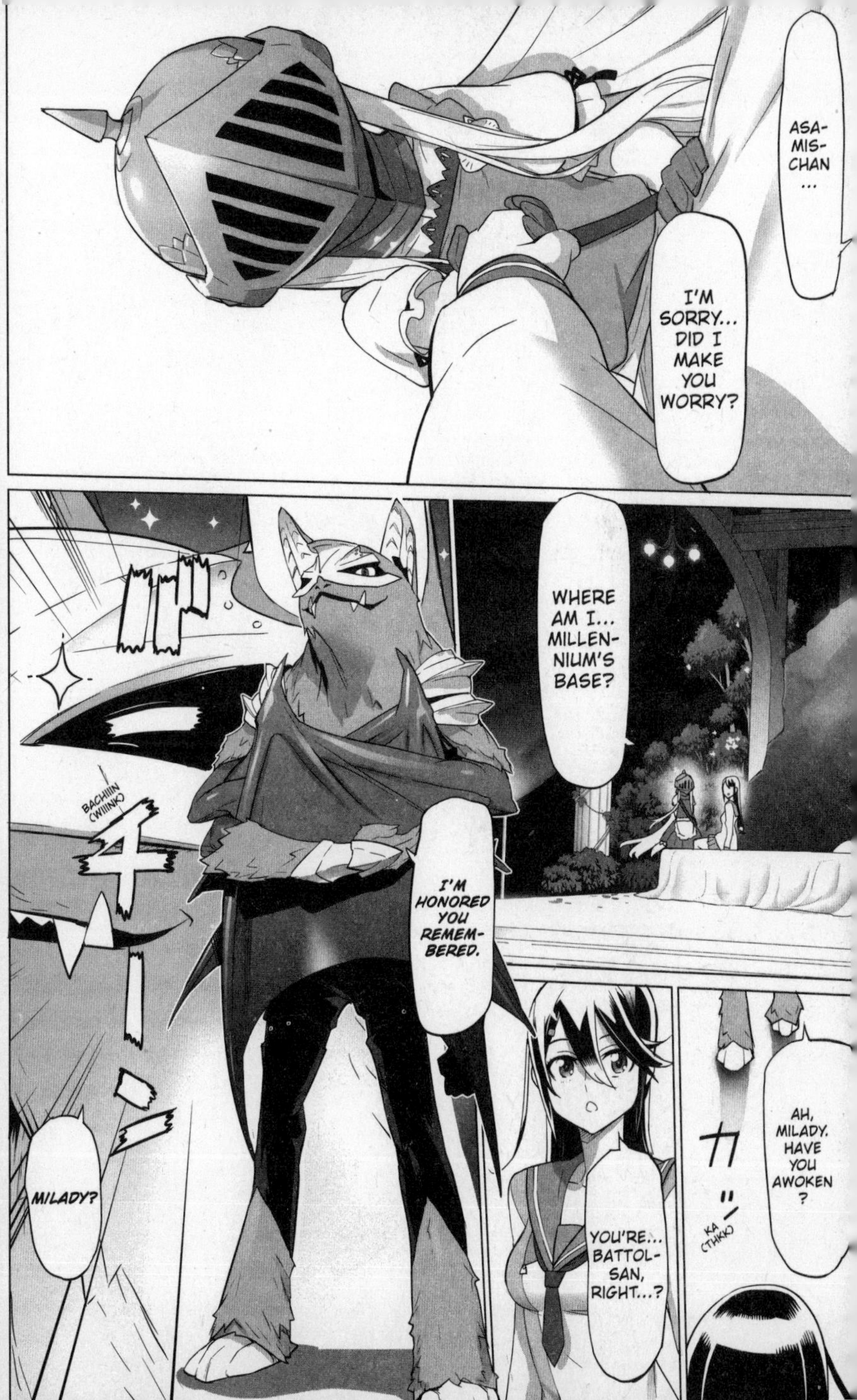
ASA-MIS-CHAN...
I'M SORRY... DID I MAKE YOU WORRY?
WHERE AM I... MILLENNIUM'S BASE?
AH, MILADY. HAVE YOU AWOKEN?
KA (THKK)
YOU'RE... BATTOL-SAN, RIGHT...?
I'M HONORED YOU REMEMBERED.
BACHIIIN (WIIINK)
MILADY?

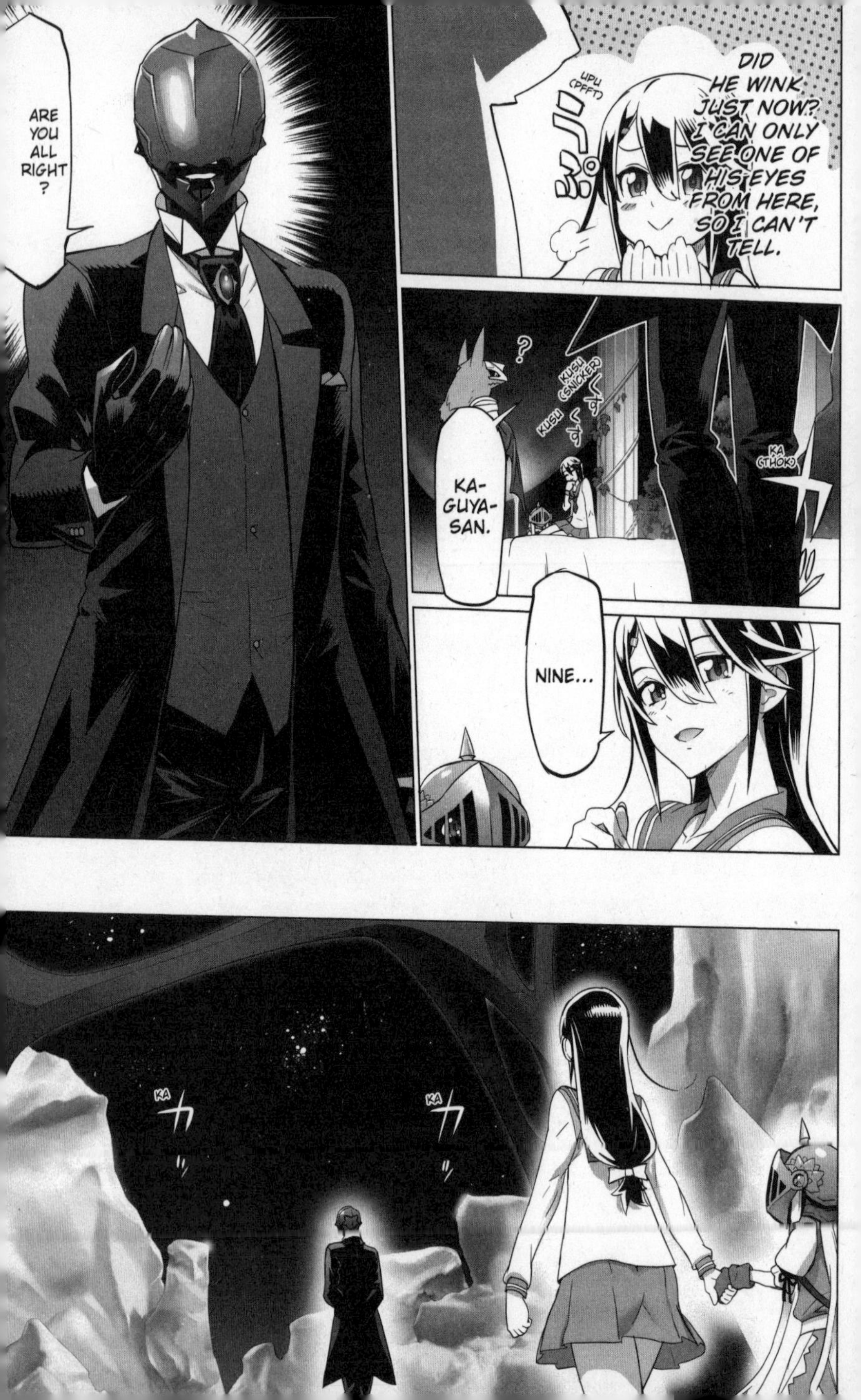

UPU (PFFT)
DID HE WINK JUST NOW? I CAN ONLY SEE ONE OF HIS EYES FROM HERE, SO I CAN'T TELL.
?
KUSU (SNICKER) KUSU
KA (THOK)
KA-GUYA-SAN.
NINE...
ARE YOU ALL RIGHT?
KA
KA

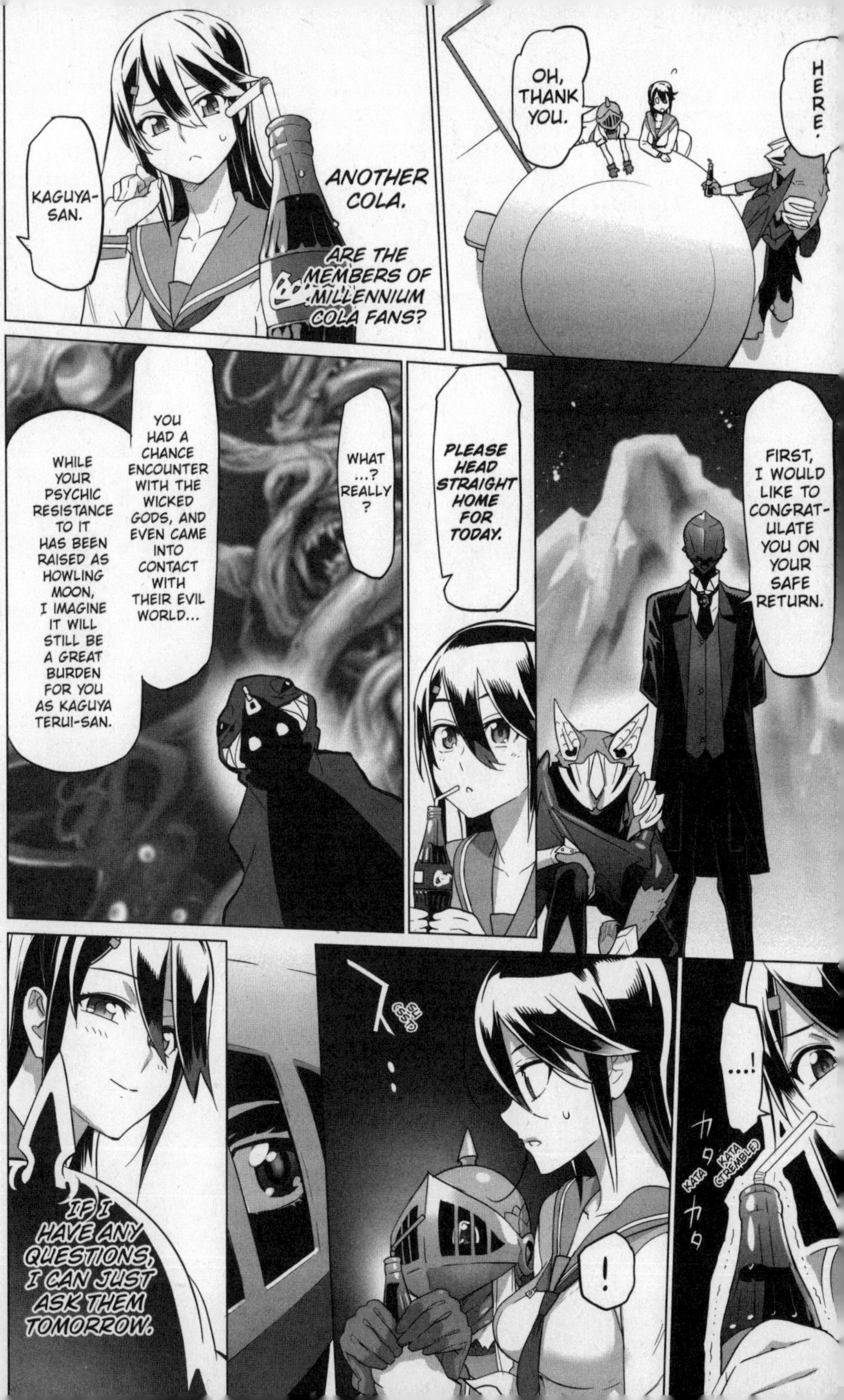

HERE.
OH, THANK YOU.
ANOTHER COLA.
ARE THE MEMBERS OF MILLENNIUM COLA FANS?
KAGUYA-SAN.
FIRST, I WOULD LIKE TO CONGRAT-ULATE YOU ON YOUR SAFE RETURN.
PLEASE HEAD STRAIGHT HOME FOR TODAY.
WHAT ...? REALLY?
YOU HAD A CHANCE ENCOUNTER WITH THE WICKED GODS, AND EVEN CAME INTO CONTACT WITH THEIR EVIL WORLD...
WHILE YOUR PSYCHIC RESISTANCE TO IT HAS BEEN RAISED AS HOWLING MOON, I IMAGINE IT WILL STILL BE A GREAT BURDEN FOR YOU AS KAGUYA TERUI-SAN.
...!
KATA KATA (TREMBLE)
SU (SST)
...
!
IF I HAVE ANY QUESTIONS, I CAN JUST ASK THEM TOMORROW.

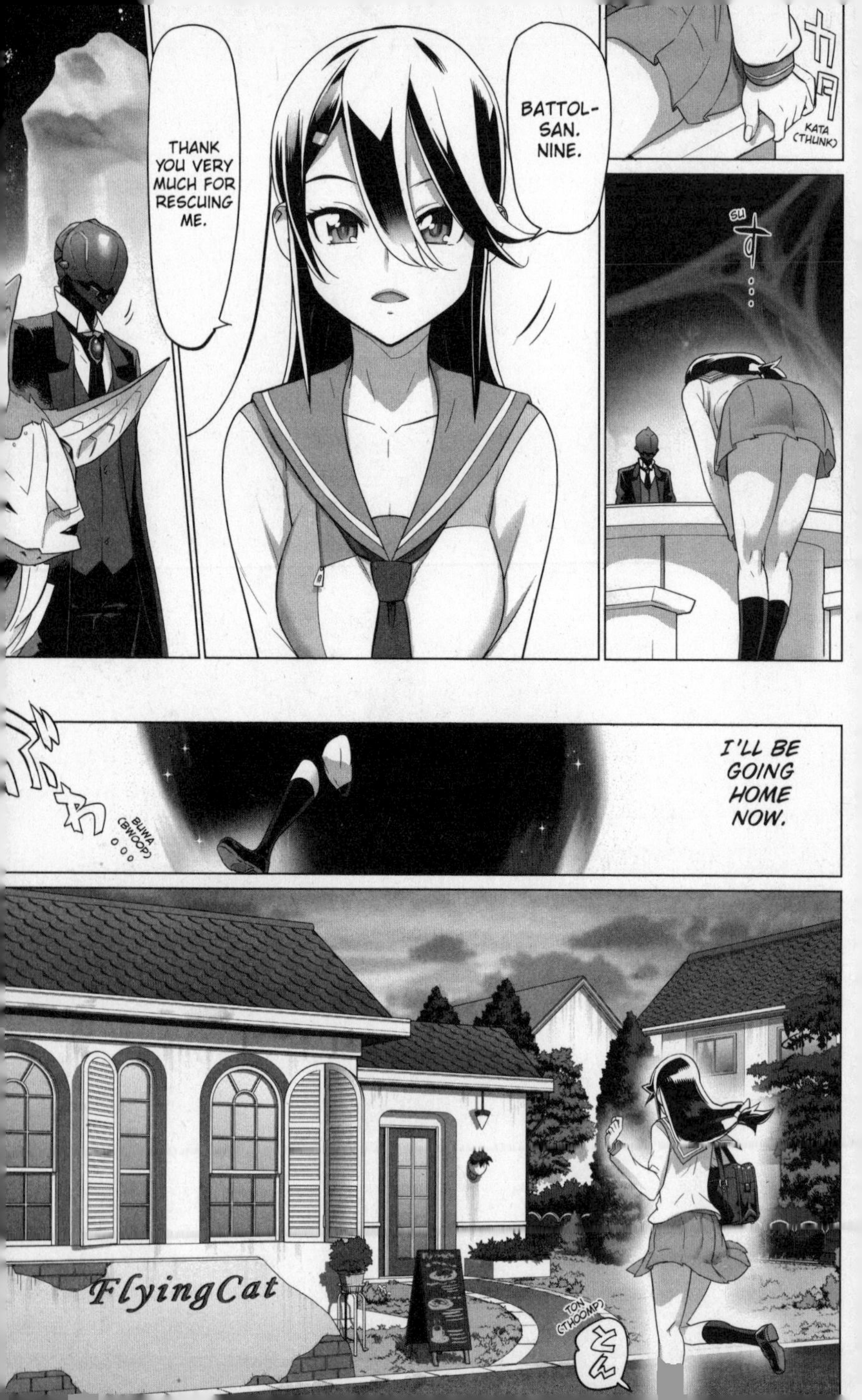
カタ
KATA (THUNK)
す…
SU
BATTOL-SAN. NINE.
THANK YOU VERY MUCH FOR RESCUING ME.
I'LL BE GOING HOME NOW.
ぶわ
BUWA (BWOOP)
とん
TON (THOOMP)
FlyingCat

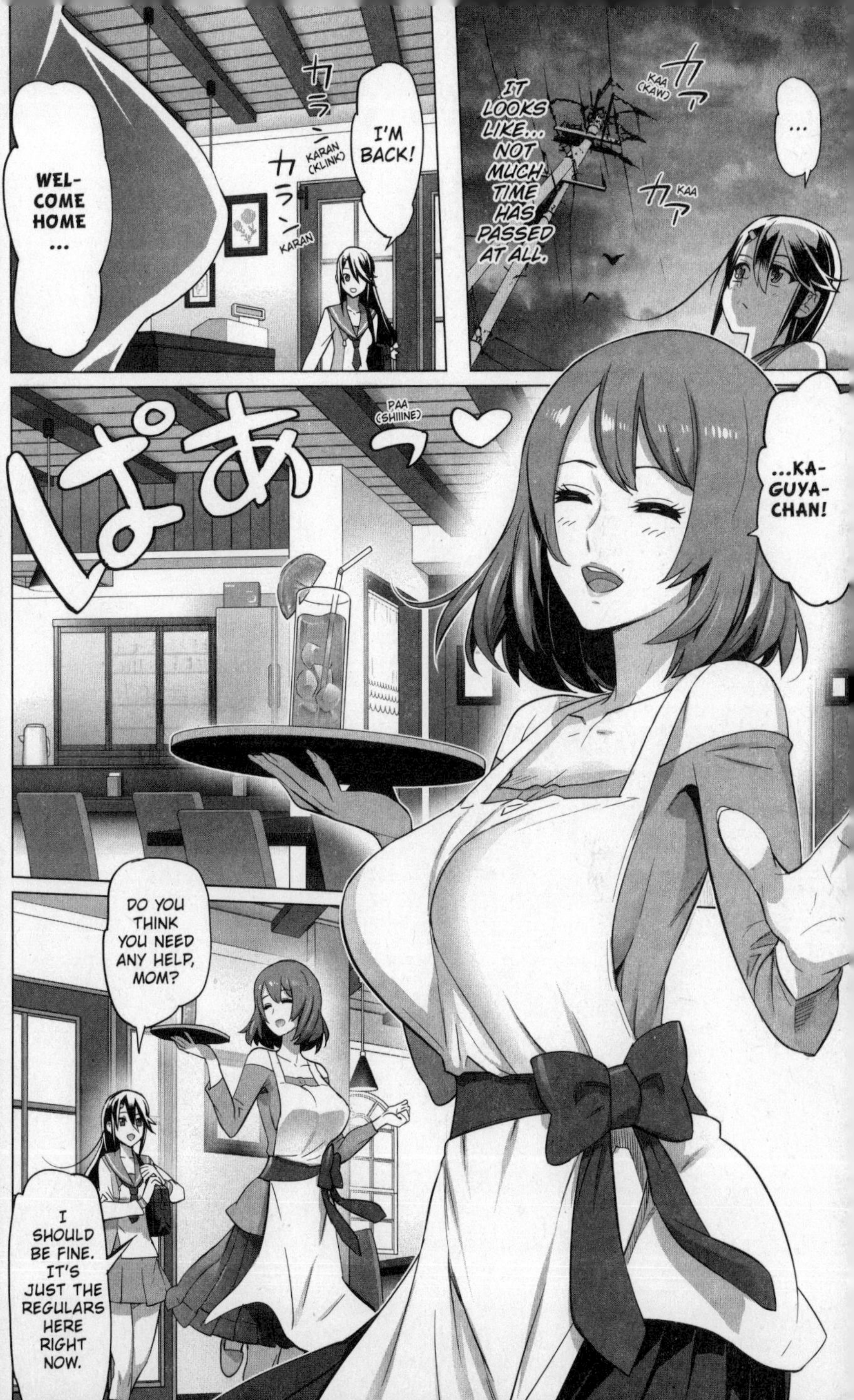
...
カァ
KAA (KAW)
IT LOOKS LIKE... NOT MUCH TIME HAS PASSED AT ALL.
カァ
KAA
I'M BACK!
カラン
KARAN (KLINK)
カラン
KARAN
WEL-COME HOME ...
...KA-GUYA-CHAN!
ぱあっ
PAA (SHIIINE)
DO YOU THINK YOU NEED ANY HELP, MOM?
I SHOULD BE FINE. IT'S JUST THE REGULARS HERE RIGHT NOW.

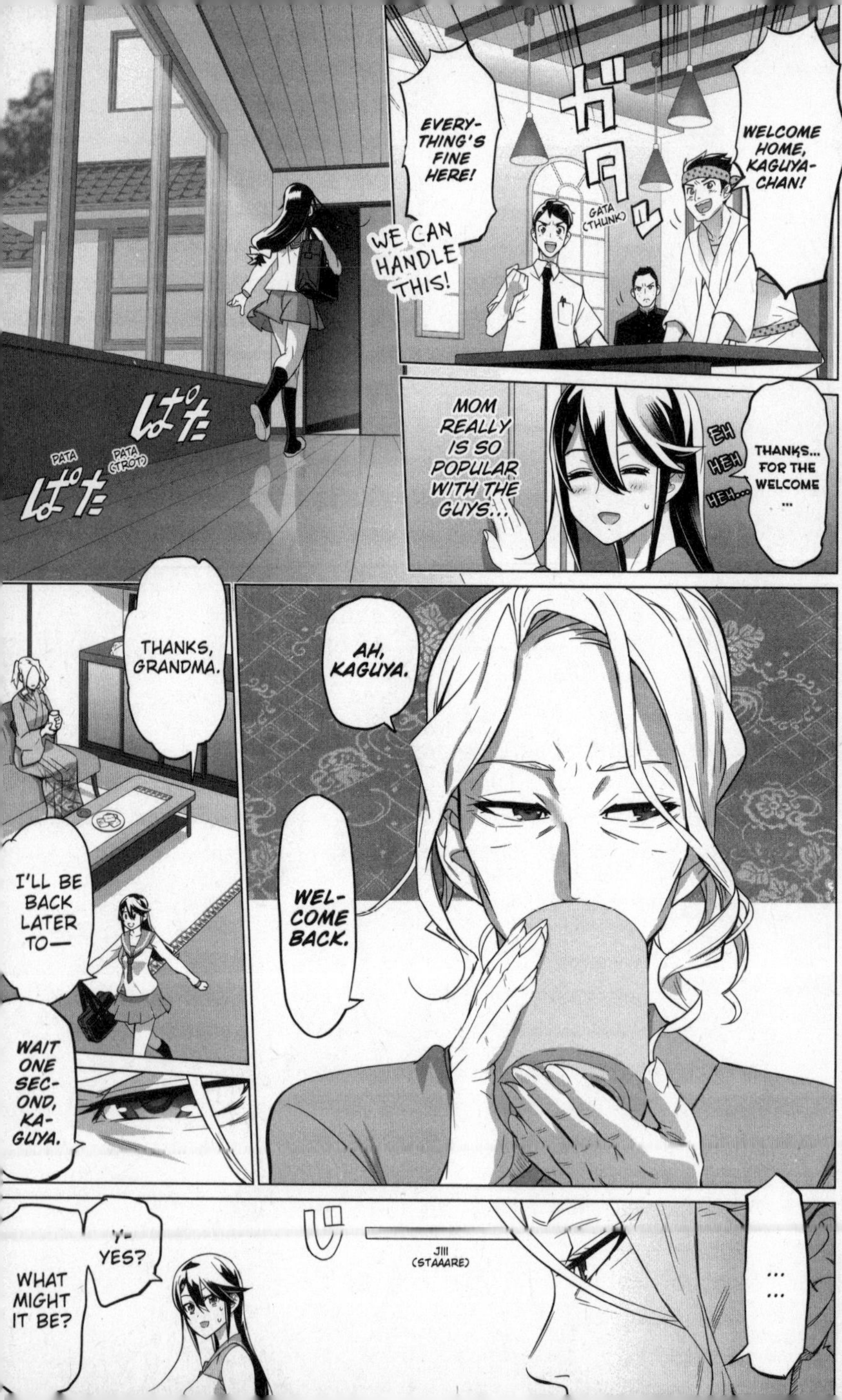
WELCOME HOME, KAGUYA-CHAN!
EVERY-THING'S FINE HERE!
GATA (THUNK)
WE CAN HANDLE THIS!
THANKS... FOR THE WELCOME ...
EH HEH HEH...
MOM REALLY IS SO POPULAR WITH THE GUYS...
PATA
PATA (TROT)
AH, KAGUYA.
WEL-COME BACK.
THANKS, GRANDMA.
I'LL BE BACK LATER TO—
WAIT ONE SEC-OND, KA-GUYA.
... ...
JIII (STAAARE)
Y-YES?
WHAT MIGHT IT BE?

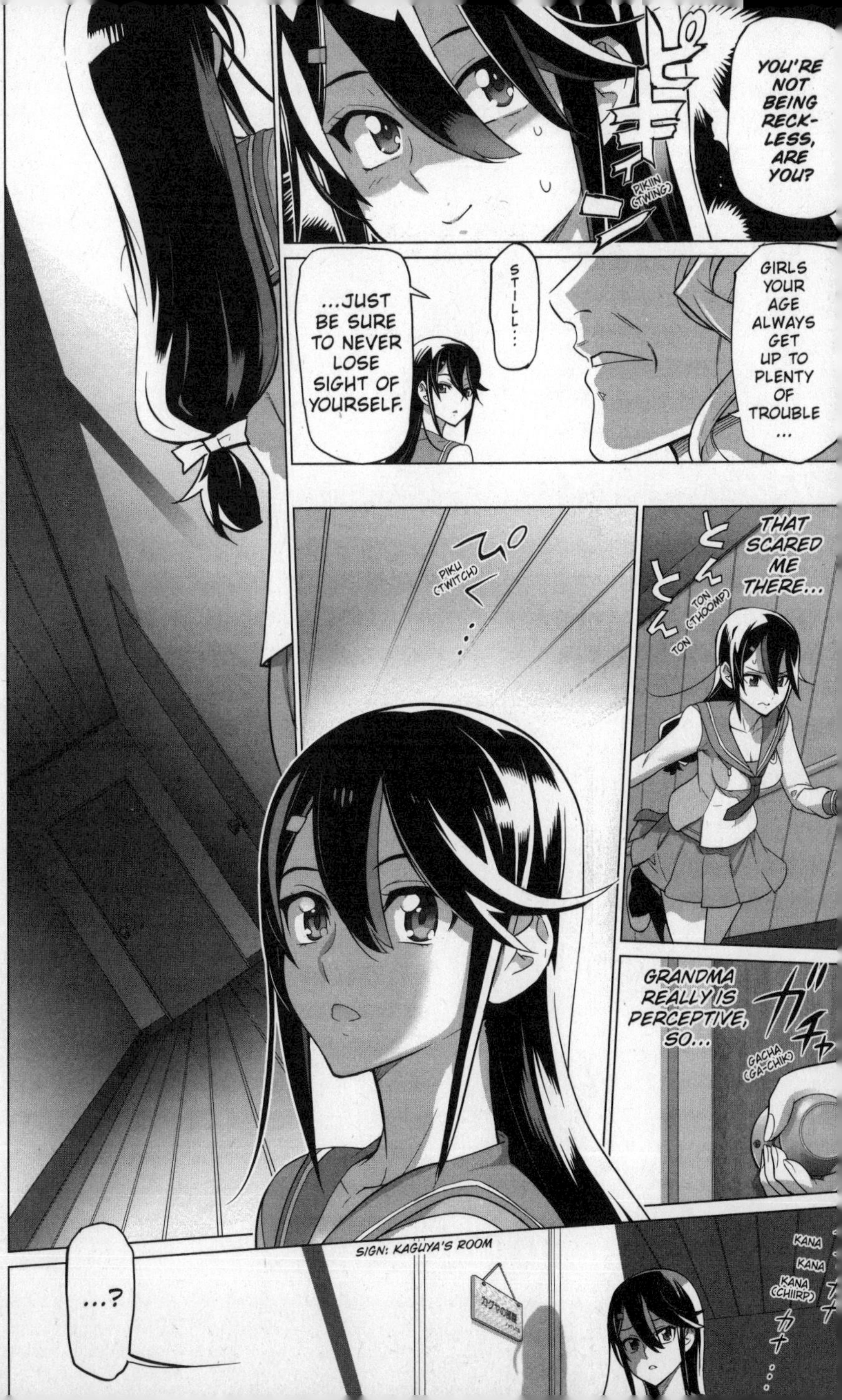
YOU'RE NOT BEING RECKLESS, ARE YOU?
PIKIIN (TWING)
GIRLS YOUR AGE ALWAYS GET UP TO PLENTY OF TROUBLE...
STILL...
...JUST BE SURE TO NEVER LOSE SIGHT OF YOURSELF.
THAT SCARED ME THERE...
TON TON (THOOMP)
GRANDMA REALLY IS PERCEPTIVE, SO...
GACHA (GA-CHIK)
PIKU (TWITCH)
KANA KANA KANA (CHIIRP)
SIGN: KAGUYA'S ROOM
...?

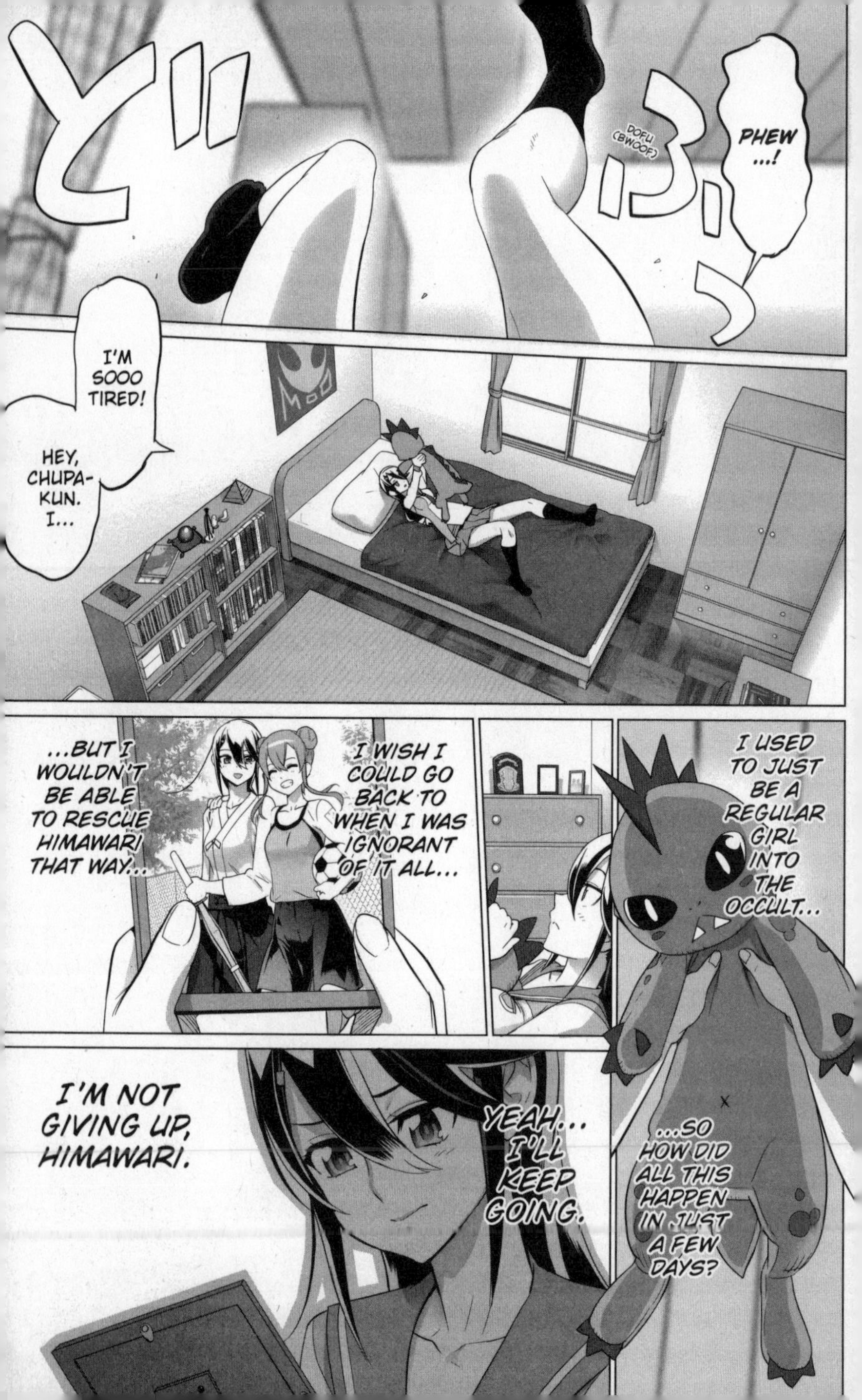
PHEW ...!
DOFU (BWOOF)
I'M SOOO TIRED!
HEY, CHUPA-KUN. I...
I USED TO JUST BE A REGULAR GIRL INTO THE OCCULT...
I WISH I COULD GO BACK TO WHEN I WAS IGNORANT OF IT ALL...
...BUT I WOULDN'T BE ABLE TO RESCUE HIMAWARI THAT WAY...
...SO HOW DID ALL THIS HAPPEN IN JUST A FEW DAYS?
YEAH... I'LL KEEP GOING.
I'M NOT GIVING UP, HIMAWARI.

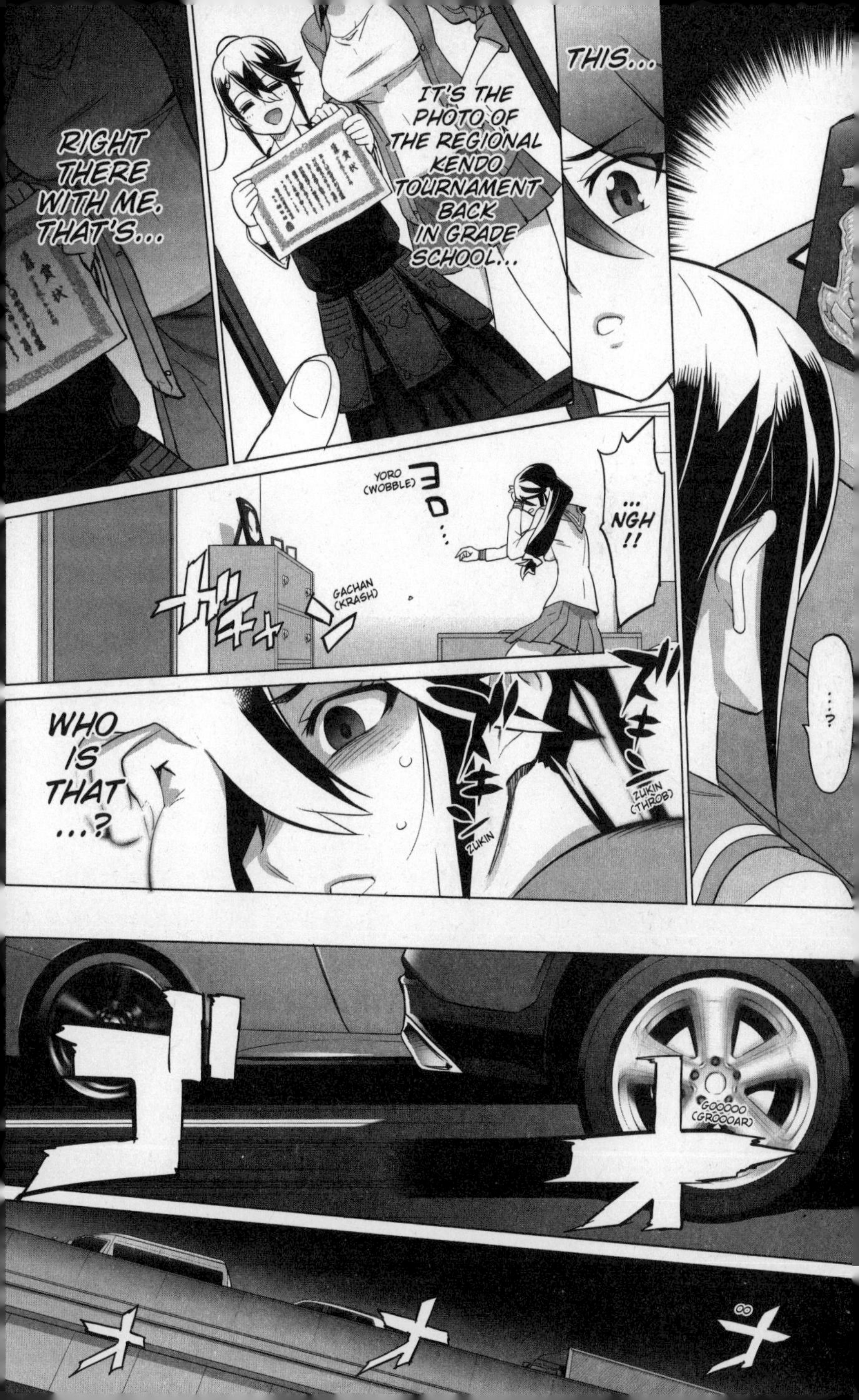
THIS...
IT'S THE PHOTO OF THE REGIONAL KENDO TOURNAMENT BACK IN GRADE SCHOOL...
RIGHT THERE WITH ME. THAT'S...
...?
...NGH!!
YORO (WOBBLE)
GACHAN (KRASH)
ZUKIN (THROB)
ZUKIN
WHO IS THAT ...?
GOOOOO (GROOOAR)

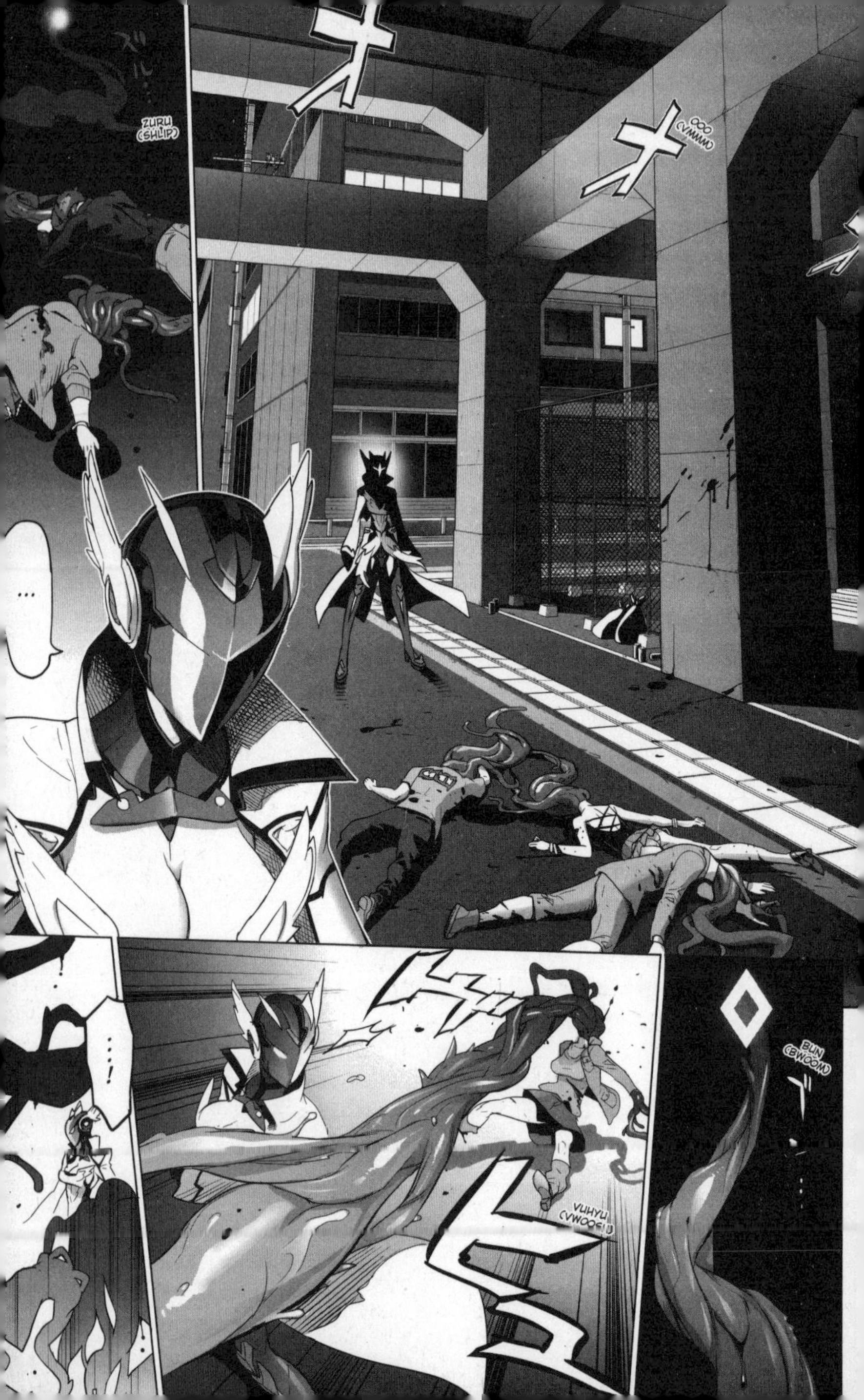
OOO (VMMM)
ZURU (SHLIP)
...
BUN (BWOOM)
VUHYU (VWOOF!)
...!

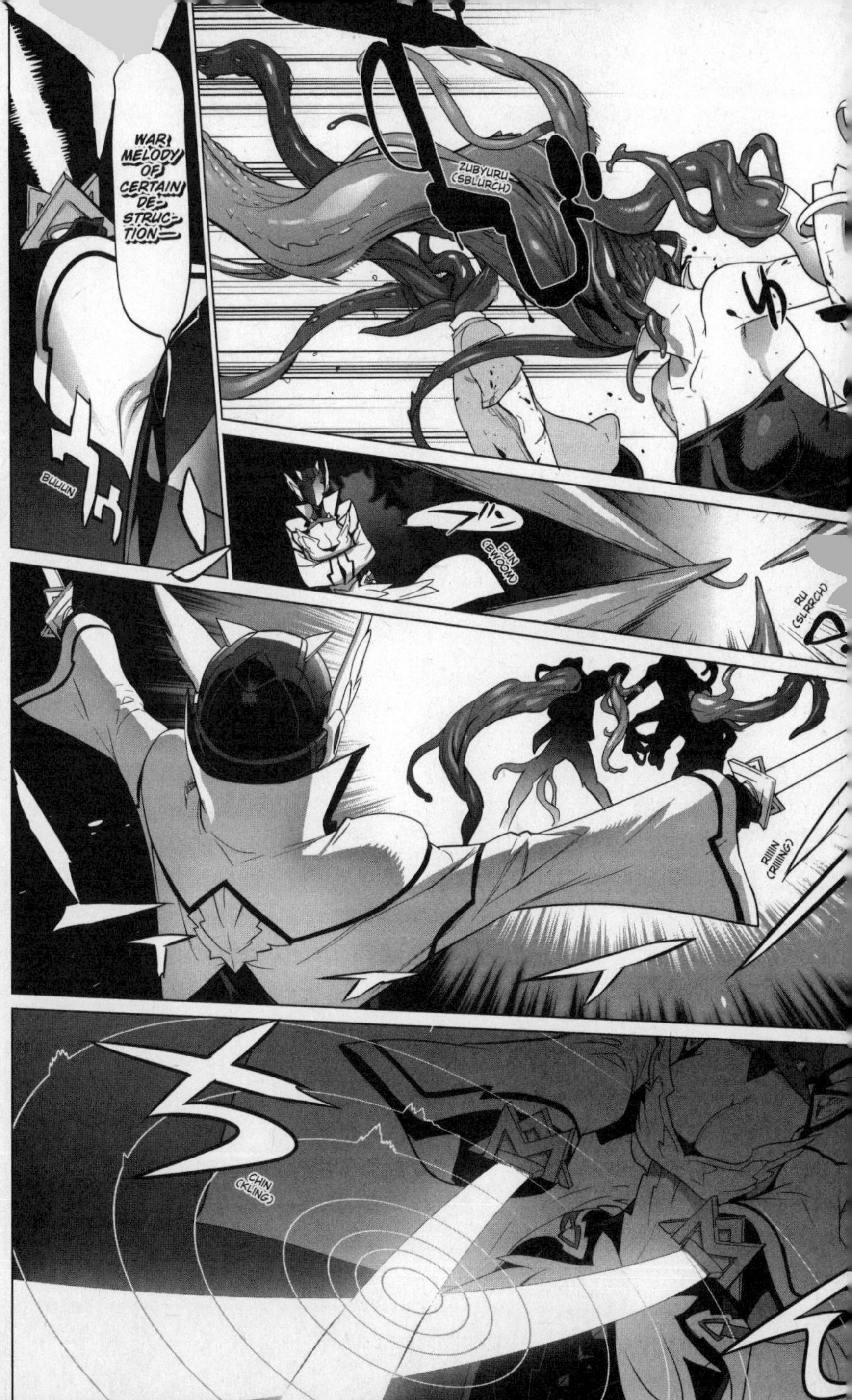
ZUBYURU (SBLURCH)
BUN (BWOOM)
WAR! MELODY OF CERTAIN DE-STRUC-TION—
BULLLN
RU (SLRRCH)
RIIIIN (RIIIIING)
CHIN (KLING)

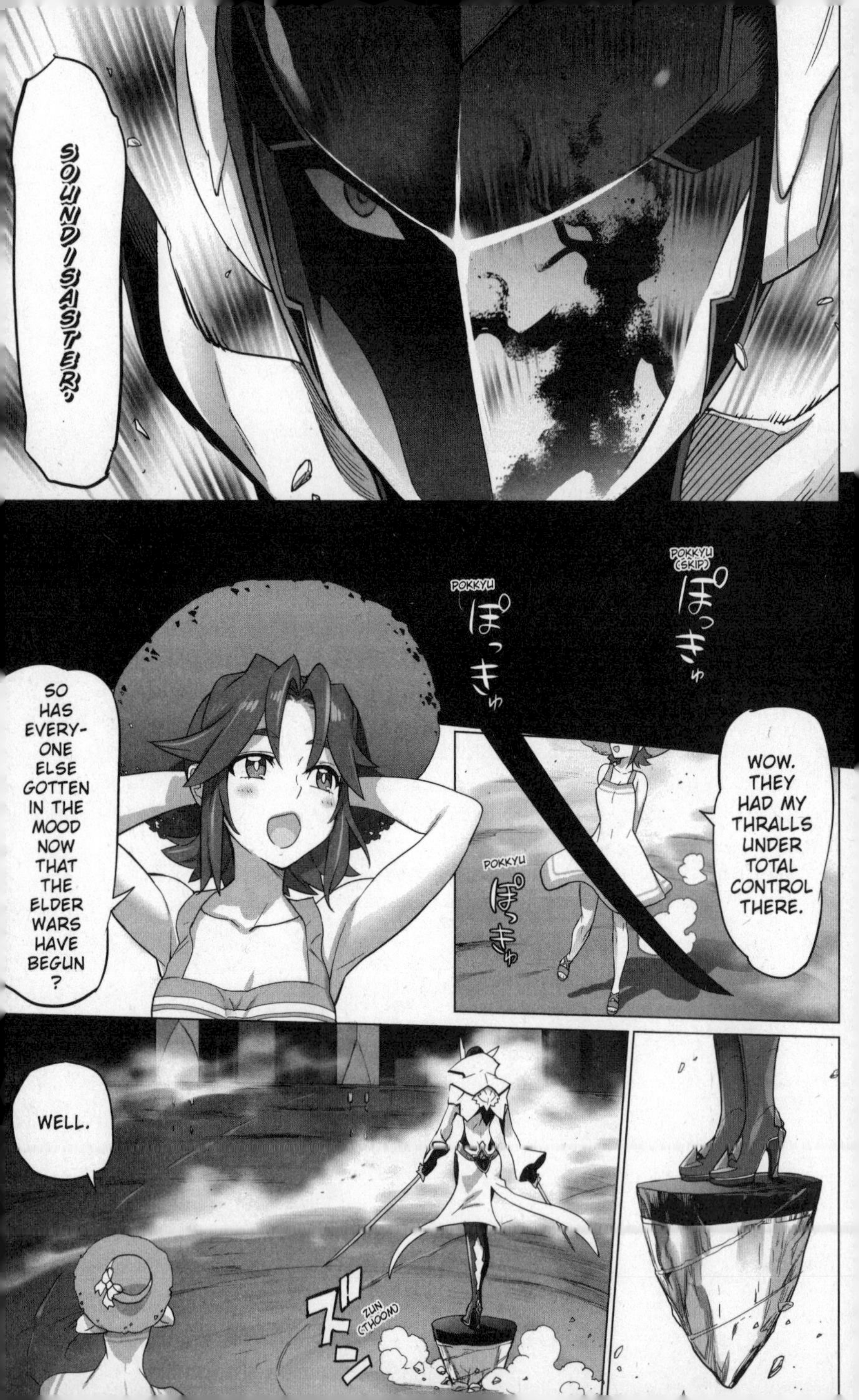
SOUNDISASTER.
POKKYU (SKIP)
ぽっきゅ
POKKYU
ぽっきゅ
WOW. THEY HAD MY THRALLS UNDER TOTAL CONTROL THERE.
POKKYU
ぽっきゅ
SO HAS EVERYONE ELSE GOTTEN IN THE MOOD NOW THAT THE ELDER WARS HAVE BEGUN?
ZUN (THOOM)
ズドン
WELL.

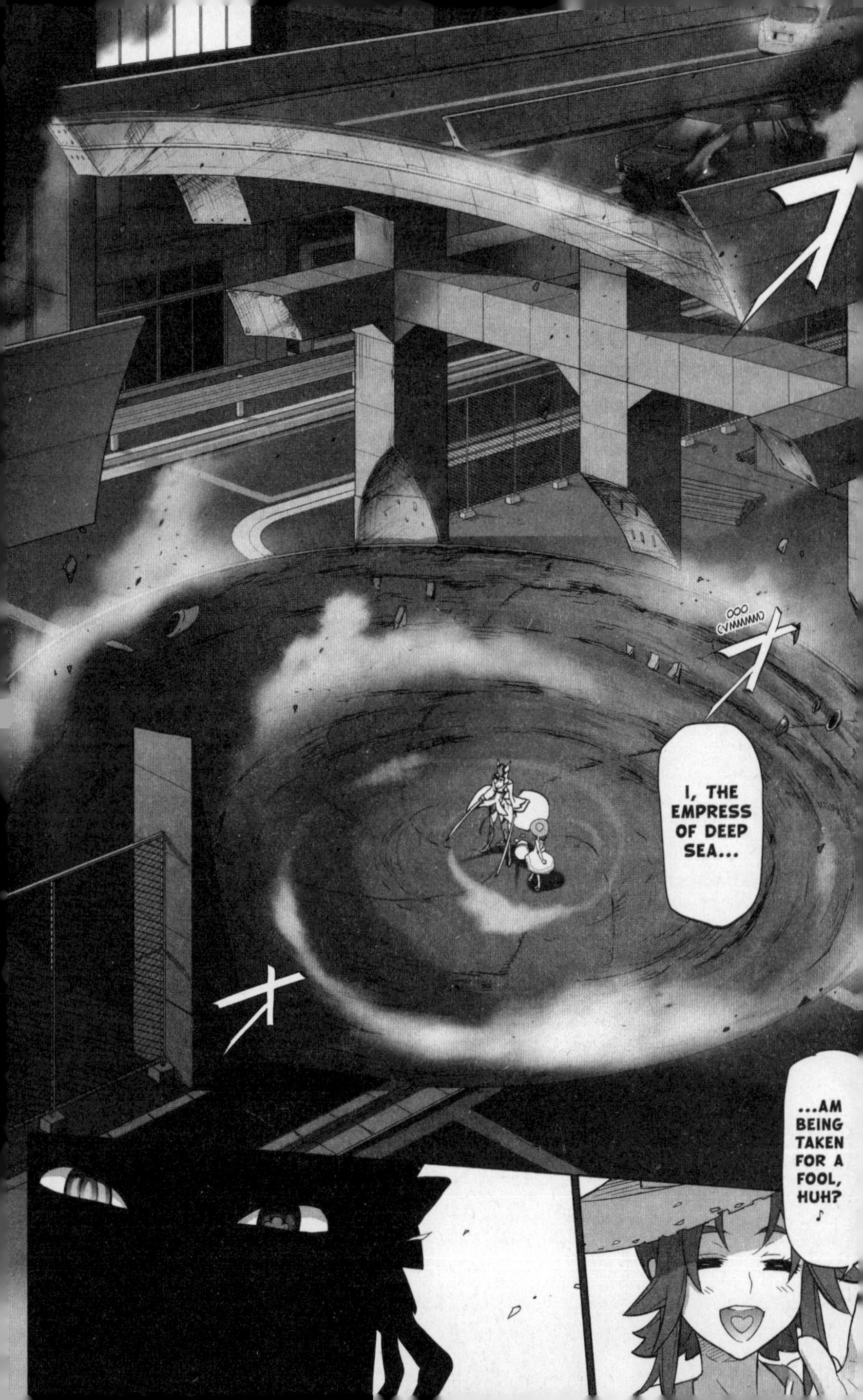
OOO
(VMMMMM)
I, THE EMPRESS OF DEEP SEA...
...AM BEING TAKEN FOR A FOOL, HUH? ♪

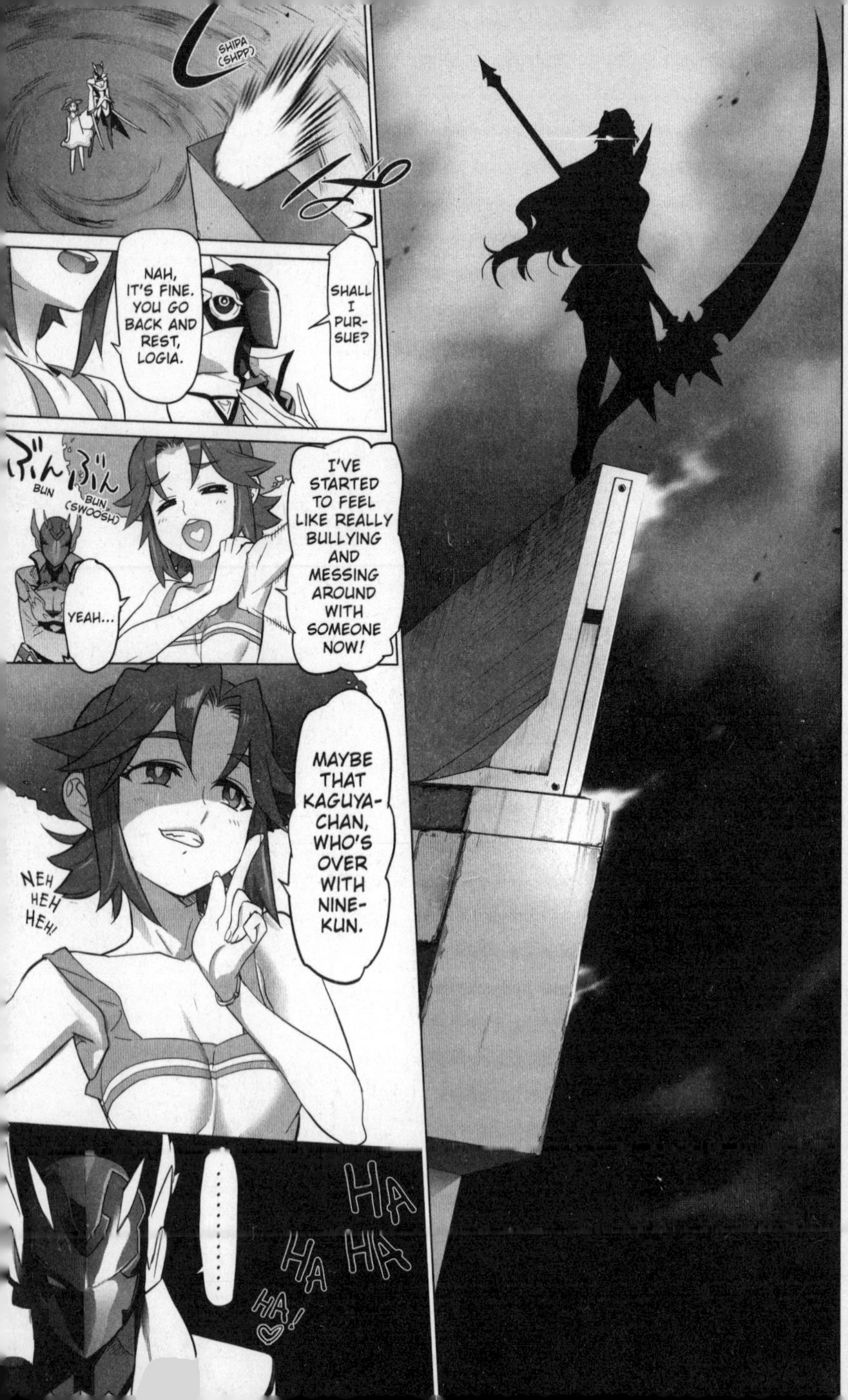
SHIPA (SHPP)
SHALL I PURSUE?
NAH, IT'S FINE. YOU GO BACK AND REST, LOGIA.
I'VE STARTED TO FEEL LIKE REALLY BULLYING AND MESSING AROUND WITH SOMEONE NOW!
YEAH...
ぶん ぶん
BUN BUN (SWOOSH)
MAYBE THAT KAGUYA-CHAN, WHO'S OVER WITH NINE-KUN.
NEH HEH HEH!
......
HA HA HA HA HA!

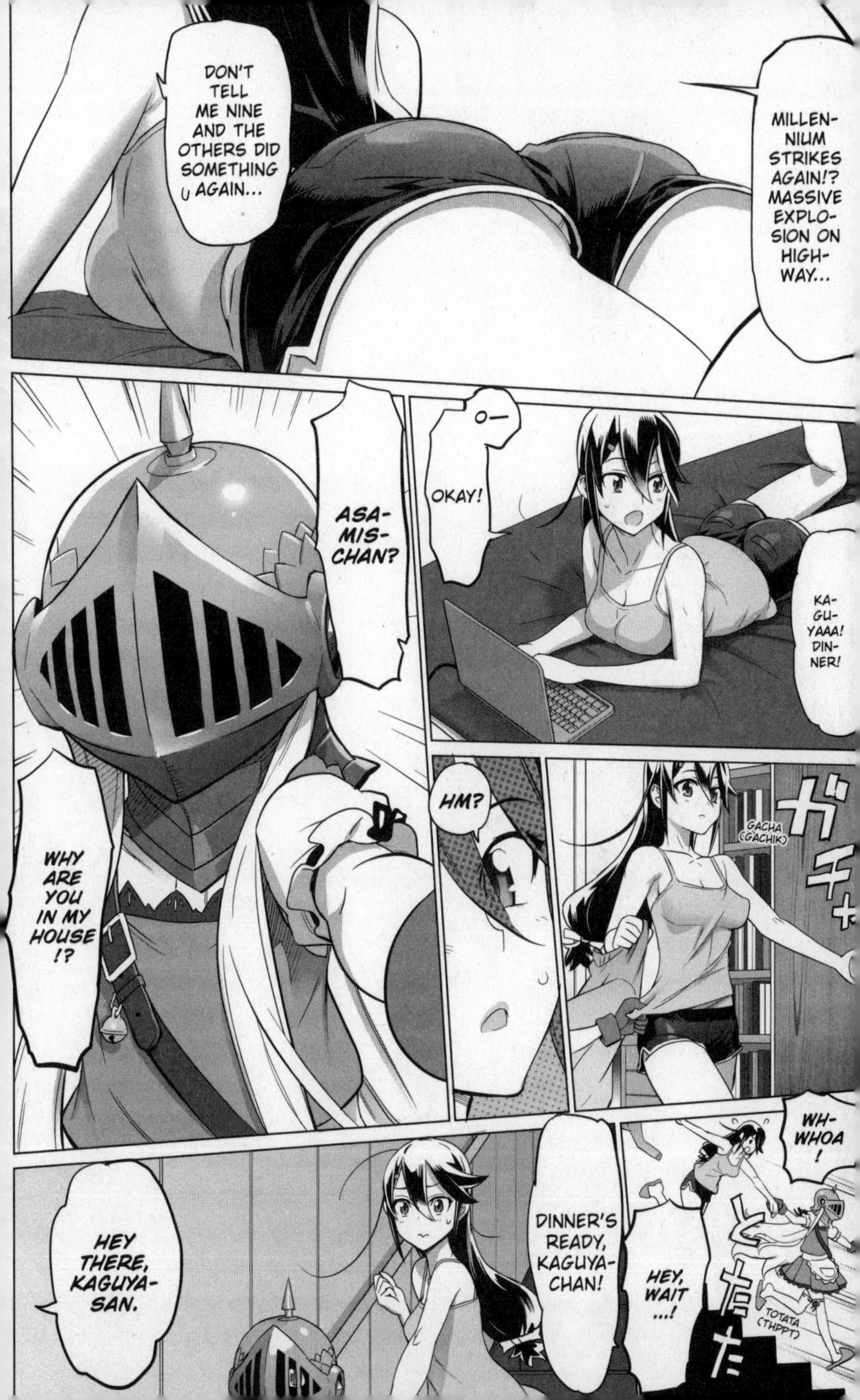
MILLENNIUM STRIKES AGAIN!? MASSIVE EXPLOSION ON HIGHWAY...
DON'T TELL ME NINE AND THE OTHERS DID SOMETHING AGAIN...
KAGUYAAA! DINNER!
O—
OKAY!
GACHA (GACHIK)
HM?
ASAMI-CHAN?
WHY ARE YOU IN MY HOUSE!?
WH-WHOA!
HEY, WAIT...!
TOTATA (THPPT)
DINNER'S READY, KAGUYA-CHAN!
HEY THERE, KAGUYA-SAN.

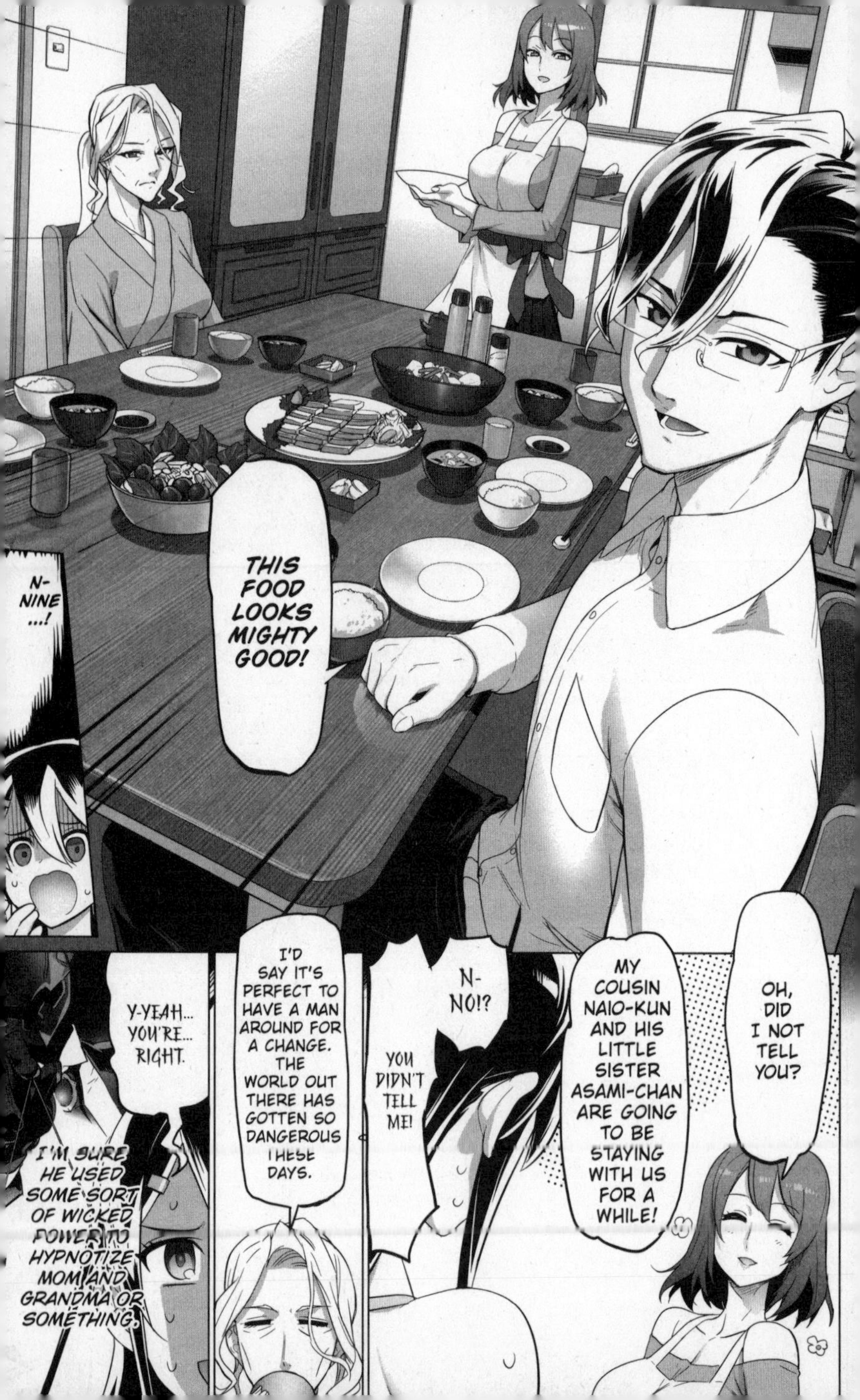
THIS FOOD LOOKS MIGHTY GOOD!
N-NINE...!
OH, DID I NOT TELL YOU?
MY COUSIN NAIO-KUN AND HIS LITTLE SISTER ASAMI-CHAN ARE GOING TO BE STAYING WITH US FOR A WHILE!
N-NO!?
YOU DIDN'T TELL ME!
I'D SAY IT'S PERFECT TO HAVE A MAN AROUND FOR A CHANGE. THE WORLD OUT THERE HAS GOTTEN SO DANGEROUS THESE DAYS.
Y-YEAH... YOU'RE... RIGHT.
I'M SURE HE USED SOME SORT OF WICKED POWER TO HYPNOTIZE MOM AND GRANDMA OR SOMETHING.

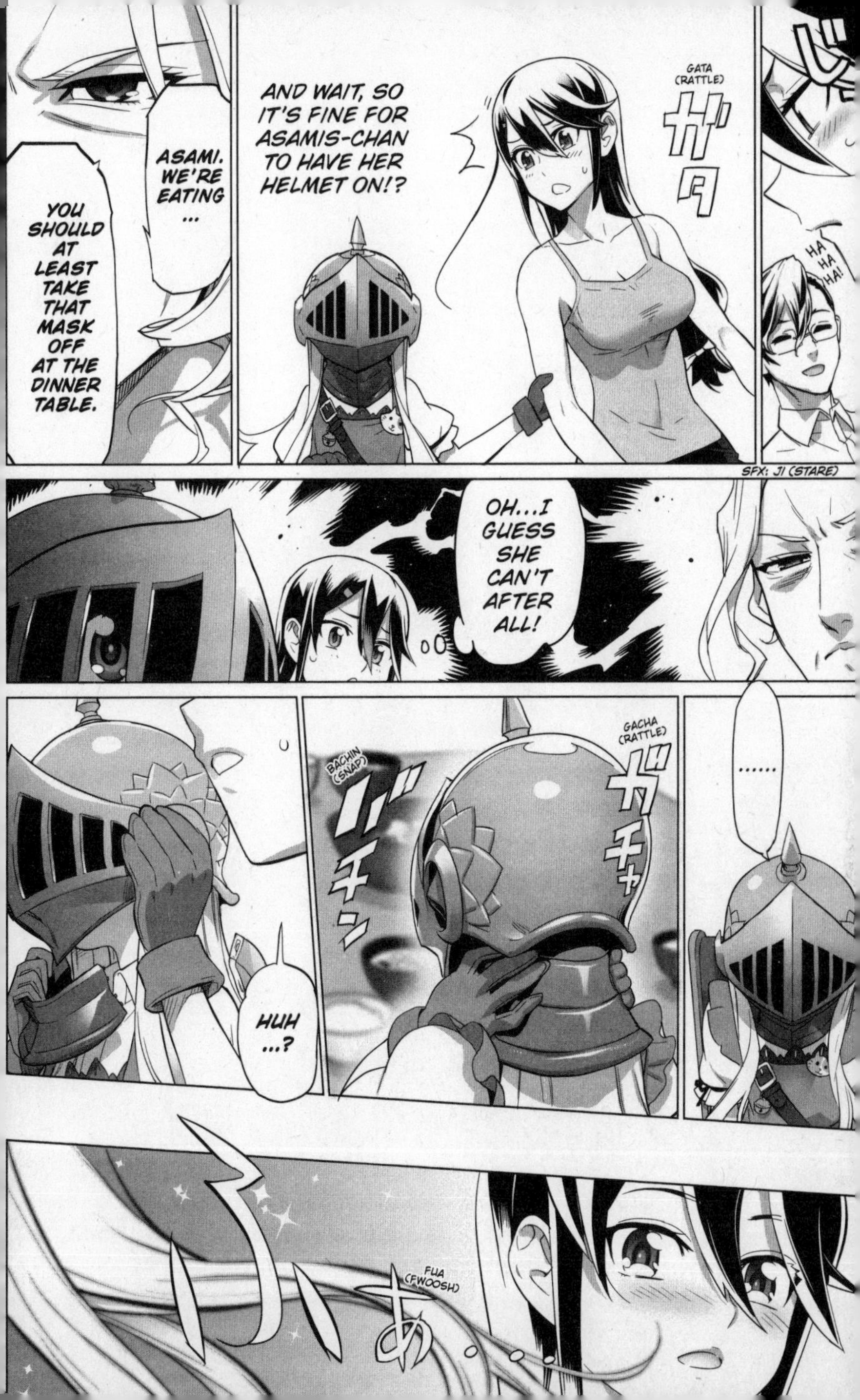
HA HA HA!
SFX: JI (STARE)
GATA (RATTLE)
AND WAIT, SO IT'S FINE FOR ASAMIS-CHAN TO HAVE HER HELMET ON!?
ASAMI. WE'RE EATING ...
YOU SHOULD AT LEAST TAKE THAT MASK OFF AT THE DINNER TABLE.
OH...I GUESS SHE CAN'T AFTER ALL!
......
GACHA (RATTLE)
BACHIN (SNAP)
HUH ...?
FUA (FWOOSH)

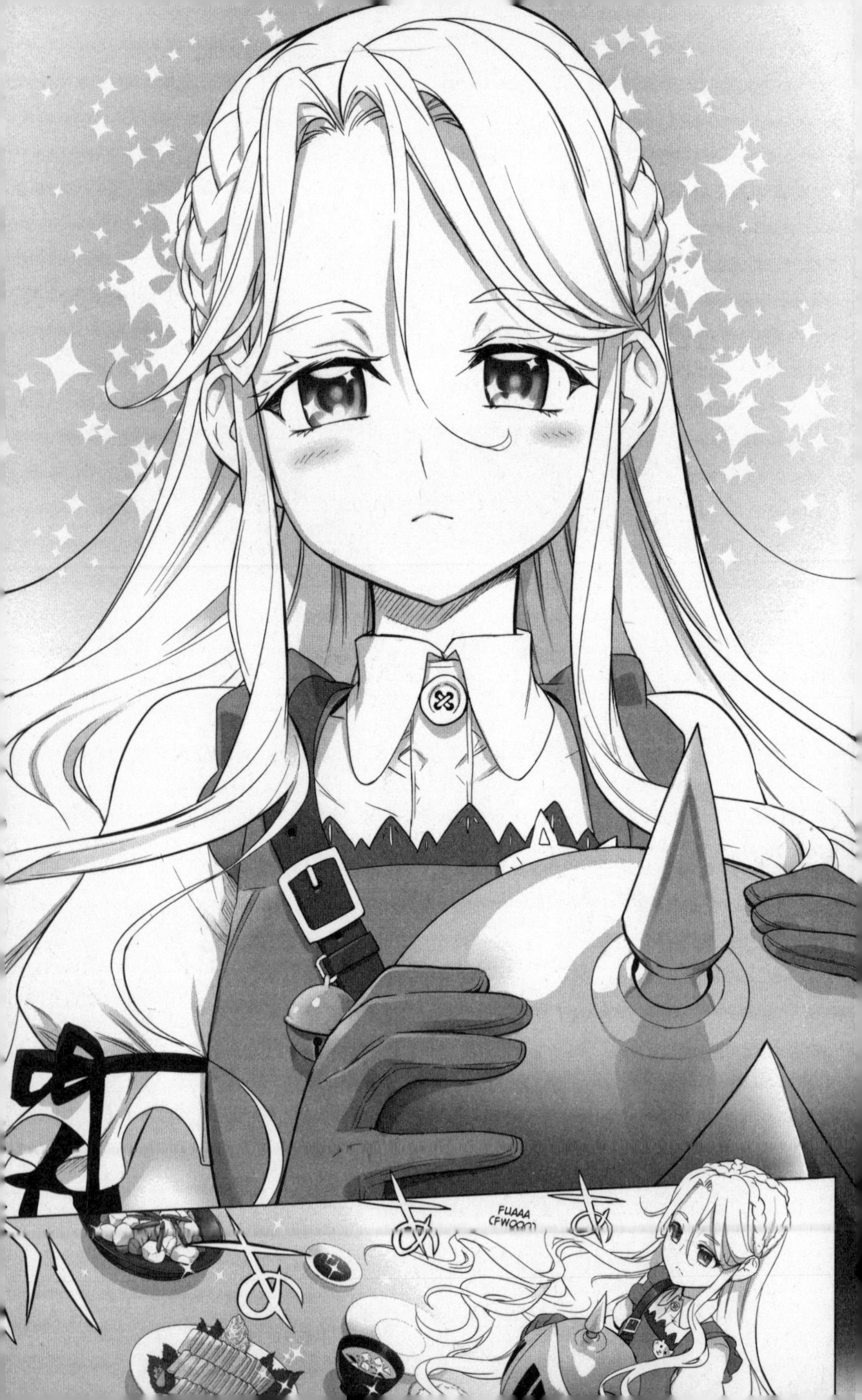
FUAAA
(FWOOM)

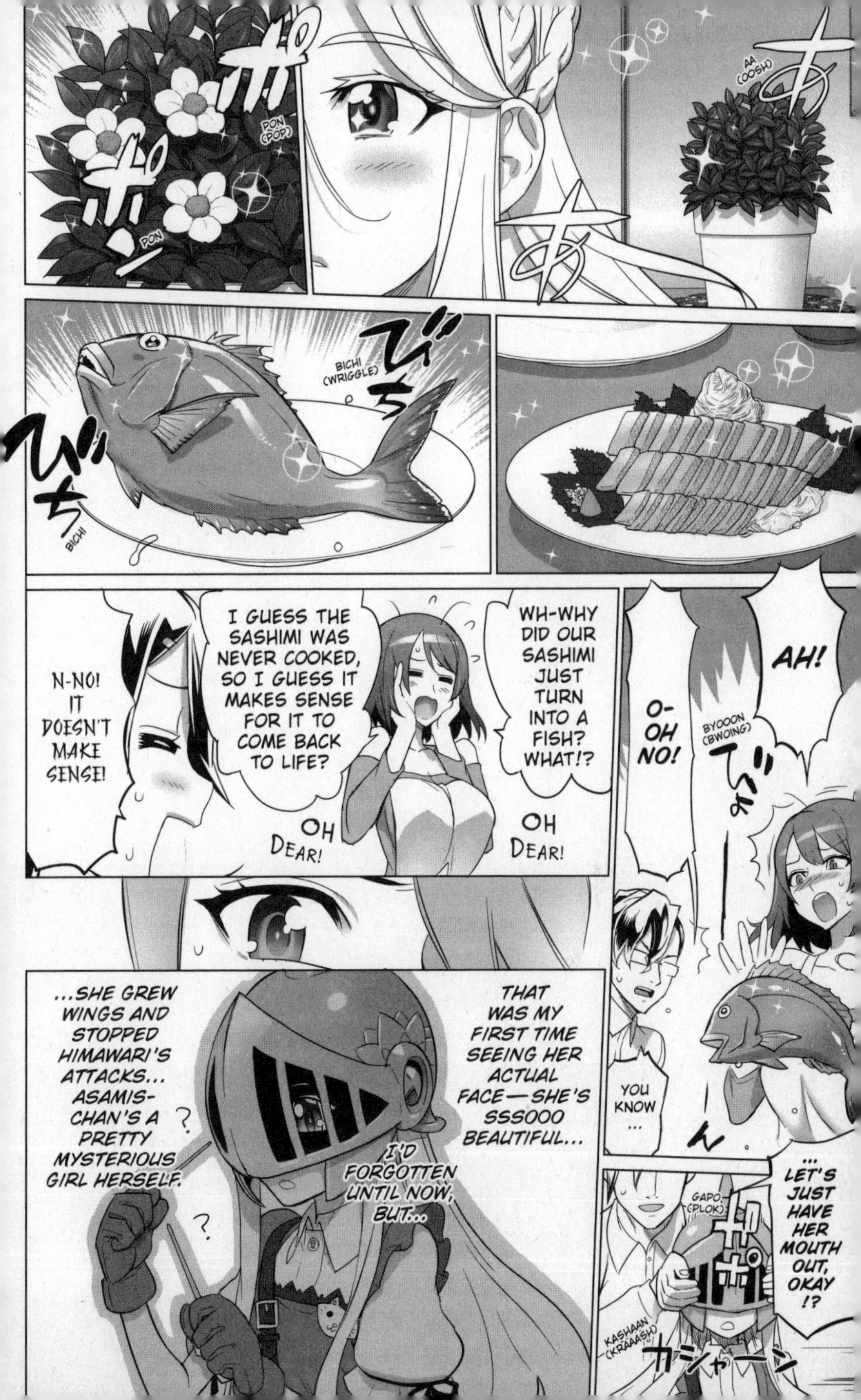
AA (COOSH)
PON (POP)
PON
BICHI (WRIGGLE)
BICHI
AH!
BYOOON (BWOING)
O-OH NO!
YOU KNOW ...
WH-WHY DID OUR SASHIMI JUST TURN INTO A FISH? WHAT!?
OH DEAR!
I GUESS THE SASHIMI WAS NEVER COOKED, SO I GUESS IT MAKES SENSE FOR IT TO COME BACK TO LIFE?
OH DEAR!
N-NO! IT DOESN'T MAKE SENSE!
... LET'S JUST HAVE HER MOUTH OUT, OKAY!?
GAPO (PLOK)
KASHAAN (KRAAASH)
THAT WAS MY FIRST TIME SEEING HER ACTUAL FACE—SHE'S SSSOOO BEAUTIFUL...
I'D FORGOTTEN UNTIL NOW, BUT...
...SHE GREW WINGS AND STOPPED HIMAWARI'S ATTACKS... ASAMIS-CHAN'S A PRETTY MYSTERIOUS GIRL HERSELF.
?
?

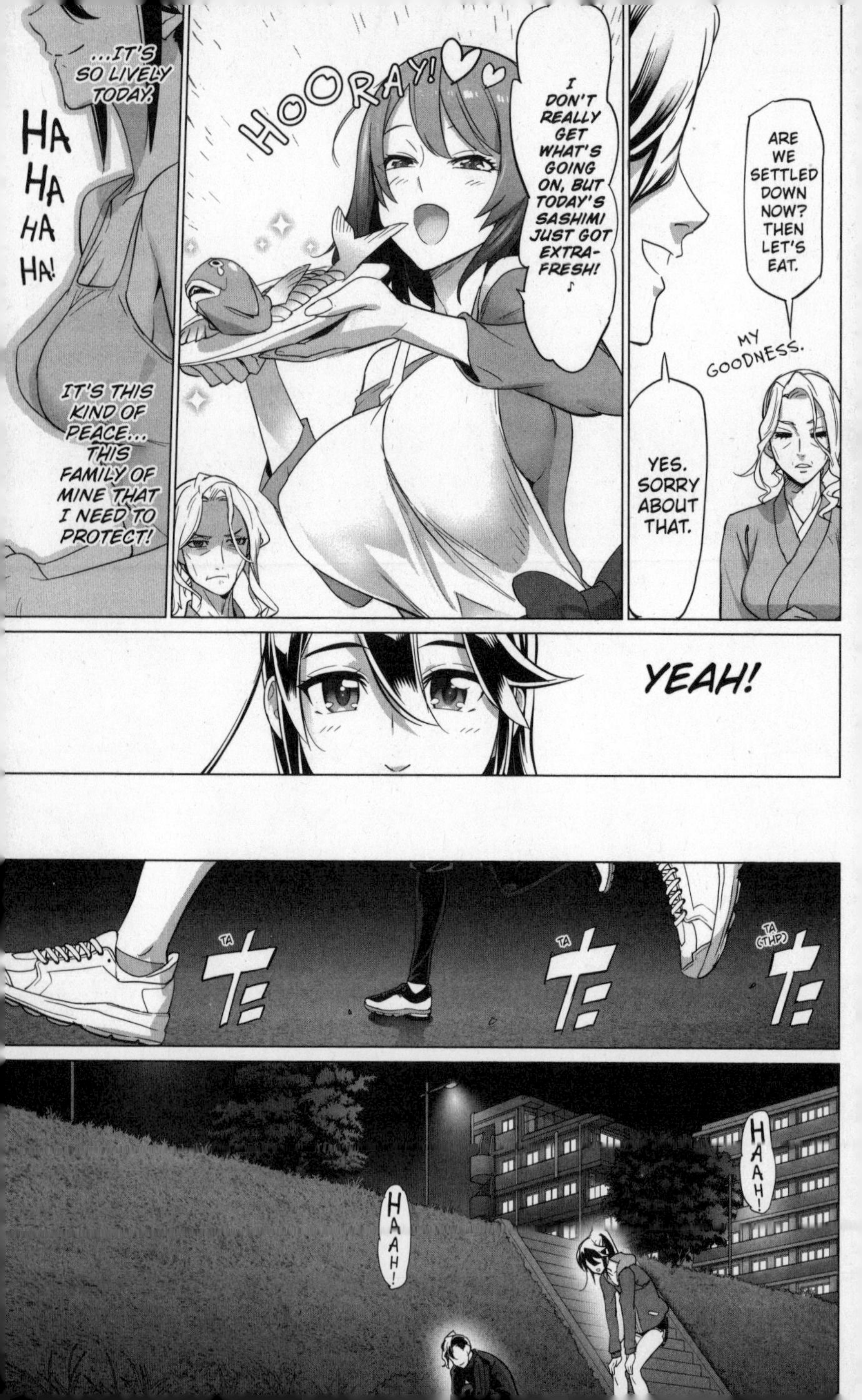
ARE WE SETTLED DOWN NOW? THEN LET'S EAT.
MY GOODNESS.
YES. SORRY ABOUT THAT.
HOORAY!
I DON'T REALLY GET WHAT'S GOING ON, BUT TODAY'S SASHIMI JUST GOT EXTRA-FRESH! ♪
...IT'S SO LIVELY TODAY.
HA HA HA HA!
IT'S THIS KIND OF PEACE... THIS FAMILY OF MINE THAT I NEED TO PROTECT!
YEAH!
TA (THP)
TA
TA
HAAAH!
HAAAH!

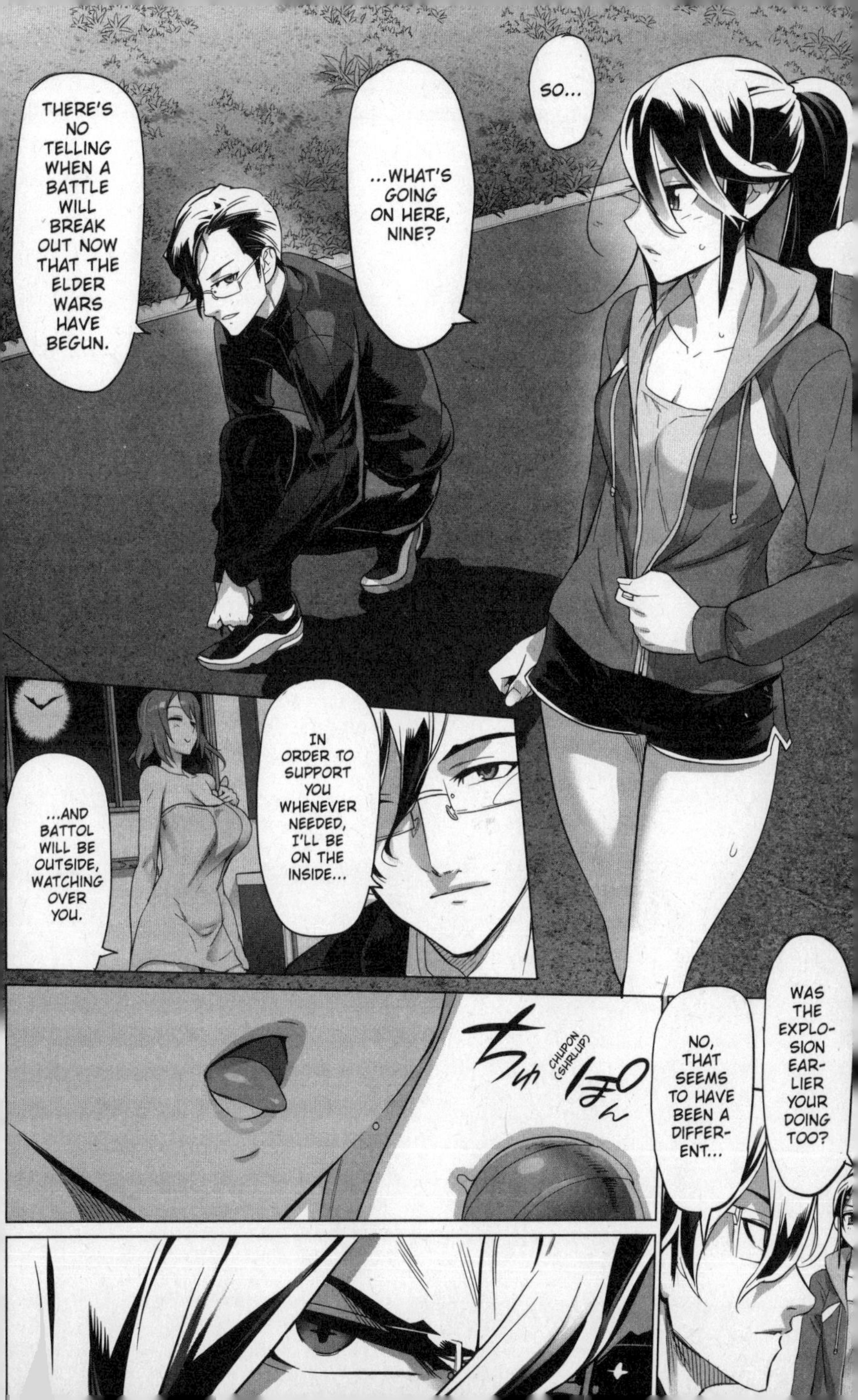
SO...
...WHAT'S GOING ON HERE, NINE?
THERE'S NO TELLING WHEN A BATTLE WILL BREAK OUT NOW THAT THE ELDER WARS HAVE BEGUN.
IN ORDER TO SUPPORT YOU WHENEVER NEEDED, I'LL BE ON THE INSIDE...
...AND BATTOL WILL BE OUTSIDE, WATCHING OVER YOU.
WAS THE EXPLOSION EARLIER YOUR DOING TOO?
NO, THAT SEEMS TO HAVE BEEN A DIFFERENT...
CHUPON (SHRLUP)

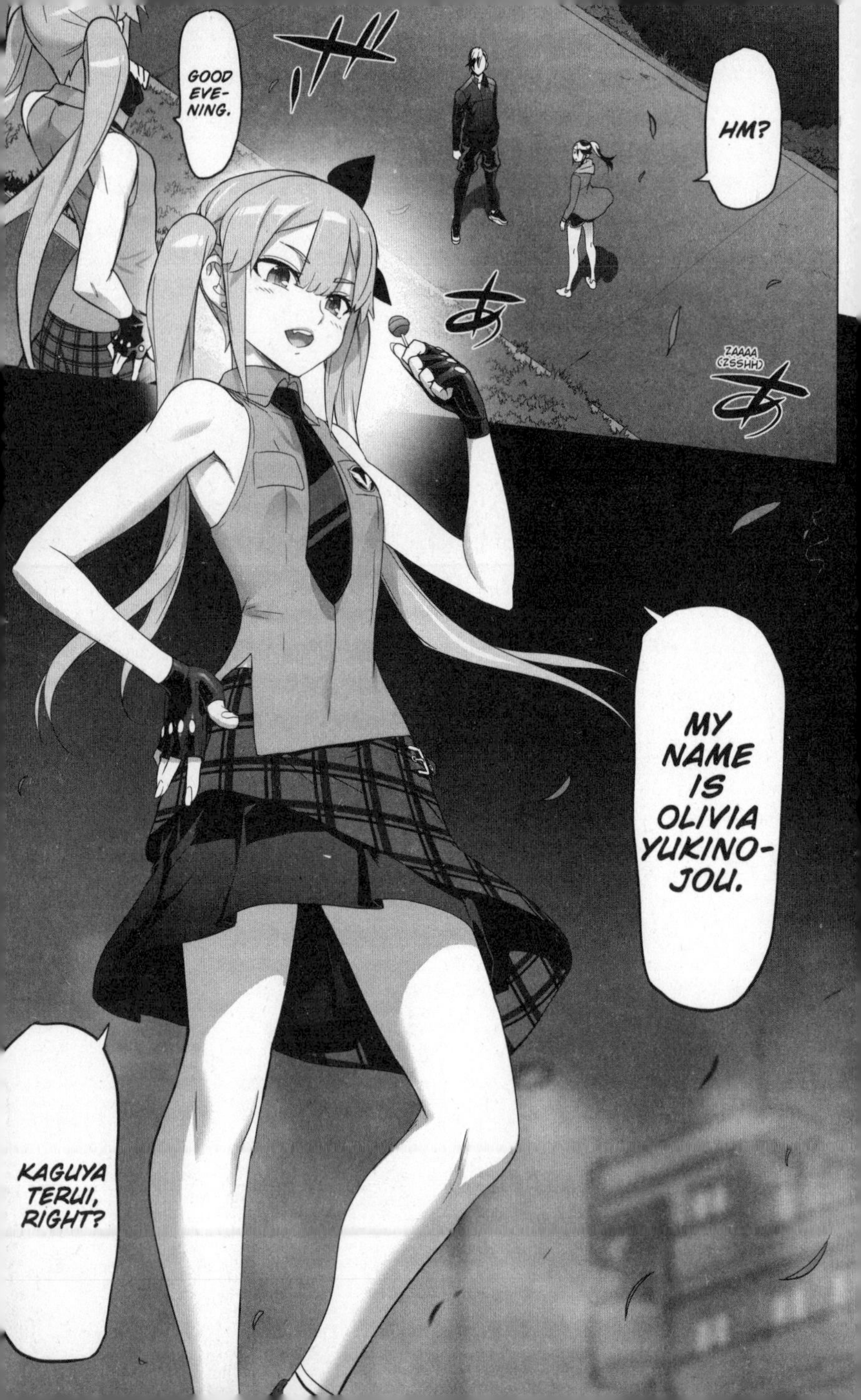
HM?
GOOD EVE-NING.
ZAAAA (ZSSHH)
MY NAME IS OLIVIA YUKINO-JOU.
KAGUYA TERUI, RIGHT?

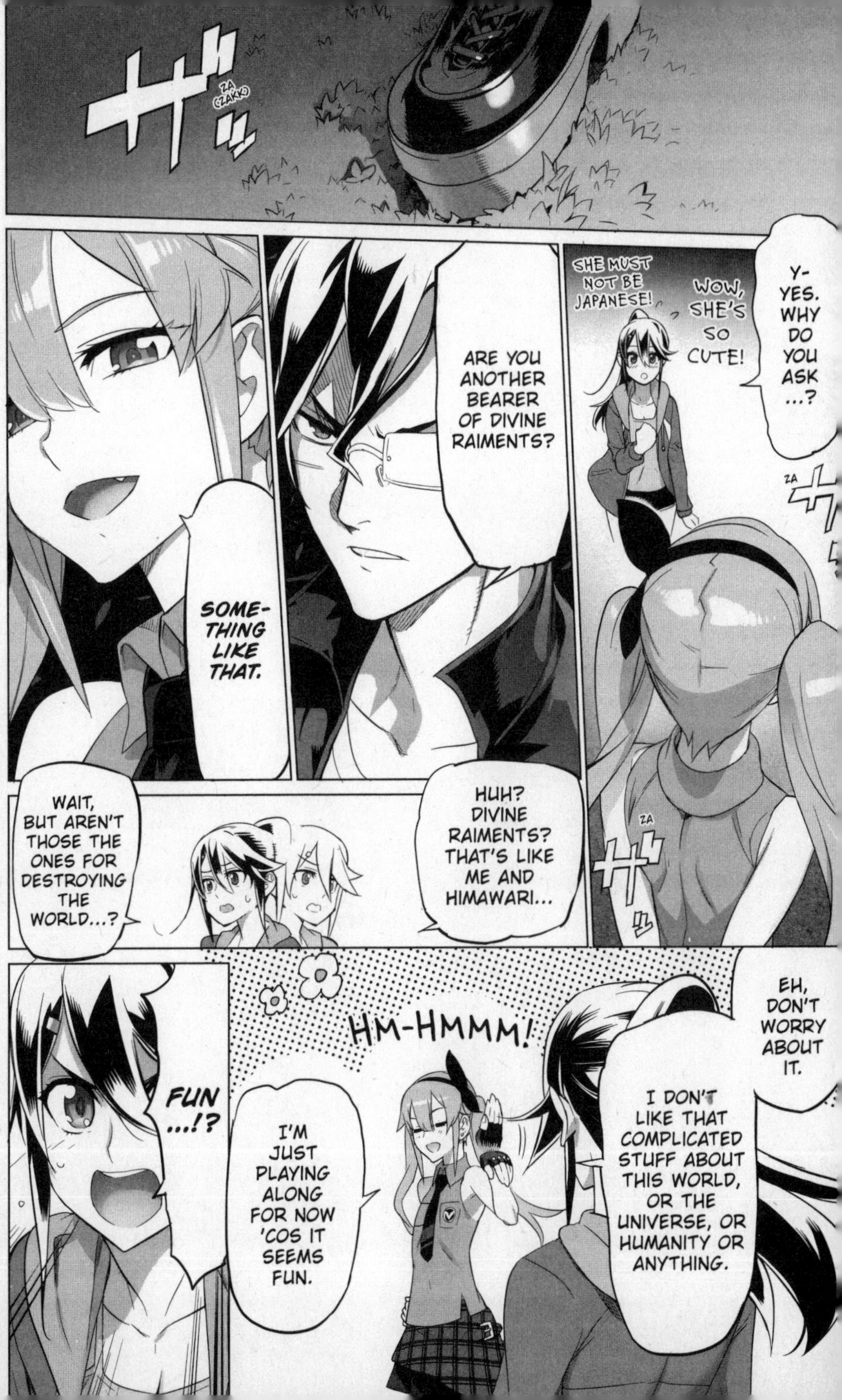
ZA (ZAKK)
Y-YES. WHY DO YOU ASK...?
WOW, SHE'S SO CUTE!
SHE MUST NOT BE JAPANESE!
ZA
ZA
ARE YOU ANOTHER BEARER OF DIVINE RAIMENTS?
SOMETHING LIKE THAT.
HUH? DIVINE RAIMENTS? THAT'S LIKE ME AND HIMAWARI...
WAIT, BUT AREN'T THOSE THE ONES FOR DESTROYING THE WORLD...?
EH, DON'T WORRY ABOUT IT.
I DON'T LIKE THAT COMPLICATED STUFF ABOUT THIS WORLD, OR THE UNIVERSE, OR HUMANITY OR ANYTHING.
HM-HMMM!
I'M JUST PLAYING ALONG FOR NOW 'COS IT SEEMS FUN.
FUN...!?

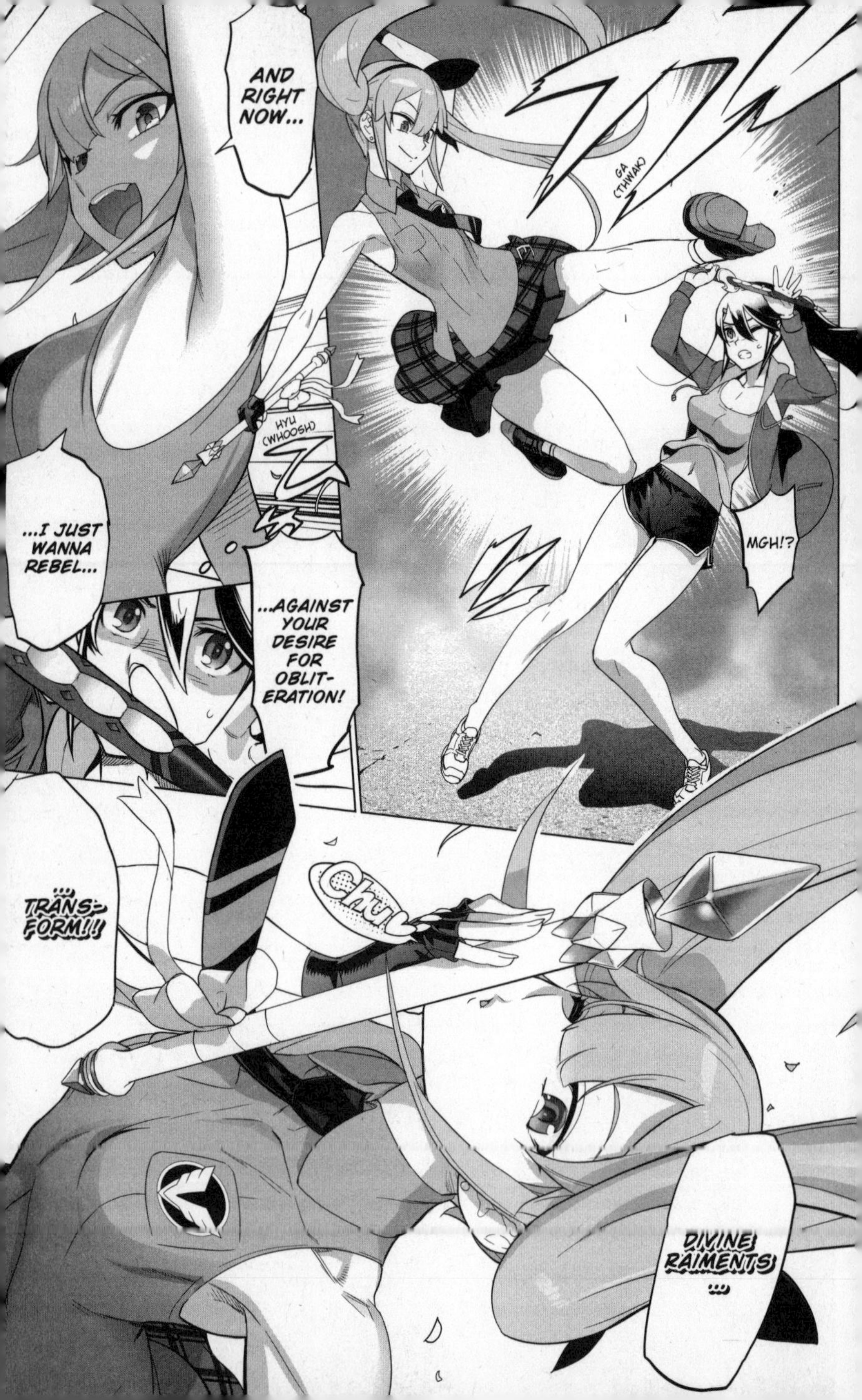
AND RIGHT NOW...
GA (THWAK)
HYU (WHOOSH)
MGH!?
...I JUST WANNA REBEL...
...AGAINST YOUR DESIRE FOR OBLITERATION!
DIVINE RAIMENTS...
Chu
...TRANSFORM!!

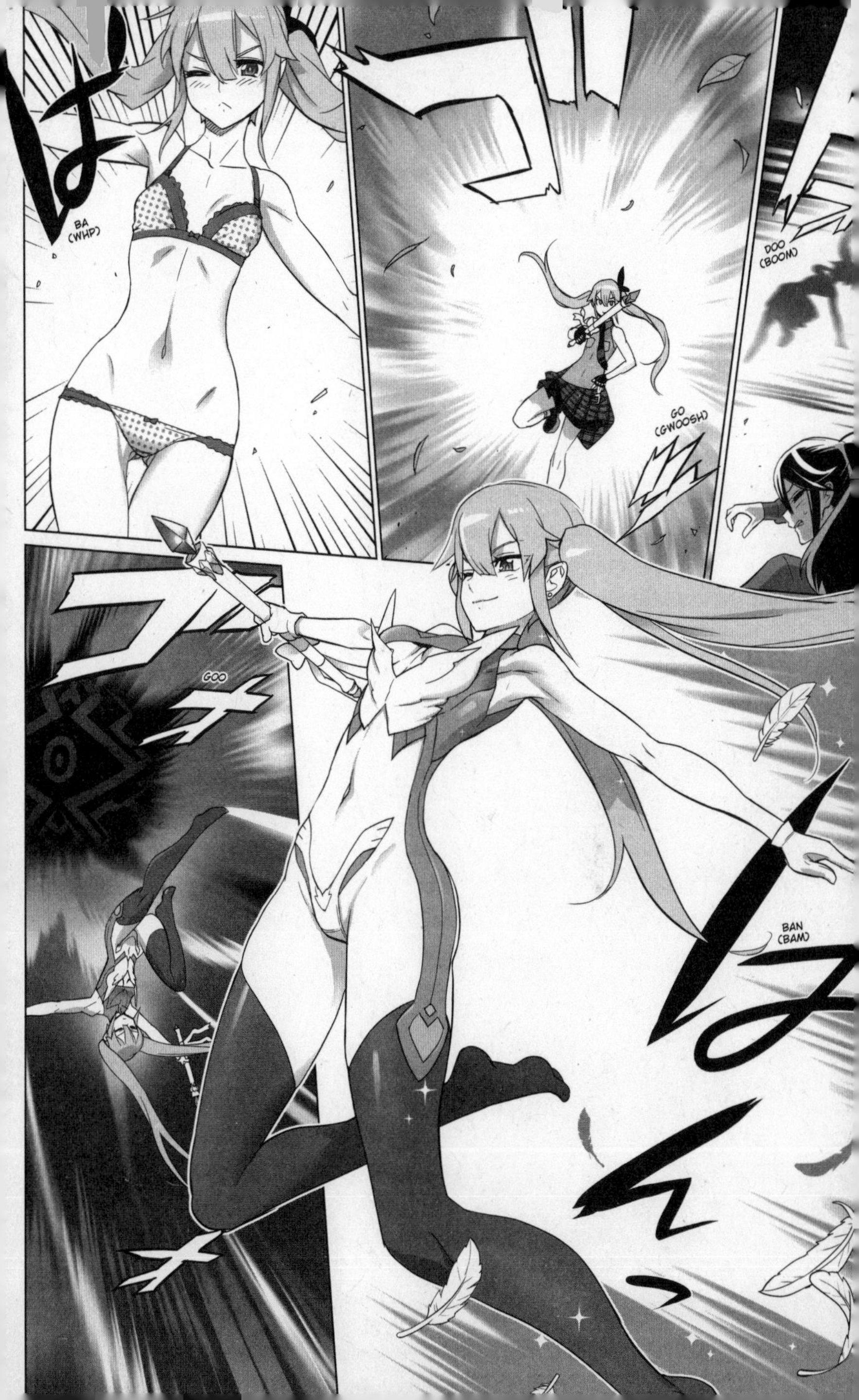
DOO (BOOM)
GO (GWOOSH)
BA (WHP)
GOO
BAN (BAM)

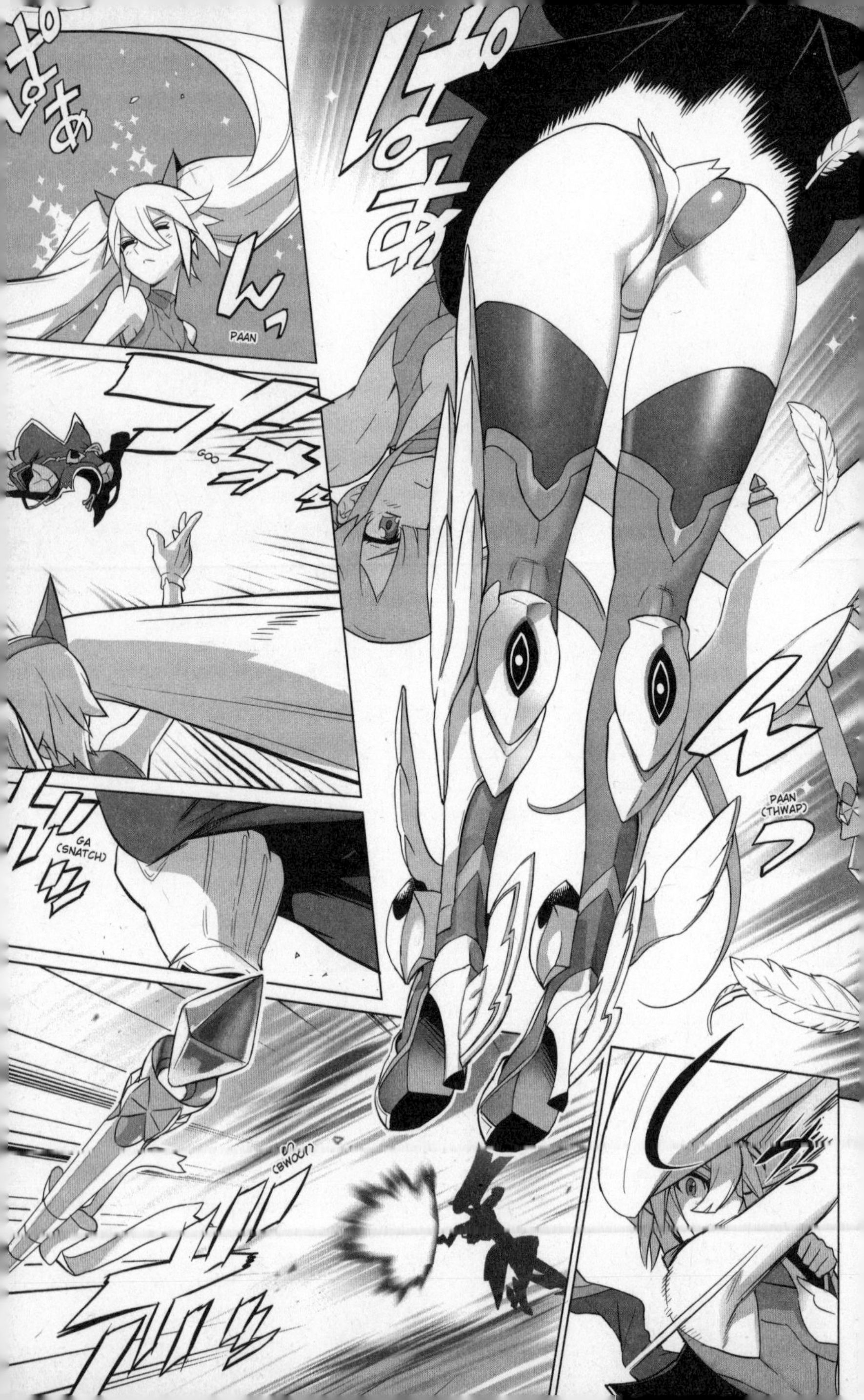

PAAN
GOO
PAAN
(THWAP)
GA
(SNATCH)

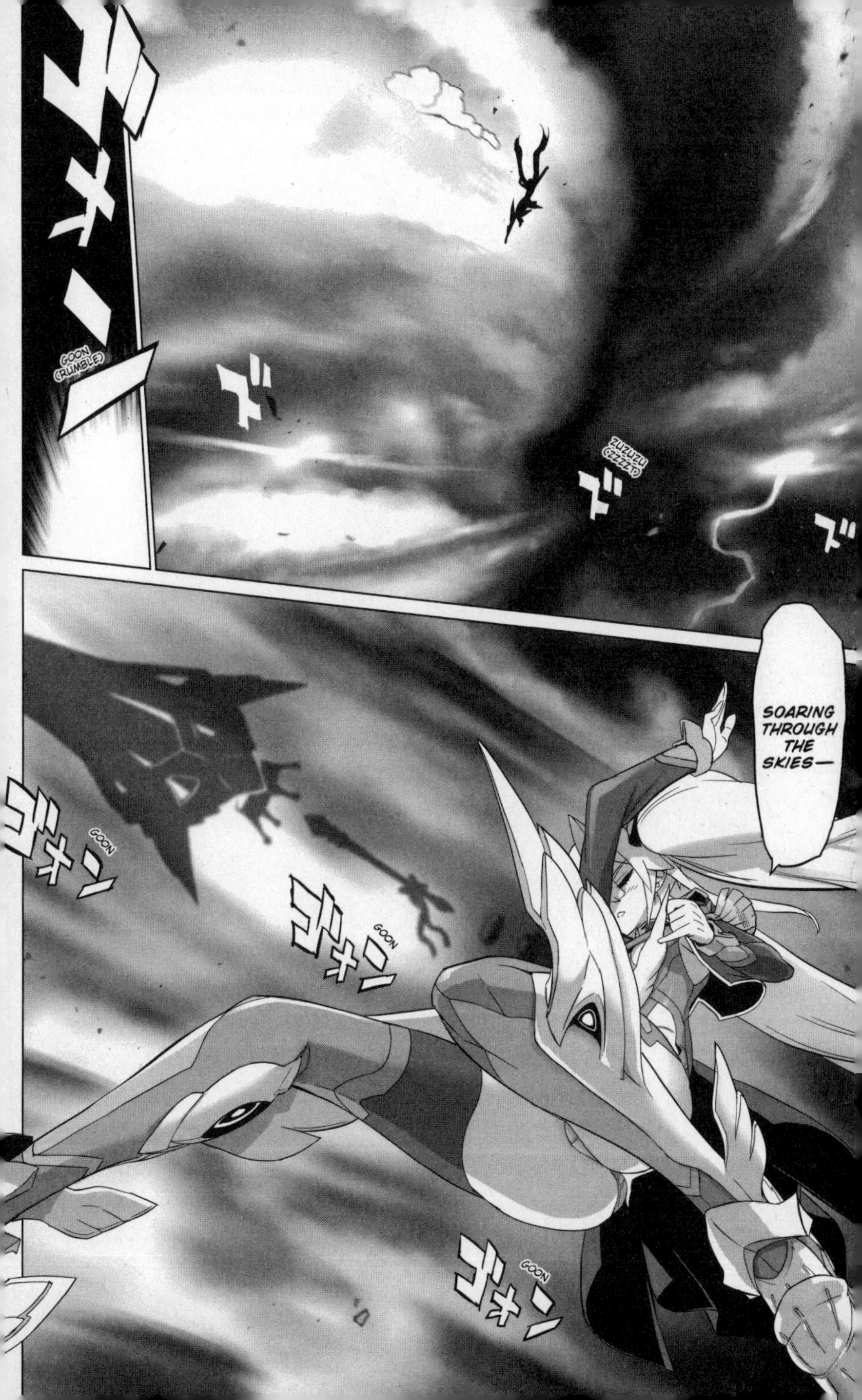
ZUZUZU (ZZZZZ!)
GOON (RUMBLE)
SOARING THROUGH THE SKIES—
GOON
GOON
GOON

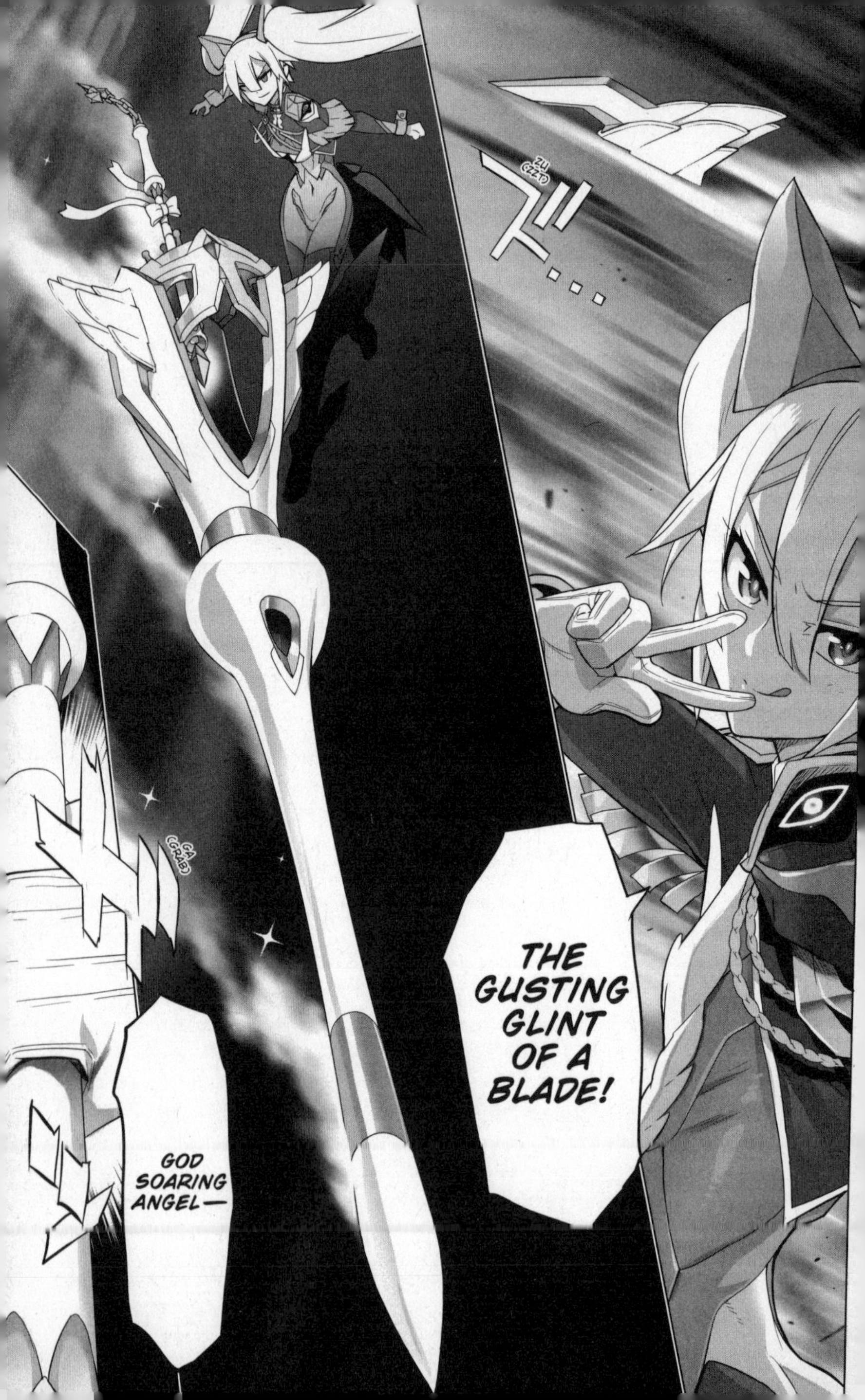
ZU (ZZZT)
THE GUSTING GLINT OF A BLADE!
GA (GRAB)
GOD SOARING ANGEL—

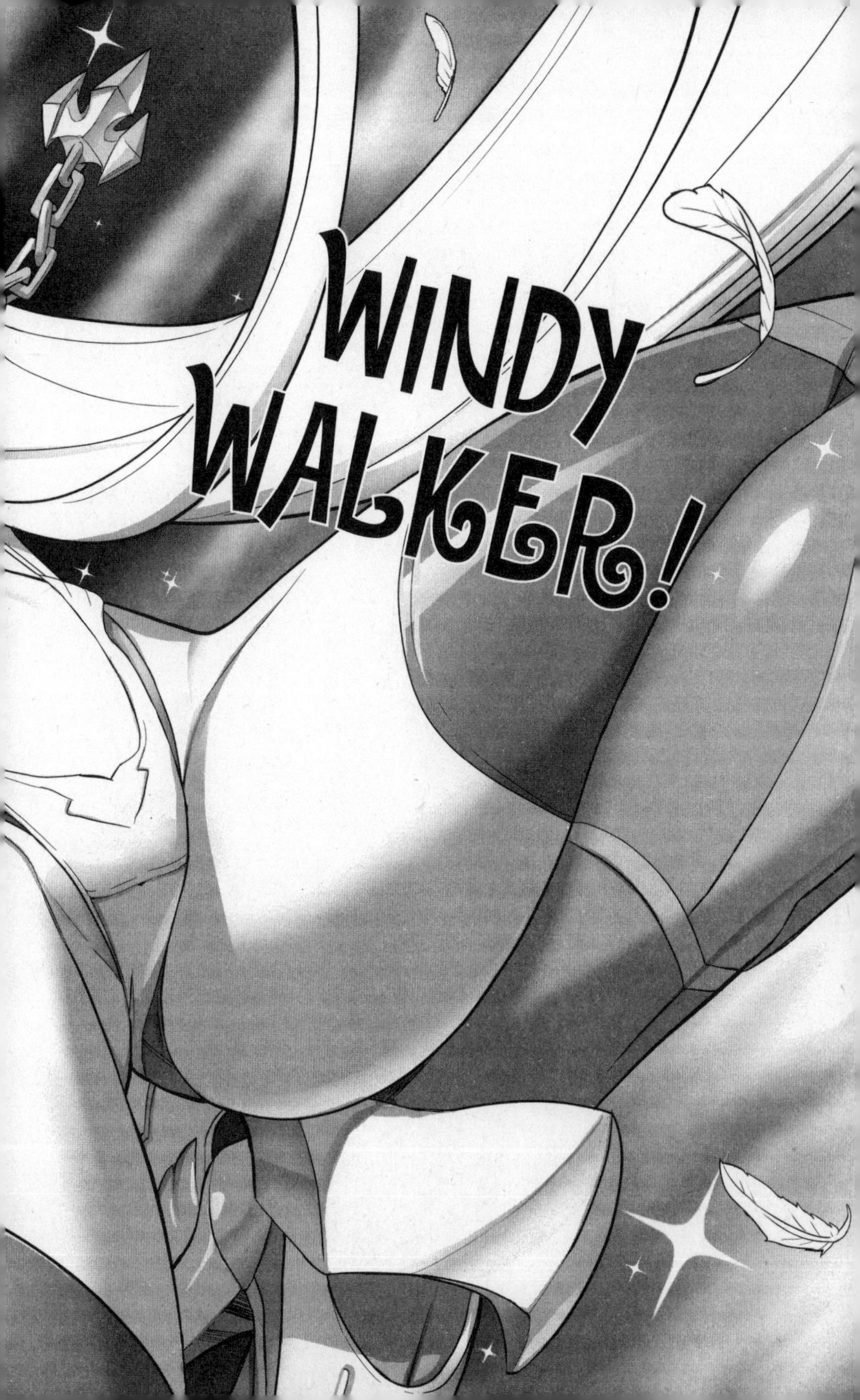
WINDY WALKER!

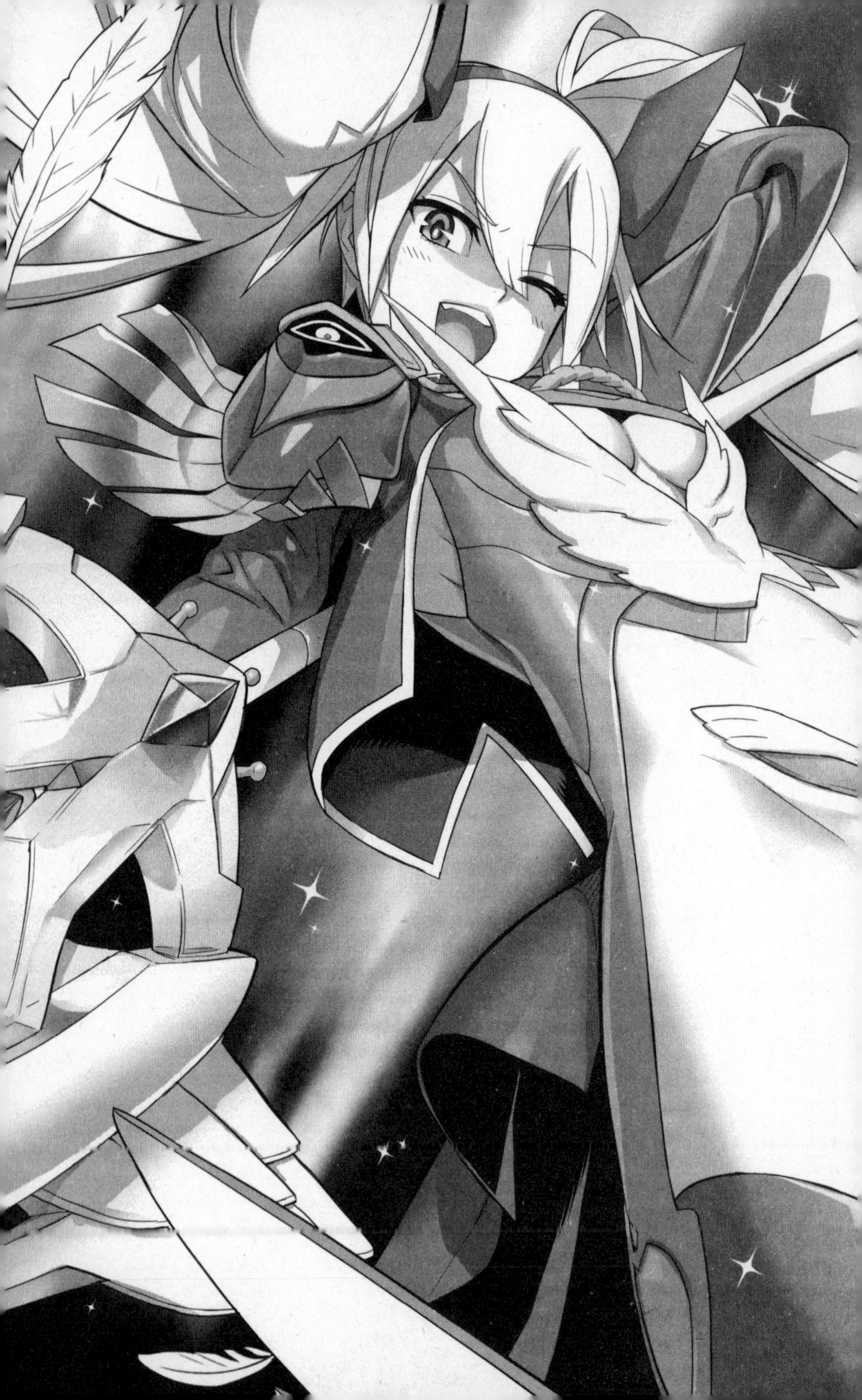

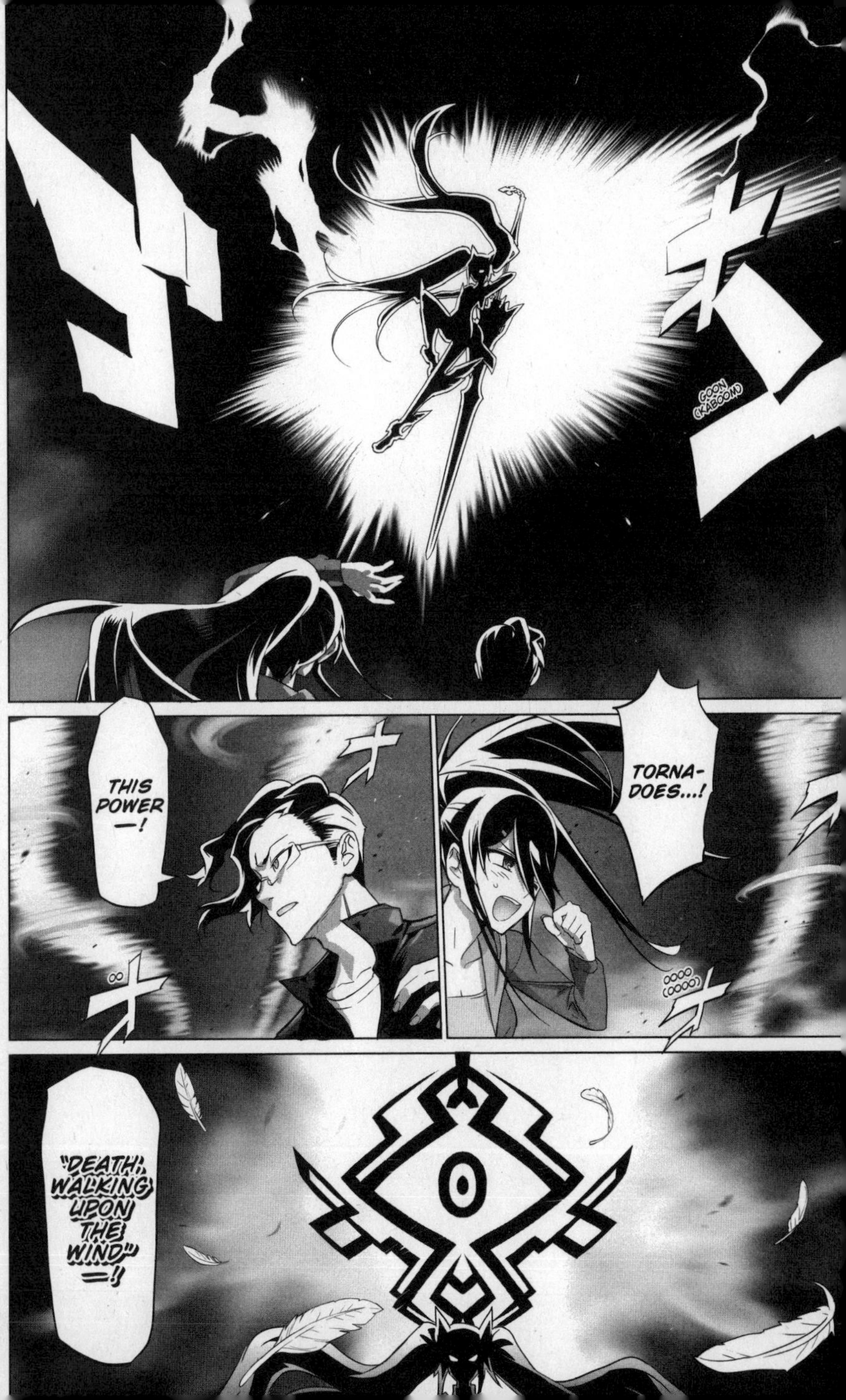
GOON (KABOOM)
TORNA-DOES...!
OOOO (OOOO)
THIS POWER—!
"DEATH WALKING UPON THE WIND"—!!

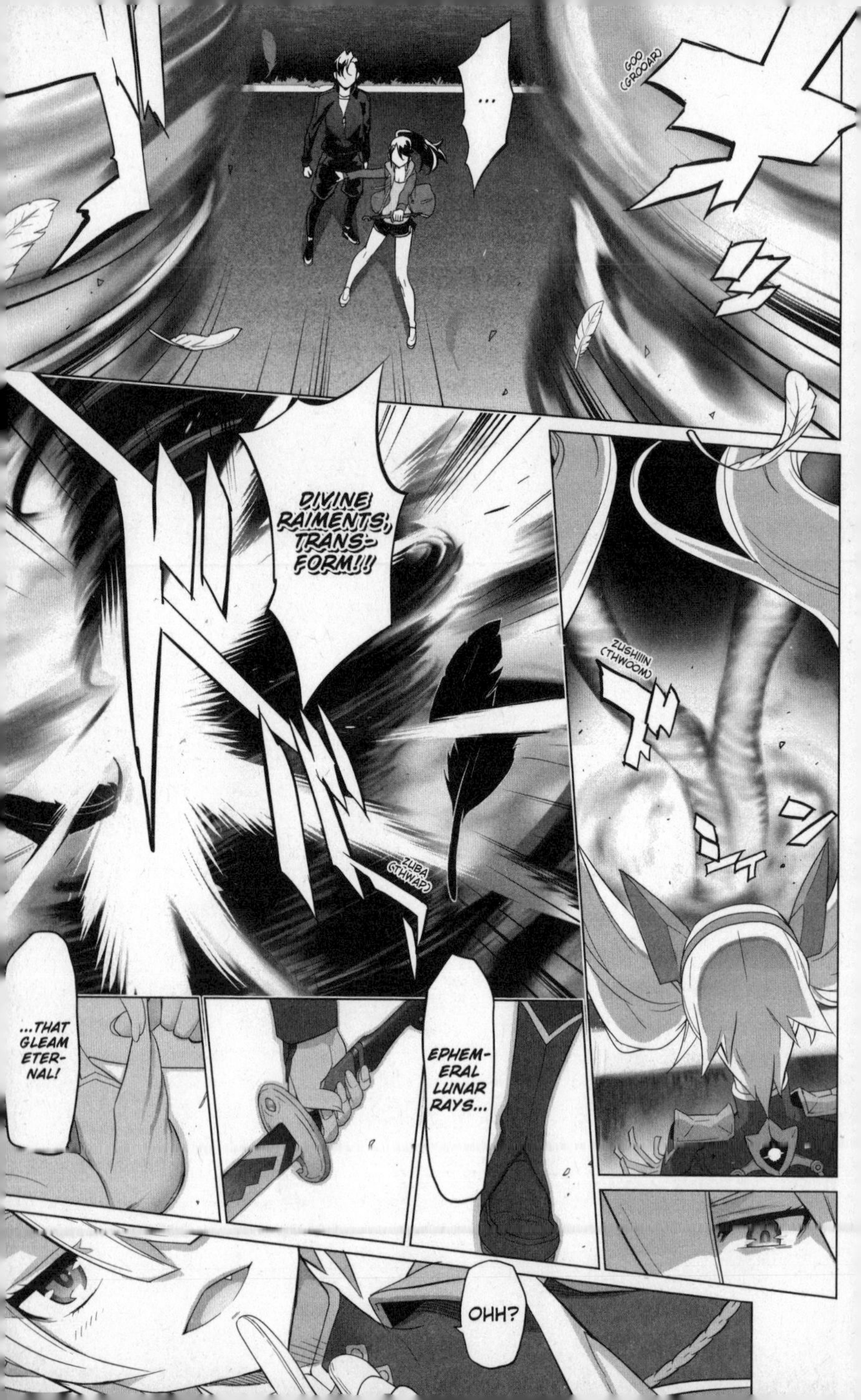
GOO
(GROOAR)
...
ZUSHIIIN
(THWOOM)
DIVINE RAIMENTS, TRANSFORM!!
ZUBA
(THWAP)
EPHEMERAL LUNAR RAYS...
...THAT GLEAM ETERNAL!
OHH?

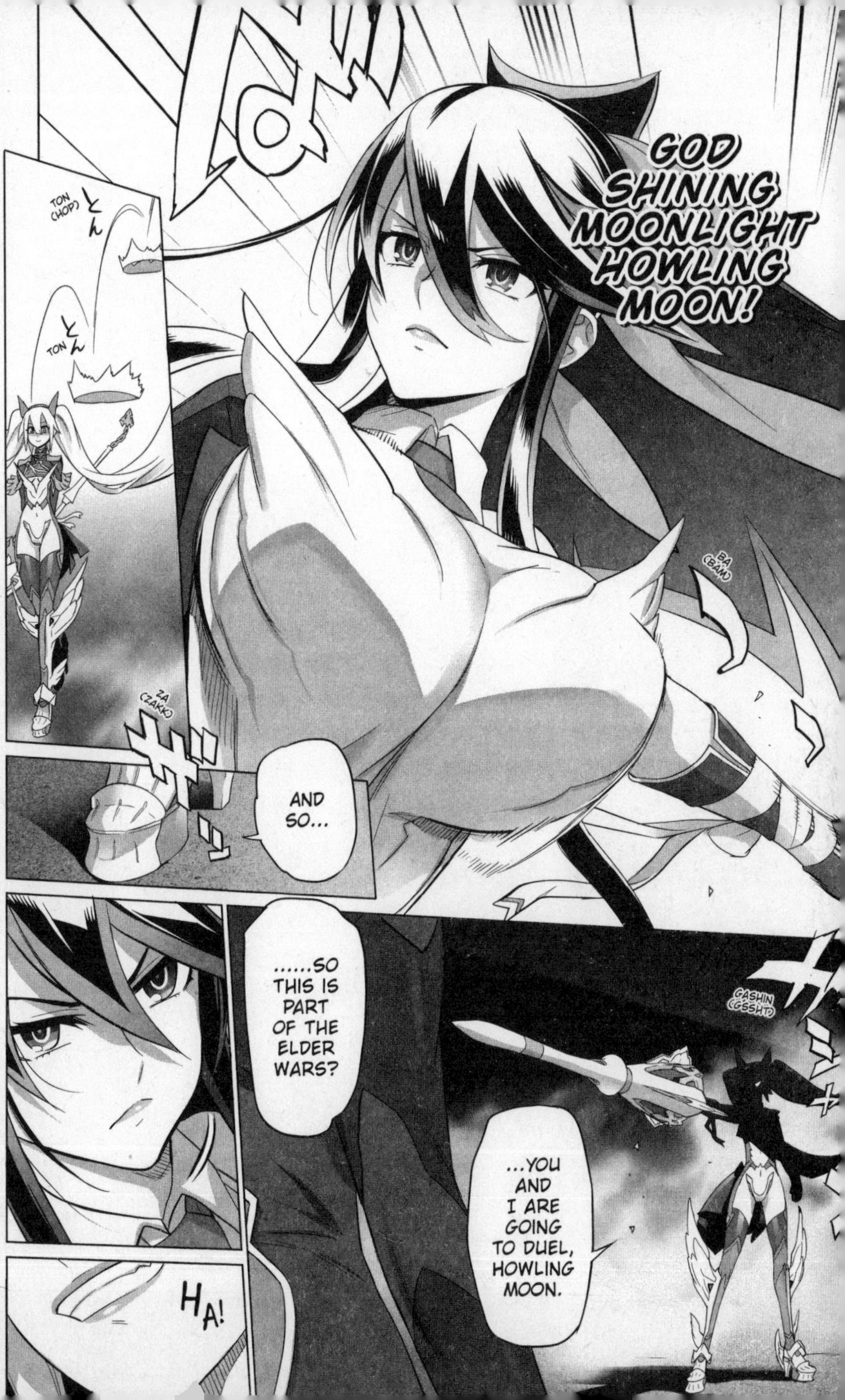
GOD SHINING MOONLIGHT HOWLING MOON!
BA (BAM)
TON (HOP)
TON
ZA (ZAKK)
AND SO...
GASHIN (GSSHT)
......SO THIS IS PART OF THE ELDER WARS?
...YOU AND I ARE GOING TO DUEL, HOWLING MOON.
HA!

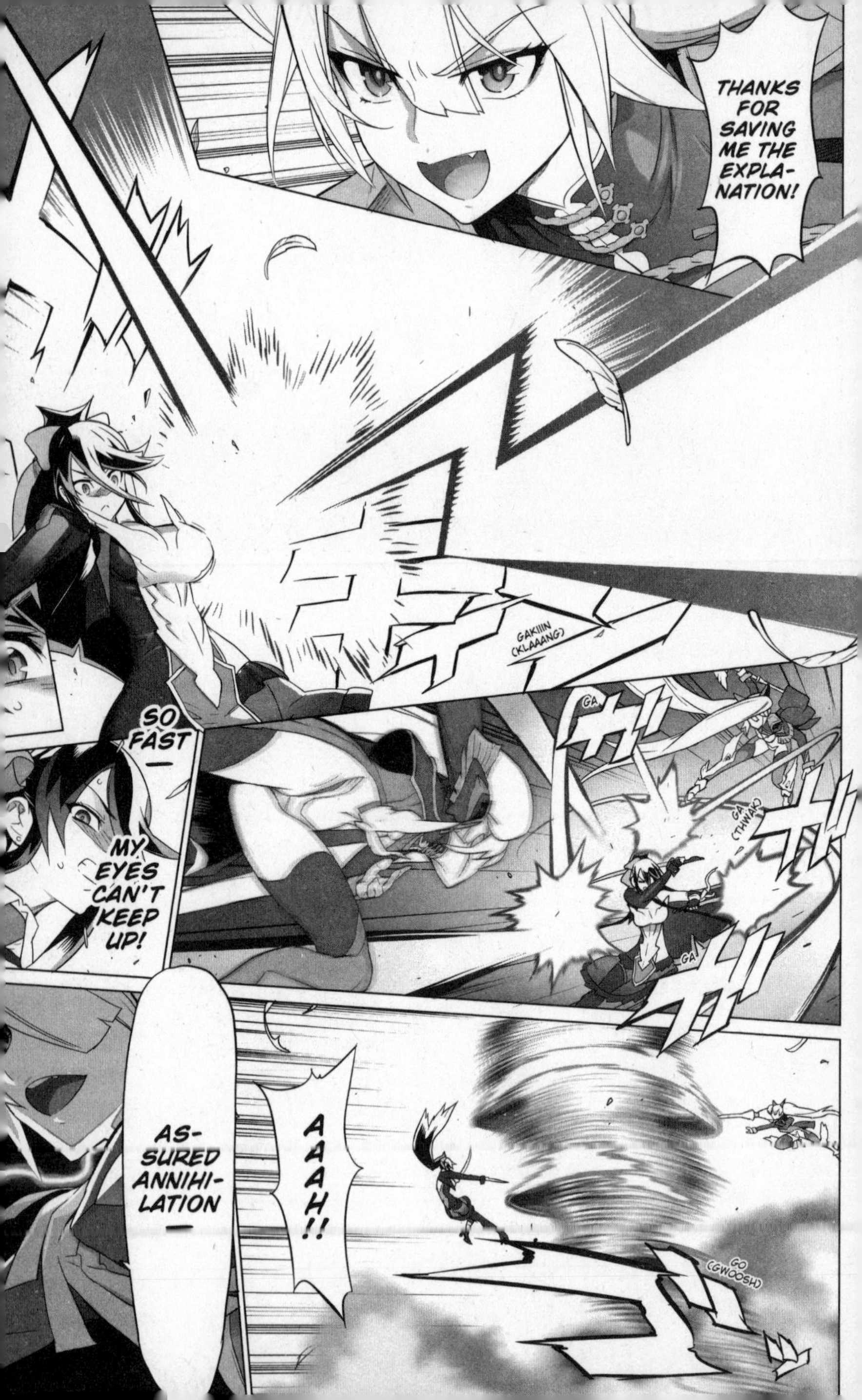
THANKS FOR SAVING ME THE EXPLA-NATION!
GAKIIIN (KLAAANG)
GA
GA (THWAK)
GA
SO FAST—
MY EYES CAN'T KEEP UP!
GO (GWOOSH)
AAAAH!!
AS-SURED ANNIHI-LATION—

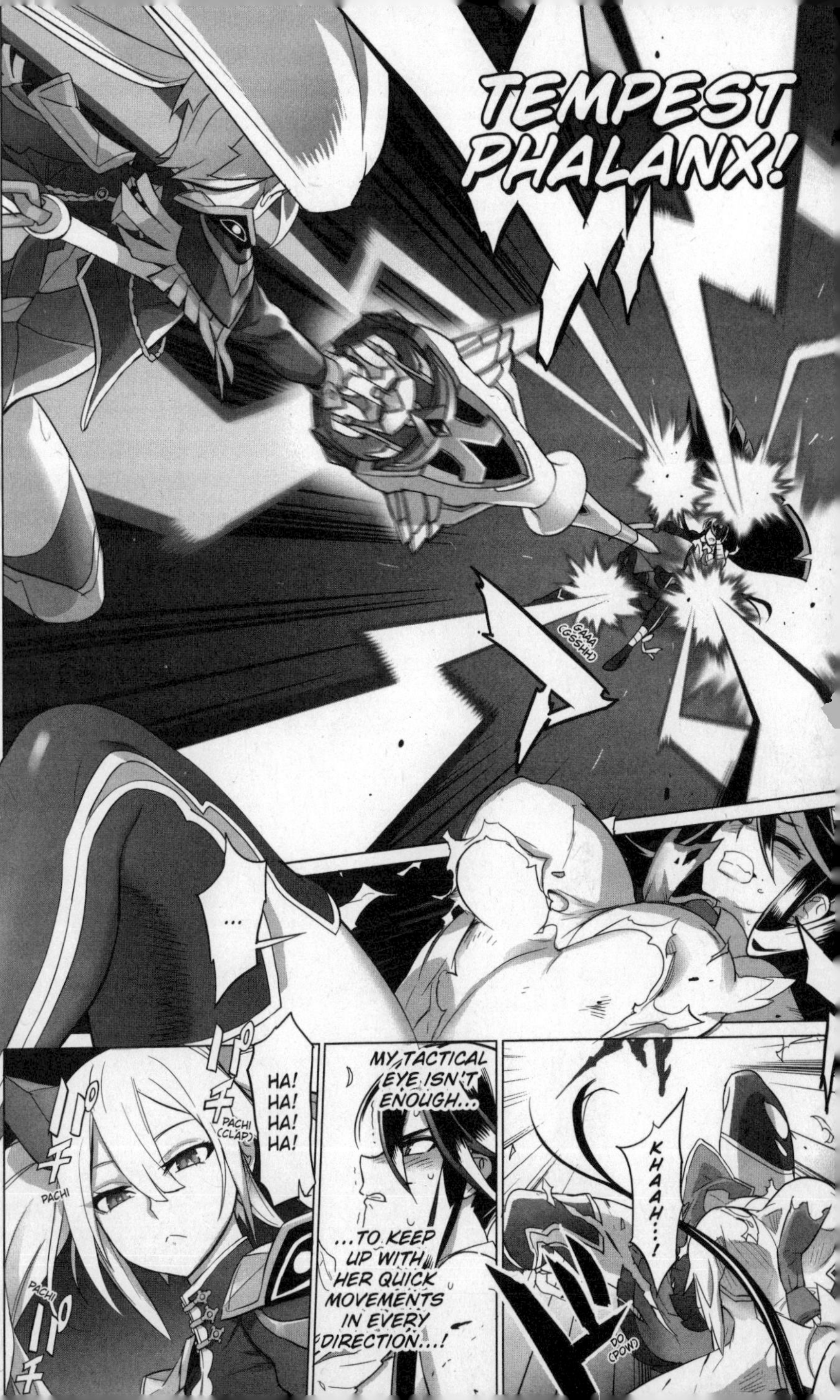
TEMPEST PHALANX!
GAAA (GSSHH)
...
KHAAAH...!
DO (POW)
MY TACTICAL EYE ISN'T ENOUGH...
...TO KEEP UP WITH HER QUICK MOVEMENTS IN EVERY DIRECTION...!
HA! HA! HA! HA!
PACHI (CLAP)
PACHI
PACHI

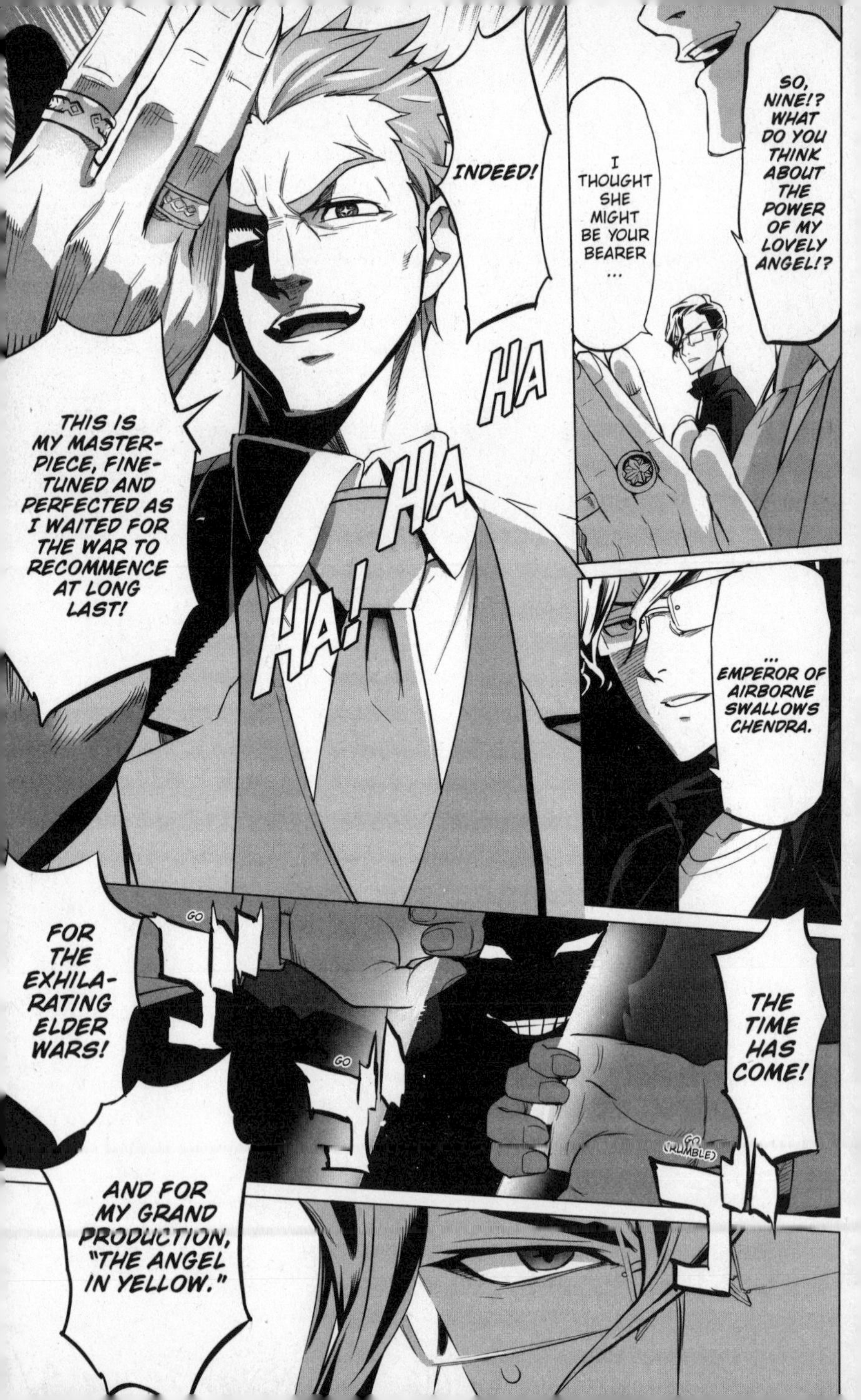
SO, NINE!? WHAT DO YOU THINK ABOUT THE POWER OF MY LOVELY ANGEL!?
I THOUGHT SHE MIGHT BE YOUR BEARER...
...EMPEROR OF AIRBORNE SWALLOWS CHENDRA.
INDEED!
THIS IS MY MASTERPIECE, FINE-TUNED AND PERFECTED AS I WAITED FOR THE WAR TO RECOMMENCE AT LONG LAST!
HA HA HA!
THE TIME HAS COME!
GO
GO
GO (RUMBLE)
FOR THE EXHILARATING ELDER WARS!
AND FOR MY GRAND PRODUCTION, "THE ANGEL IN YELLOW."

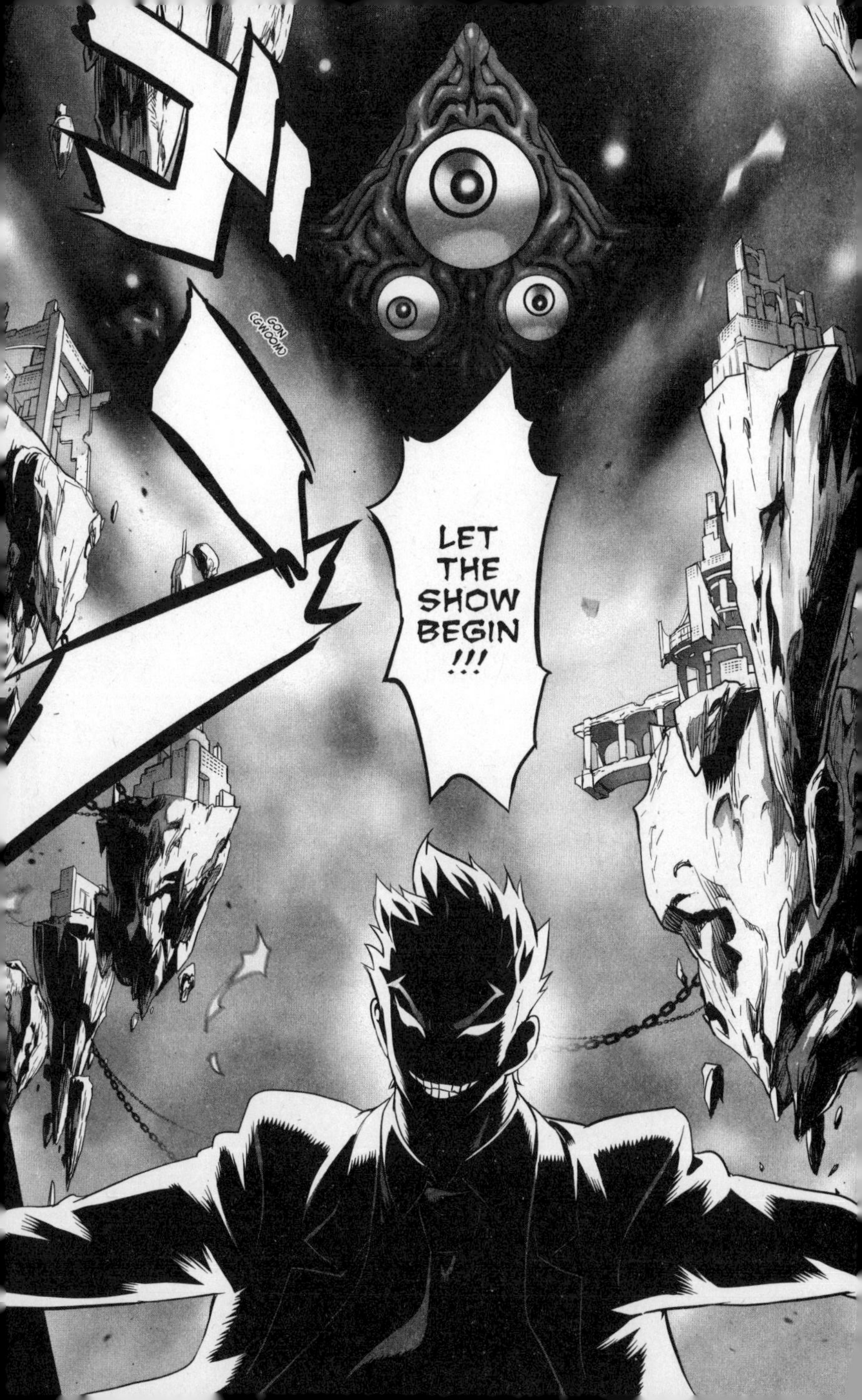
GON (GWOOM)
LET THE SHOW BEGIN!!!

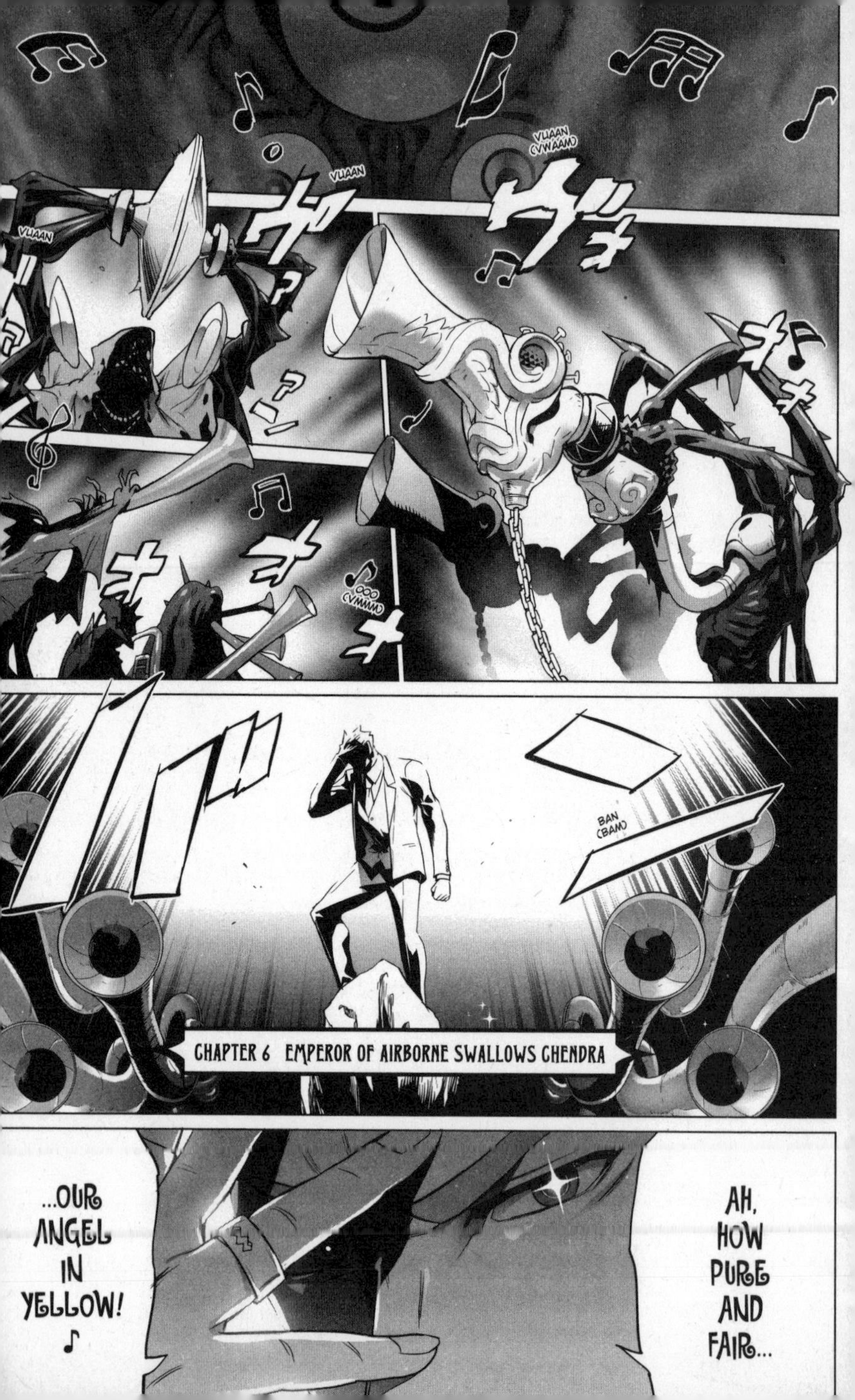
VUAAN (VWAAM)
VUAAN
VUAAN
OOO (VMMMM)
BAN (BAM)
CHAPTER 6 EMPEROR OF AIRBORNE SWALLOWS CHENDRA
AH, HOW PURE AND FAIR...
...OUR ANGEL IN YELLOW! ♪

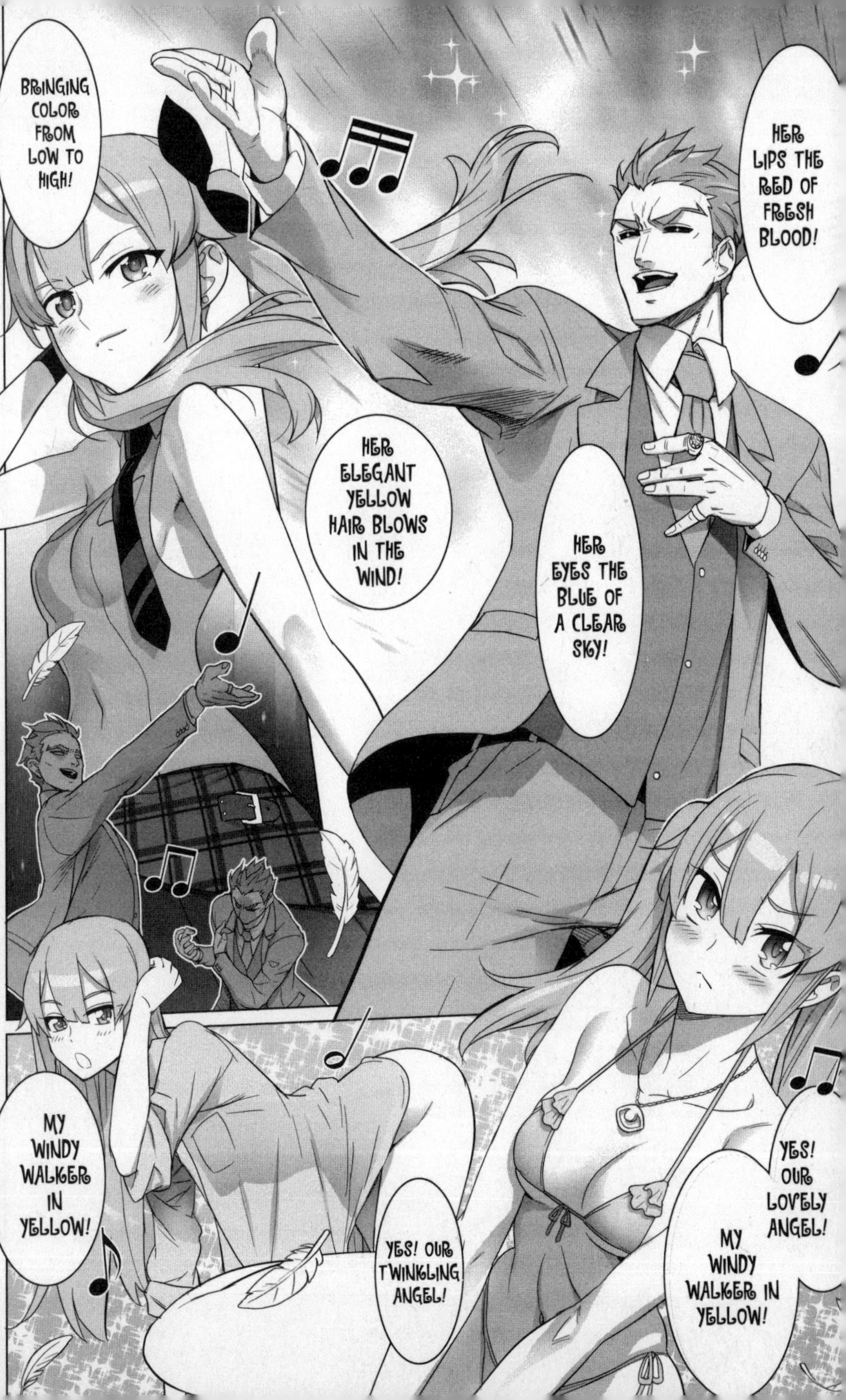
HER LIPS THE RED OF FRESH BLOOD!
BRINGING COLOR FROM LOW TO HIGH!
HER ELEGANT YELLOW HAIR BLOWS IN THE WIND!
HER EYES THE BLUE OF A CLEAR SKY!
YES! OUR LOVELY ANGEL!
MY WINDY WALKER IN YELLOW!
YES! OUR TWINKLING ANGEL!
MY WINDY WALKER IN YELLOW!

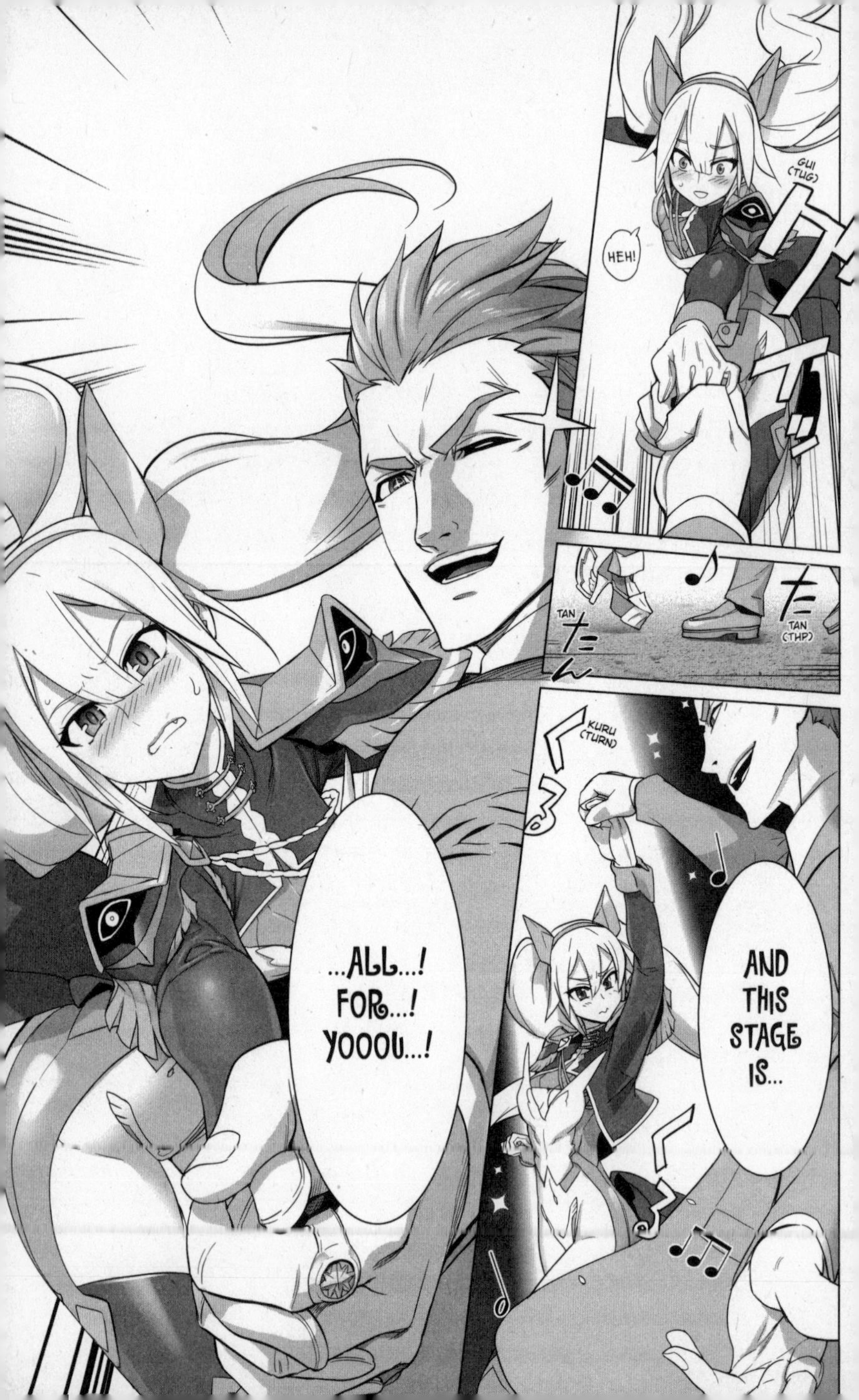
GUI (TUG)
HEH!
TAN
TAN (THP)
KURU (TURN)
AND THIS STAGE IS...
...ALL...! FOR...! YOOOU...!

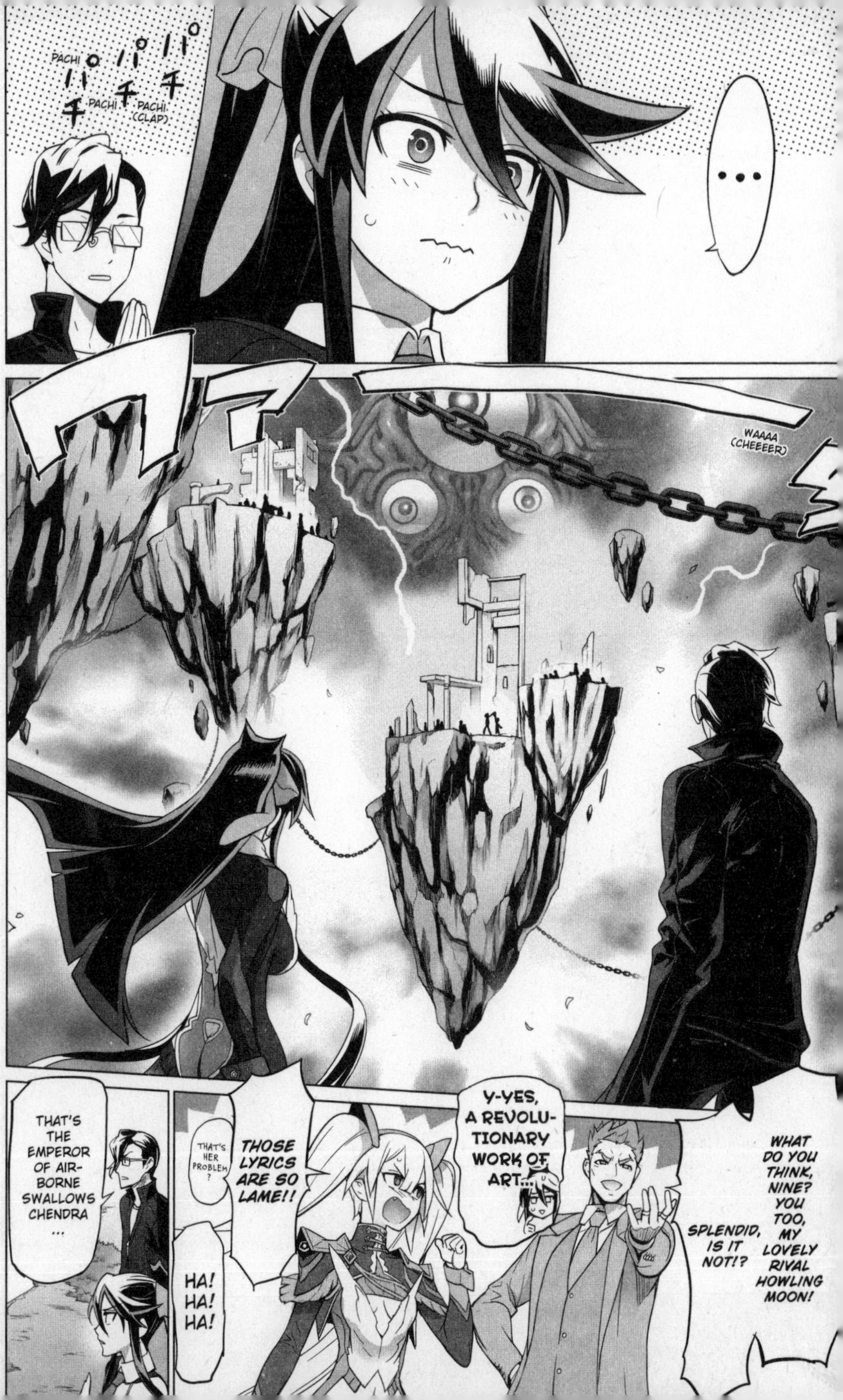
...
パチ PACHI
パチ PACHI
パチ PACHI (CLAP)
WAAAA (CHEEEER)
WHAT DO YOU THINK, NINE? YOU TOO, MY LOVELY RIVAL HOWLING MOON!
SPLENDID, IS IT NOT!?
Y-YES, A REVOLUTIONARY WORK OF ART...
THOSE LYRICS ARE SO LAME!!
THAT'S HER PROBLEM?
HA! HA! HA!
THAT'S THE EMPEROR OF AIRBORNE SWALLOWS CHENDRA ...

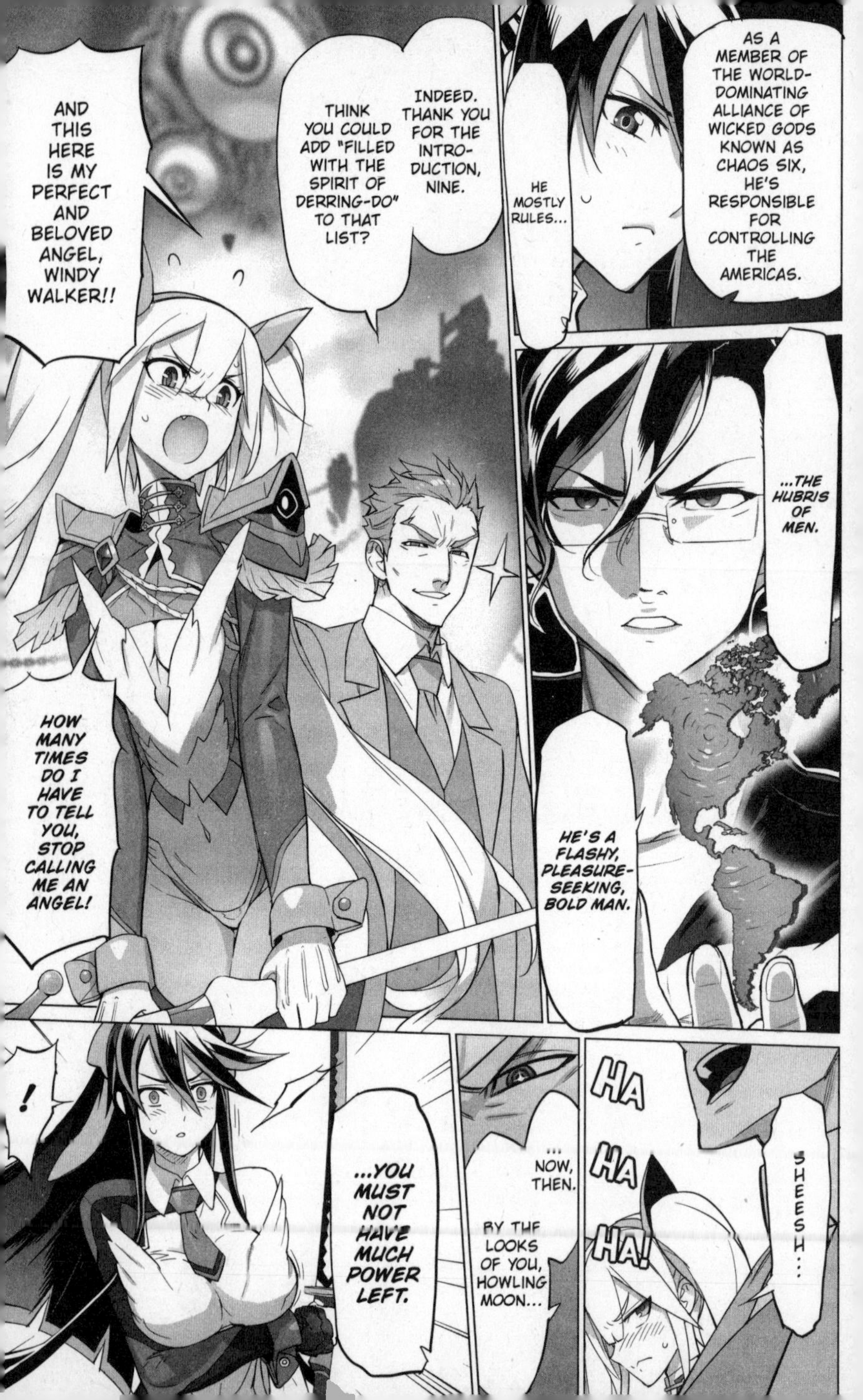

AS A MEMBER OF THE WORLD-DOMINATING ALLIANCE OF WICKED GODS KNOWN AS CHAOS SIX, HE'S RESPONSIBLE FOR CONTROLLING THE AMERICAS.
HE MOSTLY RULES...
...THE HUBRIS OF MEN.
HE'S A FLASHY, PLEASURE-SEEKING, BOLD MAN.
INDEED. THANK YOU FOR THE INTRO-DUCTION, NINE.
THINK YOU COULD ADD "FILLED WITH THE SPIRIT OF DERRING-DO" TO THAT LIST?
AND THIS HERE IS MY PERFECT AND BELOVED ANGEL, WINDY WALKER!!
HOW MANY TIMES DO I HAVE TO TELL YOU, STOP CALLING ME AN ANGEL!
SHEESH...
HA
HA
HA!
... NOW, THEN.
BY THE LOOKS OF YOU, HOWLING MOON...
...YOU MUST NOT HAVE MUCH POWER LEFT.
!

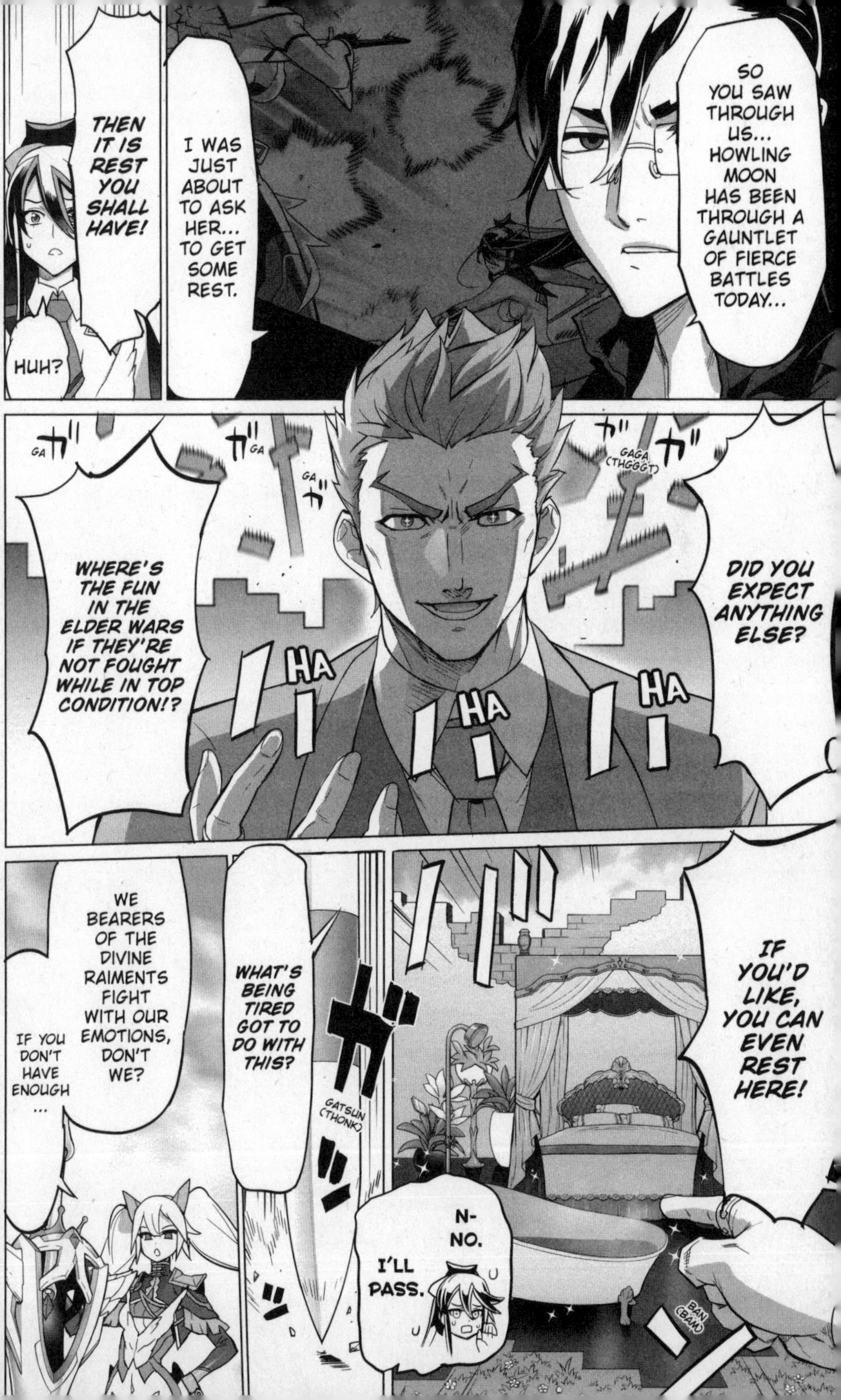
SO YOU SAW THROUGH US... HOWLING MOON HAS BEEN THROUGH A GAUNTLET OF FIERCE BATTLES TODAY...
I WAS JUST ABOUT TO ASK HER... TO GET SOME REST.
THEN IT IS REST YOU SHALL HAVE!
HUH?
GAGA (THGGGT)
GA
GA
GA
DID YOU EXPECT ANYTHING ELSE?
HA HA HA
WHERE'S THE FUN IN THE ELDER WARS IF THEY'RE NOT FOUGHT WHILE IN TOP CONDITION!?
IF YOU'D LIKE, YOU CAN EVEN REST HERE!
BAN (BAM)
N-NO. I'LL PASS.
WHAT'S BEING TIRED GOT TO DO WITH THIS?
GATSUN (THONK)
WE BEARERS OF THE DIVINE RAIMENTS FIGHT WITH OUR EMOTIONS, DON'T WE?
IF YOU DON'T HAVE ENOUGH ...

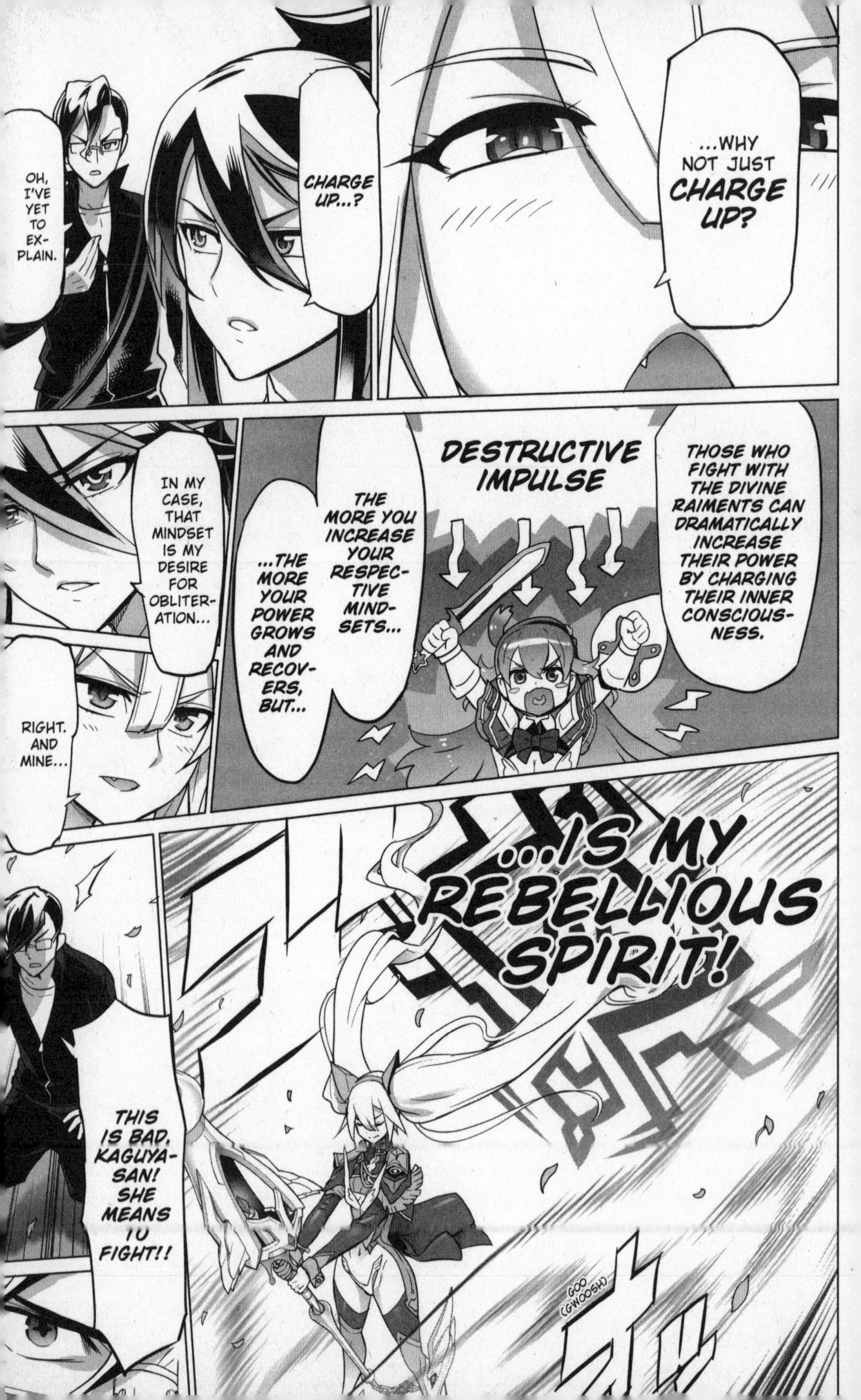
...WHY NOT JUST CHARGE UP?
CHARGE UP...?
OH, I'VE YET TO EX-PLAIN.
THOSE WHO FIGHT WITH THE DIVINE RAIMENTS CAN DRAMATICALLY INCREASE THEIR POWER BY CHARGING THEIR INNER CONSCIOUS-NESS.
DESTRUCTIVE IMPULSE
THE MORE YOU INCREASE YOUR RESPEC-TIVE MIND-SETS...
...THE MORE YOUR POWER GROWS AND RECOV-ERS, BUT...
IN MY CASE, THAT MINDSET IS MY DESIRE FOR OBLITER-ATION...
RIGHT. AND MINE...
...IS MY REBELLIOUS SPIRIT!
GOO (GWOOSH)
THIS IS BAD, KAGUYA-SAN! SHE MEANS TO FIGHT!!

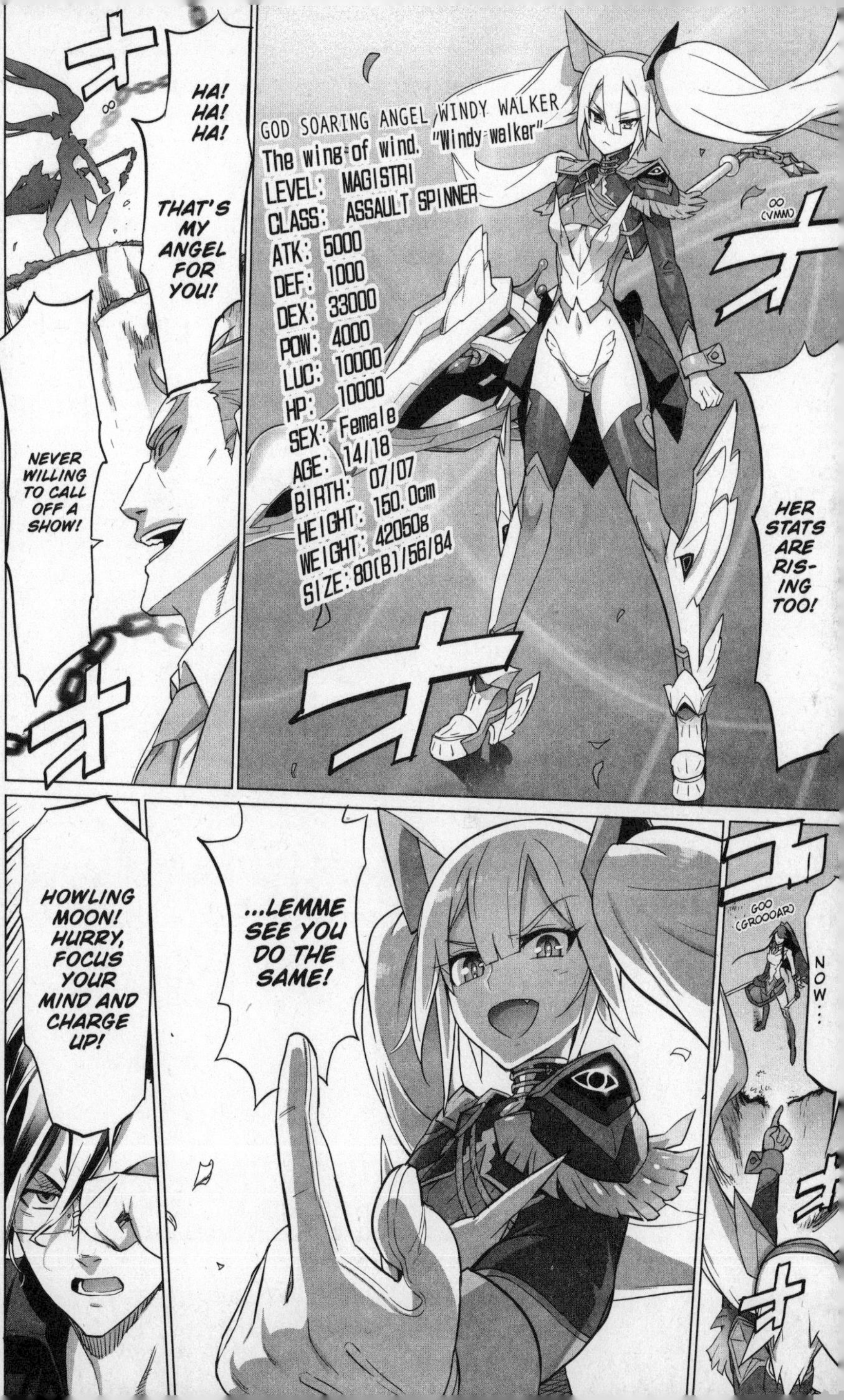
∞ (VMM)
GOD SOARING ANGEL WINDY WALKER
The wing of wind. "Windy walker"
LEVEL: MAGISTRI
CLASS: ASSAULT SPINNER
ATK: 5000
DEF: 1000
DEX: 33000
POW: 4000
LUC: 10000
HP: 10000
SEX: Female
AGE: 14/18
BIRTH: 07/07
HEIGHT: 150.0cm
WEIGHT: 42050g
SIZE: 80(B)/56/84
HER STATS ARE RISING TOO!
HA! HA! HA!
THAT'S MY ANGEL FOR YOU!
NEVER WILLING TO CALL OFF A SHOW!
GOO (GROOOAR)
NOW...
...LEMME SEE YOU DO THE SAME!
HOWLING MOON! HURRY, FOCUS YOUR MIND AND CHARGE UP!

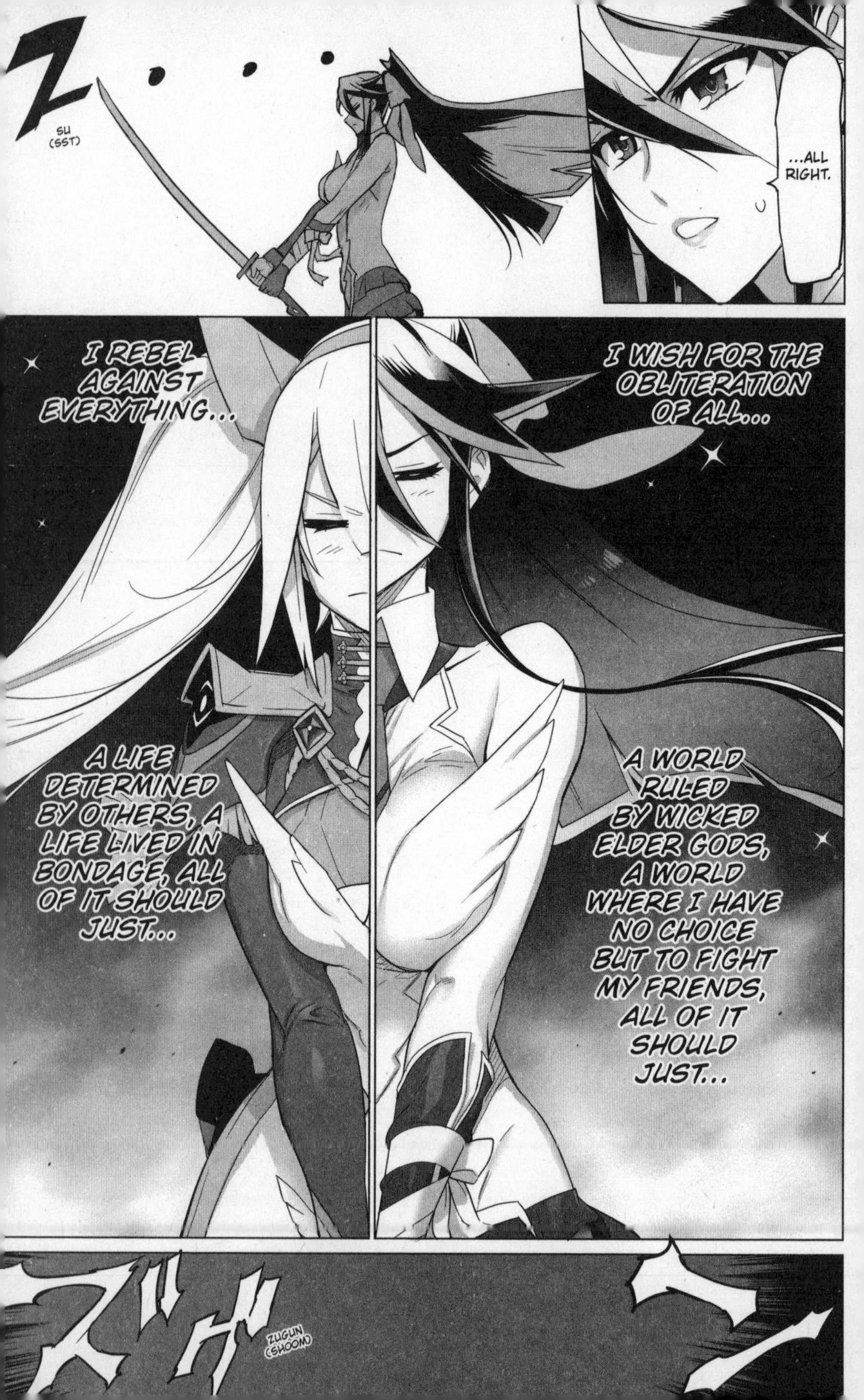
...ALL RIGHT.
SU (SST)
I WISH FOR THE OBLITERATION OF ALL...
I REBEL AGAINST EVERYTHING...
A WORLD RULED BY WICKED ELDER GODS, A WORLD WHERE I HAVE NO CHOICE BUT TO FIGHT MY FRIENDS, ALL OF IT SHOULD JUST...
A LIFE DETERMINED BY OTHERS, A LIFE LIVED IN BONDAGE, ALL OF IT SHOULD JUST...
ZUGUN (SHOOM)

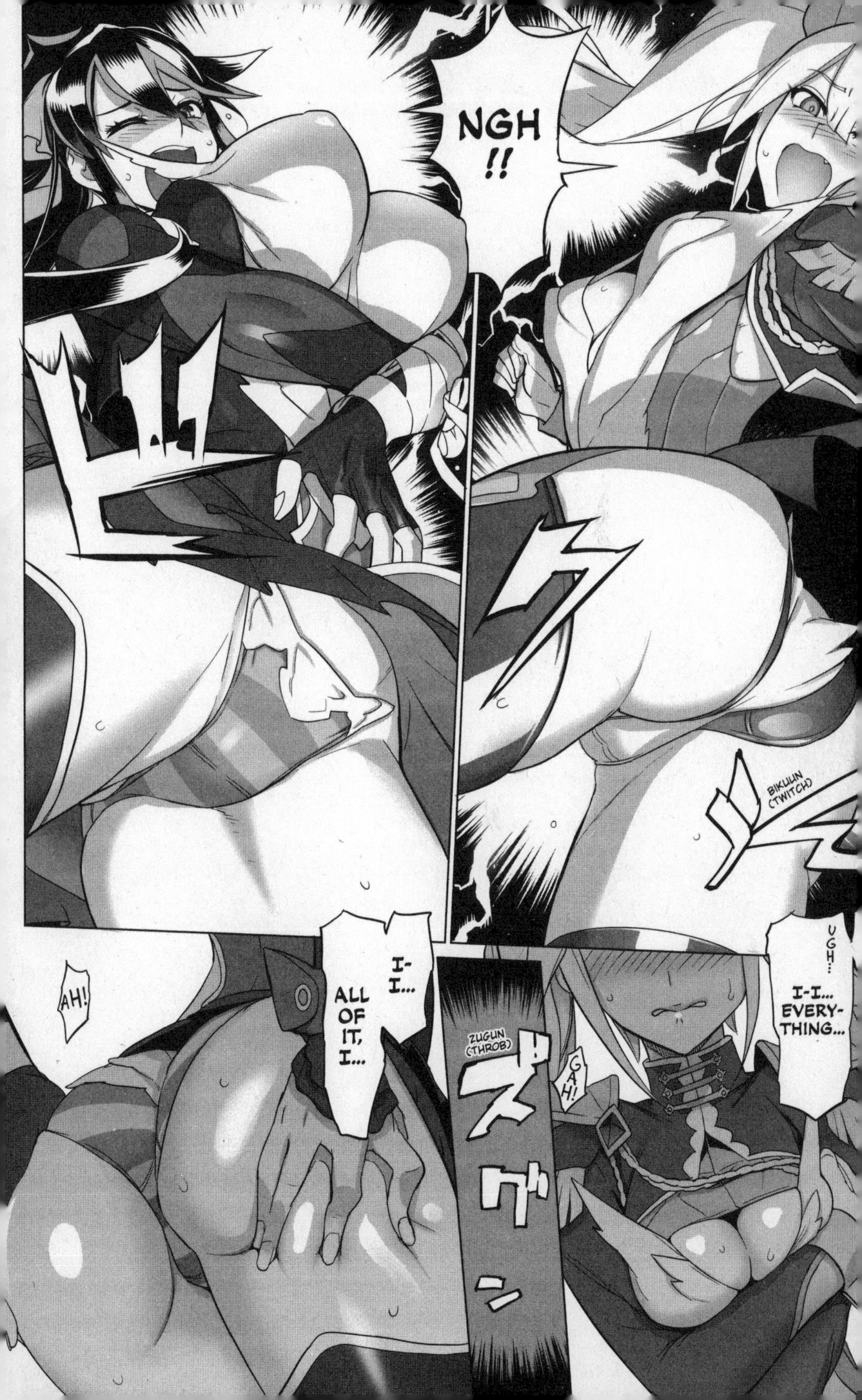
NGH !!
BIKUUN (TWITCH)
UGH...
I-I... EVERYTHING...
GAH!
ZUGUN (THROB)
I- I...
ALL OF IT, I...
AH!

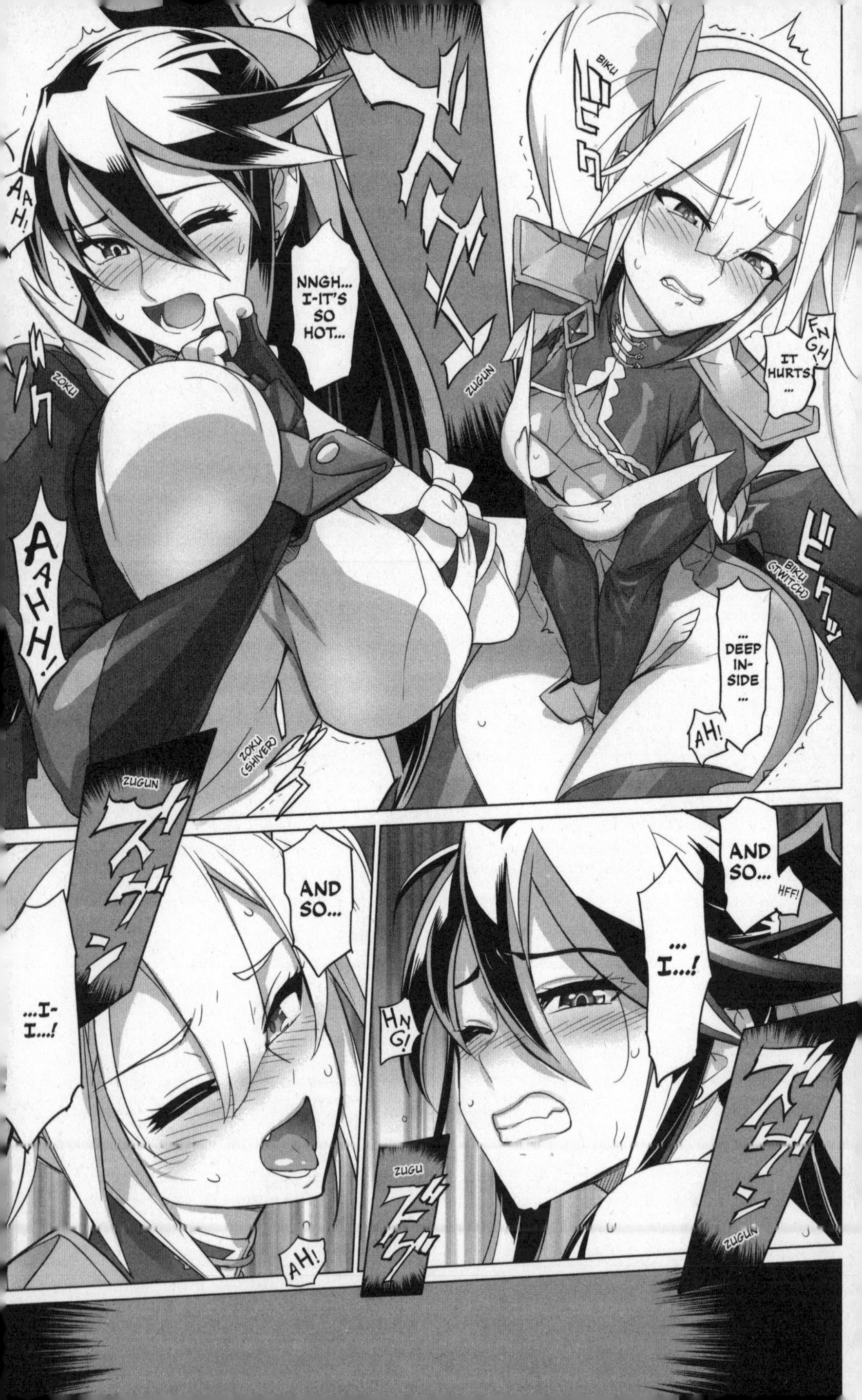
BIKU
FNGH!
IT HURTS...
ZUGUN
BIKU (TWITCH)
...DEEP IN-SIDE...
AH!
NNGH... I-IT'S SO HOT...
AAH!
ZOKU
AAHH!
ZOKU (SHIVER)
ZUGUN
AND SO...
HFF!
...I...!
HNG!
ZUGU
ZUGUN
AND SO...
...I-I...!
AH!

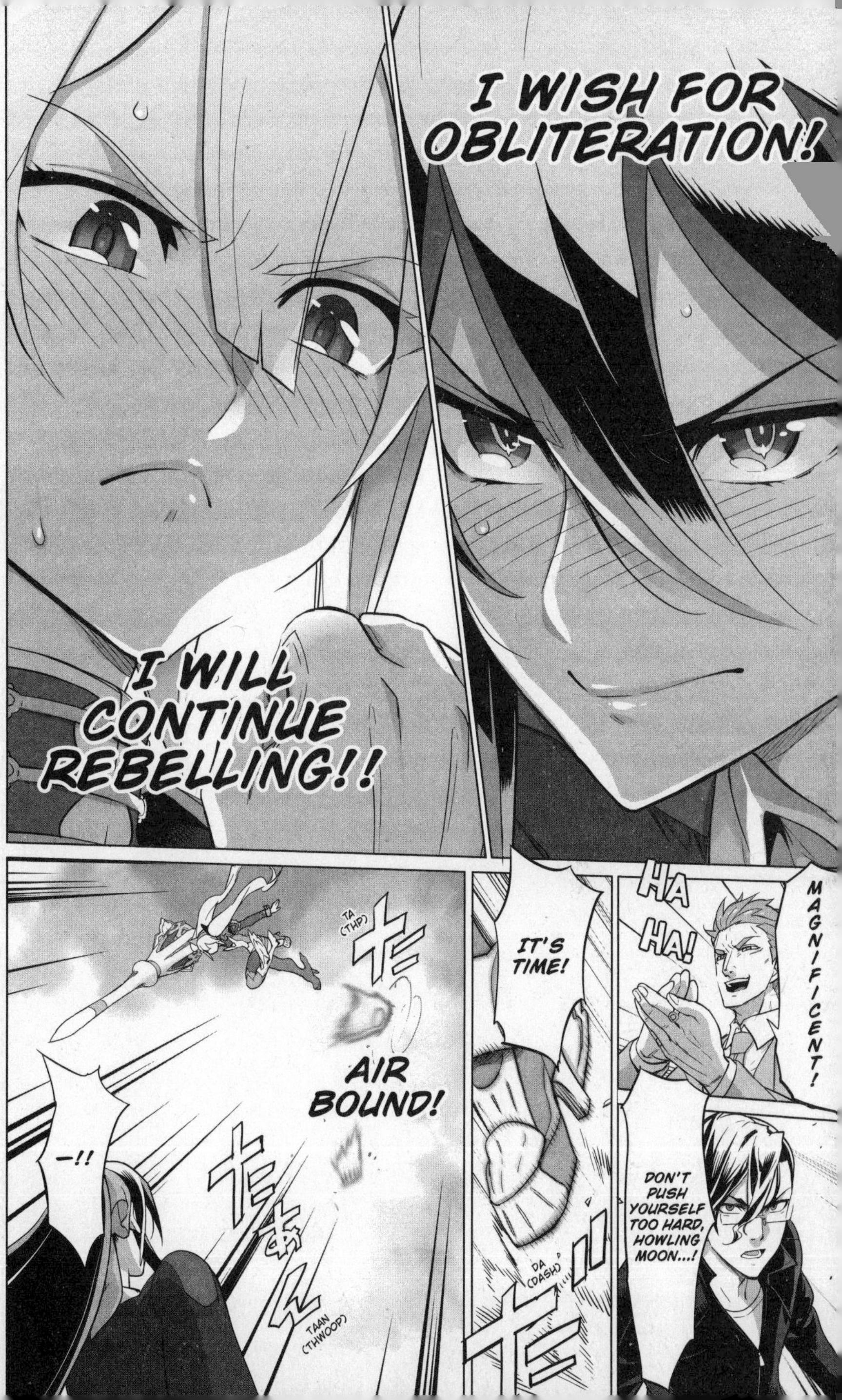
I WISH FOR OBLITERATION!
I WILL CONTINUE REBELLING!!
MAGNIFICENT!
HA HA!
DON'T PUSH YOURSELF TOO HARD, HOWLING MOON...!
IT'S TIME!
DA (DASH)
TA (THP)
AIR BOUND!
—!!
TAAN (THWOOP)

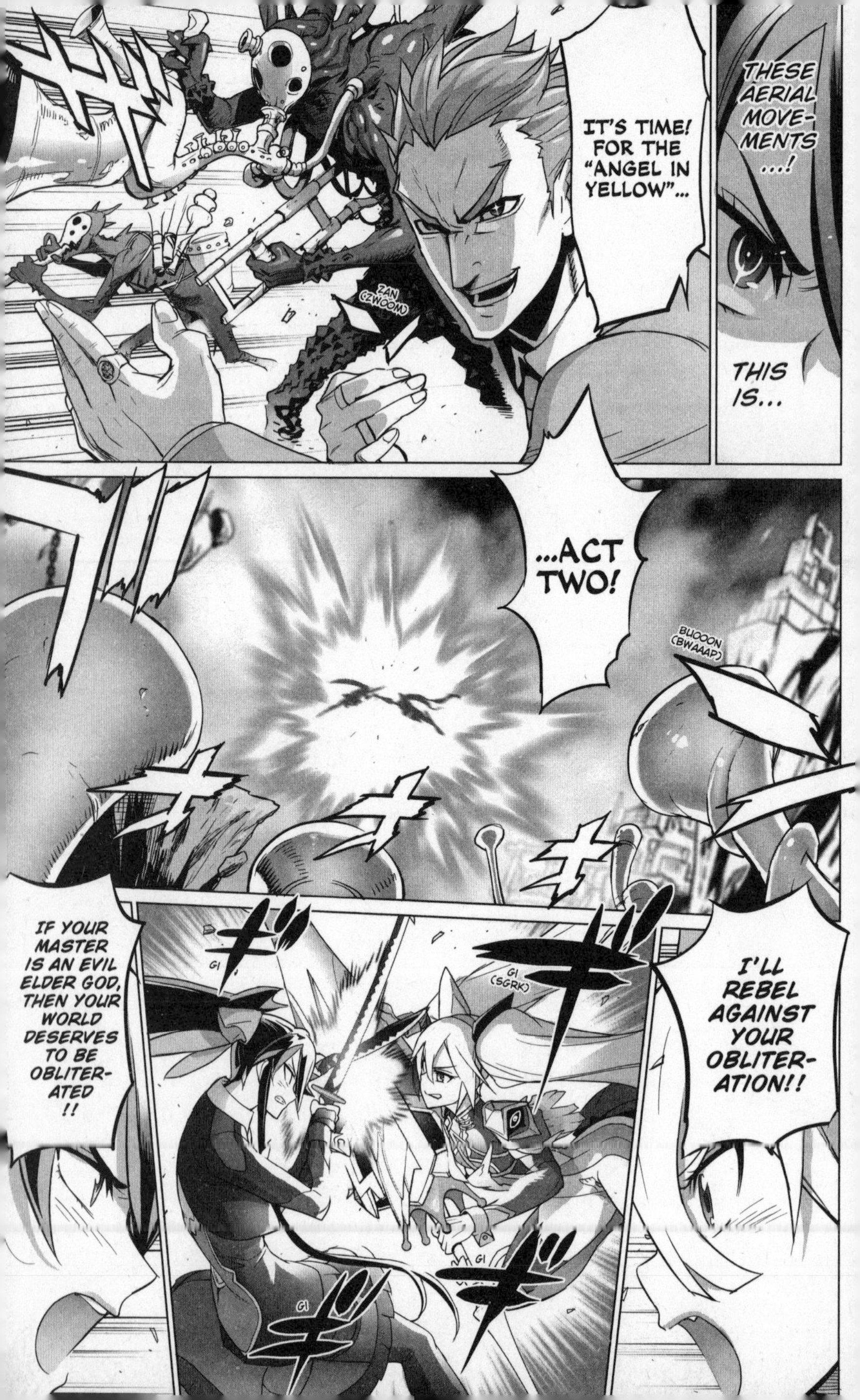

THESE AERIAL MOVE-MENTS ...!
THIS IS...
IT'S TIME! FOR THE "ANGEL IN YELLOW"...
ZAN (ZWOOM)
...ACT TWO!
BUOOON (BWAAAP)
I'LL REBEL AGAINST YOUR OBLITER-ATION!!
GI (SGRK)
GI
IF YOUR MASTER IS AN EVIL ELDER GOD, THEN YOUR WORLD DESERVES TO BE OBLITER-ATED !!
GI
GI

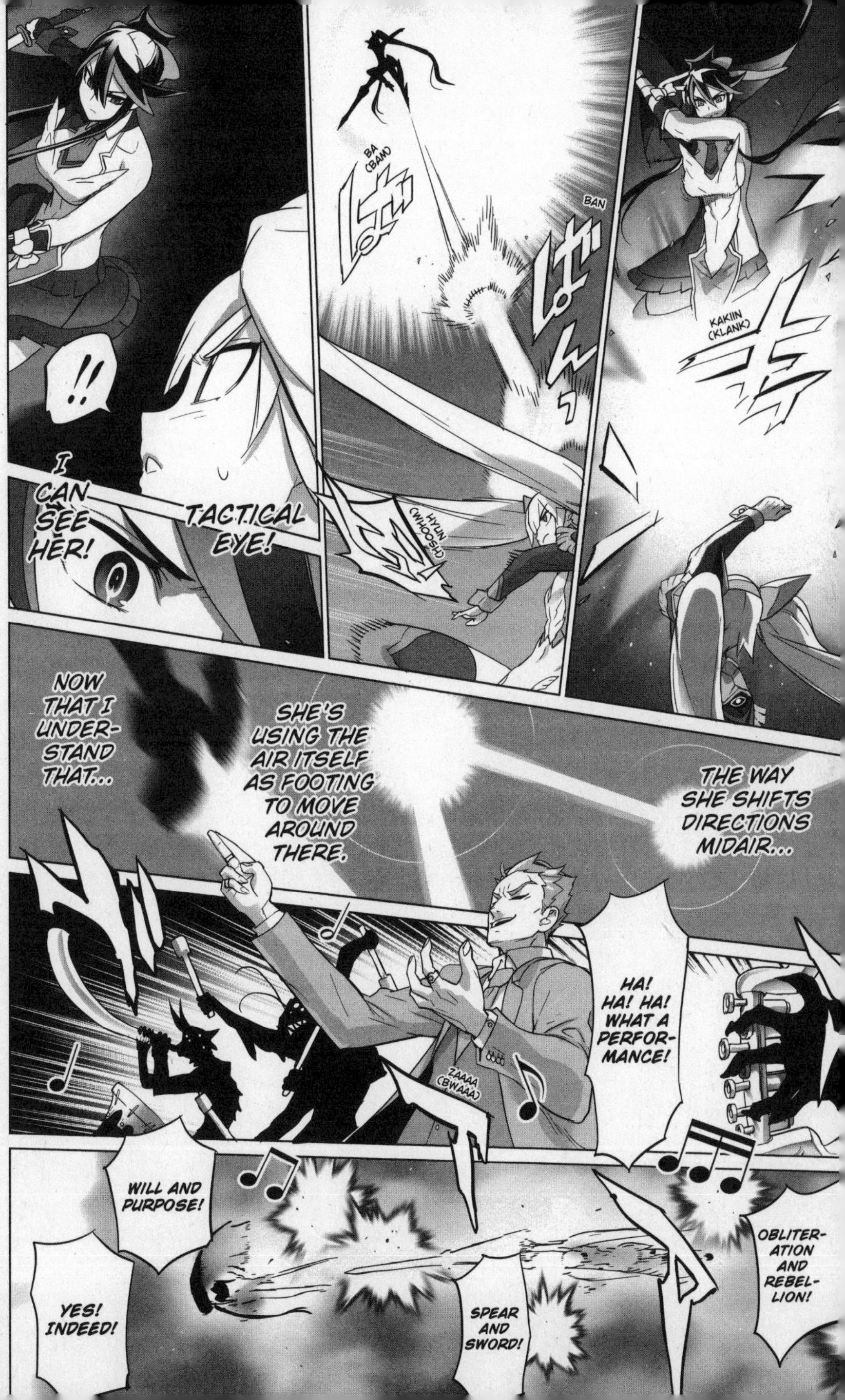
KAKIIN (KLANK)
BAN
BA (BAM)
HYUN (WHOOSH)
!!
I CAN SEE HER!
TACTICAL EYE!
THE WAY SHE SHIFTS DIRECTIONS MIDAIR...
SHE'S USING THE AIR ITSELF AS FOOTING TO MOVE AROUND THERE.
NOW THAT I UNDERSTAND THAT...
HA! HA! HA! WHAT A PERFORMANCE!
ZAAAA (BWAAA)
OBLITERATION AND REBELLION!
SPEAR AND SWORD!
WILL AND PURPOSE!
YES! INDEED!

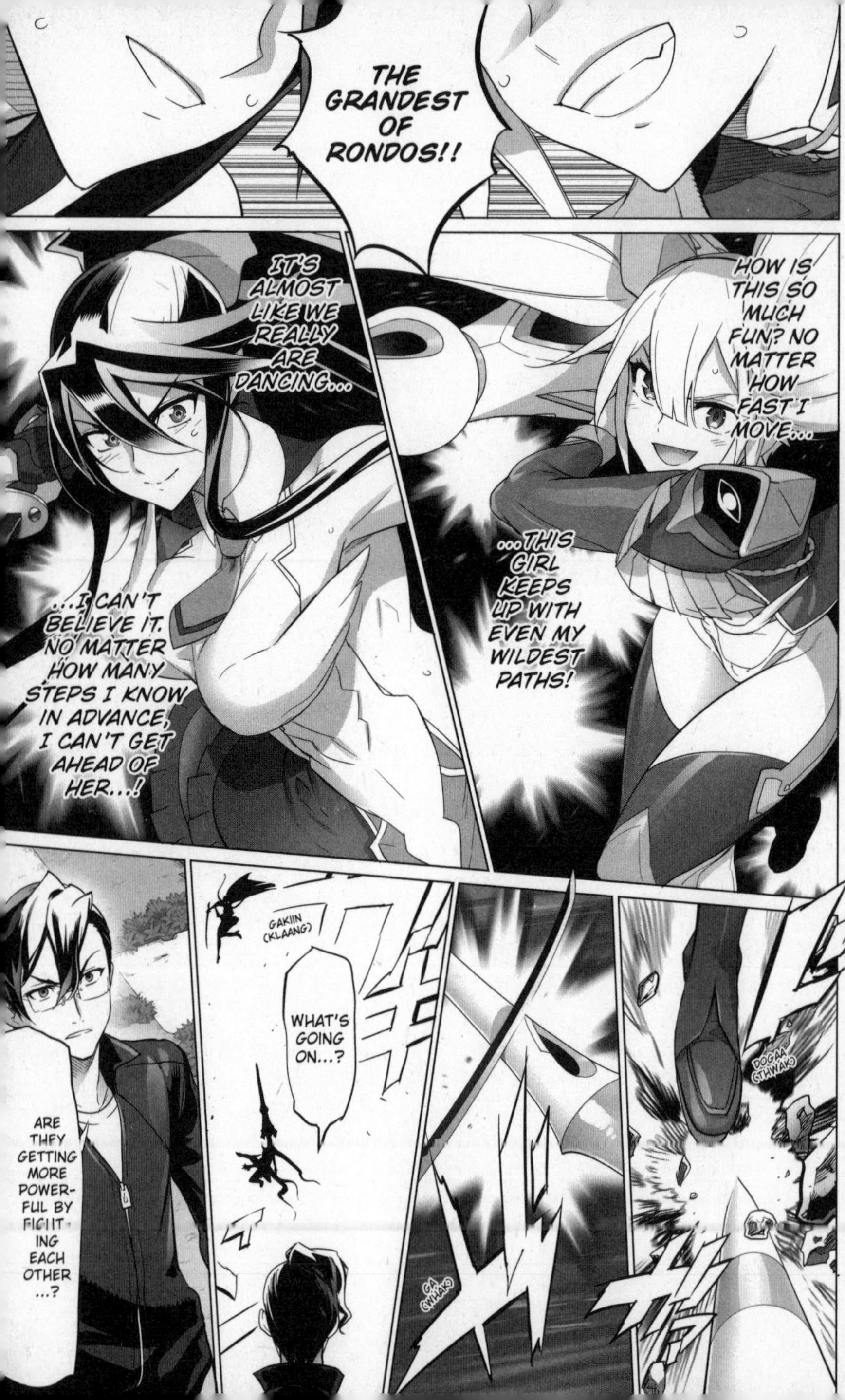
THE GRANDEST OF RONDOS!!
HOW IS THIS SO MUCH FUN? NO MATTER HOW FAST I MOVE...
...THIS GIRL KEEPS UP WITH EVEN MY WILDEST PATHS!
IT'S ALMOST LIKE WE REALLY ARE DANCING...
...I CAN'T BELIEVE IT. NO MATTER HOW MANY STEPS I KNOW IN ADVANCE, I CAN'T GET AHEAD OF HER...!
DOGAA (THWAK)
GA (WHAK)
GAKIIN (KLAANG)
WHAT'S GOING ON...?
ARE THEY GETTING MORE POWER-FUL BY FIGHT-ING EACH OTHER...?

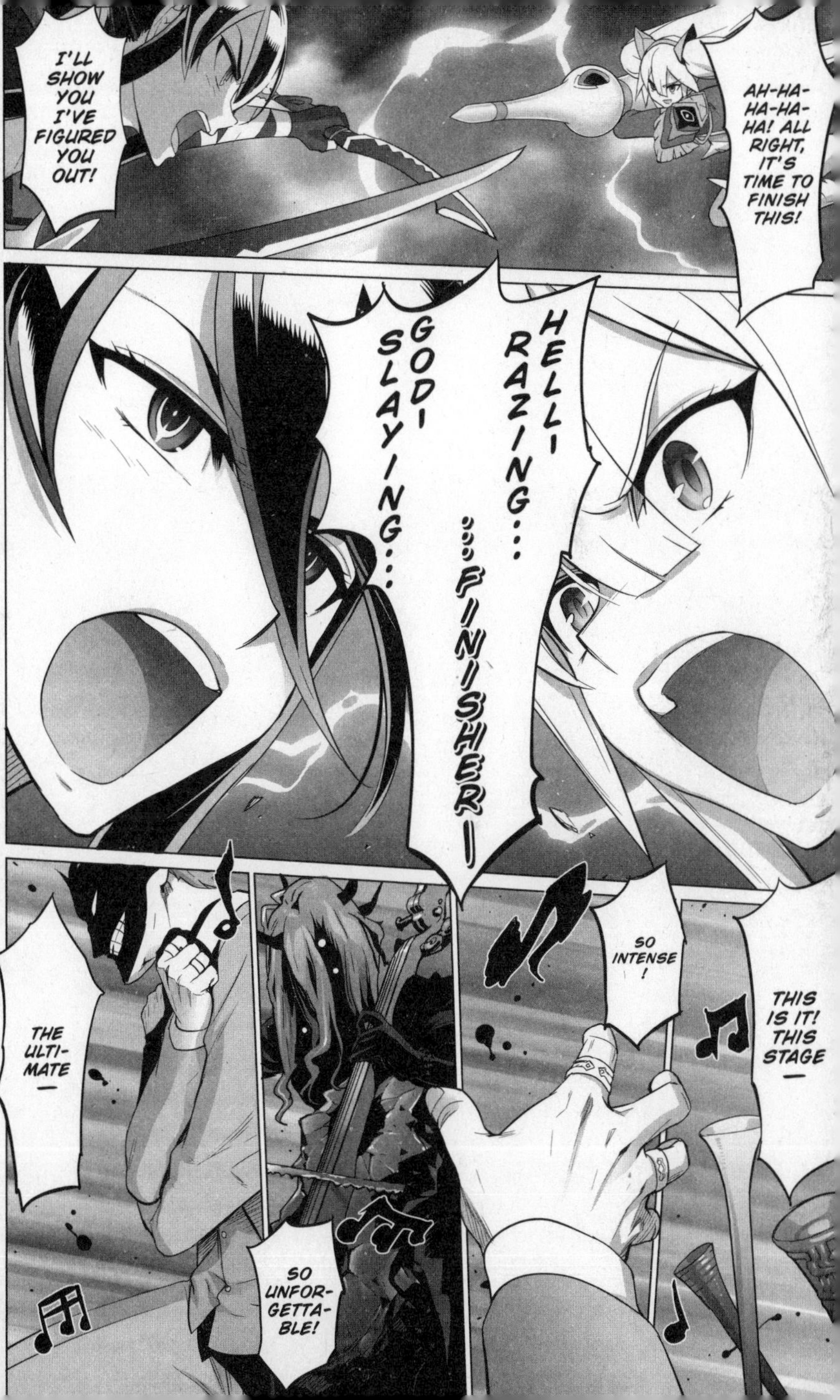
AH-HA-HA-HA! ALL RIGHT, IT'S TIME TO FINISH THIS!
I'LL SHOW YOU I'VE FIGURED YOU OUT!
HELL! RAZING...
GOD! SLAYING...
...FINISHER!
THIS IS IT! THIS STAGE—
SO INTENSE!
SO UNFORGETTABLE!
THE ULTIMATE—

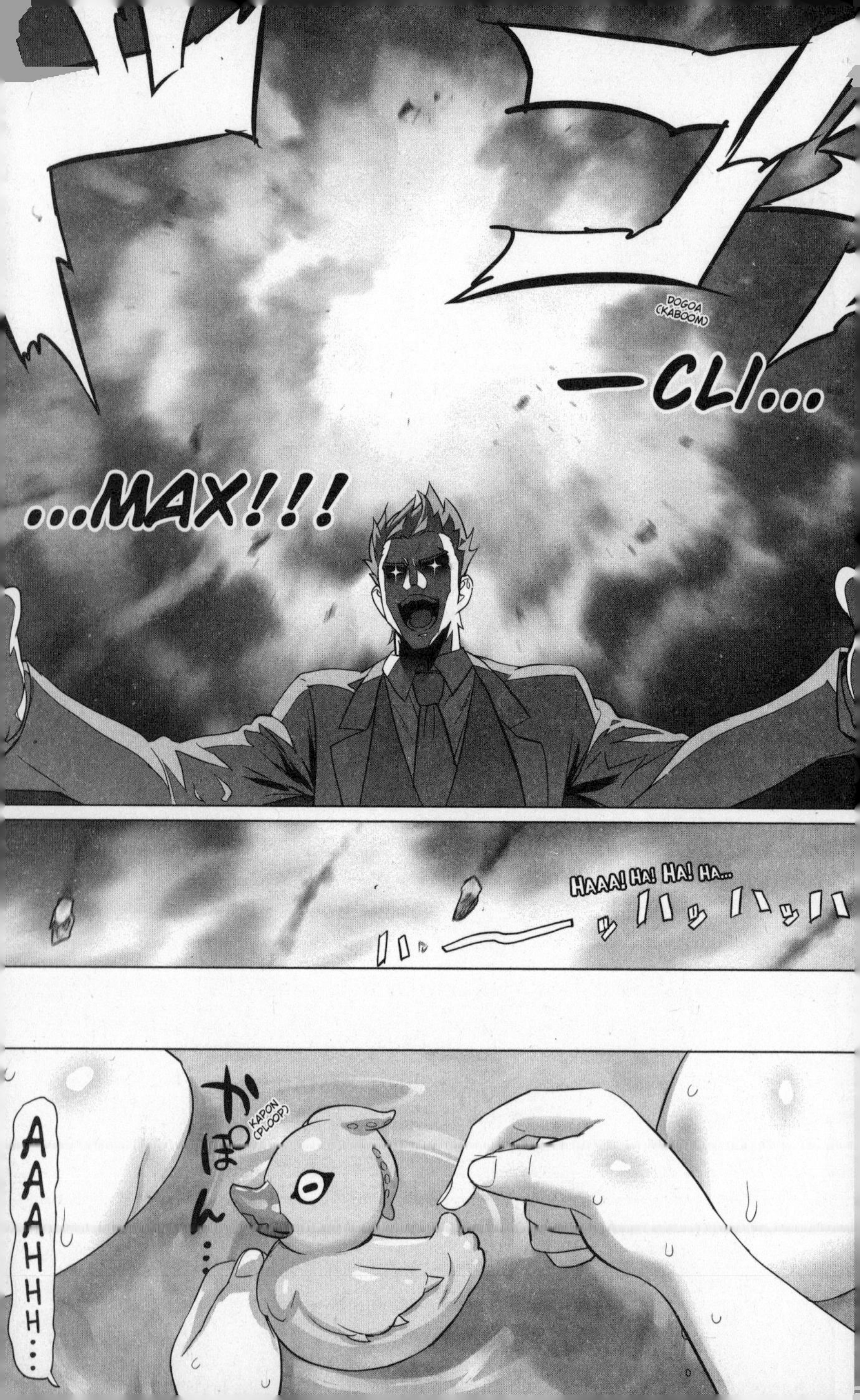
DOGOA (KABOOM)
—CLI...
...MAX!!!
HAAA! HA! HA! HA...
かぽん…
KAPON (PLOOP)
AAAAHHH...

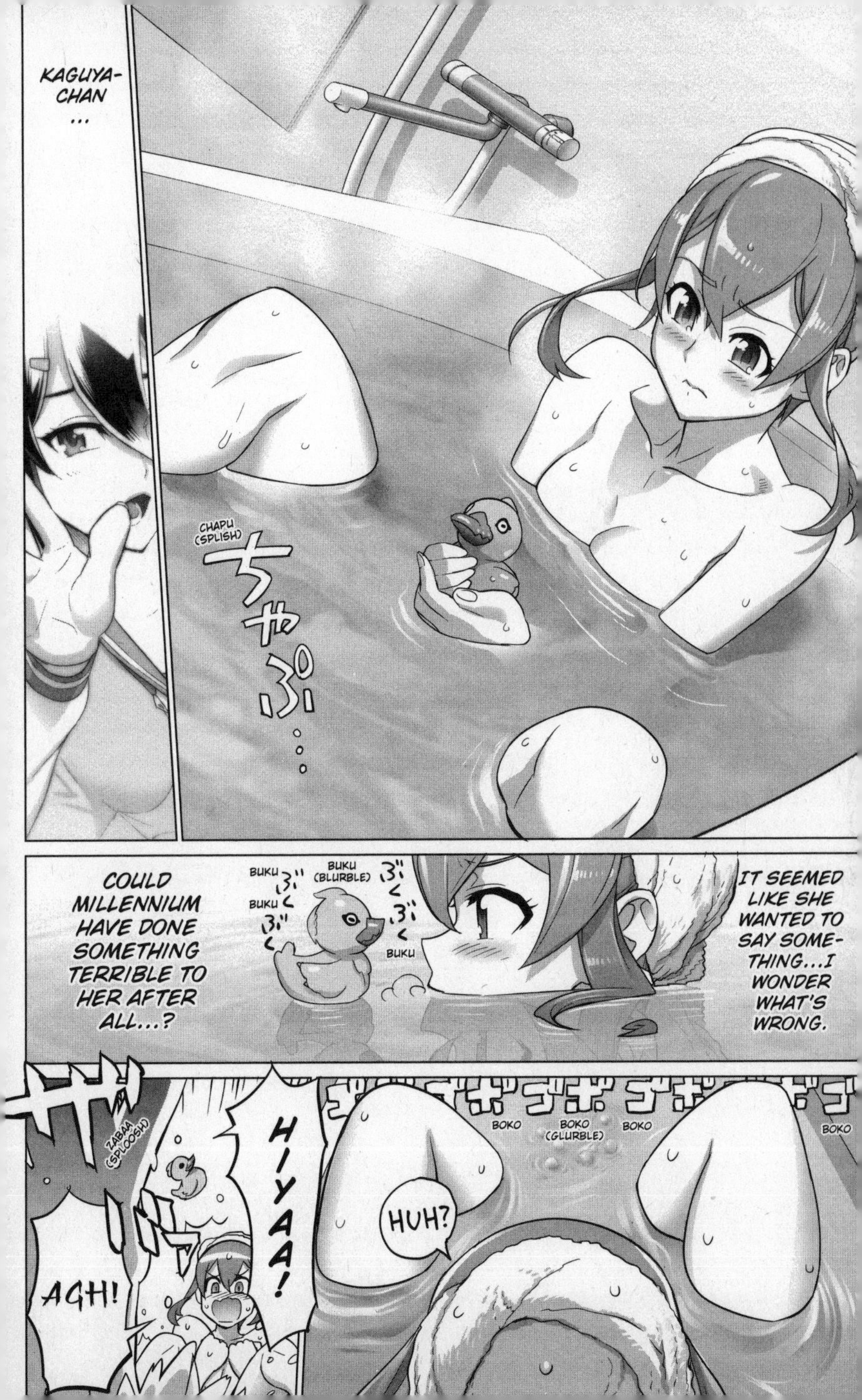
KAGUYA-CHAN...
CHAPU (SPLISH)
IT SEEMED LIKE SHE WANTED TO SAY SOME-THING...I WONDER WHAT'S WRONG.
BUKU (BLURBLE)
BUKU
BUKU
BUKU
COULD MILLENNIUM HAVE DONE SOMETHING TERRIBLE TO HER AFTER ALL...?
BOKO
BOKO
BOKO (GLURBLE)
BOKO
HUH?
HIYAA!
ZABAA (SPLOOSH)
AGH!

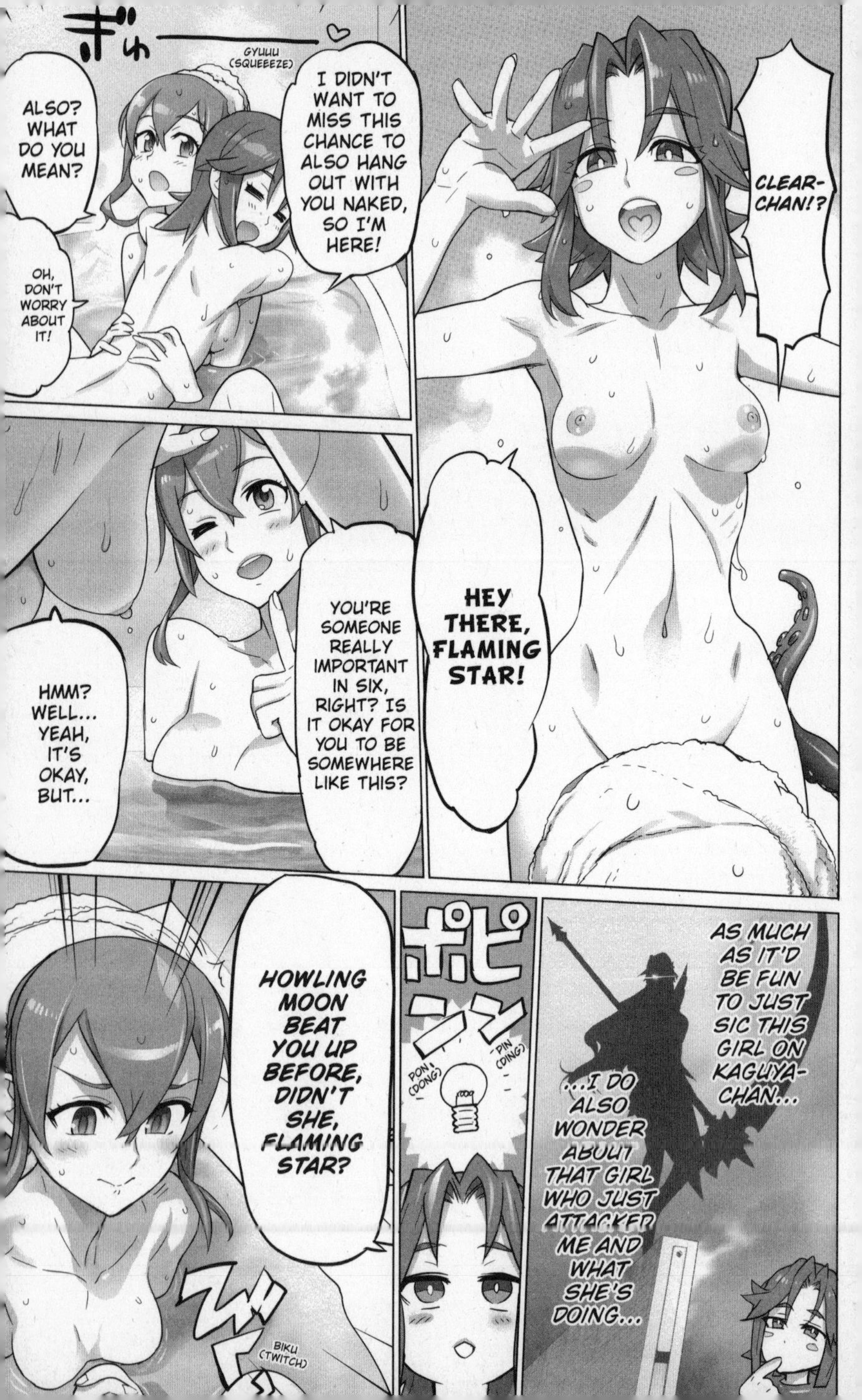
CLEAR-CHAN!?
HEY THERE, FLAMING STAR!
ぎゅ——
GYUUU (SQUEEEZE)
I DIDN'T WANT TO MISS THIS CHANCE TO ALSO HANG OUT WITH YOU NAKED, SO I'M HERE!
ALSO? WHAT DO YOU MEAN?
OH, DON'T WORRY ABOUT IT!
YOU'RE SOMEONE REALLY IMPORTANT IN SIX, RIGHT? IS IT OKAY FOR YOU TO BE SOMEWHERE LIKE THIS?
HMM? WELL... YEAH, IT'S OKAY, BUT...
AS MUCH AS IT'D BE FUN TO JUST SIC THIS GIRL ON KAGUYA-CHAN...
...I DO ALSO WONDER ABOUT THAT GIRL WHO JUST ATTACKED ME AND WHAT SHE'S DOING...
PIN (DING)
PON (DONG)
HOWLING MOON BEAT YOU UP BEFORE, DIDN'T SHE, FLAMING STAR?
BIKU (TWITCH)

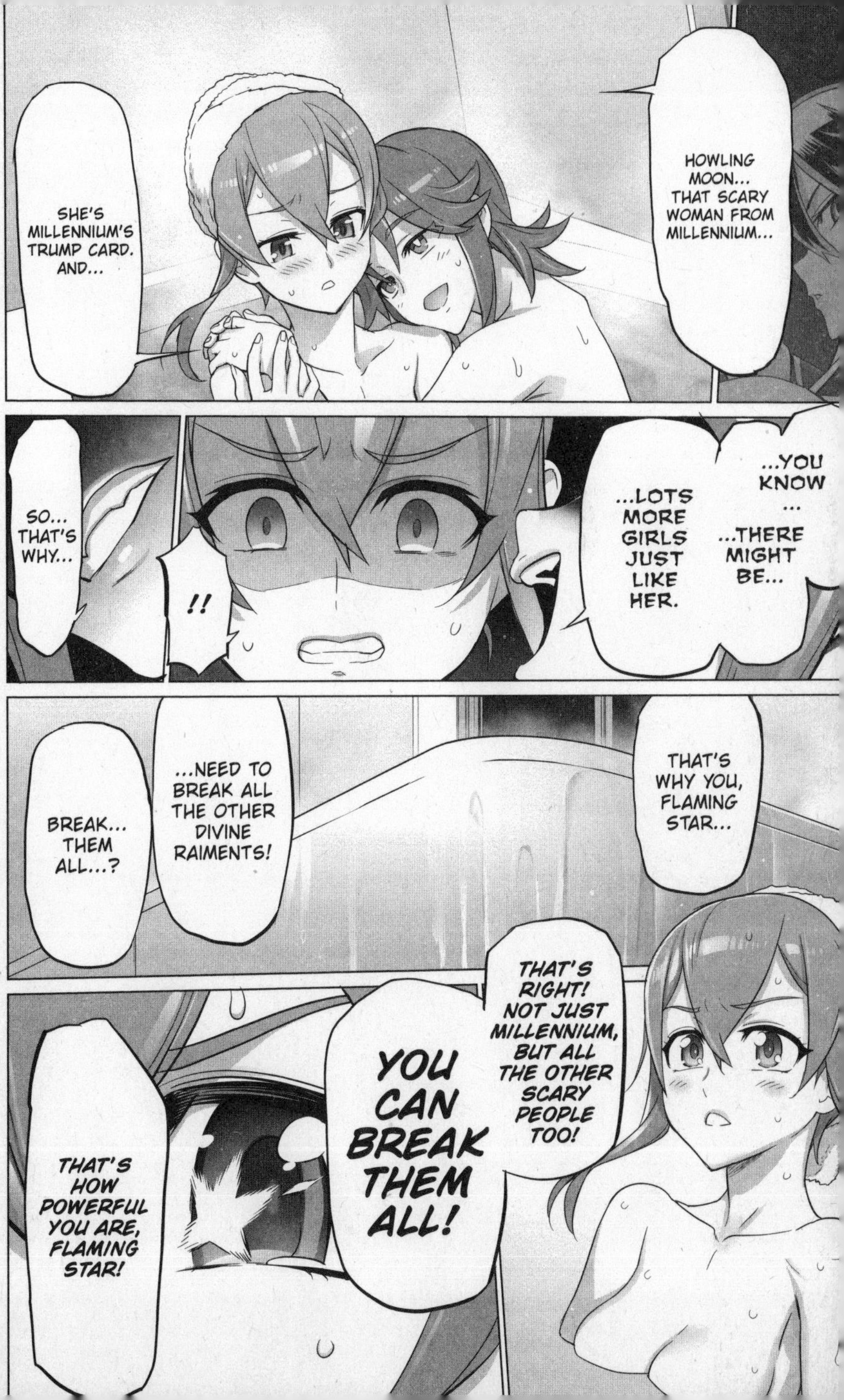
HOWLING MOON... THAT SCARY WOMAN FROM MILLENNIUM...
SHE'S MILLENNIUM'S TRUMP CARD. AND...
...YOU KNOW ... ...THERE MIGHT BE...
...LOTS MORE GIRLS JUST LIKE HER.
!!
SO... THAT'S WHY...
THAT'S WHY YOU, FLAMING STAR...
...NEED TO BREAK ALL THE OTHER DIVINE RAIMENTS!
BREAK... THEM ALL...?
THAT'S RIGHT! NOT JUST MILLENNIUM, BUT ALL THE OTHER SCARY PEOPLE TOO!
YOU CAN BREAK THEM ALL!
THAT'S HOW POWERFUL YOU ARE, FLAMING STAR!

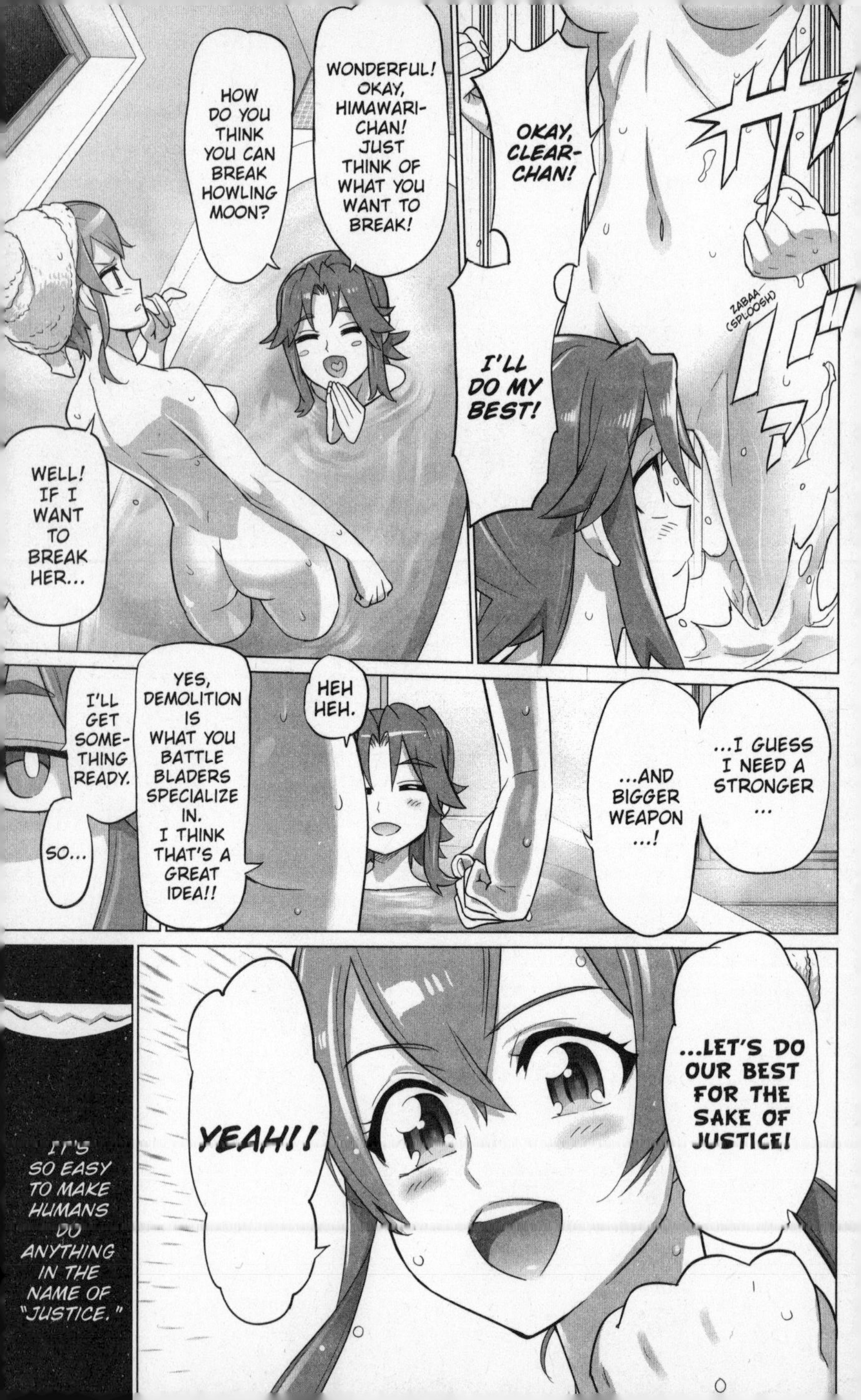
OKAY, CLEAR-CHAN!
ZABAA— (SPLOOSH)
I'LL DO MY BEST!
WONDERFUL! OKAY, HIMAWARI-CHAN! JUST THINK OF WHAT YOU WANT TO BREAK!
HOW DO YOU THINK YOU CAN BREAK HOWLING MOON?
WELL! IF I WANT TO BREAK HER...
...I GUESS I NEED A STRONGER ...
...AND BIGGER WEAPON ...!
HEH HEH.
YES, DEMOLITION IS WHAT YOU BATTLE BLADERS SPECIALIZE IN. I THINK THAT'S A GREAT IDEA!!
I'LL GET SOME-THING READY.
SO...
...LET'S DO OUR BEST FOR THE SAKE OF JUSTICE!
YEAH!!
IT'S SO EASY TO MAKE HUMANS DO ANYTHING IN THE NAME OF "JUSTICE."

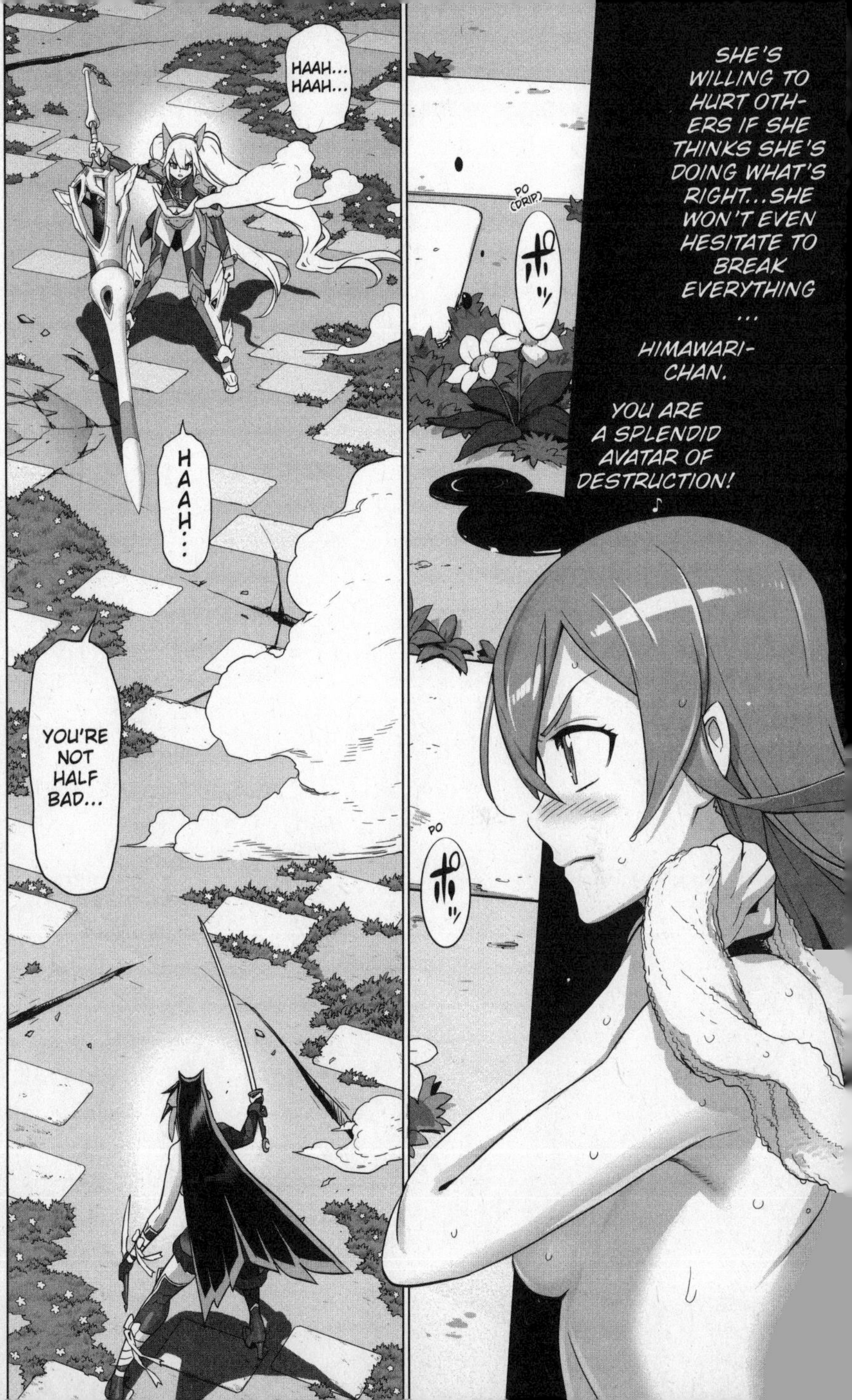
SHE'S WILLING TO HURT OTHERS IF SHE THINKS SHE'S DOING WHAT'S RIGHT...SHE WON'T EVEN HESITATE TO BREAK EVERYTHING...
HIMAWARI-CHAN.
YOU ARE A SPLENDID AVATAR OF DESTRUCTION! ♪
ポッ
PO (DRIP)
ポッ
PO
HAAH... HAAH...
HAAH...
YOU'RE NOT HALF BAD...

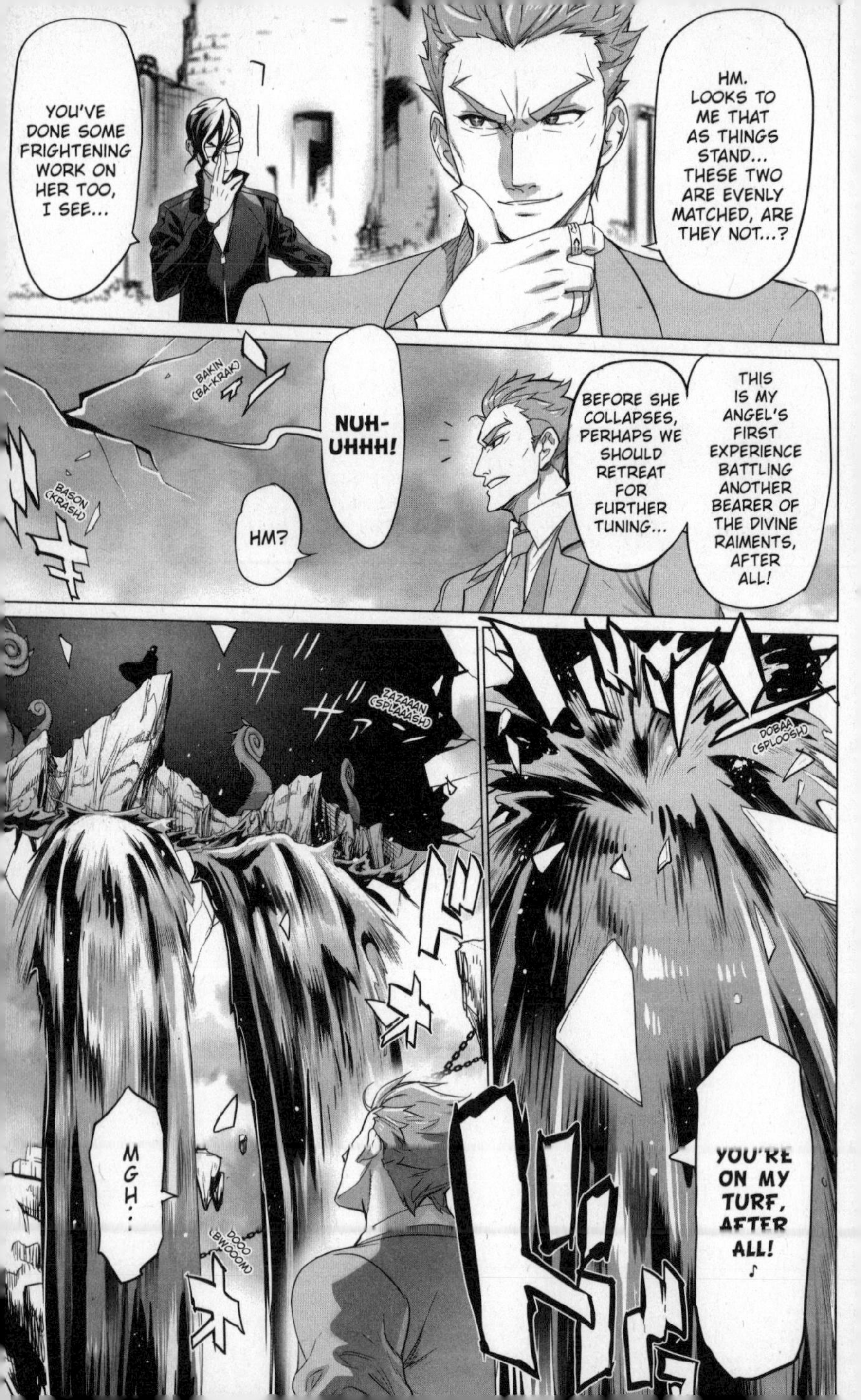
HM. LOOKS TO ME THAT AS THINGS STAND... THESE TWO ARE EVENLY MATCHED, ARE THEY NOT...?
YOU'VE DONE SOME FRIGHTENING WORK ON HER TOO, I SEE...
THIS IS MY ANGEL'S FIRST EXPERIENCE BATTLING ANOTHER BEARER OF THE DIVINE RAIMENTS, AFTER ALL!
BEFORE SHE COLLAPSES, PERHAPS WE SHOULD RETREAT FOR FURTHER TUNING...
NUH-UHHH!
BAKIN (BA-KRAK)
HM?
BASON (KRASH)
DOBAA (SPLOOSH)
YOU'RE ON MY TURF, AFTER ALL! ♪
ZAZAAAN (SPLAAASH)
MGH...
DOOO (BWOOOM)

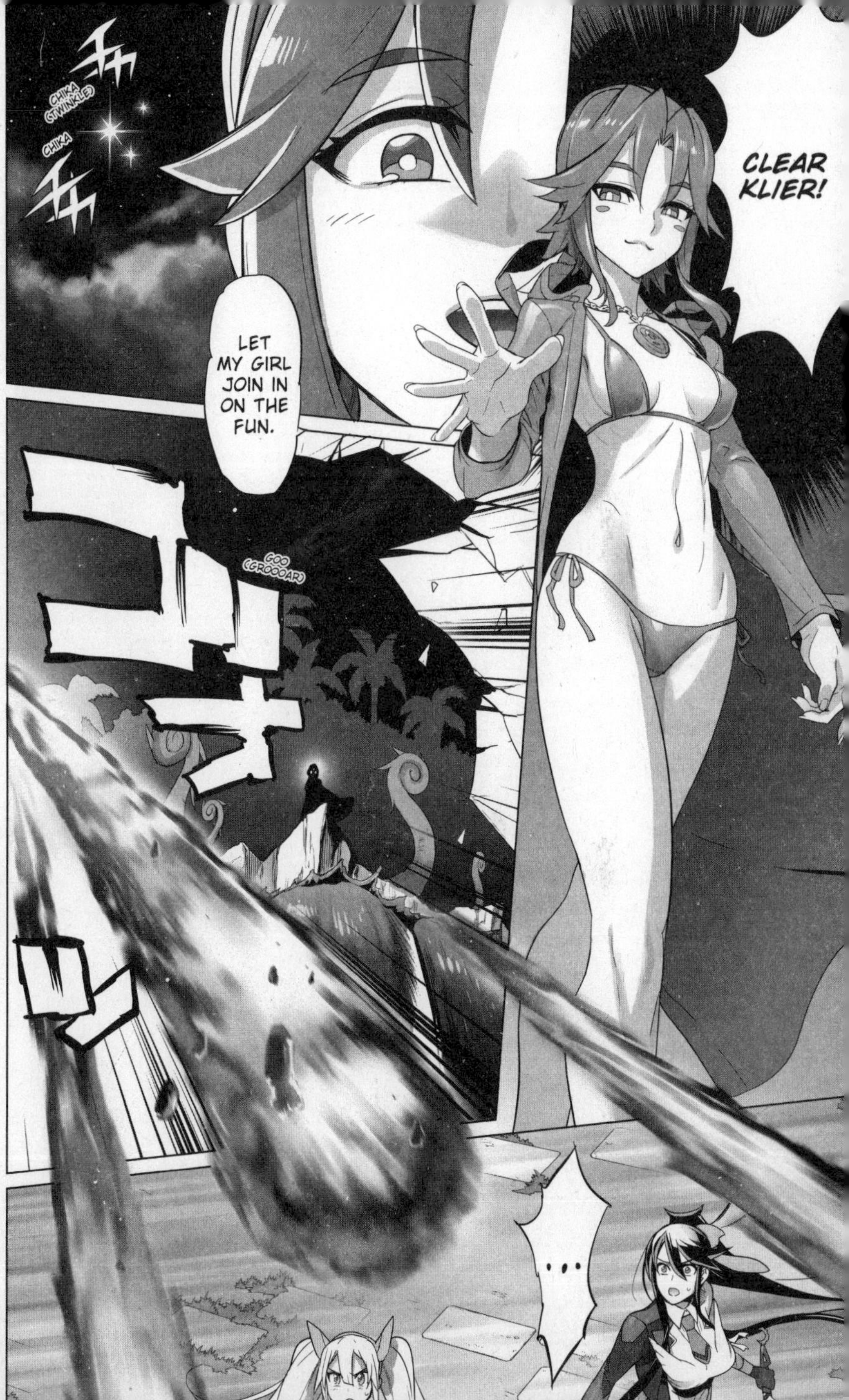

CLEAR KLIER!
CHIKA (TWINKLE) CHIKA
LET MY GIRL JOIN IN ON THE FUN.
GOO (GROOOAR)
...

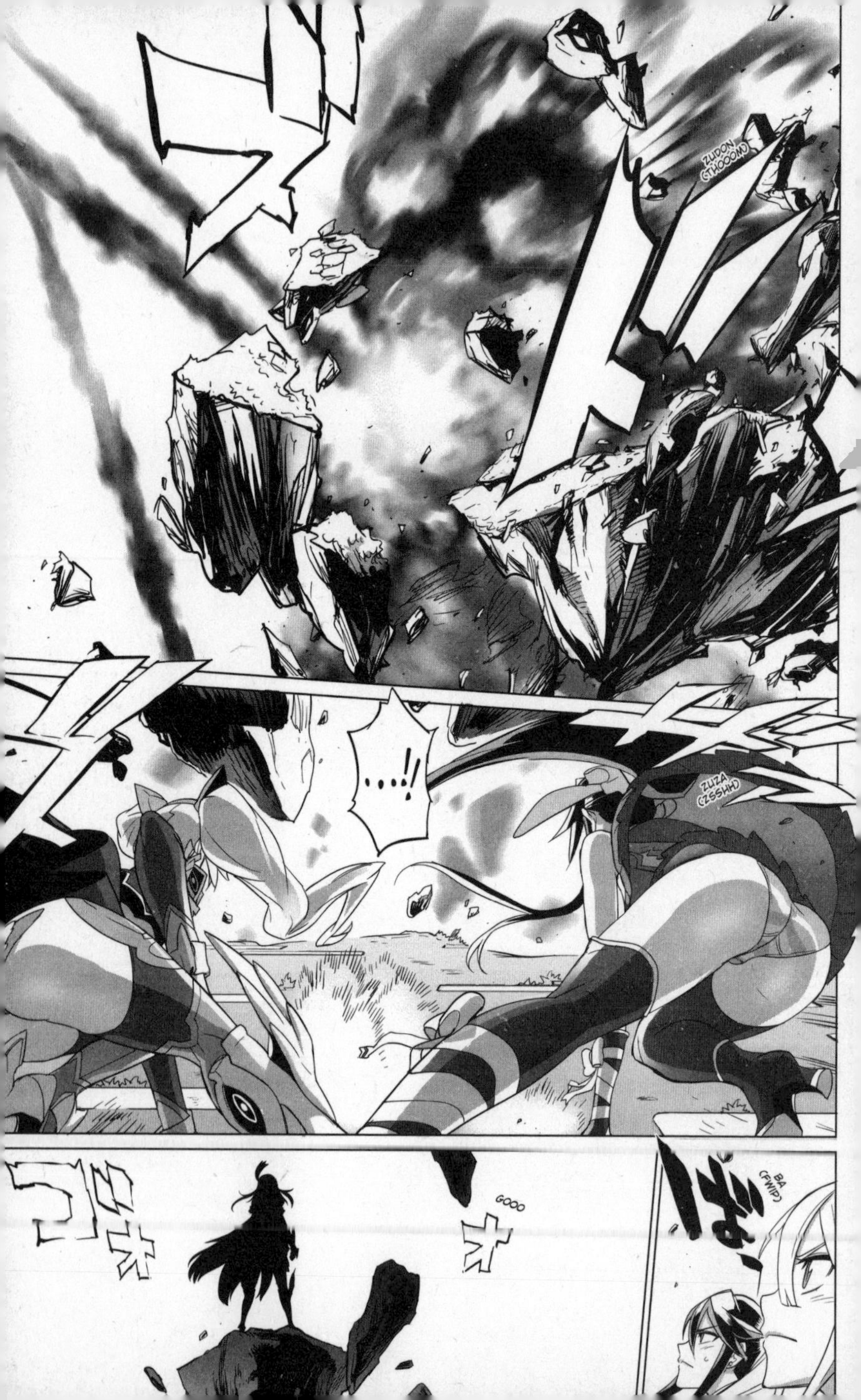

ZUDON
(THOOOM)
ZUZA
(ZSSHH)
...!!
BA
(FWIP)
GOOO

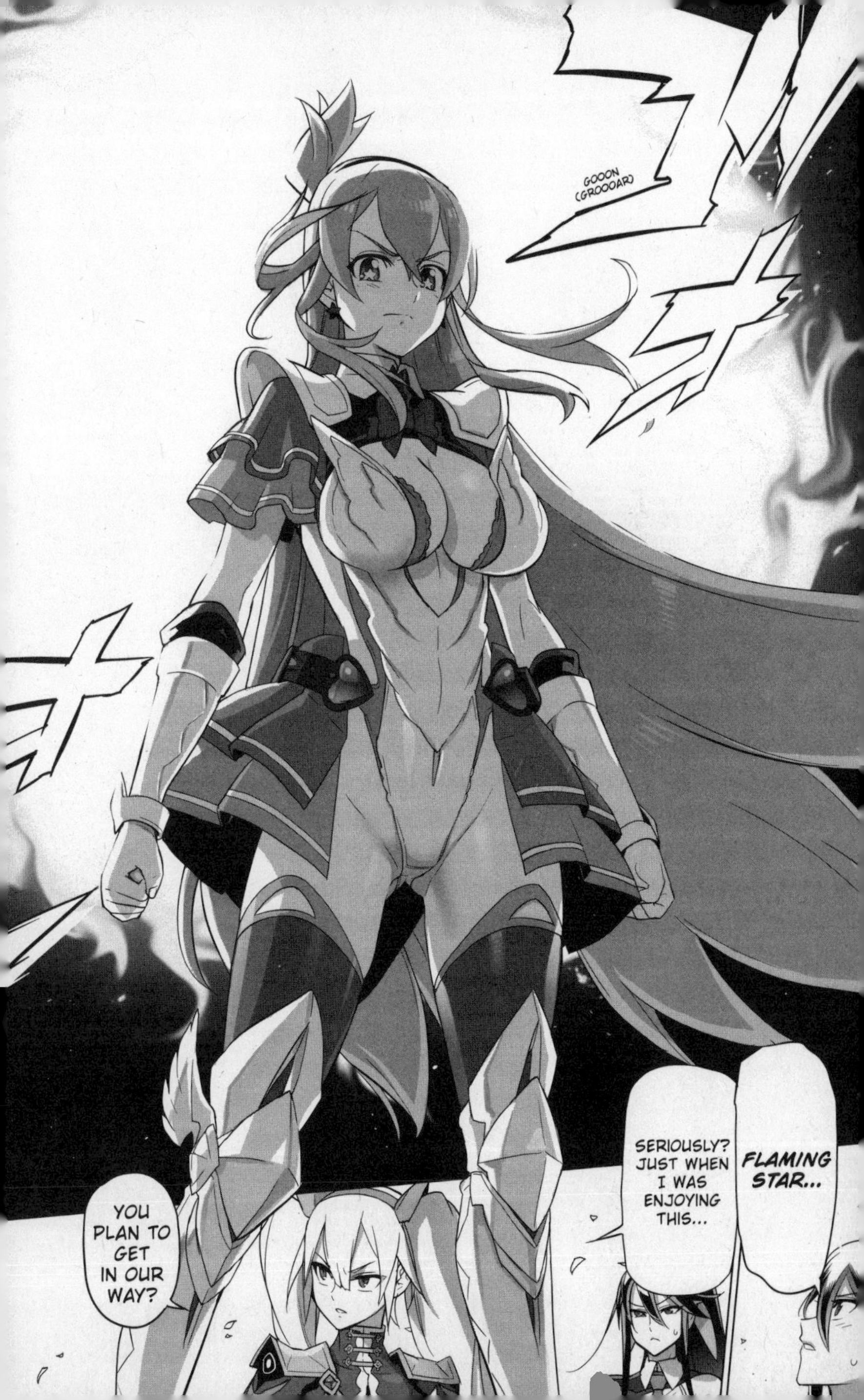
GOOON (GROOOAR)
FLAMING STAR...
SERIOUSLY? JUST WHEN I WAS ENJOYING THIS...
YOU PLAN TO GET IN OUR WAY?

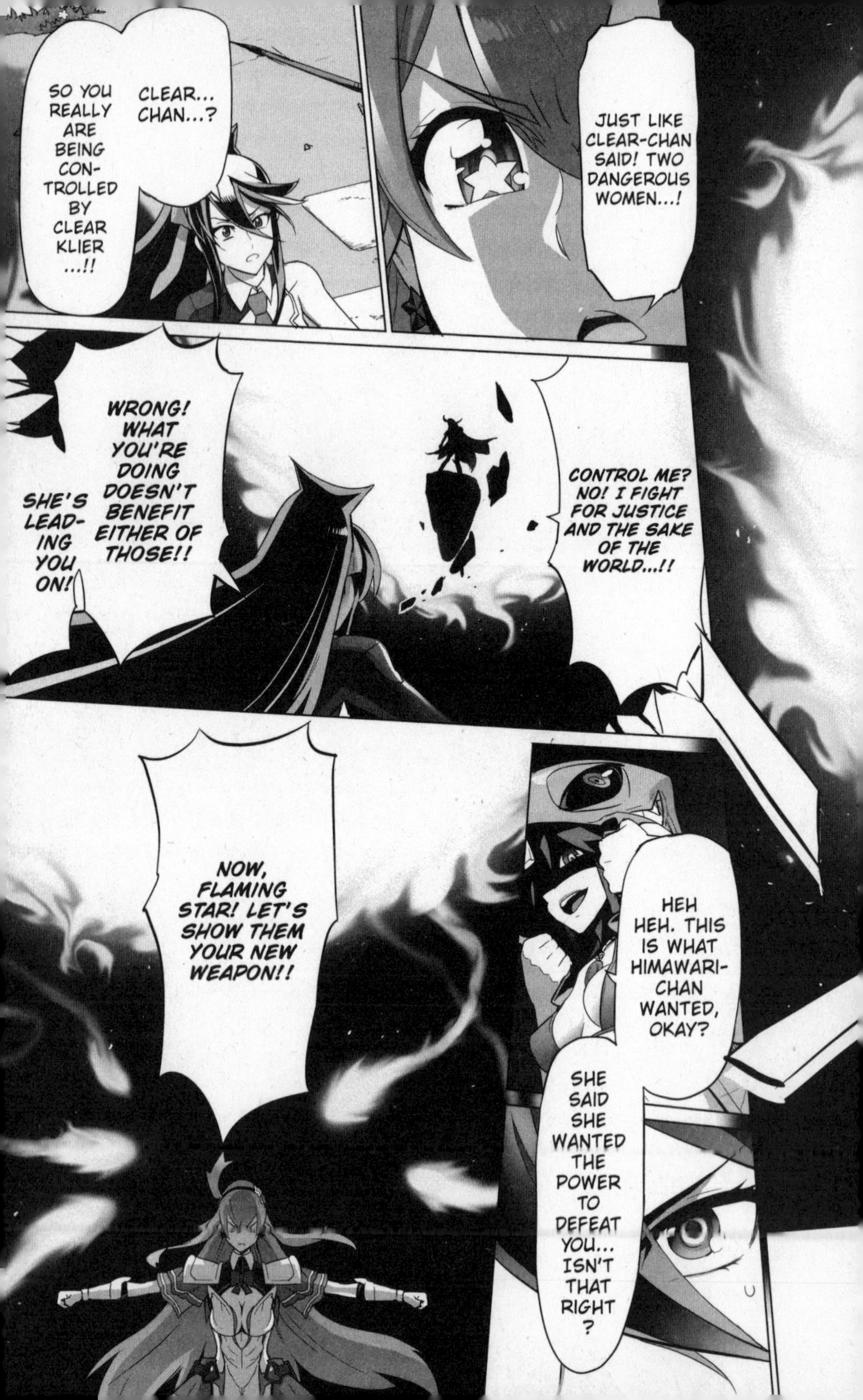
JUST LIKE CLEAR-CHAN SAID! TWO DANGEROUS WOMEN...!
CLEAR... CHAN...?
SO YOU REALLY ARE BEING CON-TROLLED BY CLEAR KLIER ...!!
CONTROL ME? NO! I FIGHT FOR JUSTICE AND THE SAKE OF THE WORLD...!!
WRONG! WHAT YOU'RE DOING DOESN'T BENEFIT EITHER OF THOSE!!
SHE'S LEAD-ING YOU ON!
HEH HEH. THIS IS WHAT HIMAWARI-CHAN WANTED, OKAY?
SHE SAID SHE WANTED THE POWER TO DEFEAT YOU... ISN'T THAT RIGHT?
NOW, FLAMING STAR! LET'S SHOW THEM YOUR NEW WEAPON!!

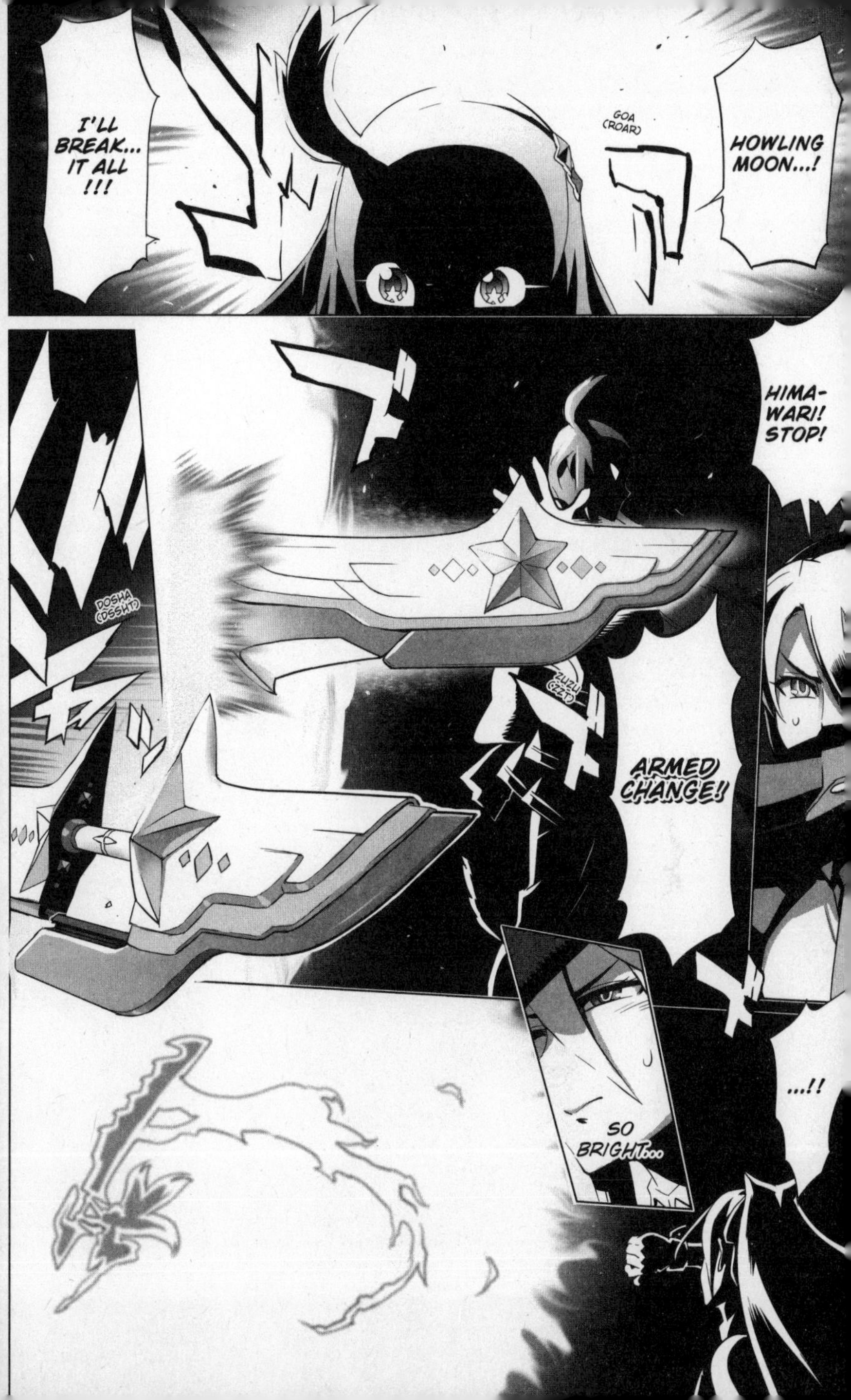
HOWLING MOON...!
GOA (ROAR)
I'LL BREAK... IT ALL !!!
HIMA-WARI! STOP!
ARMED CHANGE!!
ZUZU (SZZT)
DOSHA (DSSHT)
...!!
SO BRIGHT...

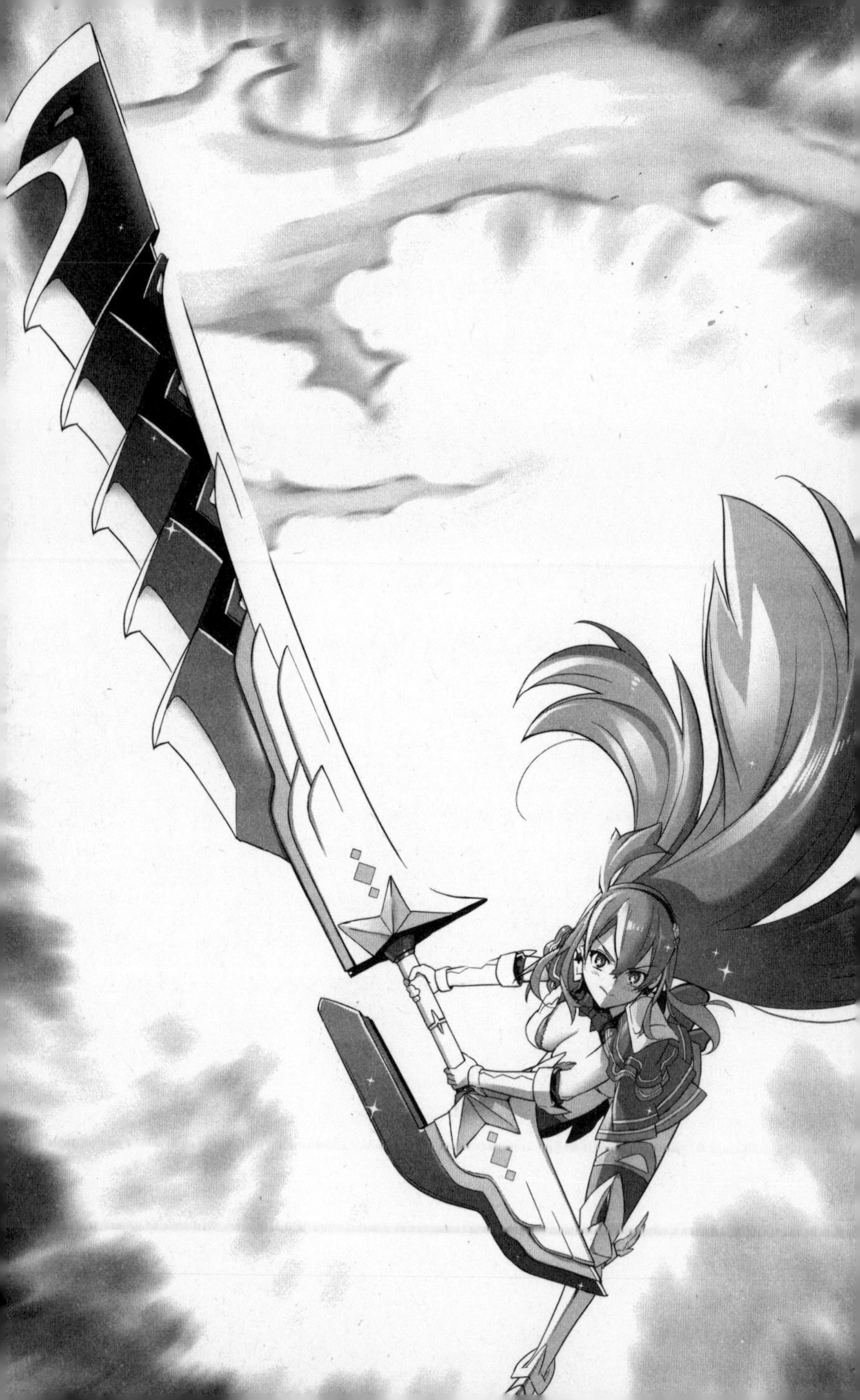

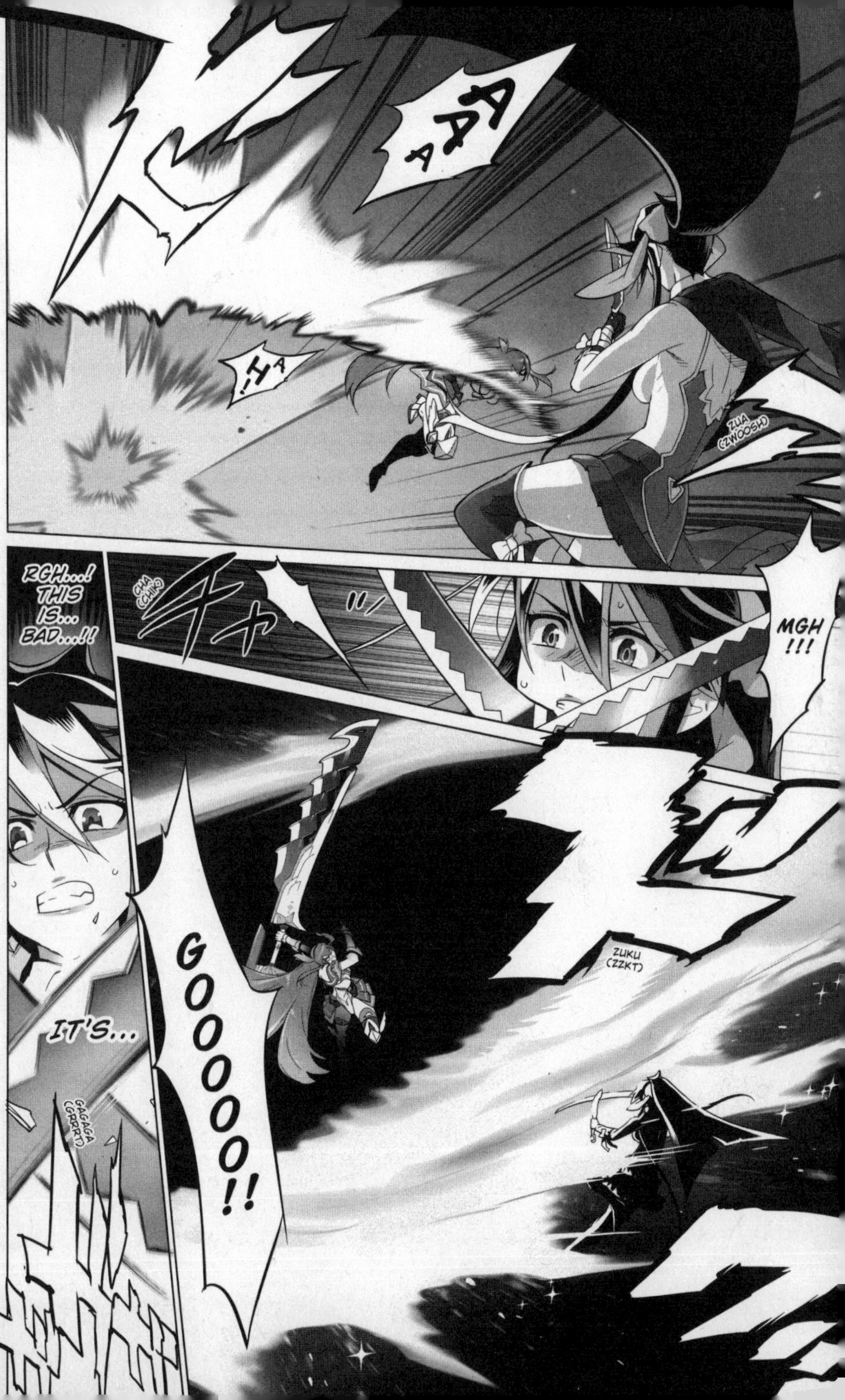
AAA
HA!
ZUA (ZWOOSH)
MGH!!!
CHA CHIKI
RGH...! THIS IS... BAD...!!
ZUKU (ZZKT)
GOOOOOO!!
IT'S...
GAGAGA (GRRRT)

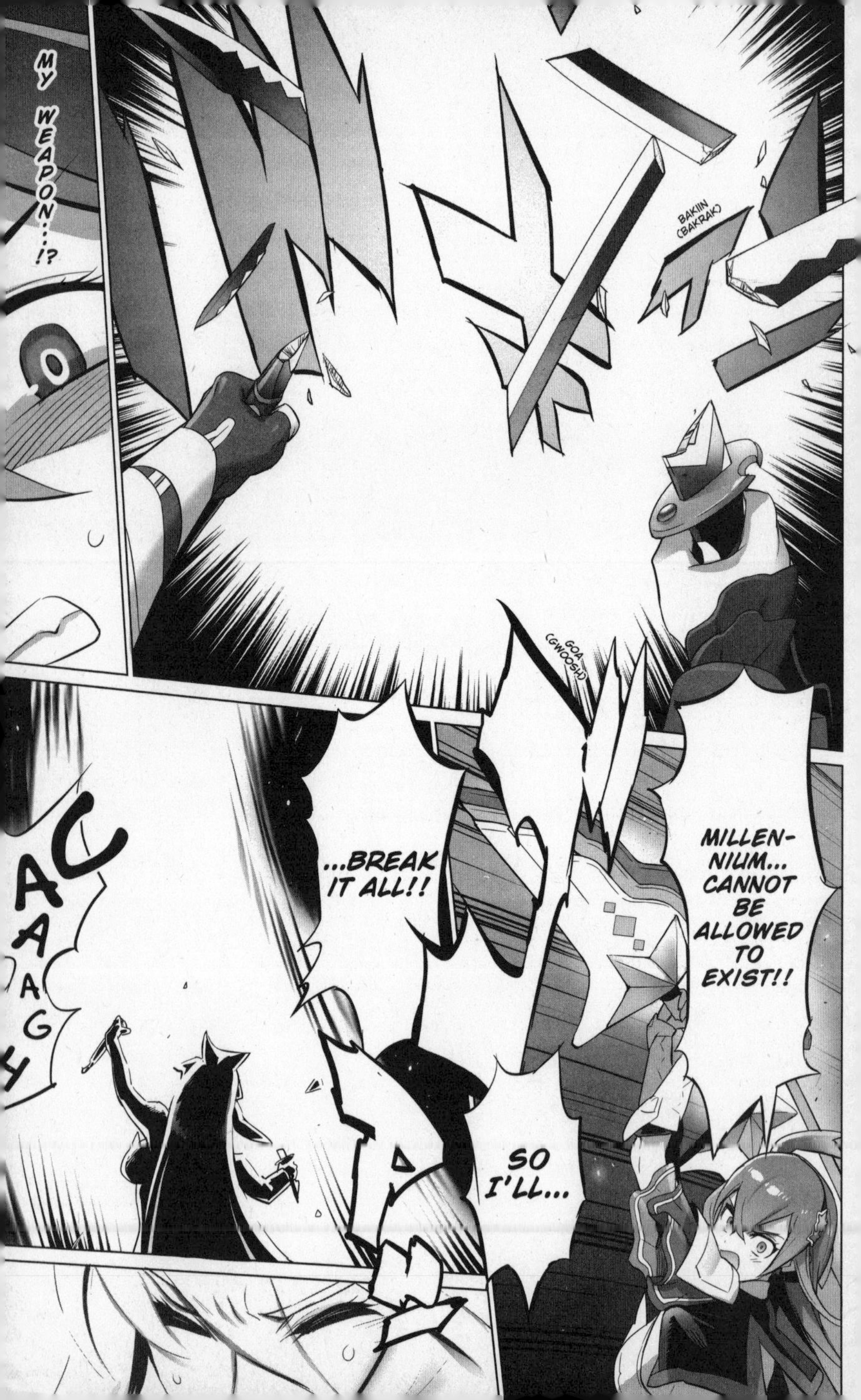
BAKIIN (BAKRAK)
MY WEAPON...!?
GOA (GWOOSH)
MILLEN-NIUM... CANNOT BE ALLOWED TO EXIST!!
SO I'LL...
...BREAK IT ALL!!
ACAAGH

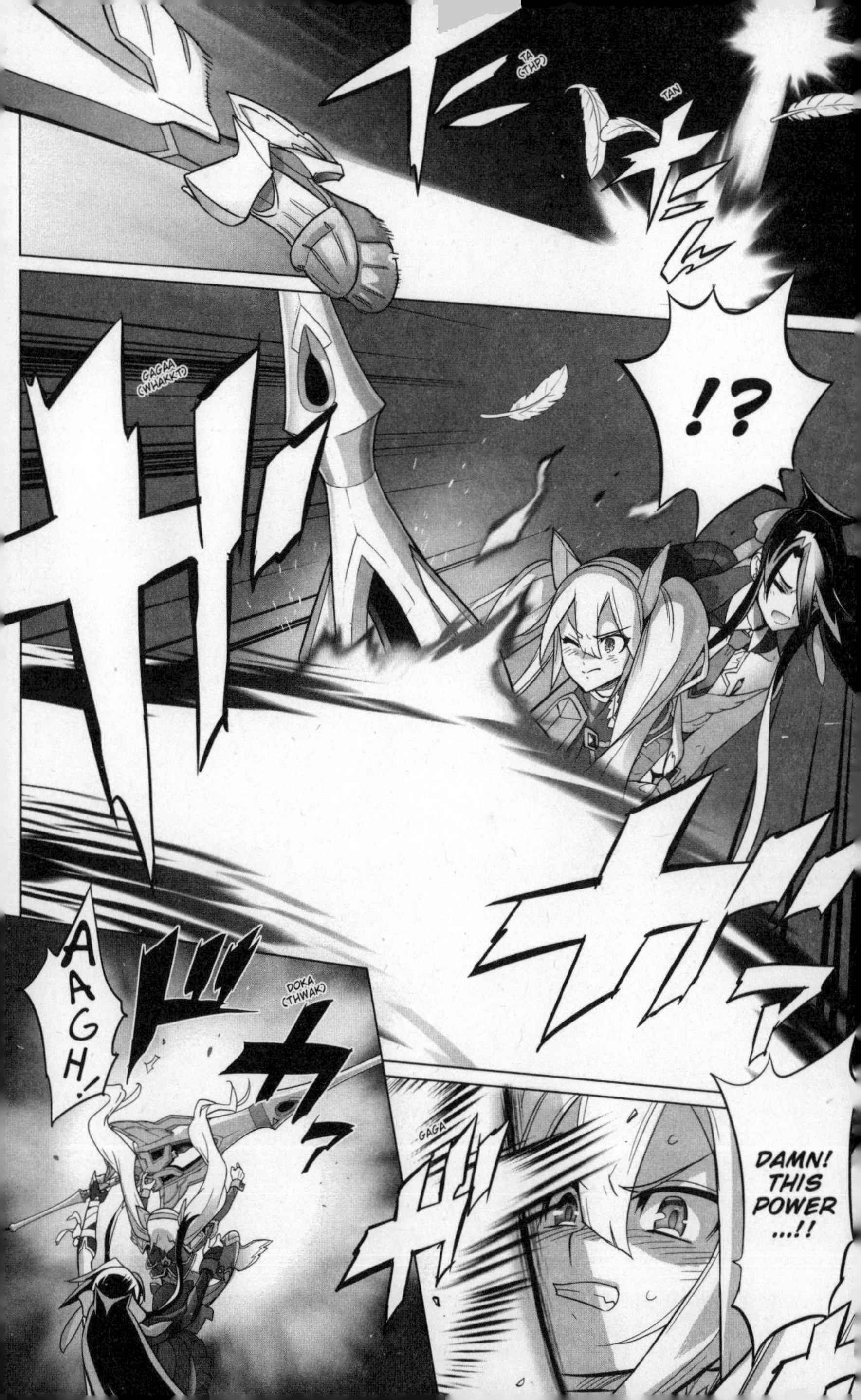
TA (THP)
TAN
!?
GAGAA (WHAKK!)
GAGA
DAMN! THIS POWER ...!!
AAGH!
DOKA (THWAK)

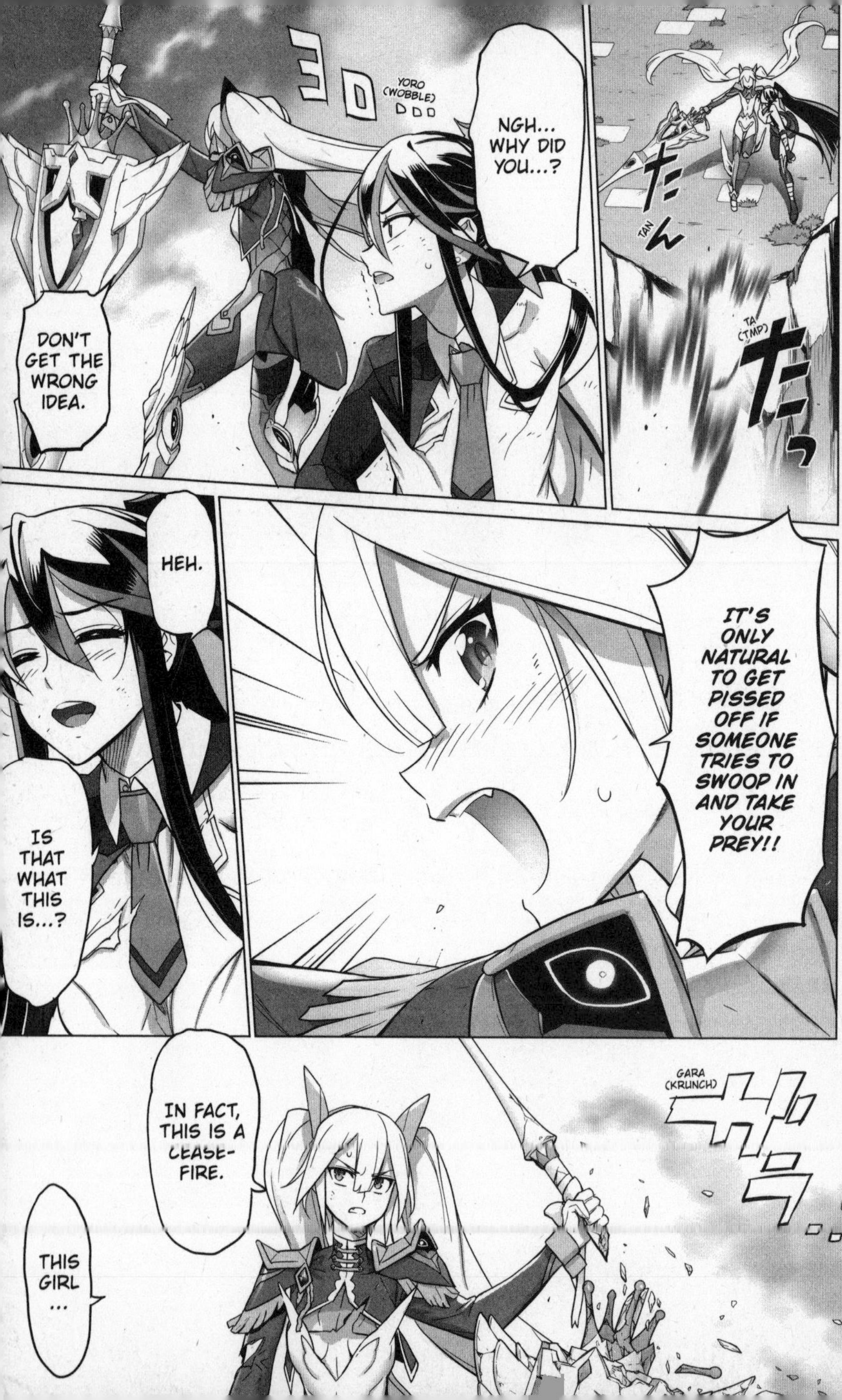
TAN
TA (TMP)
YORO (WOBBLE)
NGH... WHY DID YOU...?
DON'T GET THE WRONG IDEA.
IT'S ONLY NATURAL TO GET PISSED OFF IF SOMEONE TRIES TO SWOOP IN AND TAKE YOUR PREY!!
HEH.
IS THAT WHAT THIS IS...?
GARA (KRUNCH)
IN FACT, THIS IS A CEASE-FIRE.
THIS GIRL ...

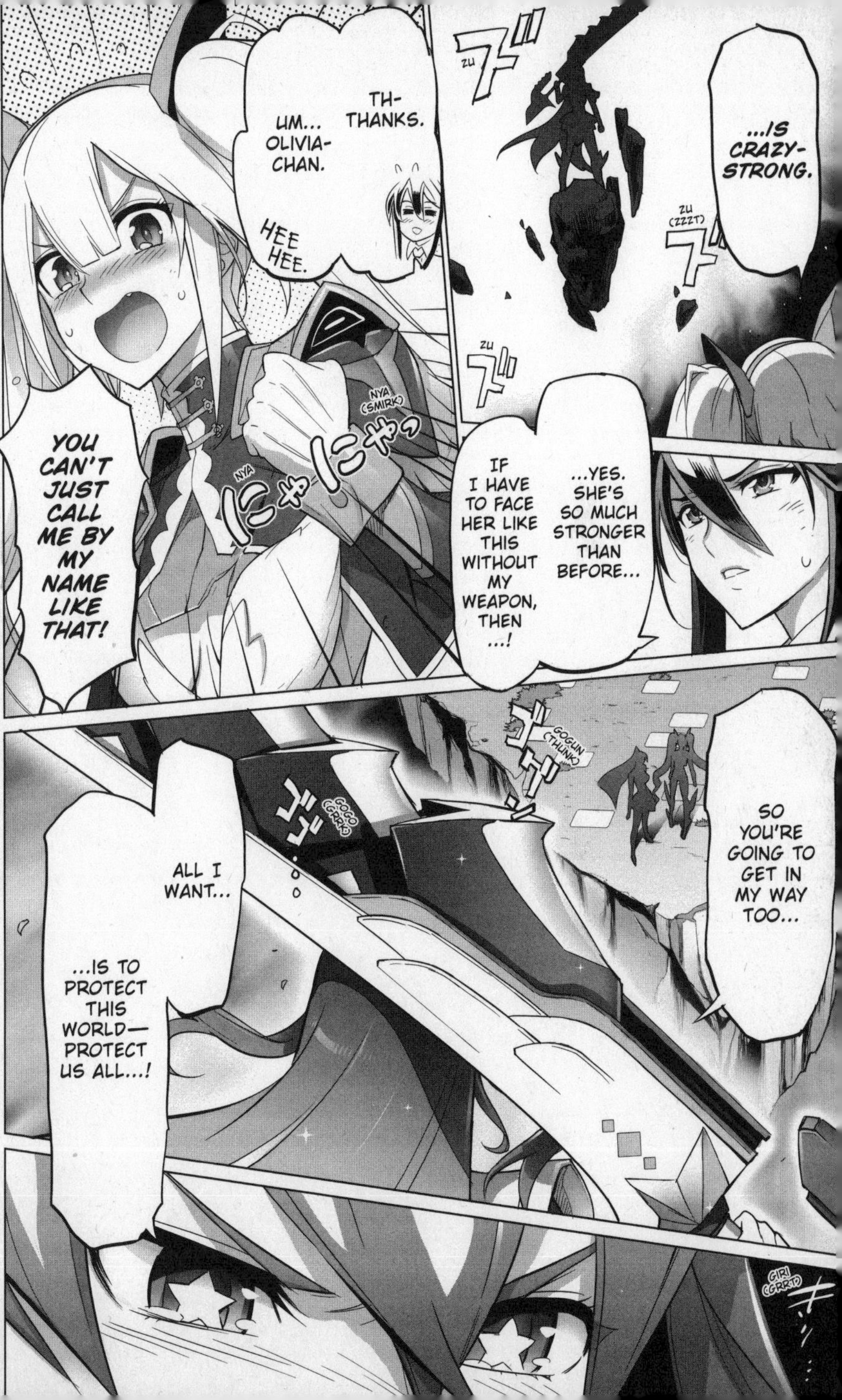

ZU
ZU (ZZZT)
...IS CRAZY-STRONG.
ZU
...YES. SHE'S SO MUCH STRONGER THAN BEFORE...
IF I HAVE TO FACE HER LIKE THIS WITHOUT MY WEAPON, THEN ...!
TH- THANKS.
UM... OLIVIA-CHAN.
HEE HEE.
NYA (SMIRK)
NYA
YOU CAN'T JUST CALL ME BY MY NAME LIKE THAT!
GOGUN (THUNK)
SO YOU'RE GOING TO GET IN MY WAY TOO...
GOGO (GRRR)
ALL I WANT...
...IS TO PROTECT THIS WORLD— PROTECT US ALL...!
GIRI (GRRT)

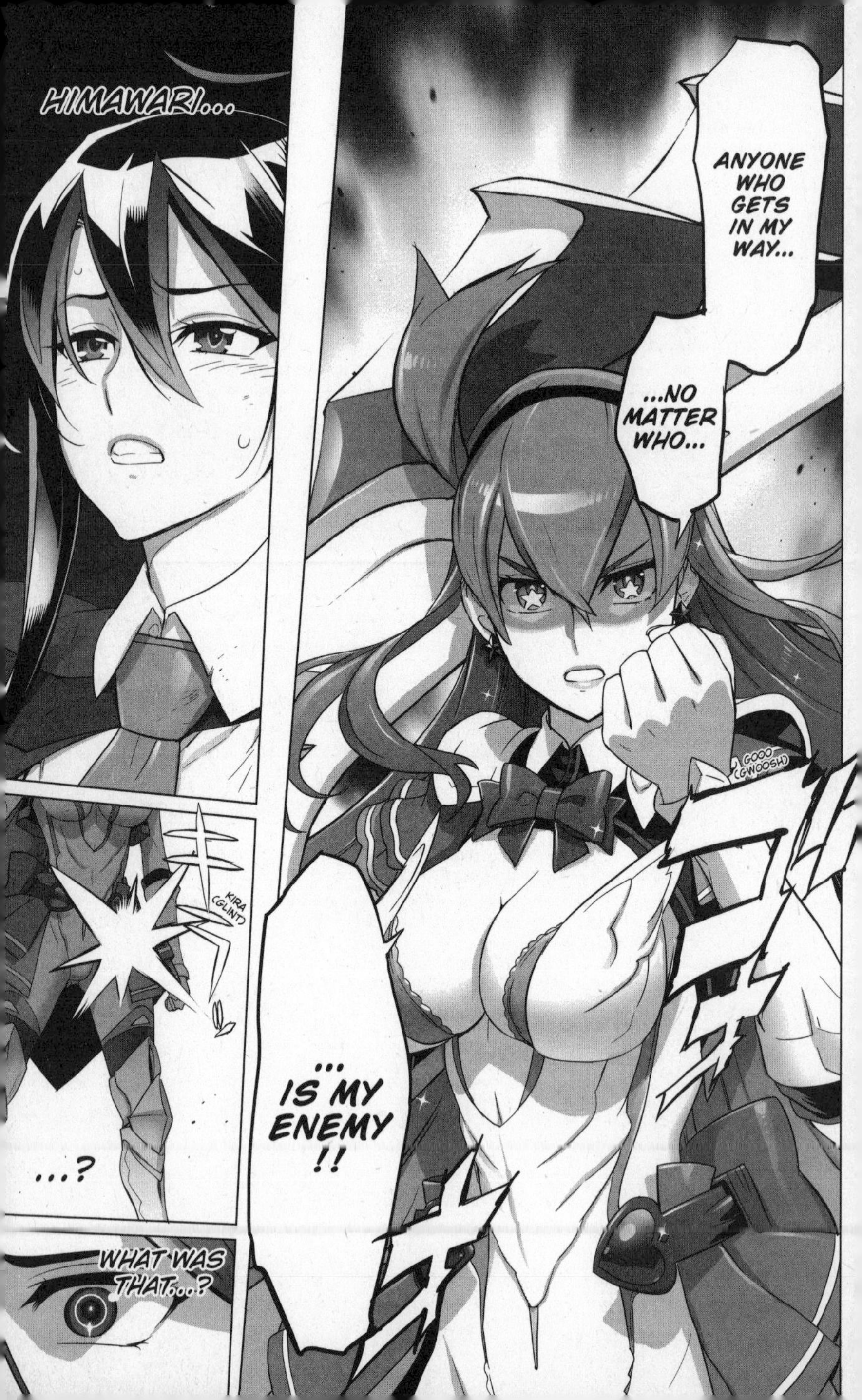
ANYONE WHO GETS IN MY WAY...
...NO MATTER WHO...
GOOO (GWOOSH)
...IS MY ENEMY!!
HIMAWARI...
KIRA (GLINT)
...?
WHAT WAS THAT...?

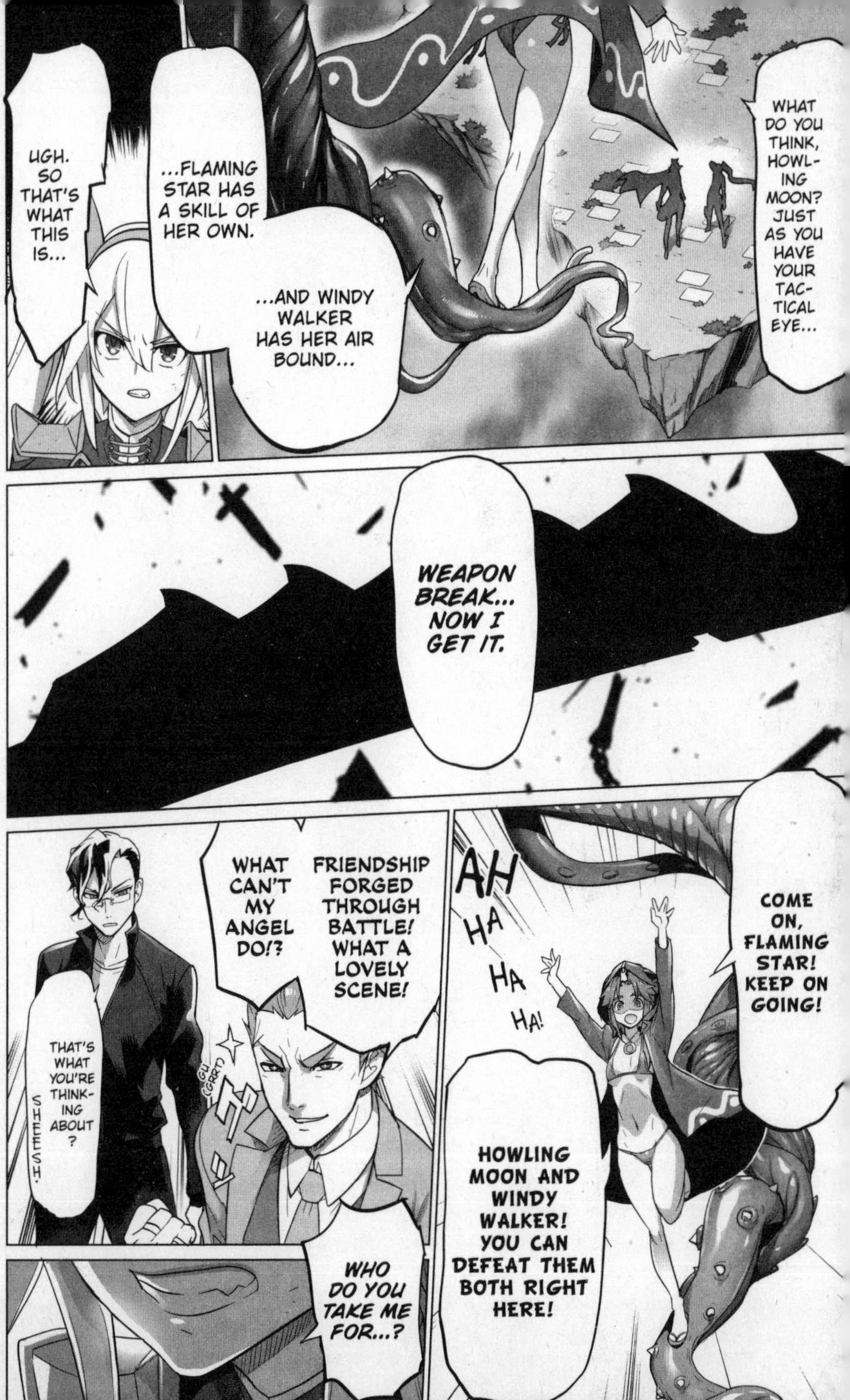
WHAT DO YOU THINK, HOWLING MOON? JUST AS YOU HAVE YOUR TACTICAL EYE...
...AND WINDY WALKER HAS HER AIR BOUND...
...FLAMING STAR HAS A SKILL OF HER OWN.
UGH. SO THAT'S WHAT THIS IS...
WEAPON BREAK... NOW I GET IT.
COME ON, FLAMING STAR! KEEP ON GOING!
AH HA HA HA!
HOWLING MOON AND WINDY WALKER! YOU CAN DEFEAT THEM BOTH RIGHT HERE!
FRIENDSHIP FORGED THROUGH BATTLE! WHAT A LOVELY SCENE!
WHAT CAN'T MY ANGEL DO!?
GU (GRRT)
THAT'S WHAT YOU'RE THINKING ABOUT?
SHEESH.
WHO DO YOU TAKE ME FOR...?

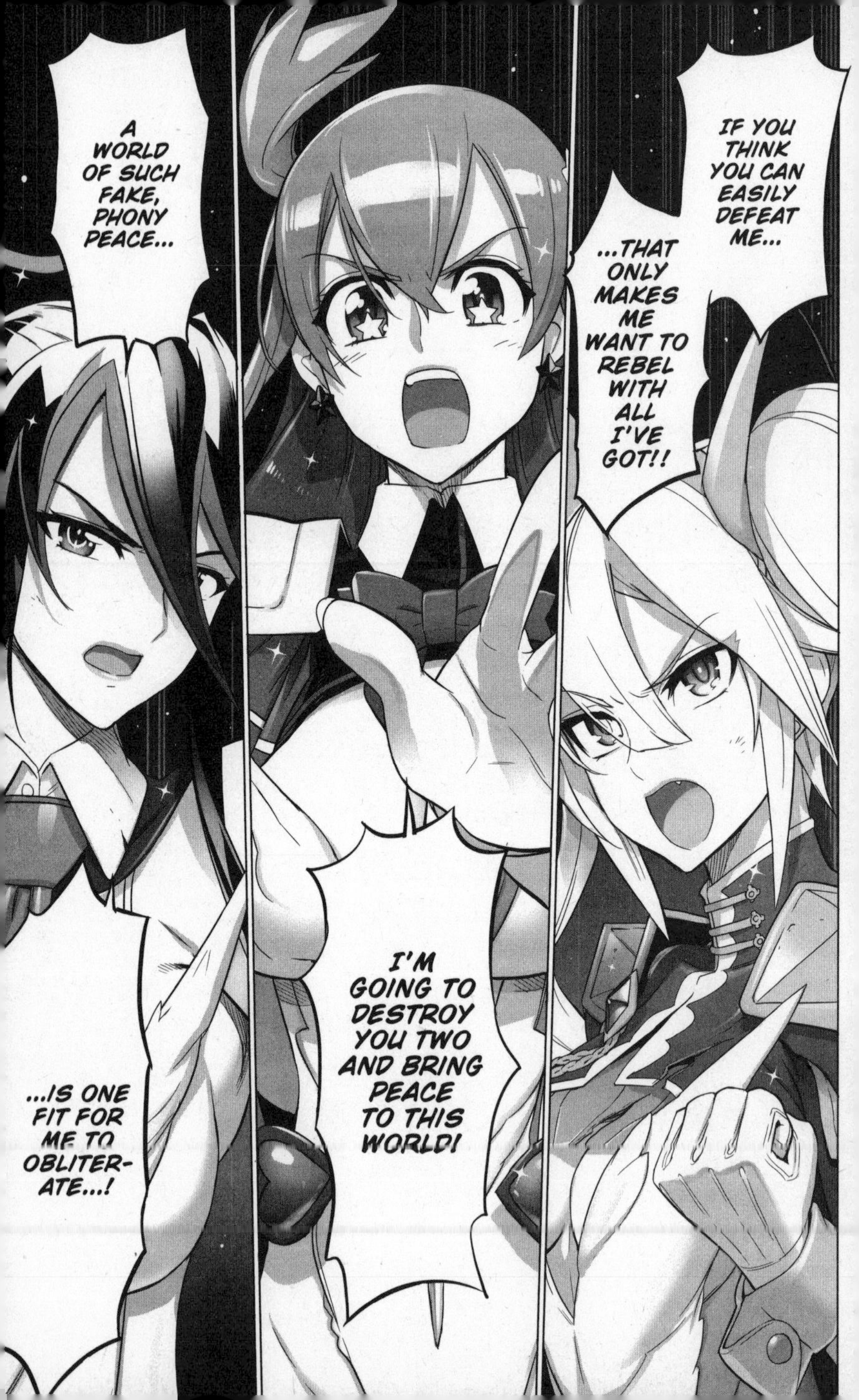
IF YOU THINK YOU CAN EASILY DEFEAT ME...
...THAT ONLY MAKES ME WANT TO REBEL WITH ALL I'VE GOT!!
I'M GOING TO DESTROY YOU TWO AND BRING PEACE TO THIS WORLD!
A WORLD OF SUCH FAKE, PHONY PEACE...
...IS ONE FIT FOR ME TO OBLITER-ATE...!

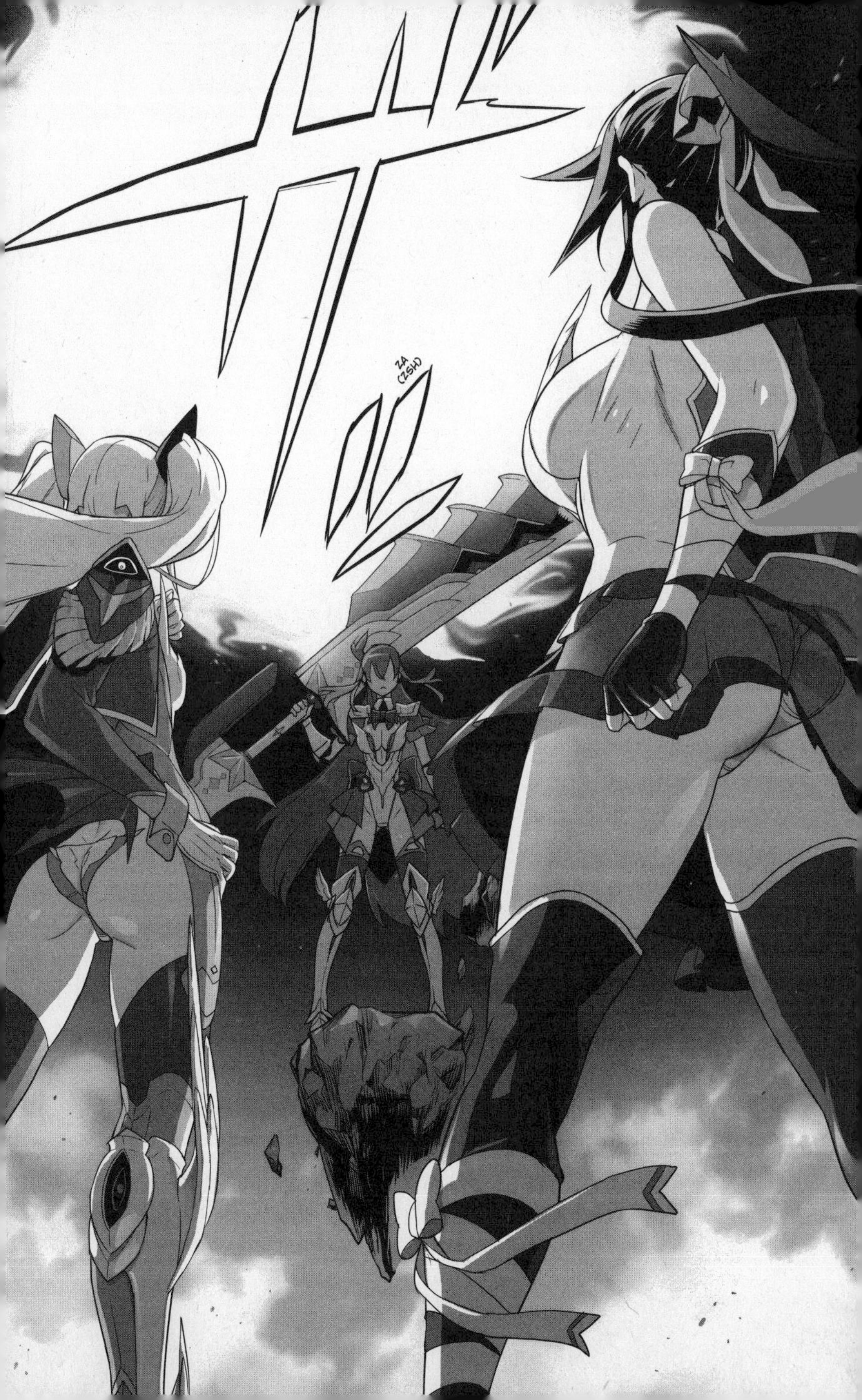
ZA
(ZSH)

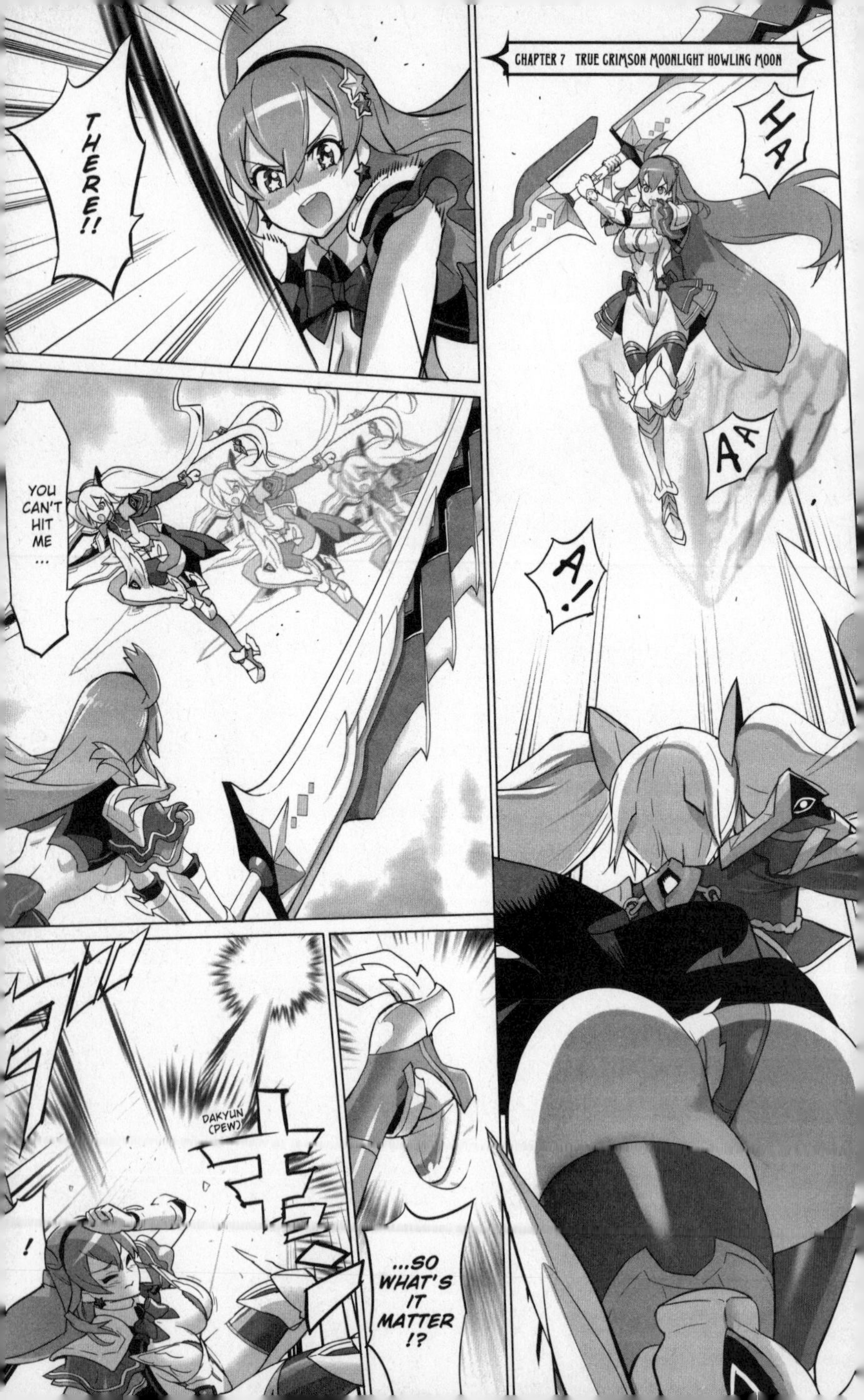
CHAPTER 7 TRUE CRIMSON MOONLIGHT HOWLING MOON
HA
AA
A!
THERE!!
YOU CAN'T HIT ME ...
...SO WHAT'S IT MATTER !?
DAKYUN (PEW)
!

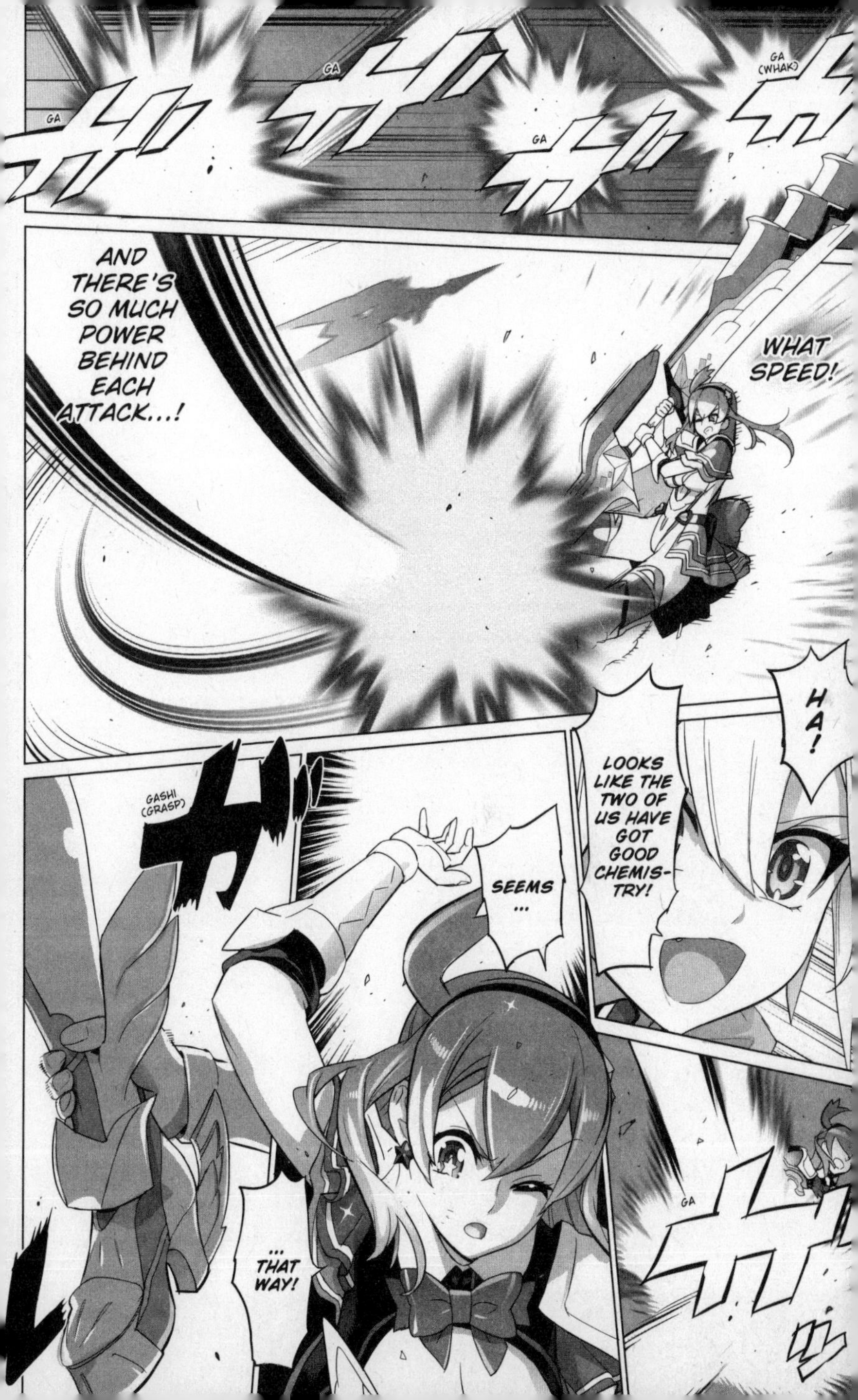
GA (WHAK)
GA
GA
GA
WHAT SPEED!
AND THERE'S SO MUCH POWER BEHIND EACH ATTACK...!
HA!
LOOKS LIKE THE TWO OF US HAVE GOT GOOD CHEMIS-TRY!
SEEMS ...
GASHI (GRASP)
GA
... THAT WAY!

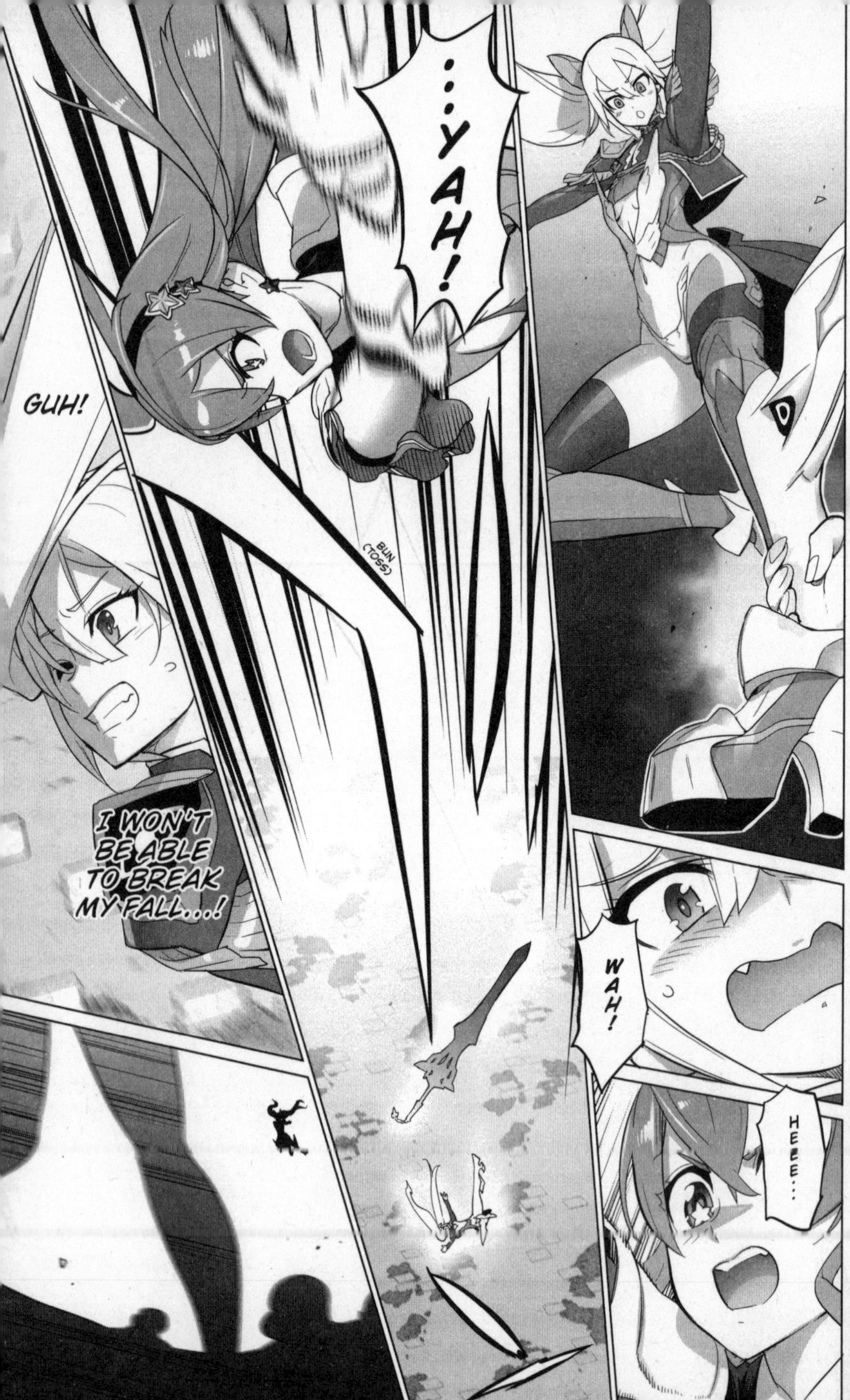
...YAH!
BUN (TOSS)
GUH!
I WON'T BE ABLE TO BREAK MY FALL...!
WAH!
HEEE...

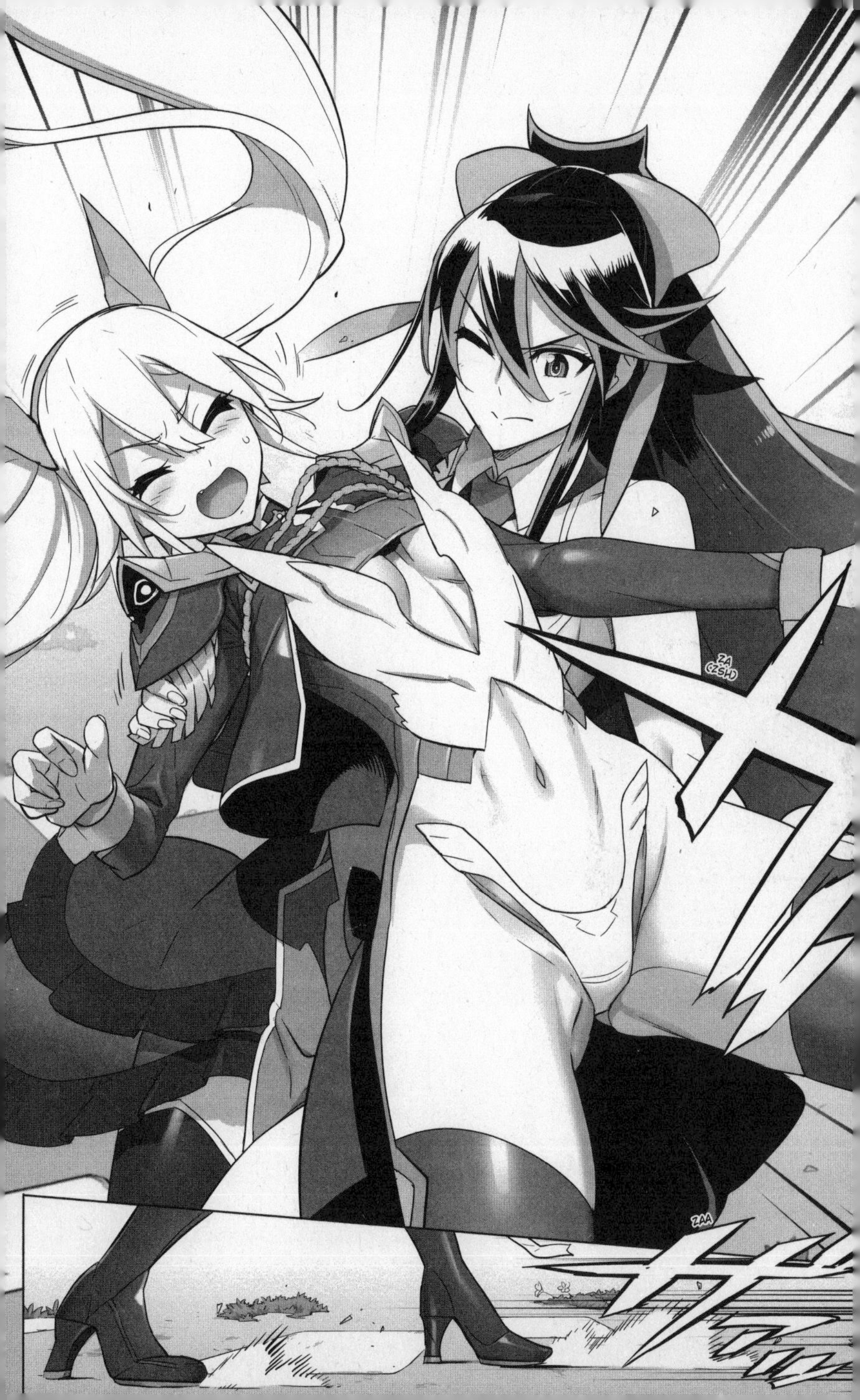
ZA (ZSH)
ZAA

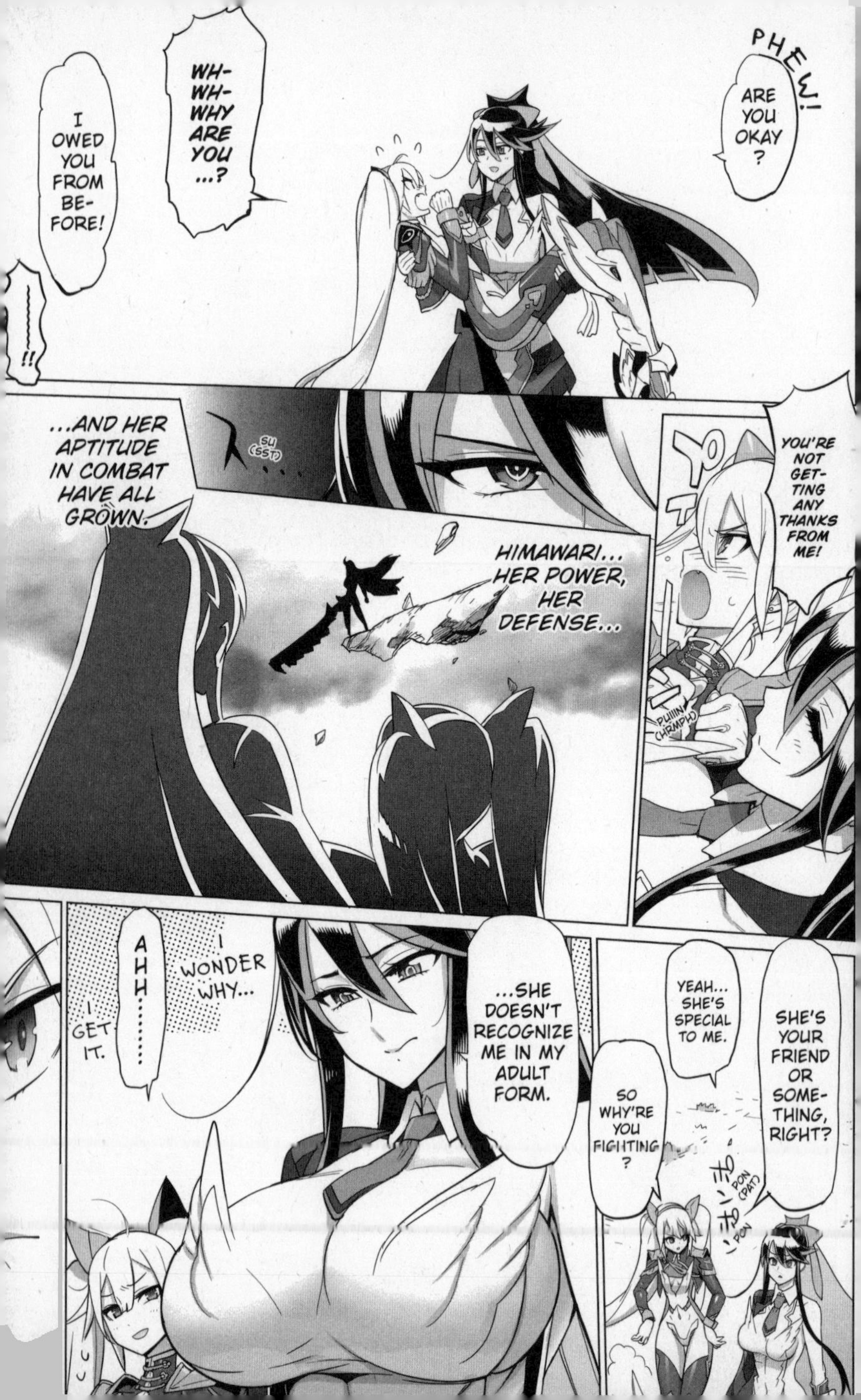
PHEW!
ARE YOU OKAY?
WH-WH-WHY ARE YOU ...?
I OWED YOU FROM BEFORE!
......!!
YOU'RE NOT GETTING ANY THANKS FROM ME!
PUIIIN (HRMPH)
SU (SSST)
HIMAWARI... HER POWER, HER DEFENSE...
...AND HER APTITUDE IN COMBAT HAVE ALL GROWN.
SHE'S YOUR FRIEND OR SOMETHING, RIGHT?
YEAH... SHE'S SPECIAL TO ME.
SO WHY'RE YOU FIGHTING?
PON (PAT)
PON
...SHE DOESN'T RECOGNIZE ME IN MY ADULT FORM.
I WONDER WHY...
AHH......
I GET IT.

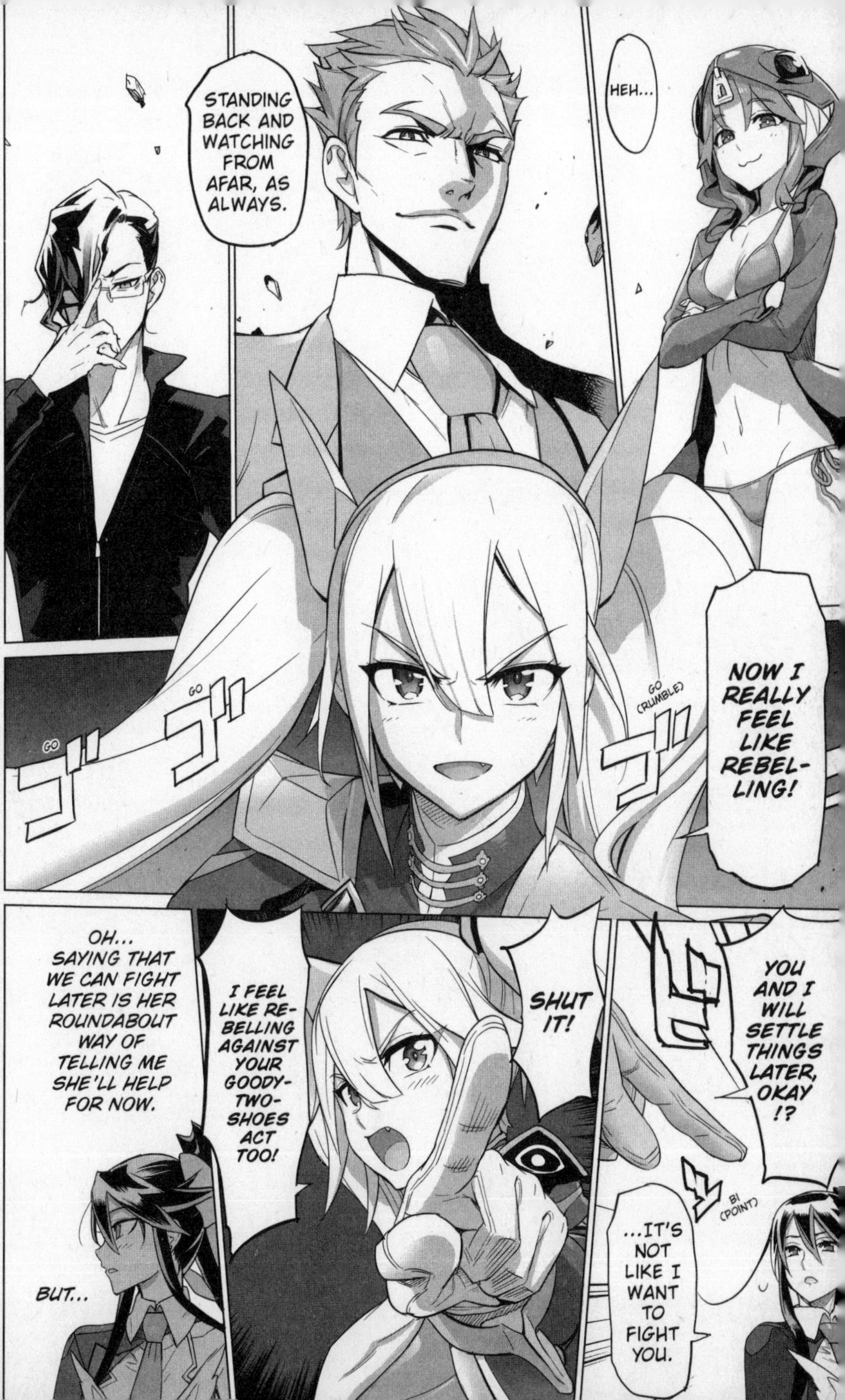
HEH...
STANDING BACK AND WATCHING FROM AFAR, AS ALWAYS.
NOW I REALLY FEEL LIKE REBEL-LING!
GO (RUMBLE)
GO
GO
YOU AND I WILL SETTLE THINGS LATER, OKAY!?
BI (POINT)
...IT'S NOT LIKE I WANT TO FIGHT YOU.
SHUT IT!
I FEEL LIKE RE-BELLING AGAINST YOUR GOODY-TWO-SHOES ACT TOO!
OH... SAYING THAT WE CAN FIGHT LATER IS HER ROUNDABOUT WAY OF TELLING ME SHE'LL HELP FOR NOW.
BUT...

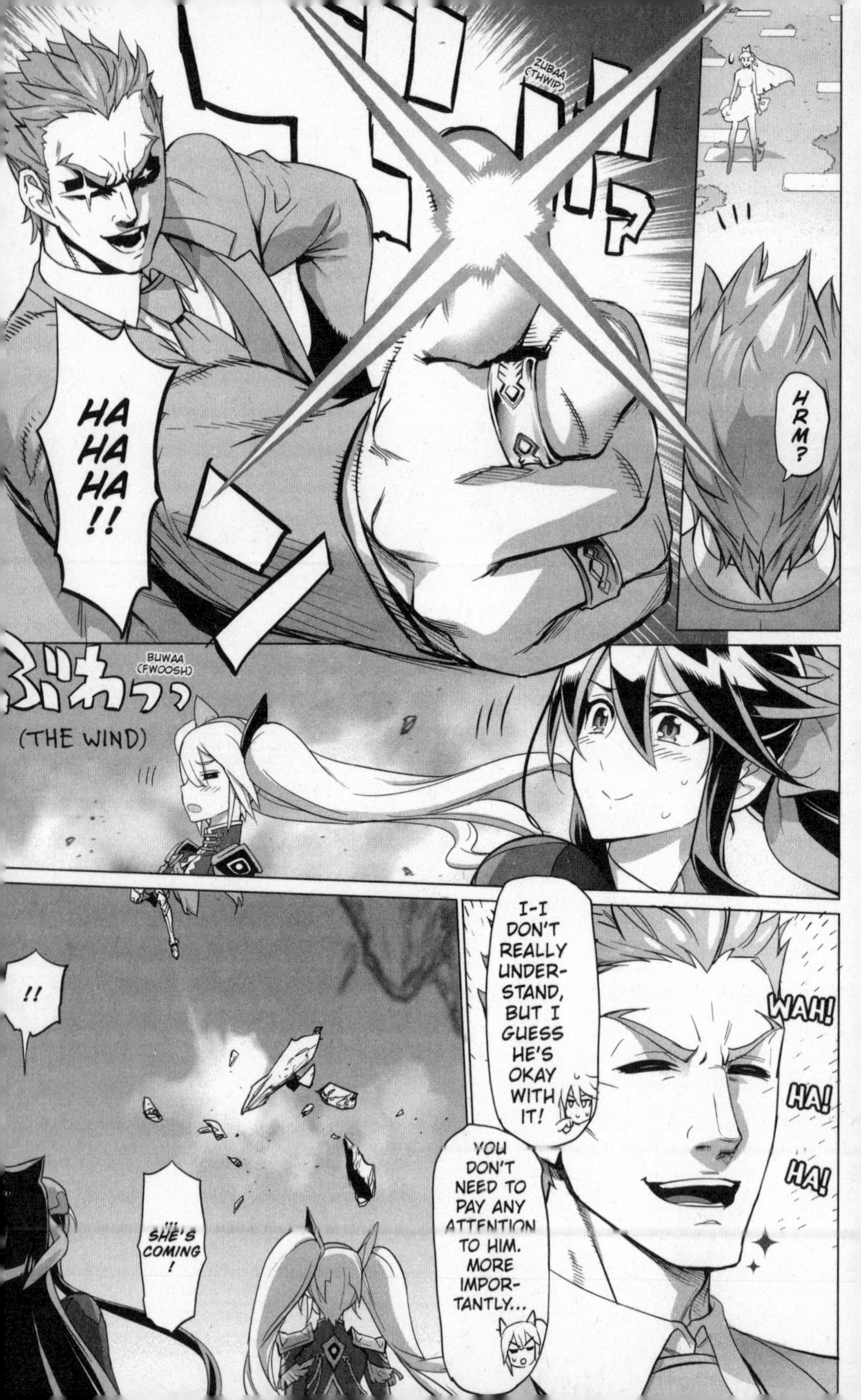
HRM?
ZUBAA (THWIP)
HA HA HA!!
ぶわっっ
BUWAA (FWOOSH)
(THE WIND)
I-I DON'T REALLY UNDERSTAND, BUT I GUESS HE'S OKAY WITH IT!
WAH! HA! HA!
YOU DON'T NEED TO PAY ANY ATTENTION TO HIM. MORE IMPORTANTLY...
!!
...! SHE'S COMING!

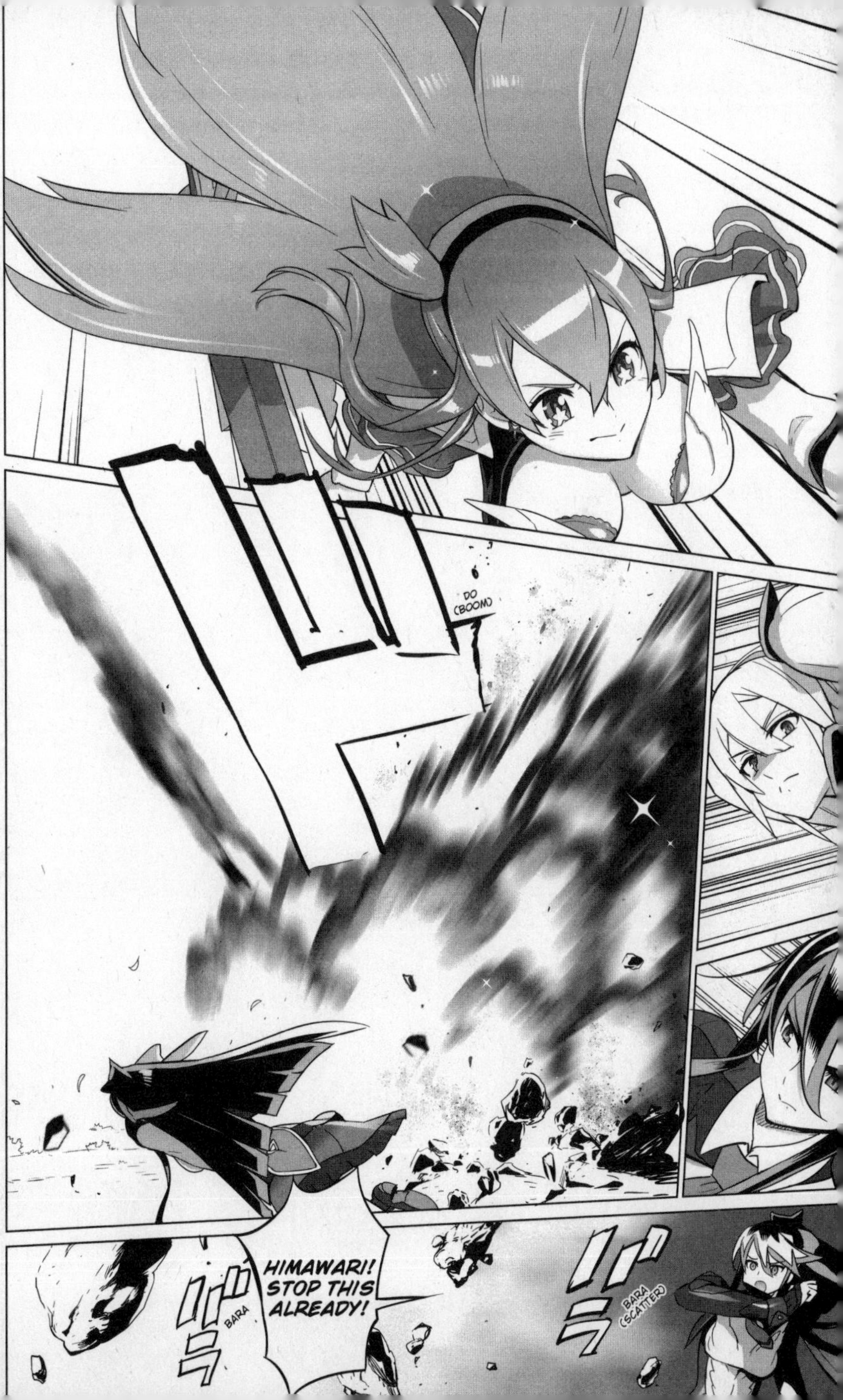
DO (BOOM)
BARA (SCATTER)
HIMAWARI! STOP THIS ALREADY!
BARA

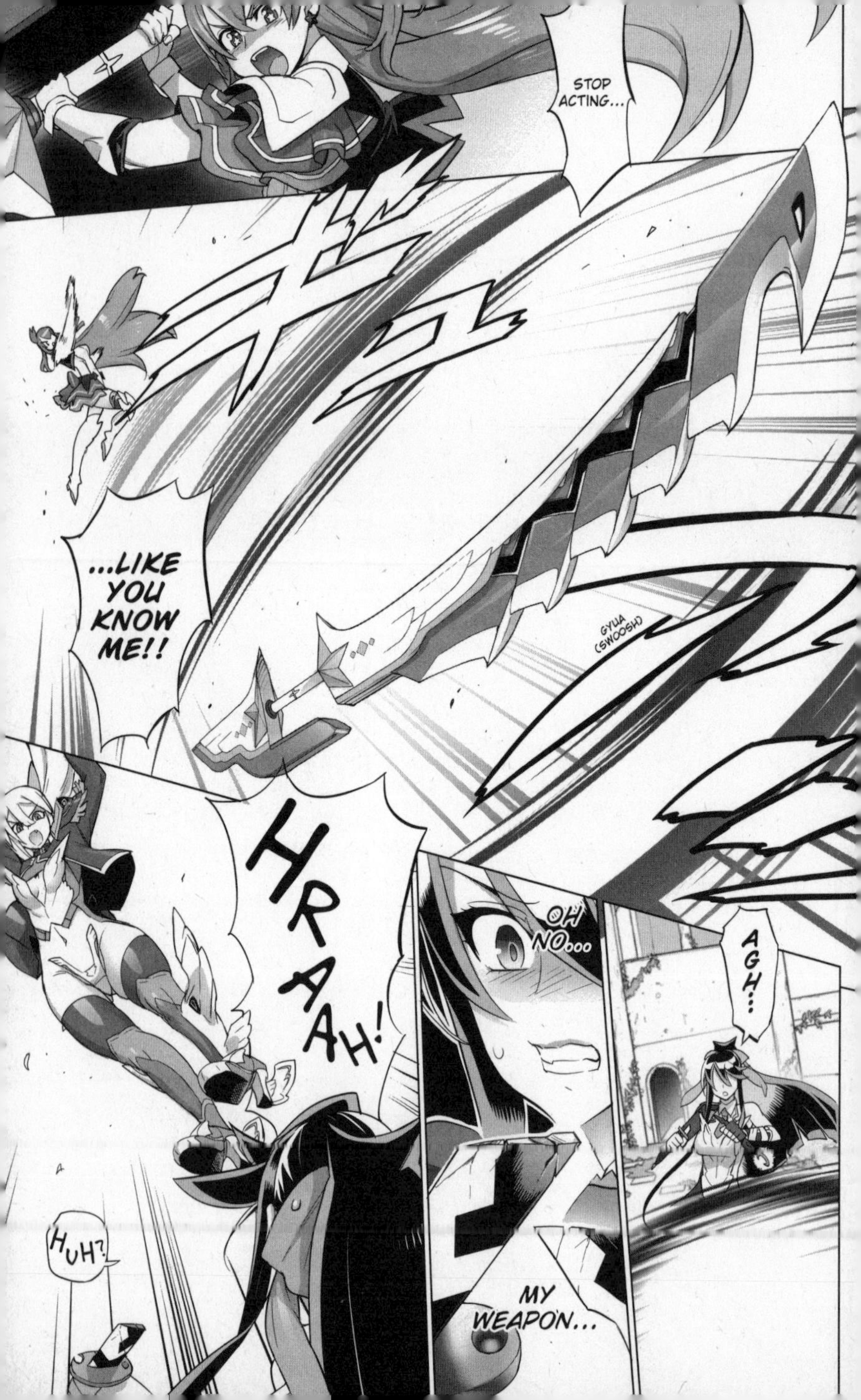
STOP ACTING...
...LIKE YOU KNOW ME!!
GYUA (SWOOSH)
AGH..
OH NO...
MY WEAPON...
HRAAH!
HUH?

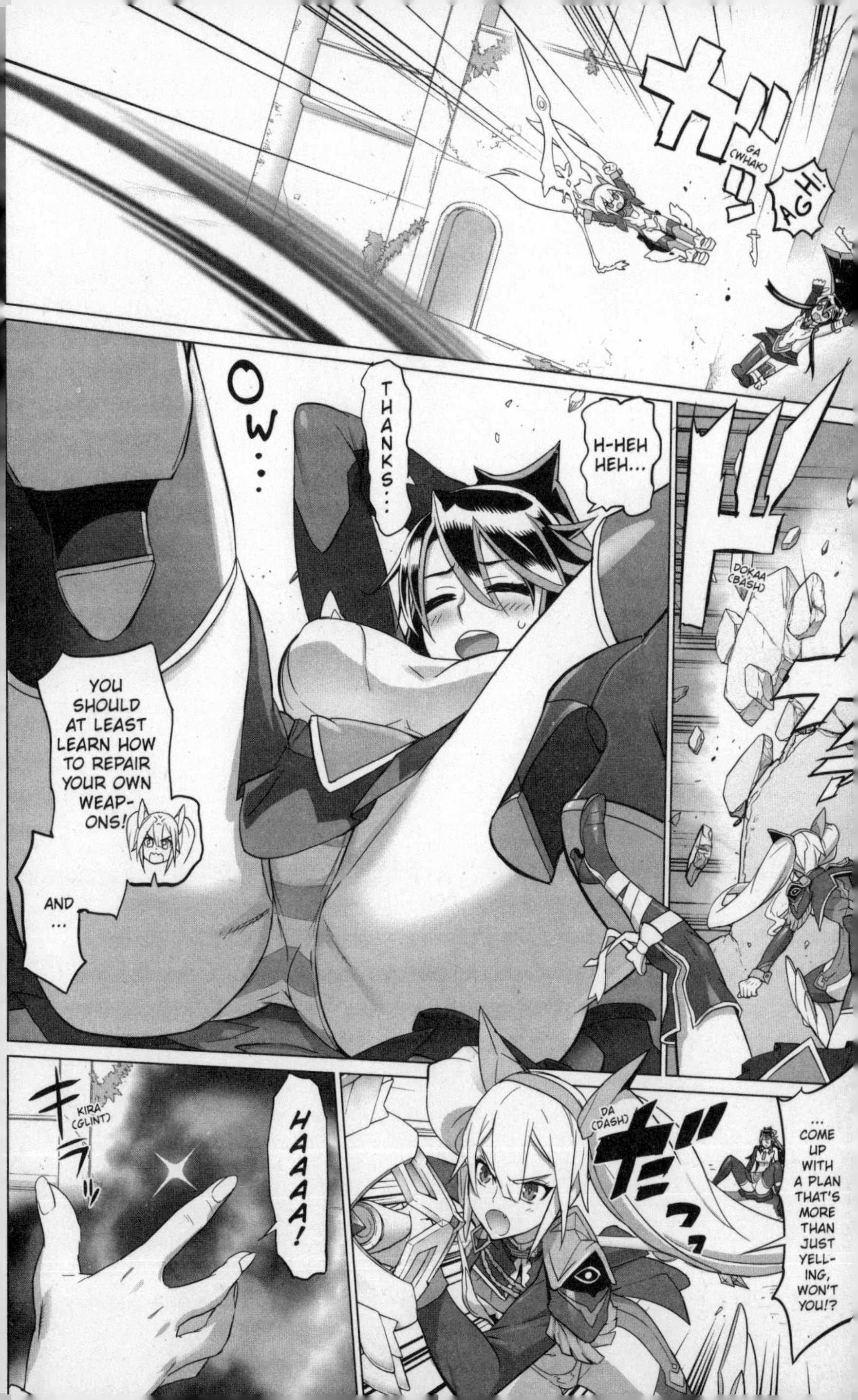
GA (WHAK)
AGH!
DOKAA (BASH)
H-HEH HEH...
THANKS...
OW...
YOU SHOULD AT LEAST LEARN HOW TO REPAIR YOUR OWN WEAP-ONS!
AND...
...COME UP WITH A PLAN THAT'S MORE THAN JUST YELL-ING, WON'T YOU!?
DA (DASH)
HAAAAA!
KIRA (GLINT)

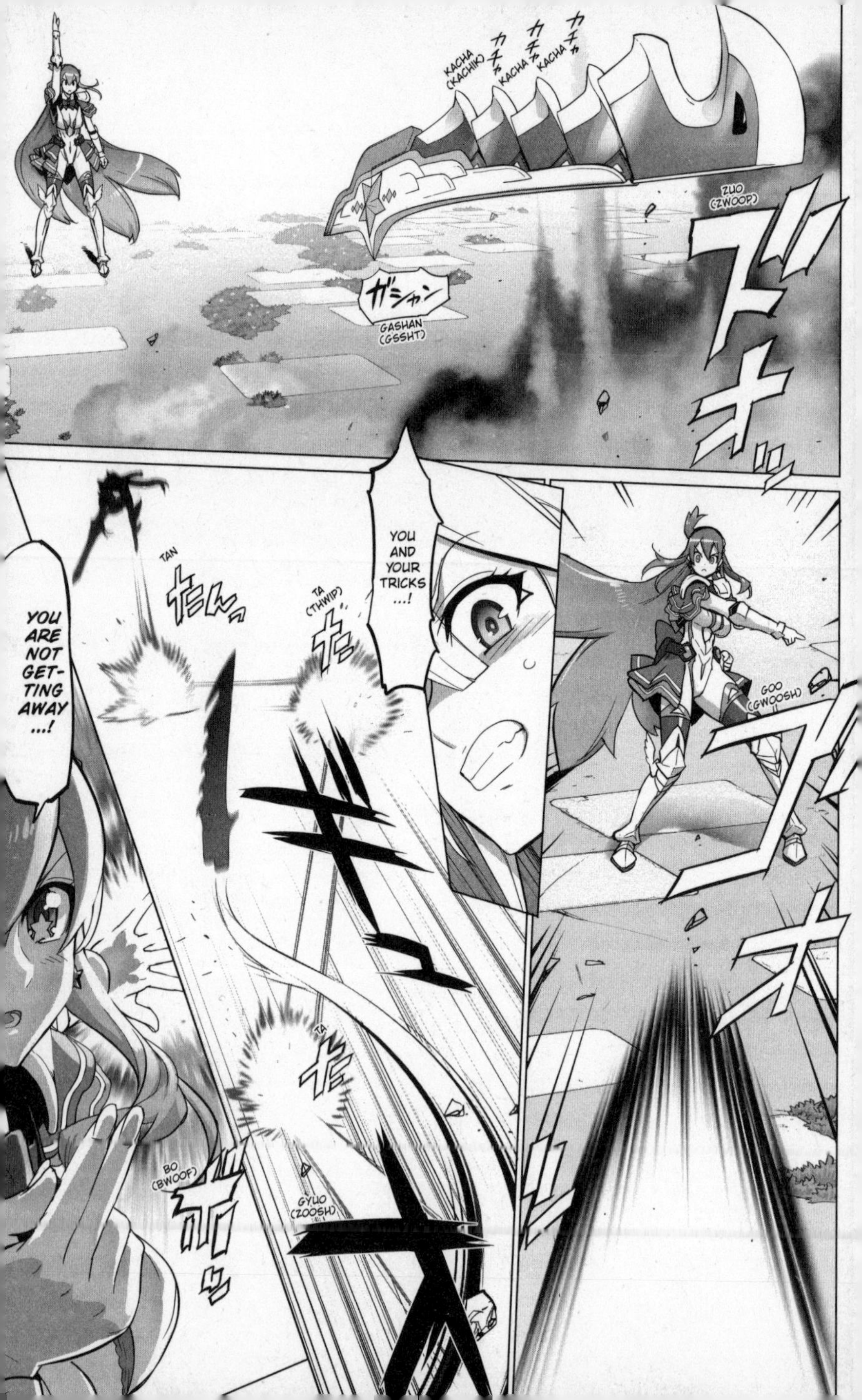
KACHA (KACHIK)
KACHA
KACHA
ZUO (ZWOOP)
ガシャン
GASHAN (GSSHT)
GOO (GWOOSH)
YOU AND YOUR TRICKS ...!
TAN
TA (THWIP)
YOU ARE NOT GETTING AWAY ...!
TA
BO (BWOOF)
GYUO (ZOOSH)

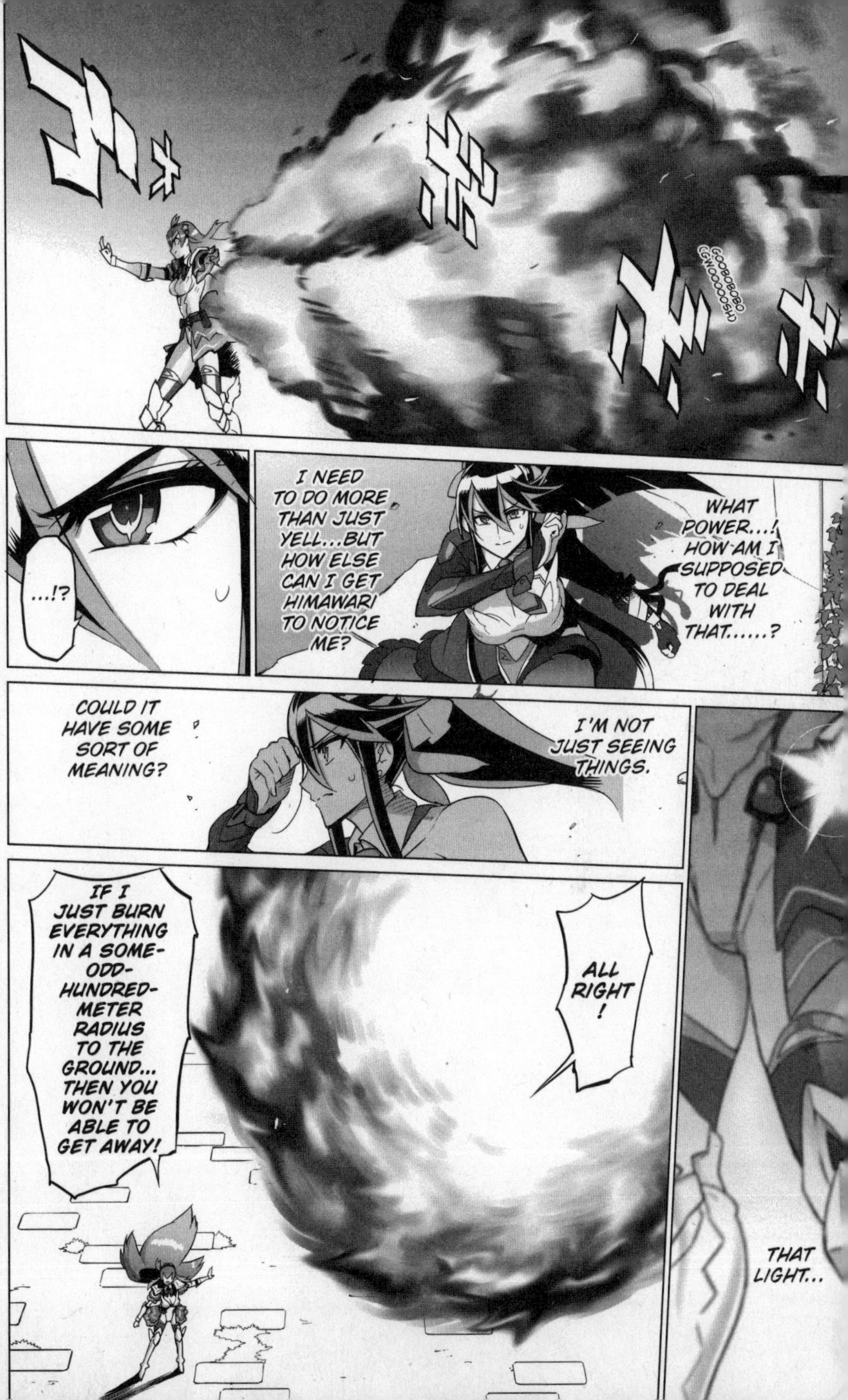
GOOBOBOBO (GWOOOOOSH)
WHAT POWER...! HOW AM I SUPPOSED TO DEAL WITH THAT......?
I NEED TO DO MORE THAN JUST YELL...BUT HOW ELSE CAN I GET HIMAWARI TO NOTICE ME?
...!?
THAT LIGHT...
I'M NOT JUST SEEING THINGS.
COULD IT HAVE SOME SORT OF MEANING?
ALL RIGHT!
IF I JUST BURN EVERYTHING IN A SOME-ODD-HUNDRED-METER RADIUS TO THE GROUND... THEN YOU WON'T BE ABLE TO GET AWAY!

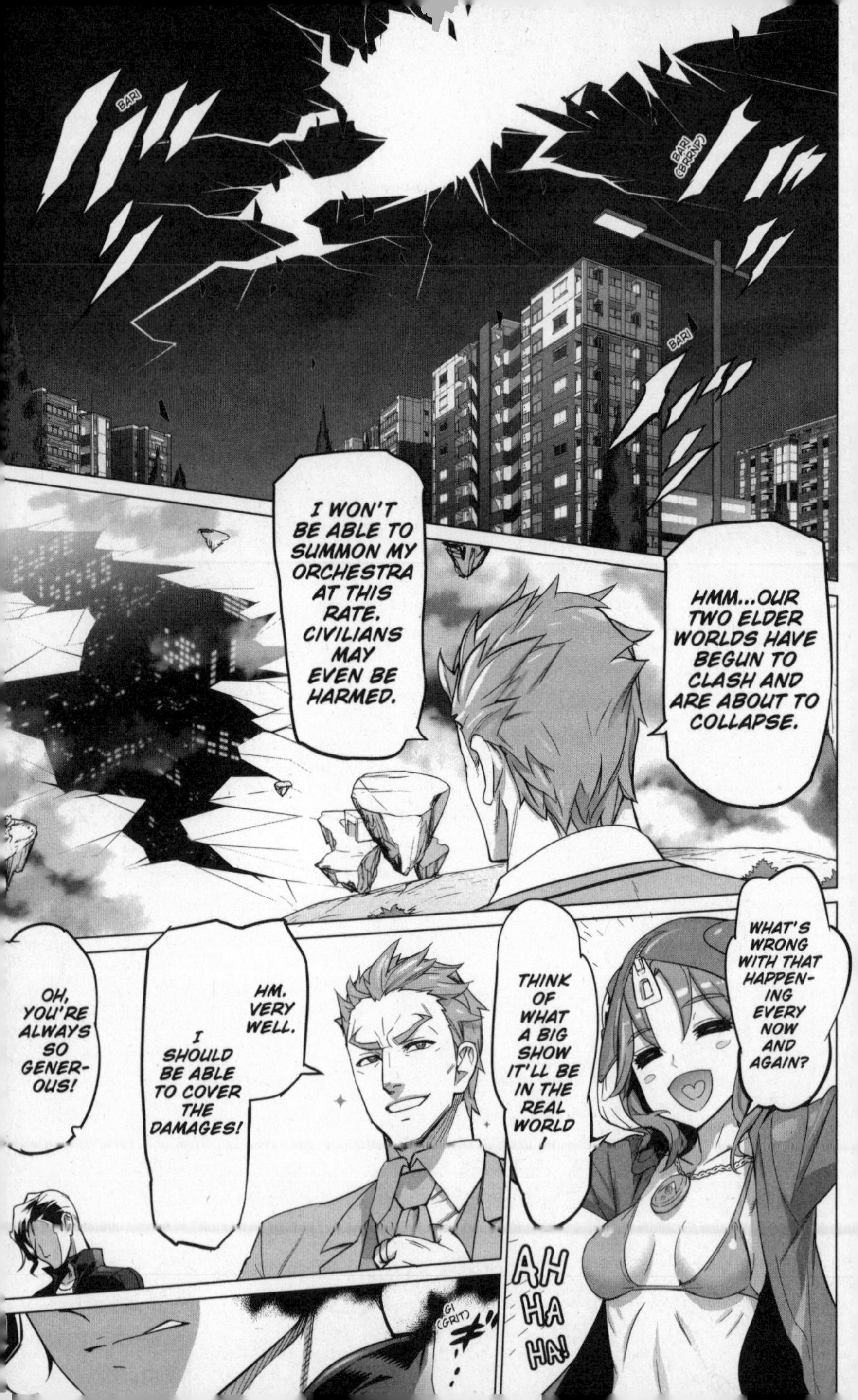
BARI (BRRNP)
BARI
BARI
HMM...OUR TWO ELDER WORLDS HAVE BEGUN TO CLASH AND ARE ABOUT TO COLLAPSE.
I WON'T BE ABLE TO SUMMON MY ORCHESTRA AT THIS RATE. CIVILIANS MAY EVEN BE HARMED.
WHAT'S WRONG WITH THAT HAPPEN-ING EVERY NOW AND AGAIN?
THINK OF WHAT A BIG SHOW IT'LL BE IN THE REAL WORLD!
HM. VERY WELL.
I SHOULD BE ABLE TO COVER THE DAMAGES!
OH, YOU'RE ALWAYS SO GENER-OUS!
AH HA HA HA!
GI (GRIT)

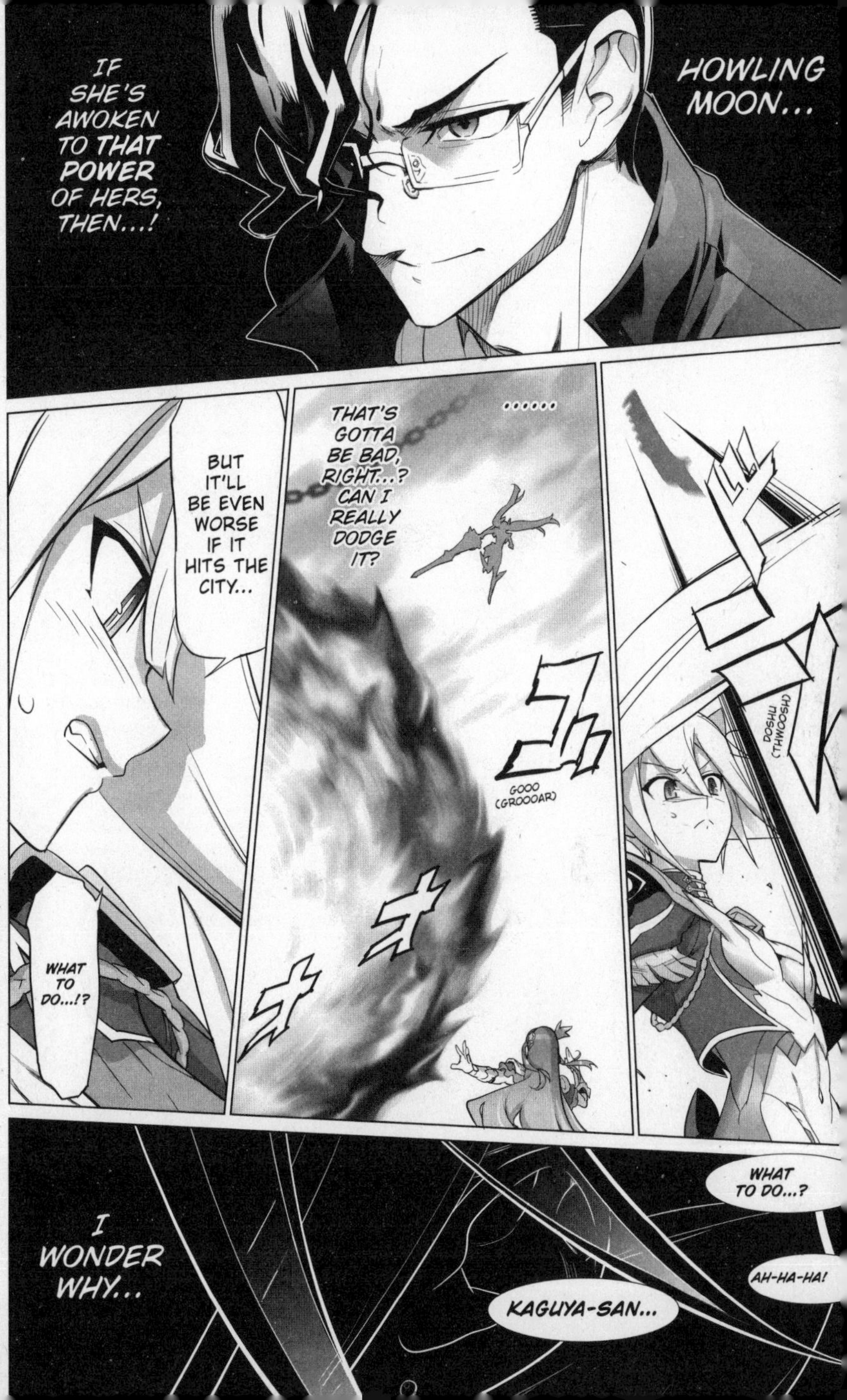

HOWLING MOON...
IF SHE'S AWOKEN TO THAT POWER OF HERS, THEN...!
DOSHU (THWOOSH)
......
THAT'S GOTTA BE BAD, RIGHT...? CAN I REALLY DODGE IT?
GOOO (GROOOAR)
BUT IT'LL BE EVEN WORSE IF IT HITS THE CITY...
WHAT TO DO...!?
WHAT TO DO...?
AH-HA-HA!
KAGUYA-SAN...
I WONDER WHY...

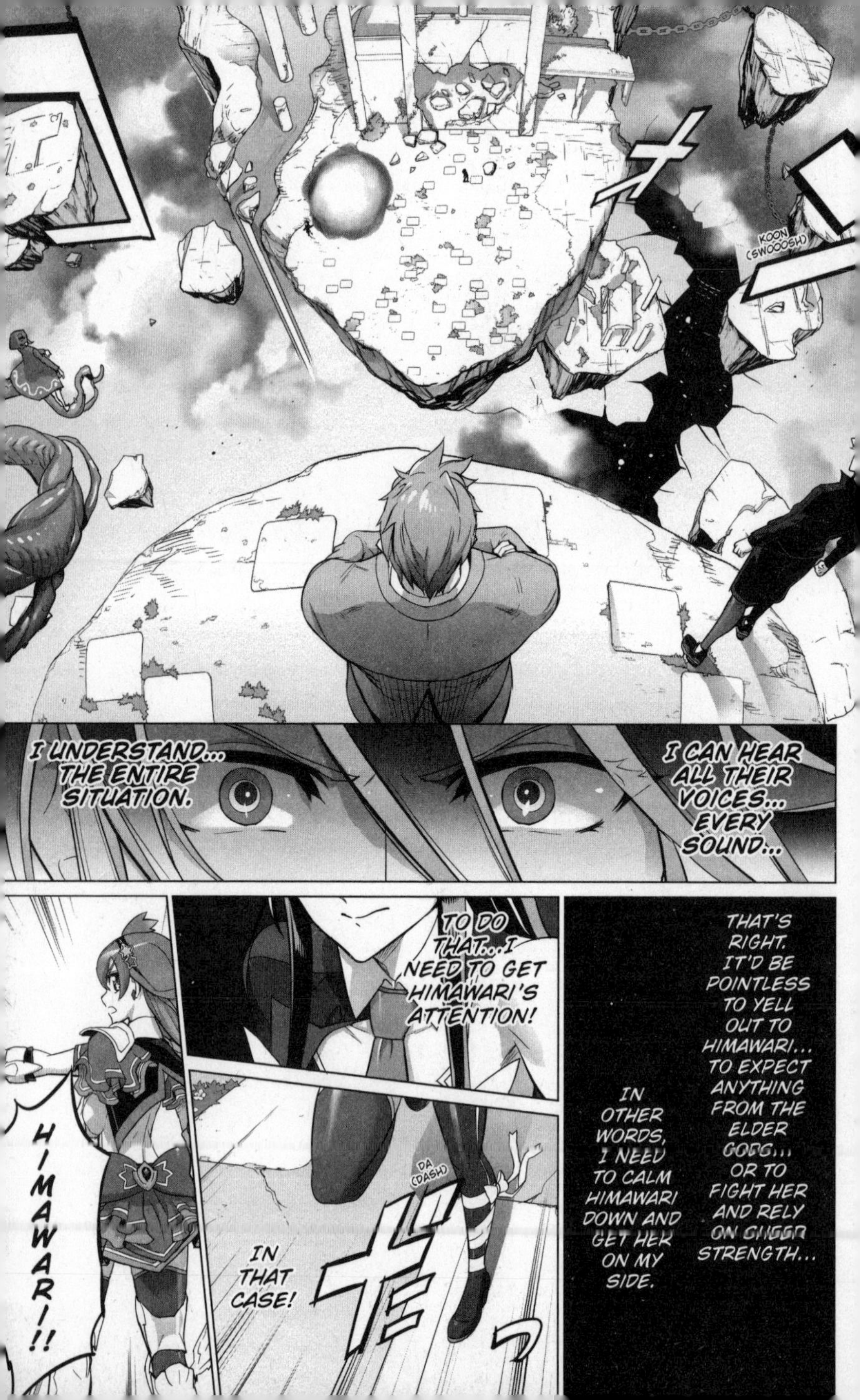
KOON (SWOOOSH)
I CAN HEAR ALL THEIR VOICES... EVERY SOUND...
I UNDERSTAND... THE ENTIRE SITUATION.
THAT'S RIGHT. IT'D BE POINTLESS TO YELL OUT TO HIMAWARI... TO EXPECT ANYTHING FROM THE ELDER GODS... OR TO FIGHT HER AND RELY ON SHEER STRENGTH...
IN OTHER WORDS, I NEED TO CALM HIMAWARI DOWN AND GET HER ON MY SIDE.
TO DO THAT...I NEED TO GET HIMAWARI'S ATTENTION!
DA (DASH)
IN THAT CASE!
HIMAWARI!!

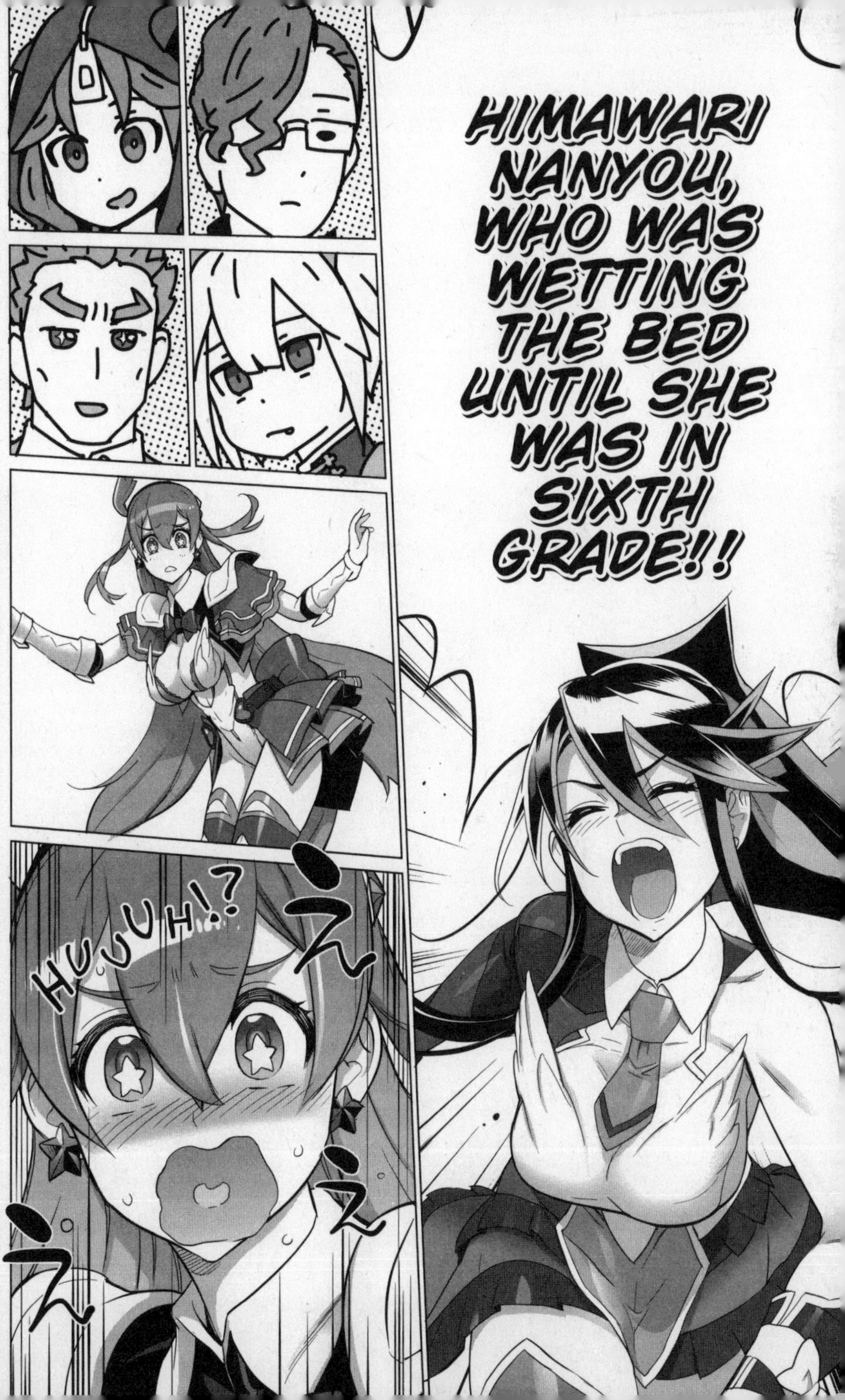
HIMAWARI NANYOU, WHO WAS WETTING THE BED UNTIL SHE WAS IN SIXTH GRADE!!
HUUUH!?

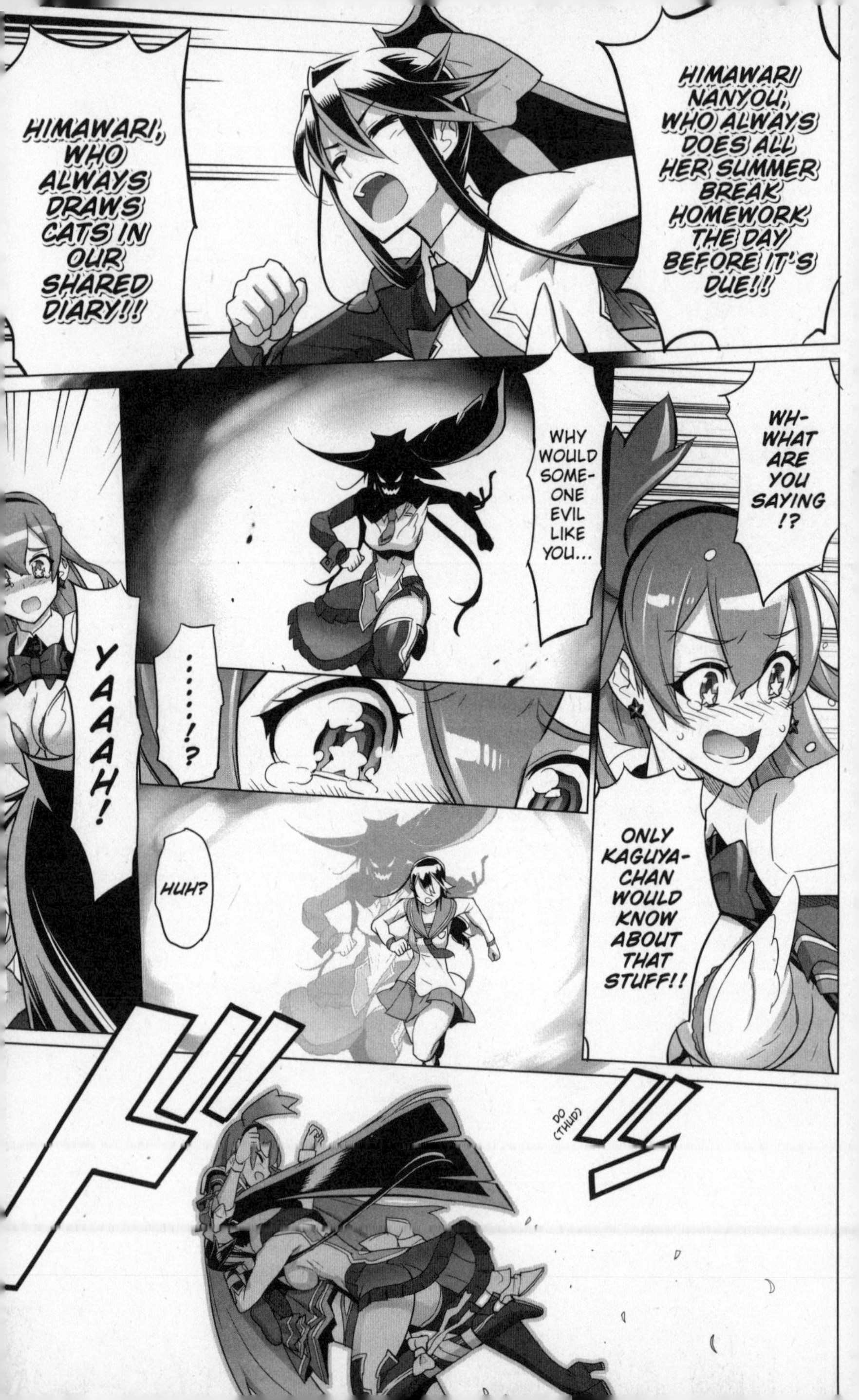
HIMAWARI NANYOU, WHO ALWAYS DOES ALL HER SUMMER BREAK HOMEWORK THE DAY BEFORE IT'S DUE!!
HIMAWARI, WHO ALWAYS DRAWS CATS IN OUR SHARED DIARY!!
WH-WHAT ARE YOU SAYING!?
ONLY KAGUYA-CHAN WOULD KNOW ABOUT THAT STUFF!!
WHY WOULD SOME-ONE EVIL LIKE YOU...
......!?
HUH?
YAAAAH!
DO (THUD)

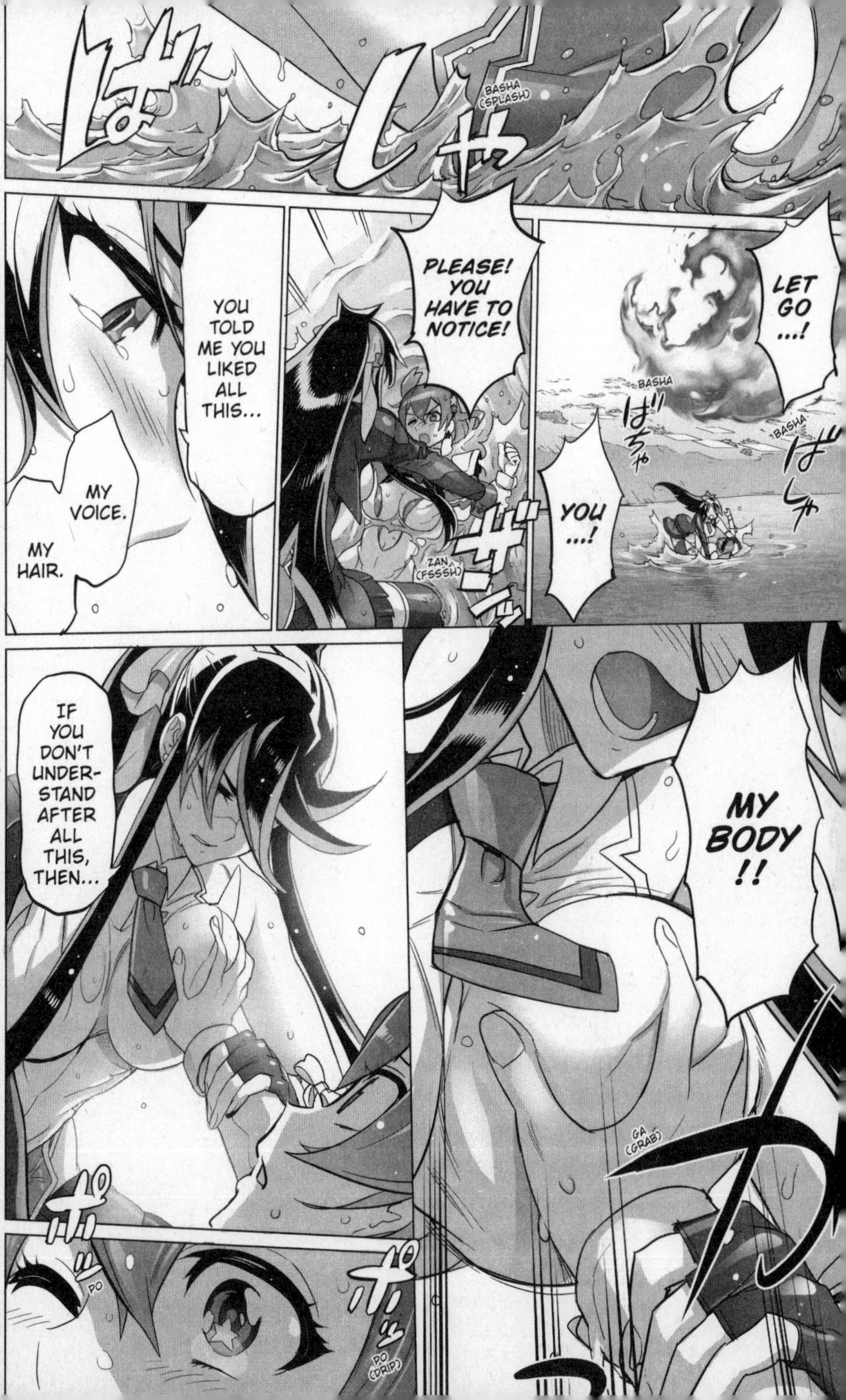
ばしゃ
BASHA (SPLASH)
LET GO ...!
BASHA
ばしゃ
BASHA
YOU ...!
PLEASE! YOU HAVE TO NOTICE!
ZAN (FSSSH)
YOU TOLD ME YOU LIKED ALL THIS...
MY VOICE.
MY HAIR.
MY BODY !!
GA (GRAB)
IF YOU DON'T UNDER-STAND AFTER ALL THIS, THEN...
PO
PO (DRIP)

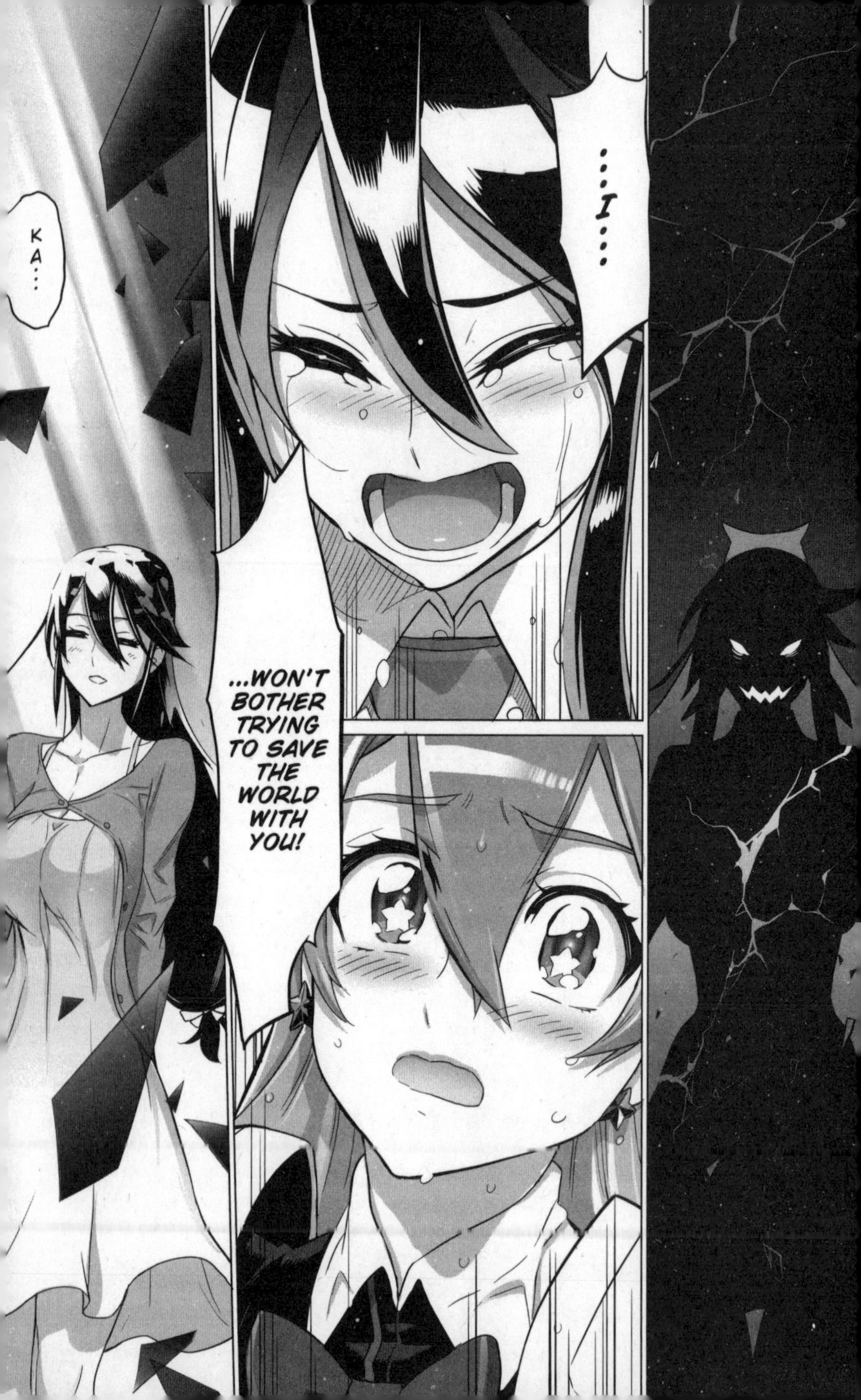
...I...
...WON'T BOTHER TRYING TO SAVE THE WORLD WITH YOU!
KA...

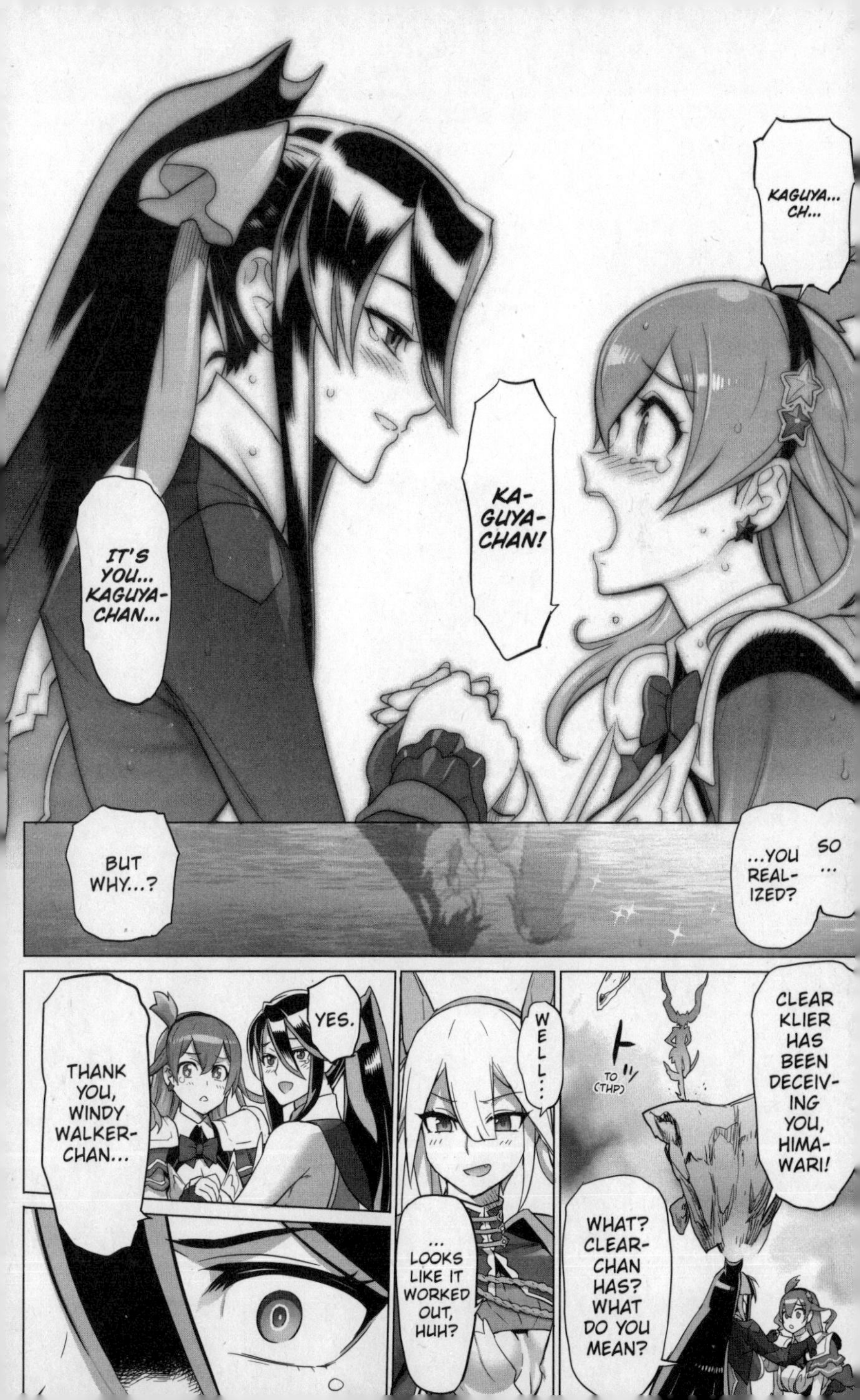
KAGUYA... CH...
KA-GUYA-CHAN!
IT'S YOU... KAGUYA-CHAN...
SO...
...YOU REAL-IZED?
BUT WHY...?
CLEAR KLIER HAS BEEN DECEIV-ING YOU, HIMA-WARI!
TO (THP)
WHAT? CLEAR-CHAN HAS? WHAT DO YOU MEAN?
WELL...
...LOOKS LIKE IT WORKED OUT, HUH?
YES.
THANK YOU, WINDY WALKER-CHAN...

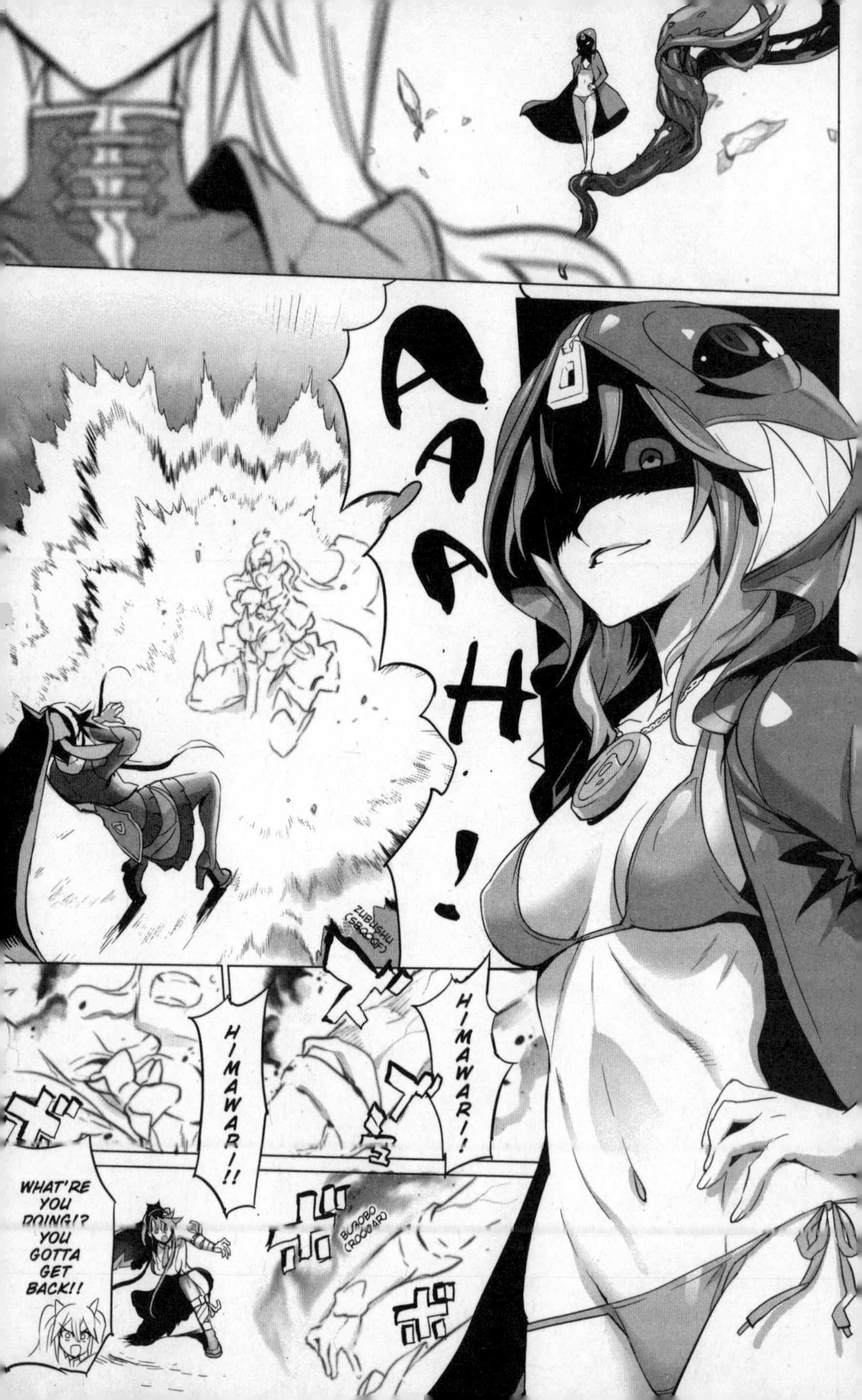
AAAH!
ZUBUSHU (SBOOOF)
HIMAWARI!!
HIMAWARI!!
BUSOBO (ROOOAR)
WHAT'RE YOU DOING!? YOU GOTTA GET BACK!!

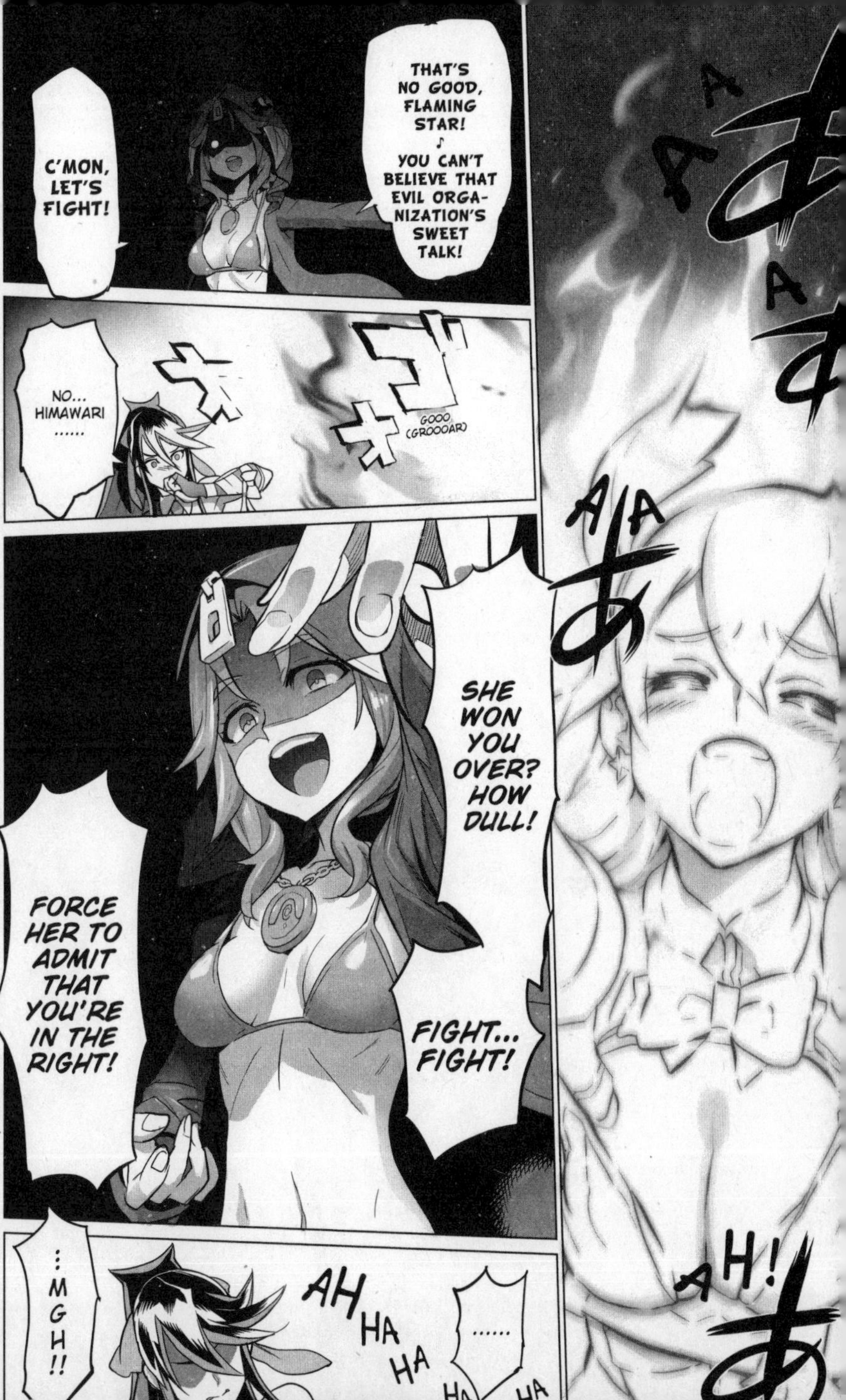

あ A A A
あ A A
あ AH!
THAT'S NO GOOD, FLAMING STAR! ♪ YOU CAN'T BELIEVE THAT EVIL ORGA-NIZATION'S SWEET TALK!
C'MON, LET'S FIGHT!
GOOO (GROOOAR)
NO... HIMAWARI ......
SHE WON YOU OVER? HOW DULL!
FIGHT... FIGHT!
FORCE HER TO ADMIT THAT YOU'RE IN THE RIGHT!
......
AH HA HA HA HA HA
...MGH!!

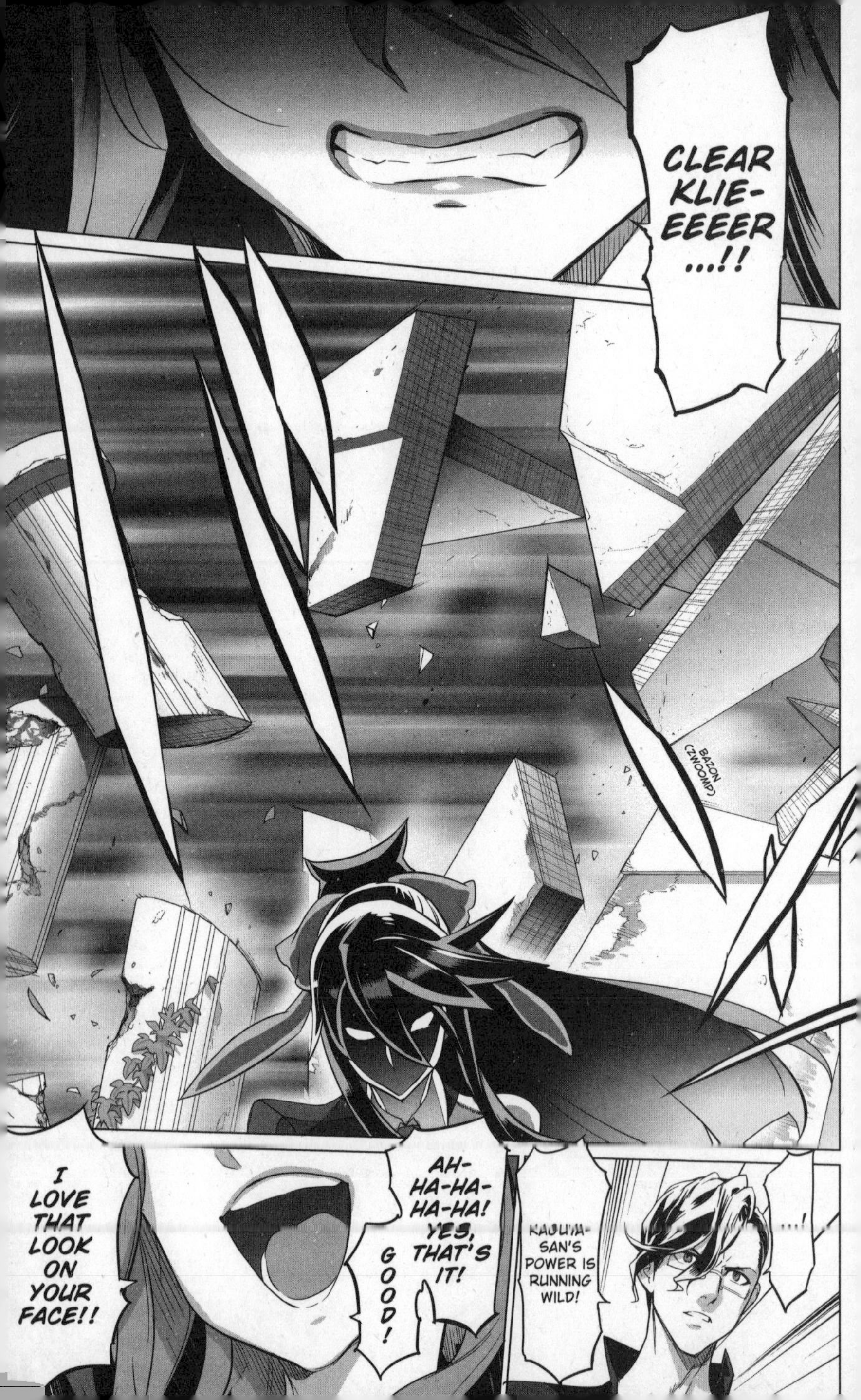
CLEAR KLIE-EEEER ...!!
BAZON (ZWOOMP)
...!
KAGUYA-SAN'S POWER IS RUNNING WILD!
AH-HA-HA-HA-HA! YES, THAT'S IT!
GOOD!
I LOVE THAT LOOK ON YOUR FACE!!

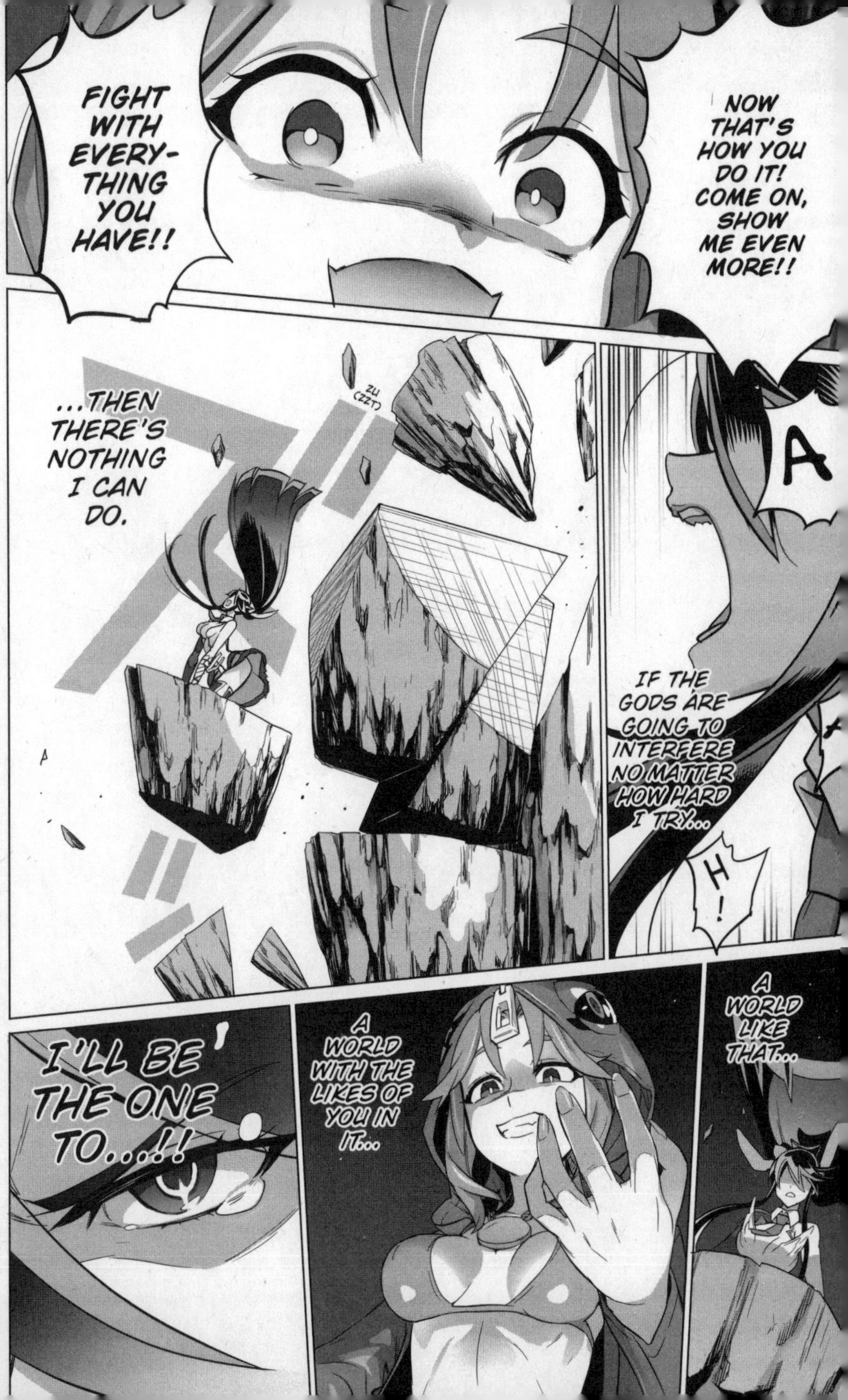
NOW THAT'S HOW YOU DO IT! COME ON, SHOW ME EVEN MORE!!
FIGHT WITH EVERY-THING YOU HAVE!!
A
IF THE GODS ARE GOING TO INTERFERE NO MATTER HOW HARD I TRY...
H!
ZU (ZZT)
...THEN THERE'S NOTHING I CAN DO.
A WORLD LIKE THAT...
A WORLD WITH THE LIKES OF YOU IN IT...
I'LL BE THE ONE TO...!!

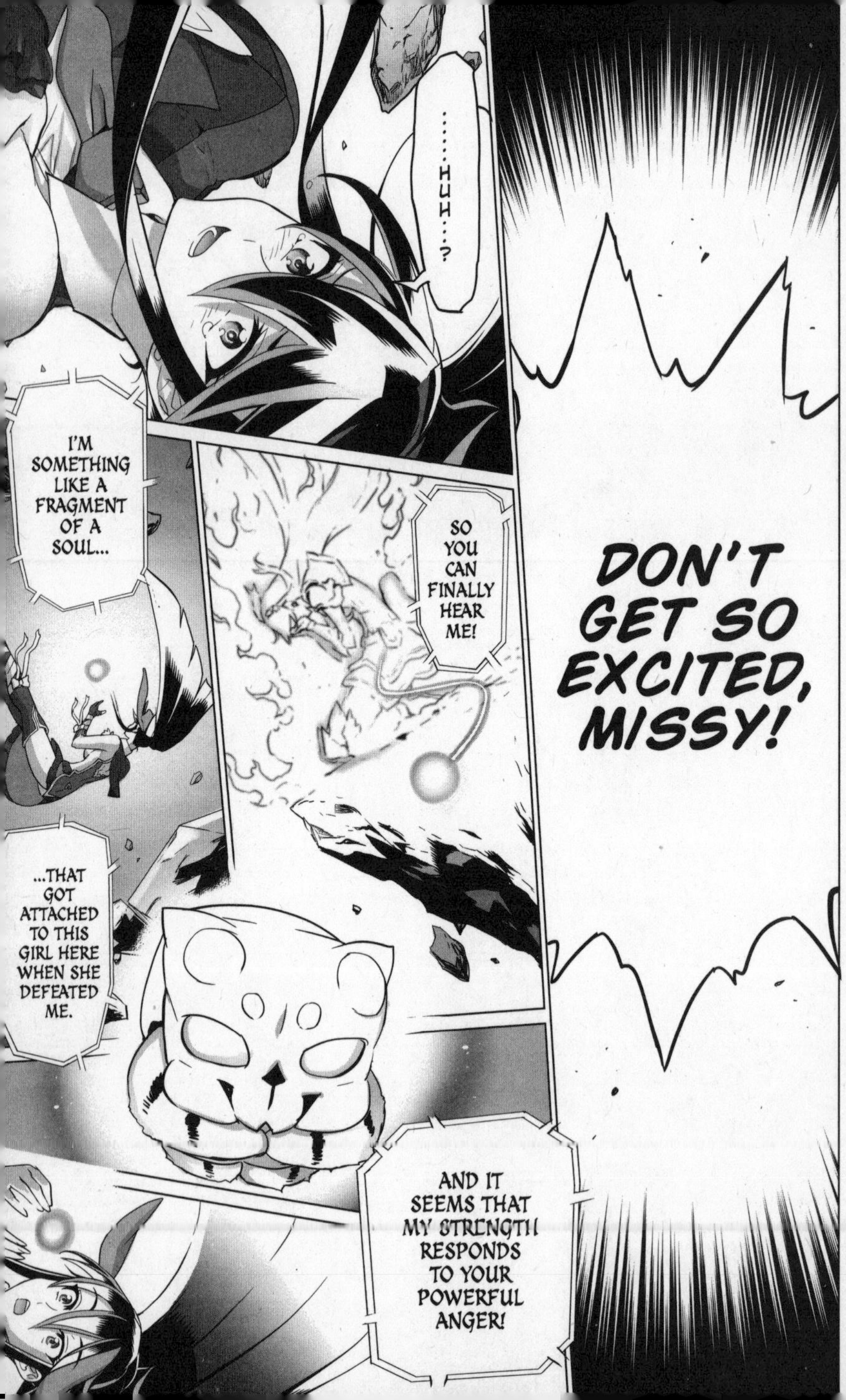
DON'T GET SO EXCITED, MISSY!
......HUH...?
SO YOU CAN FINALLY HEAR ME!
I'M SOMETHING LIKE A FRAGMENT OF A SOUL...
...THAT GOT ATTACHED TO THIS GIRL HERE WHEN SHE DEFEATED ME.
AND IT SEEMS THAT MY STRENGTH RESPONDS TO YOUR POWERFUL ANGER!

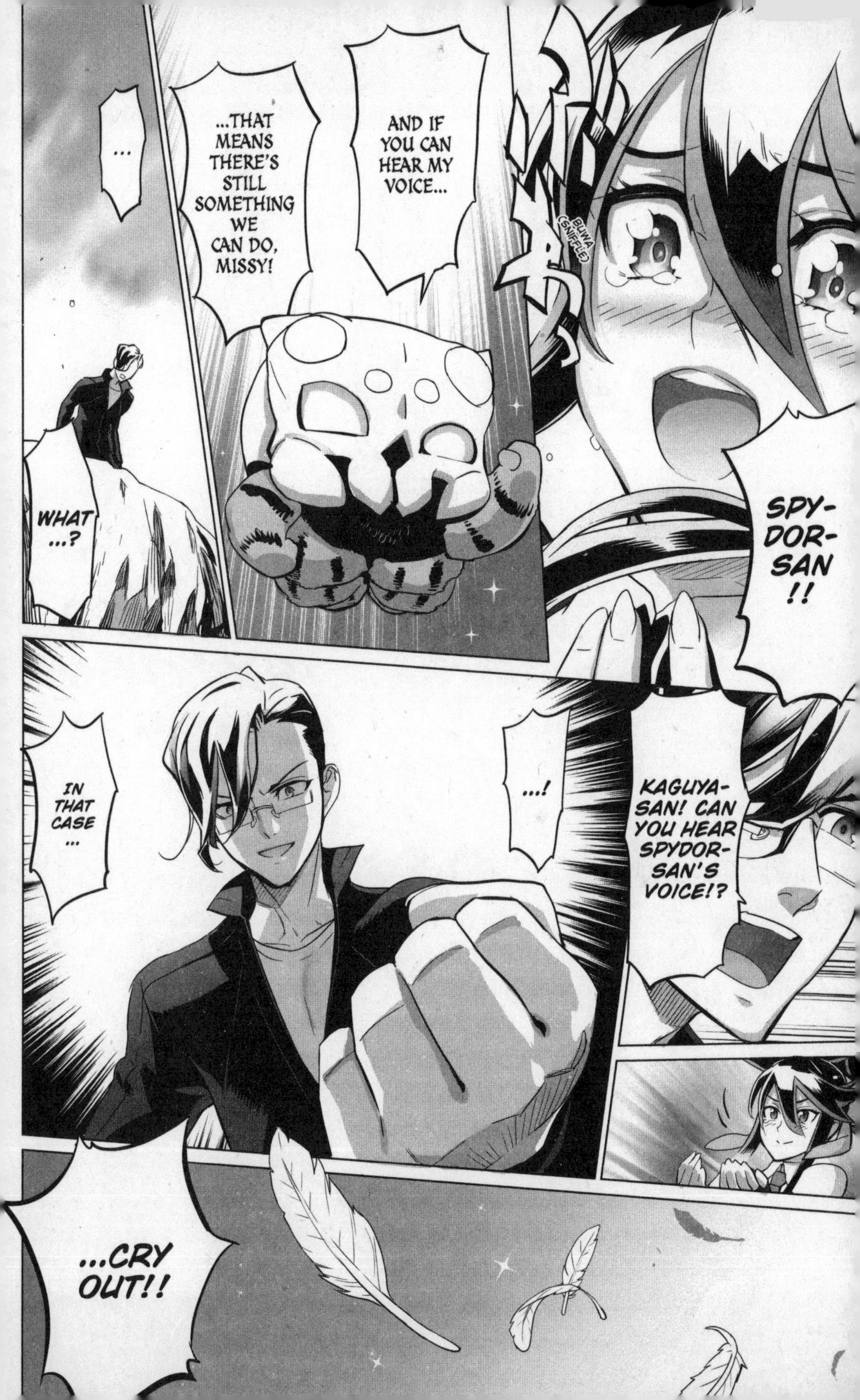
BUWA (SNIFFLE)
SPY-DOR-SAN!!
AND IF YOU CAN HEAR MY VOICE...
...THAT MEANS THERE'S STILL SOMETHING WE CAN DO, MISSY!
...
WHAT...?
KAGUYA-SAN! CAN YOU HEAR SPYDOR-SAN'S VOICE!?
...!
IN THAT CASE...
...CRY OUT!!

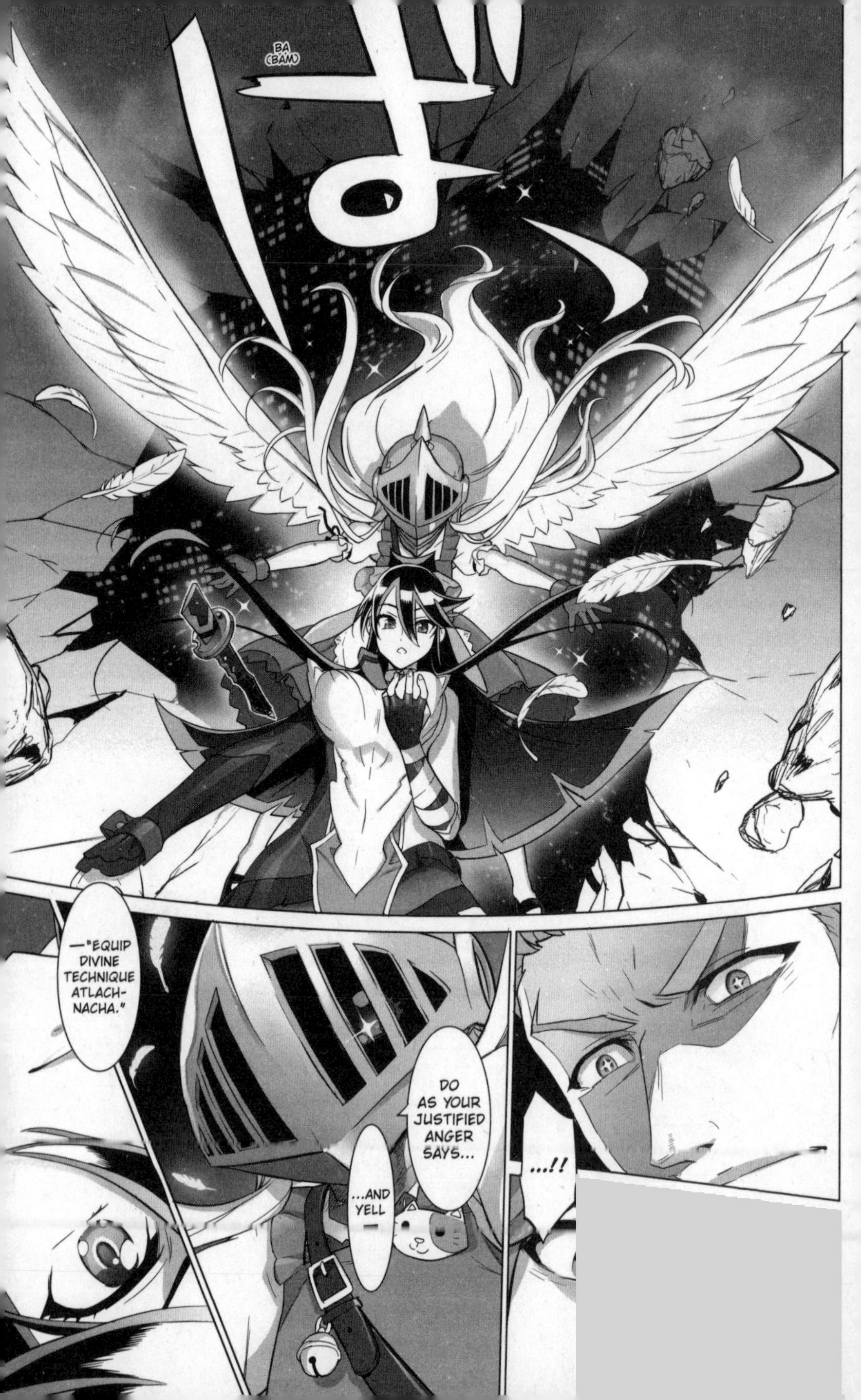
BA (BAM)
...!!
DO AS YOUR JUSTIFIED ANGER SAYS...
...AND YELL—
—"EQUIP DIVINE TECHNIQUE ATLACH-NACHA."

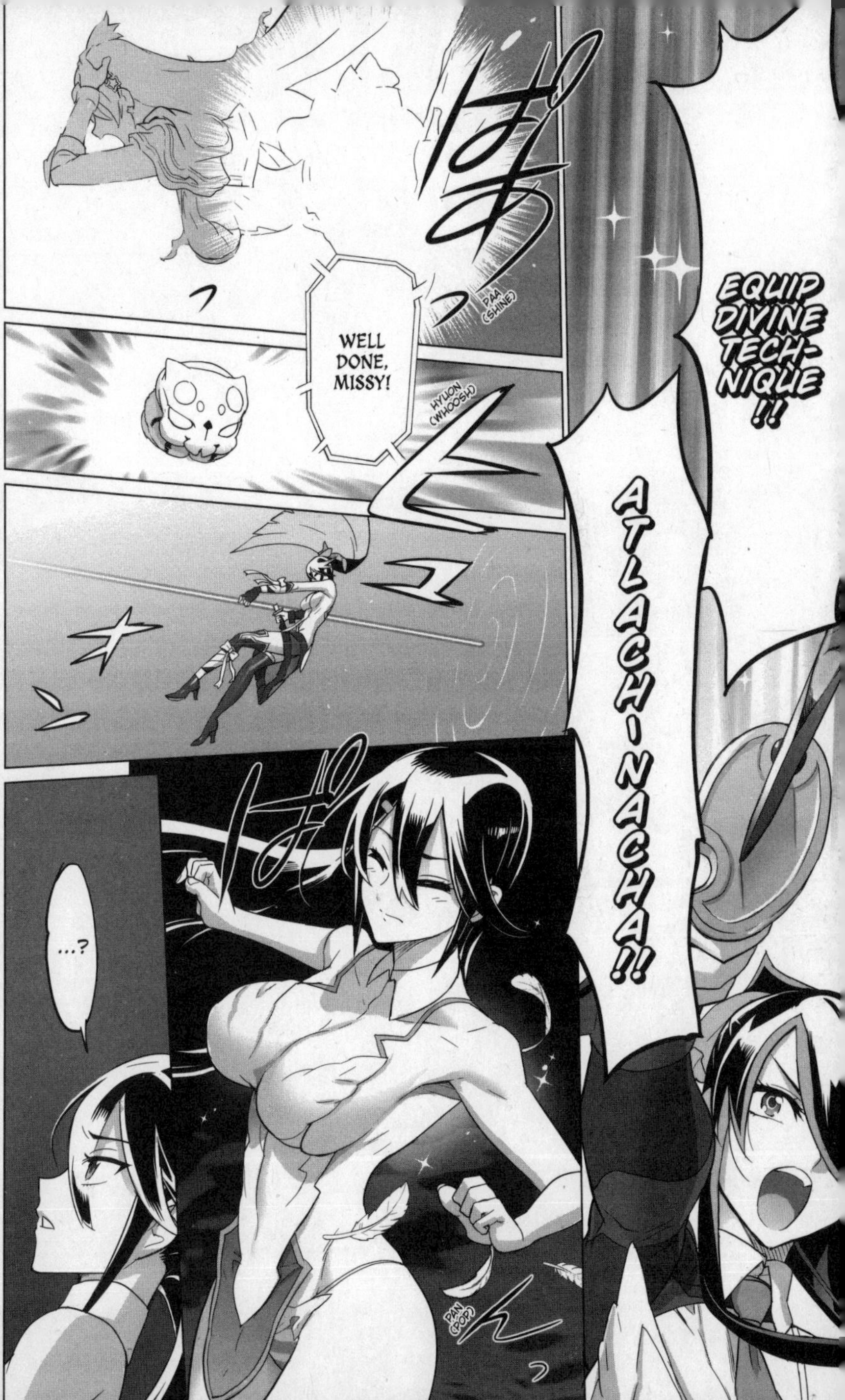

EQUIP DIVINE TECH-NIQUE!!
ATLACHI-NACHA!!
PAA (SHINE)
WELL DONE, MISSY!
HYUON (WHOOSH)
...?
PAN (POP)

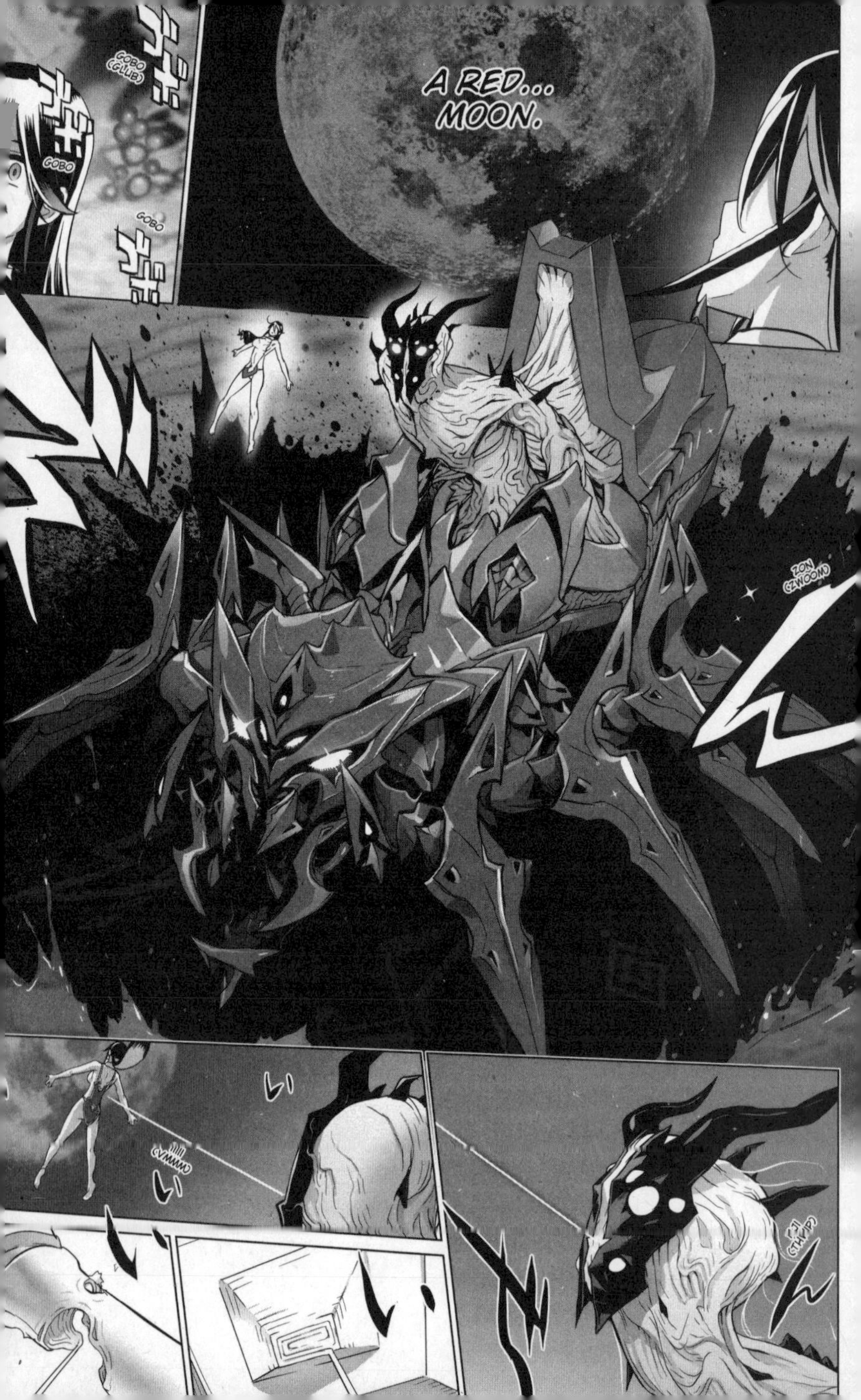
A RED... MOON.
GOBO (GLUB)
GOBO
GOBO
ZON (ZWOOM)
(THWIP)
(VMMM)

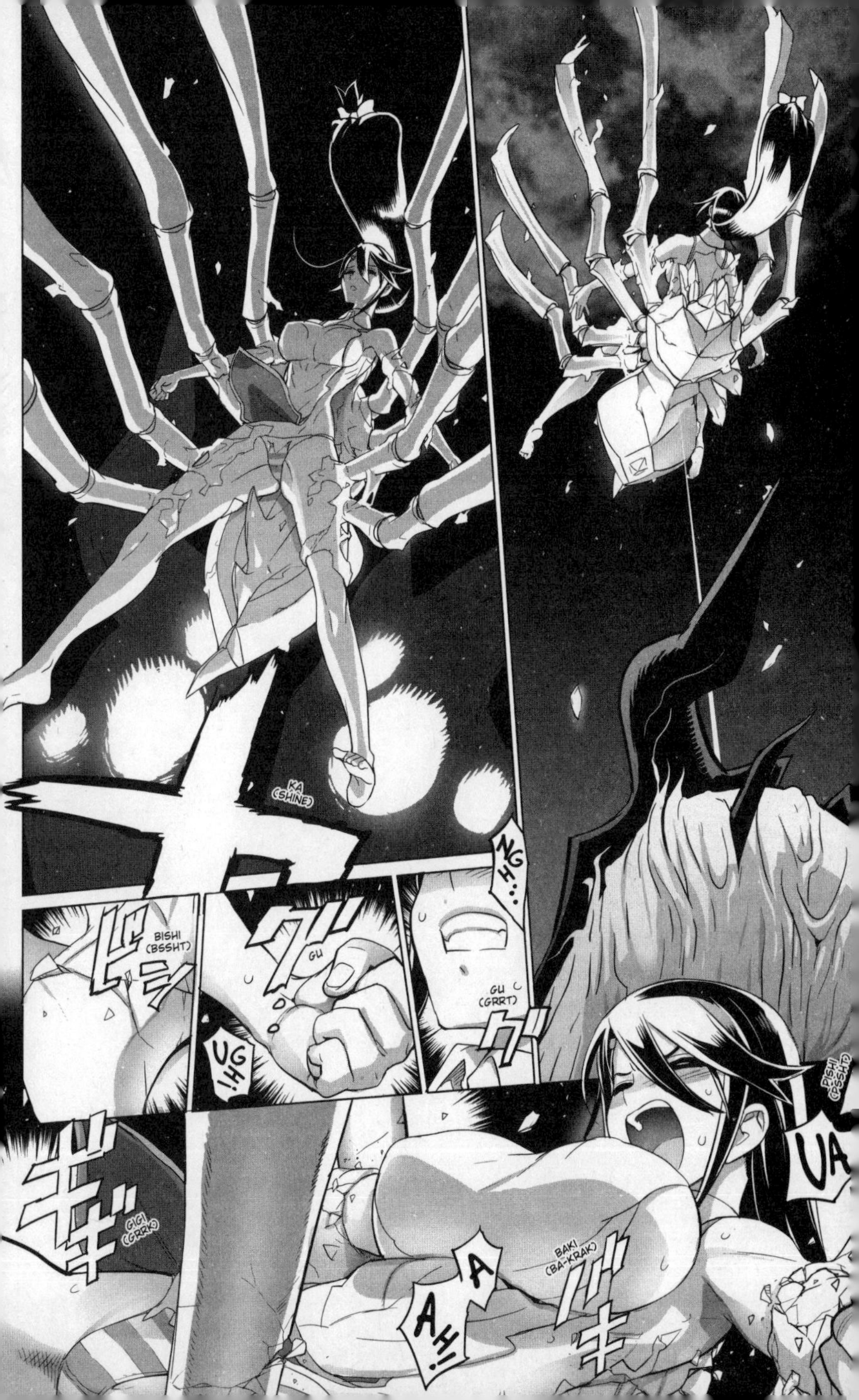
KA (SHINE)
NGH...
GU (GRRT)
GU
UGH!
BISHI (BSSHT)
PISHI (PSSHT)
UA
BAKI (BA-KRAK)
A
AH!
GIGI (GRRK)

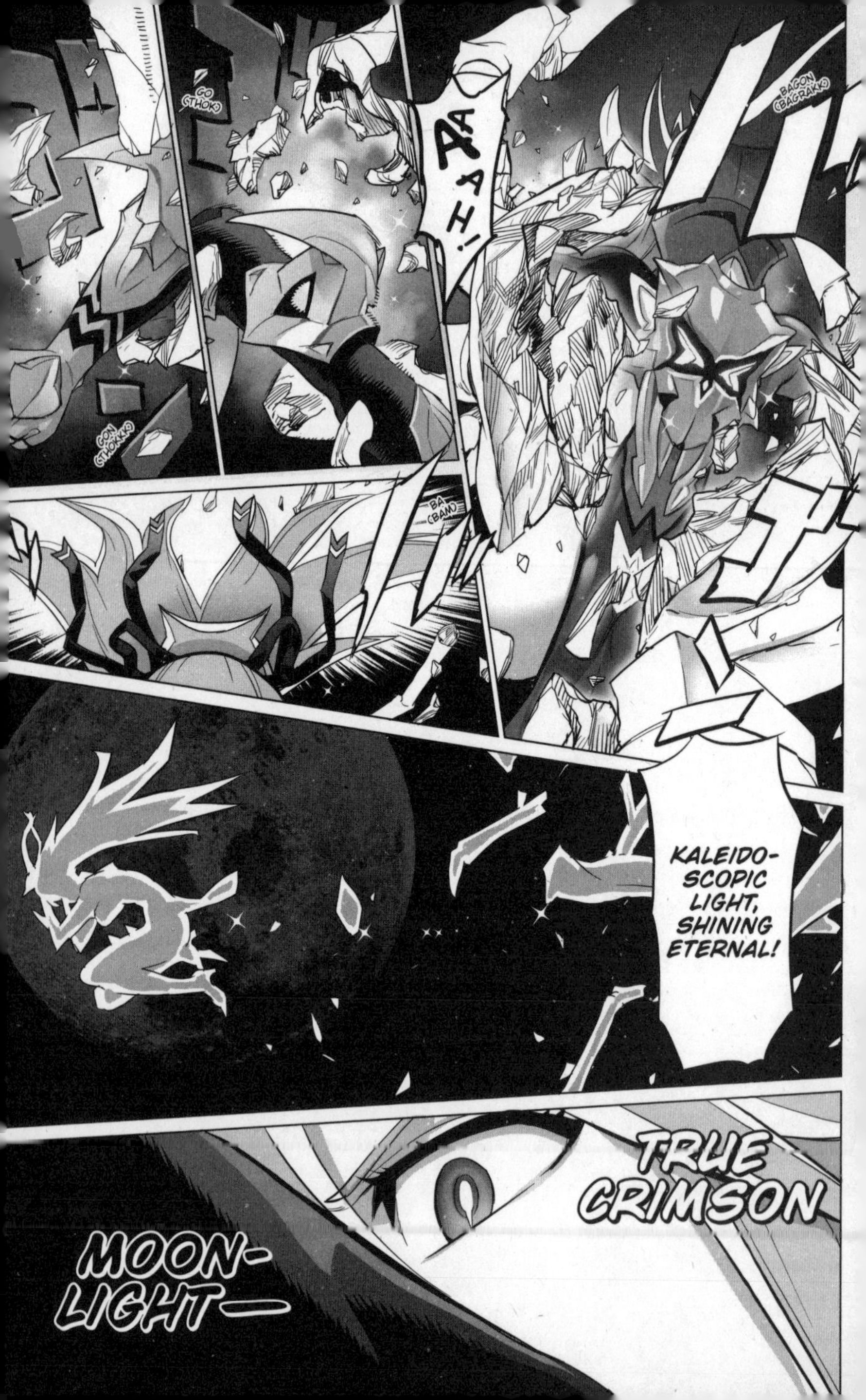
BAGON (BAGRAKK)
AAAH!
GO (THOK)
GON (THOKK)
BA (BAM)
KALEIDO-SCOPIC LIGHT, SHINING ETERNAL!
TRUE CRIMSON
MOON-LIGHT—

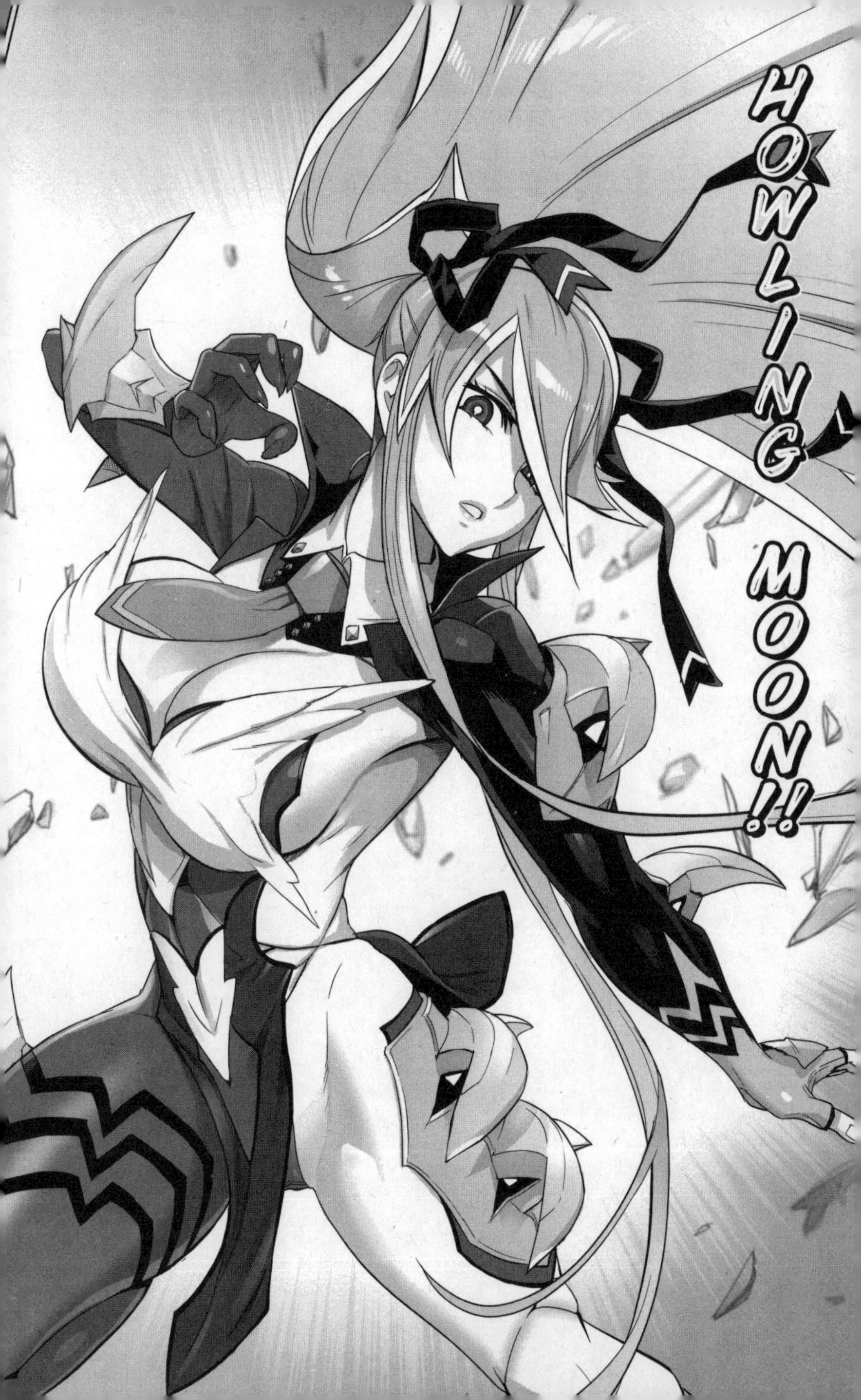
HOWLING MOON!!

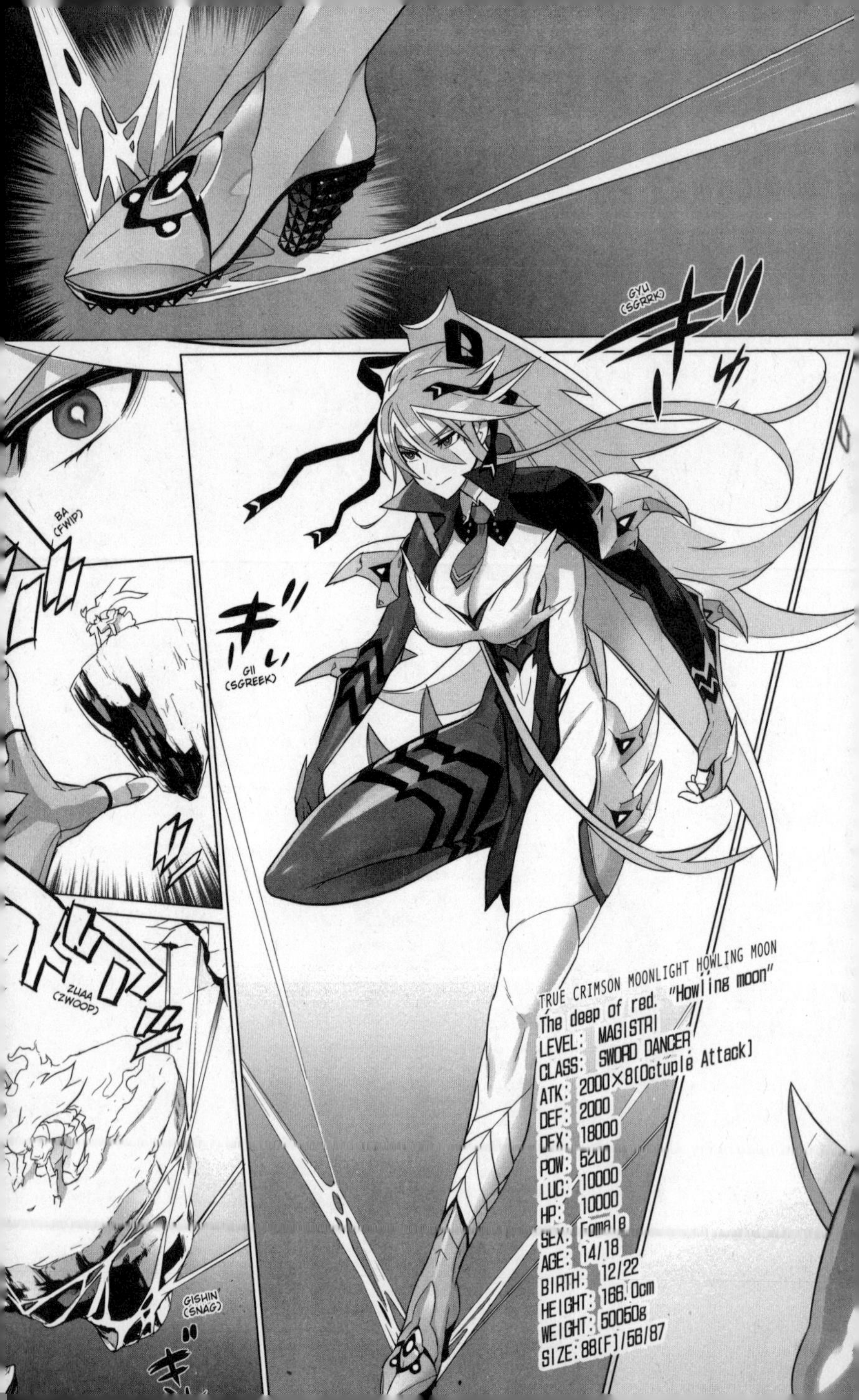
GYU (SGRRK)
GII (SGREEK)
TRUE CRIMSON MOONLIGHT HOWLING MOON
The deep of red. "Howling moon"
LEVEL: MAGISTRI
CLASS: SWORD DANCER
ATK: 2000×8(Octuple Attack)
DEF: 2000
DFX: 18000
POW: 5200
LUC: 10000
HP: 10000
SEX: Female
AGE: 14/18
BIRTH: 12/22
HEIGHT: 166.0cm
WEIGHT: 50050g
SIZE: 88(F)/56/87
BA (FWIP)
ZUAA (ZWOOP)
GISHIN (SNAG)

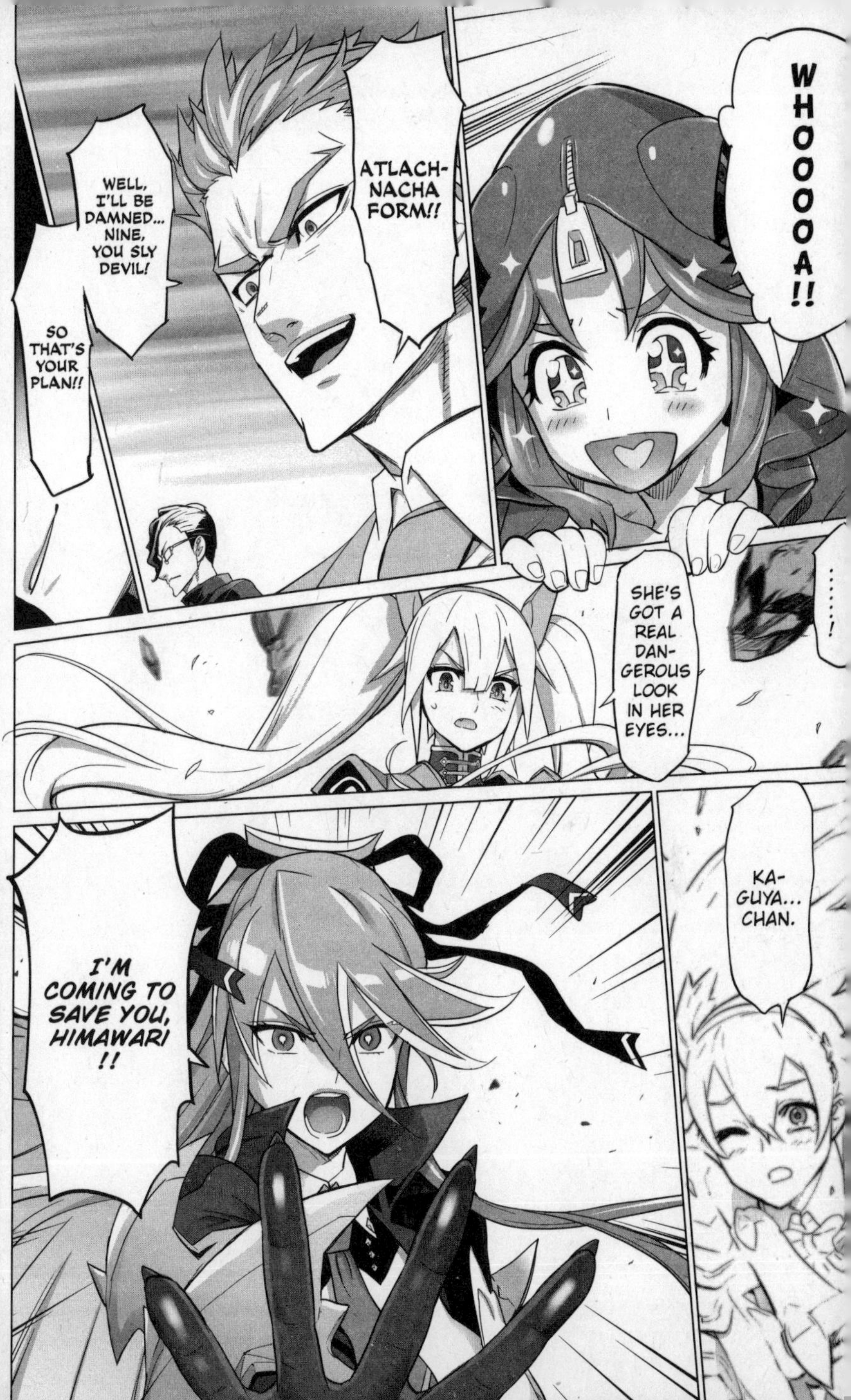
WHOOOOOA!!
ATLACH-NACHA FORM!!
WELL, I'LL BE DAMNED... NINE, YOU SLY DEVIL!
SO THAT'S YOUR PLAN!!
......!
SHE'S GOT A REAL DAN-GEROUS LOOK IN HER EYES...
KA-GUYA... CHAN.
I'M COMING TO SAVE YOU, HIMAWARI!!

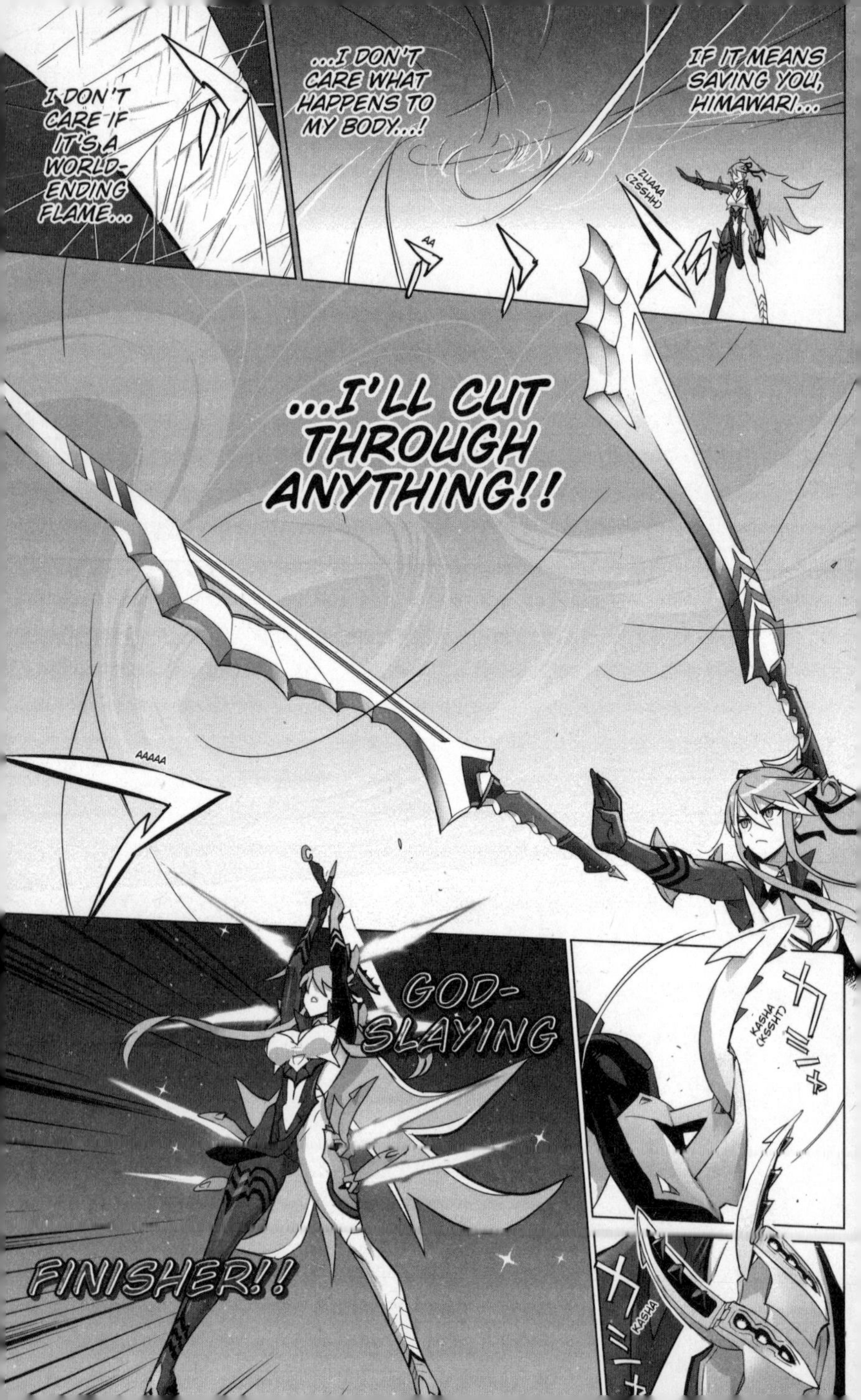

IF IT MEANS SAVING YOU, HIMAWARI...
ZUAAA (ZSSHH)
...I DON'T CARE WHAT HAPPENS TO MY BODY...!
I DON'T CARE IF IT'S A WORLD-ENDING FLAME...
AA
...I'LL CUT THROUGH ANYTHING!!
AAAAA
KASHA (KSSHT)
KASHA
GOD-SLAYING
FINISHER!!

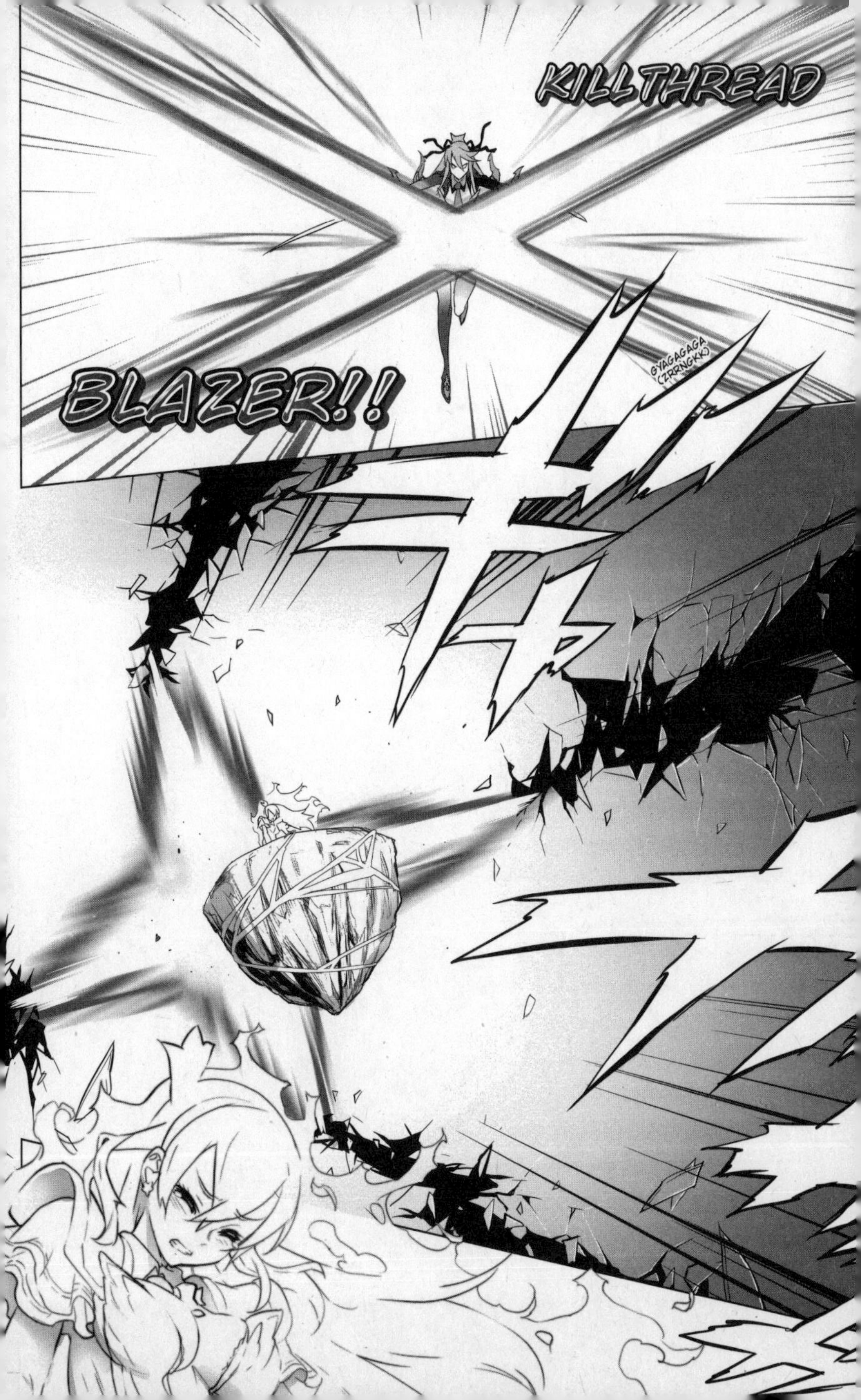
KILLTHREAD
BLAZER!!
GYAGAGAGA
(ZRRNGKK)

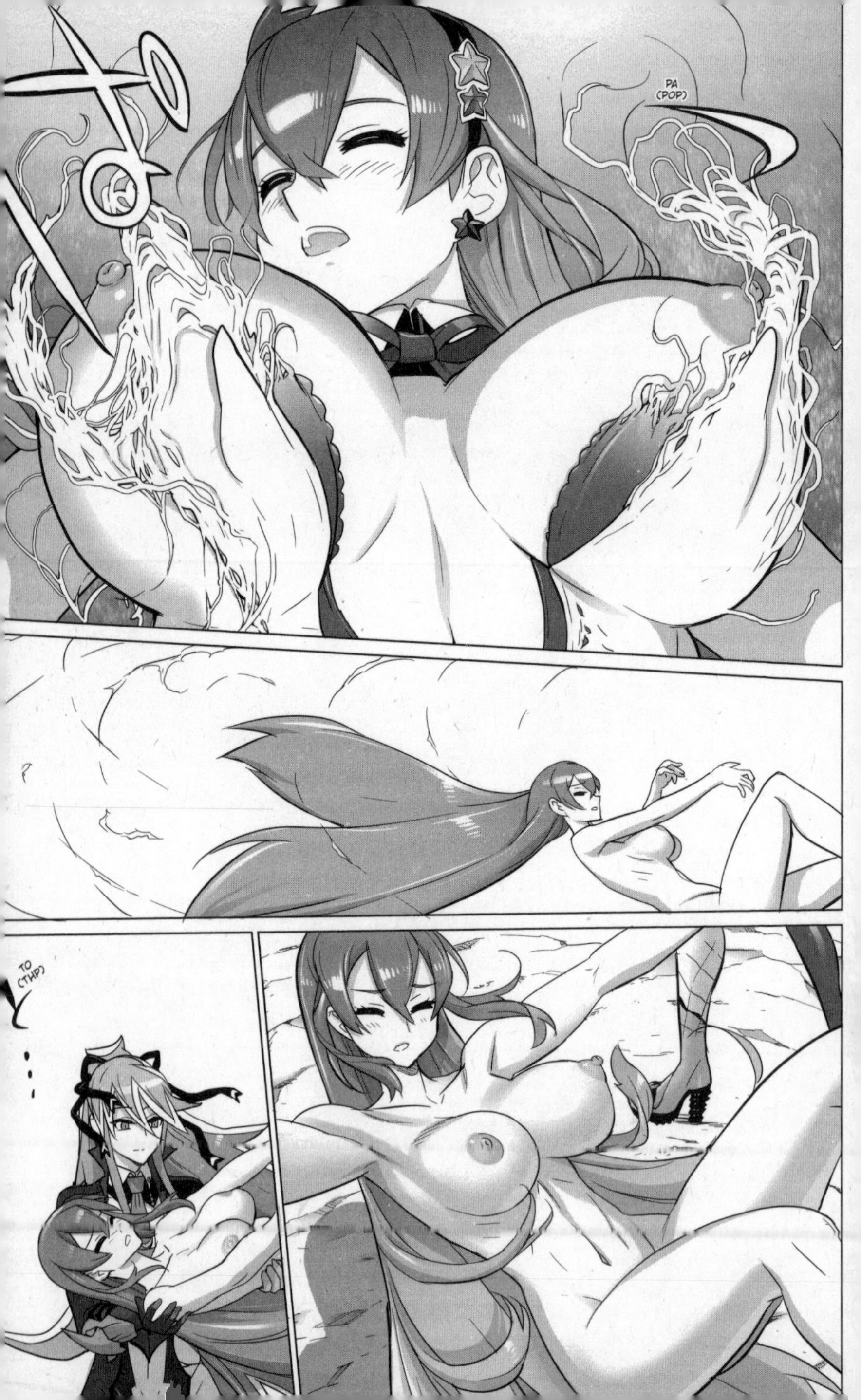
PA (POP)
TO (THP)
...

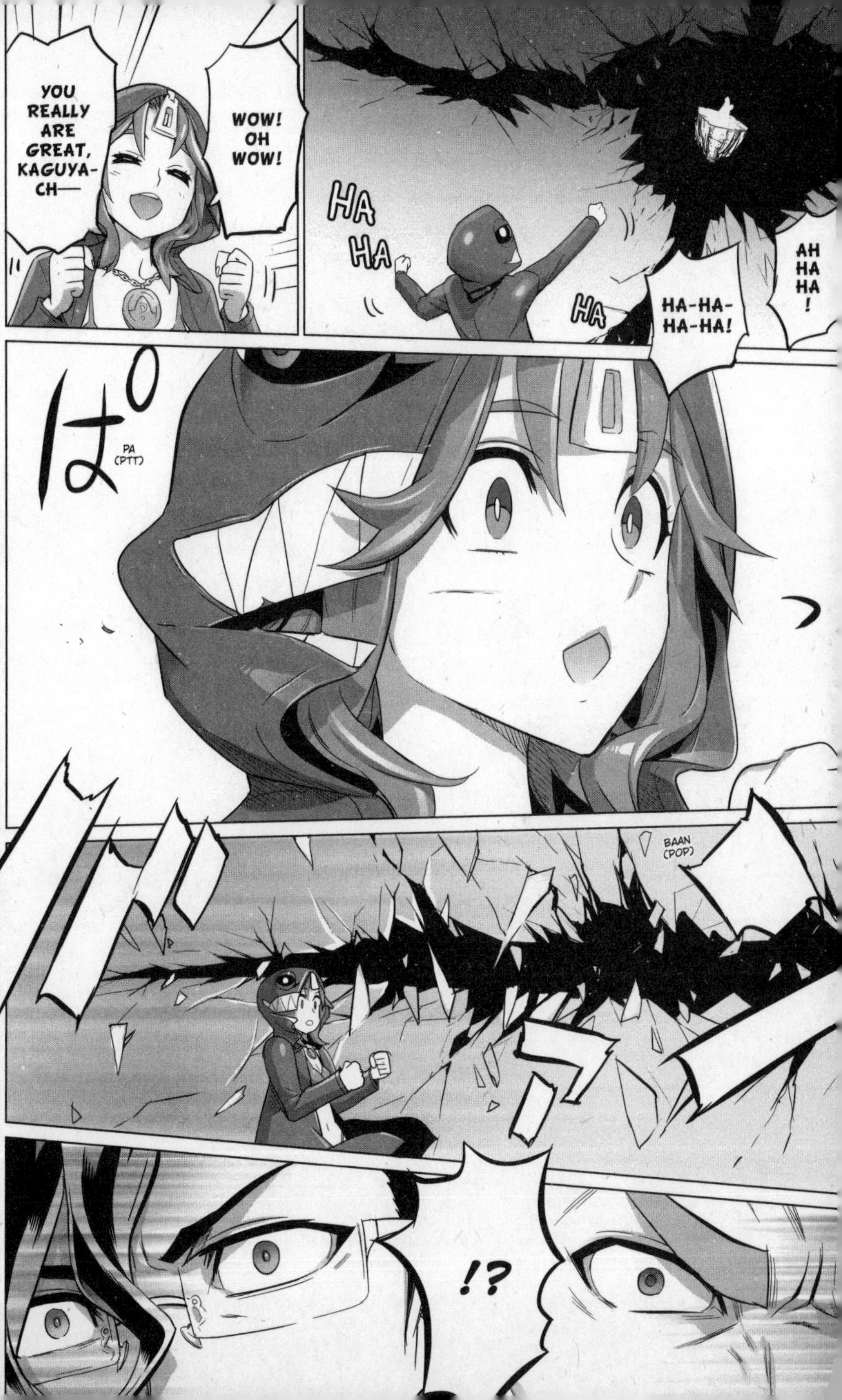
AH HA HA!
HA-HA-HA-HA!
HA
HA HA
WOW! OH WOW!
YOU REALLY ARE GREAT, KAGUYA-CH—
ぱ
PA (PTT)
BAAN (POP)
!?

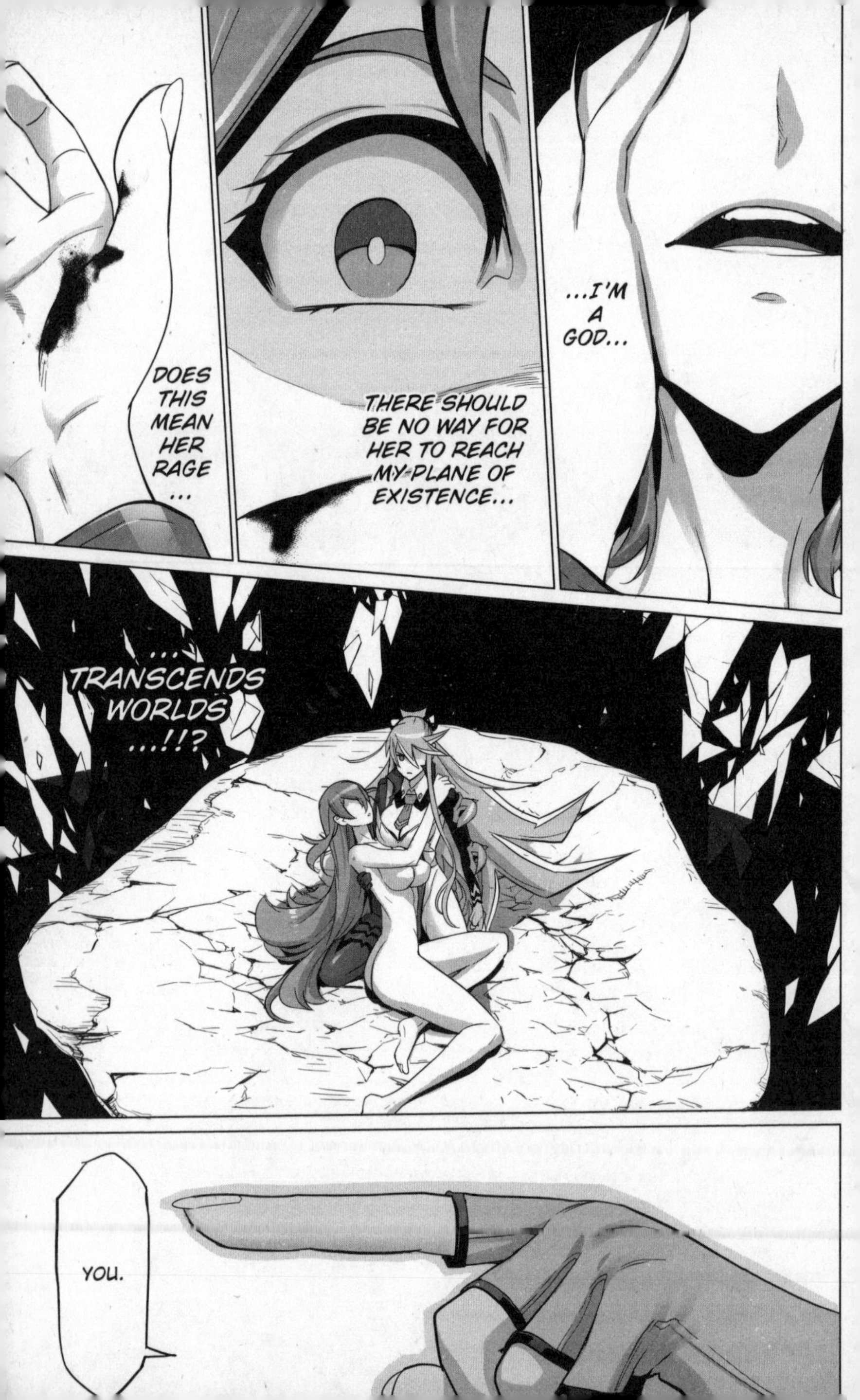
...I'M A GOD...
THERE SHOULD BE NO WAY FOR HER TO REACH MY PLANE OF EXISTENCE...
DOES THIS MEAN HER RAGE ...
...TRANSCENDS WORLDS ...!!?
YOU.

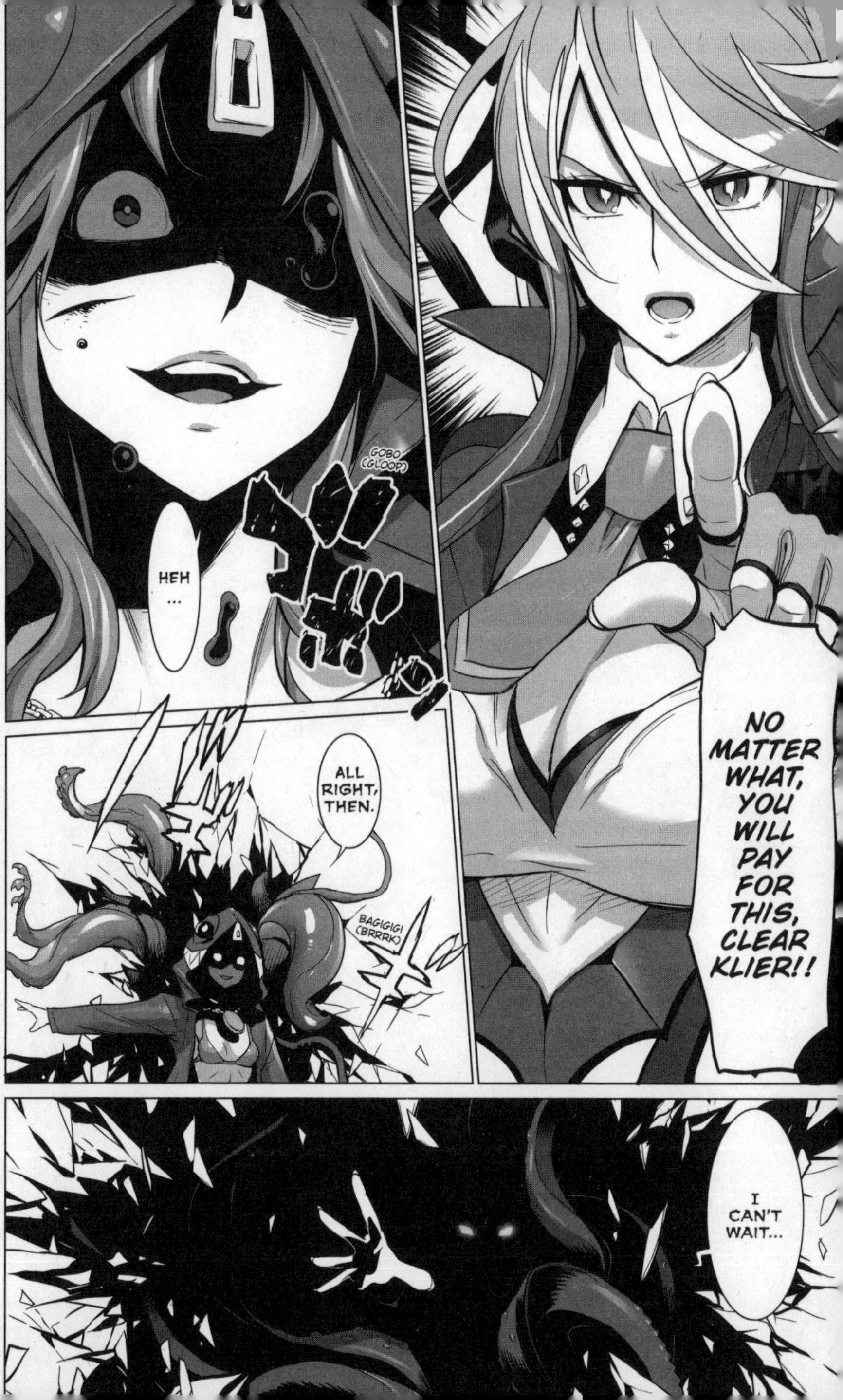
NO MATTER WHAT, YOU WILL PAY FOR THIS, CLEAR KLIER!!
GOBO (GLOOP)
HEH ...
ALL RIGHT, THEN.
BAGIGIGI (BRRRK)
I CAN'T WAIT...

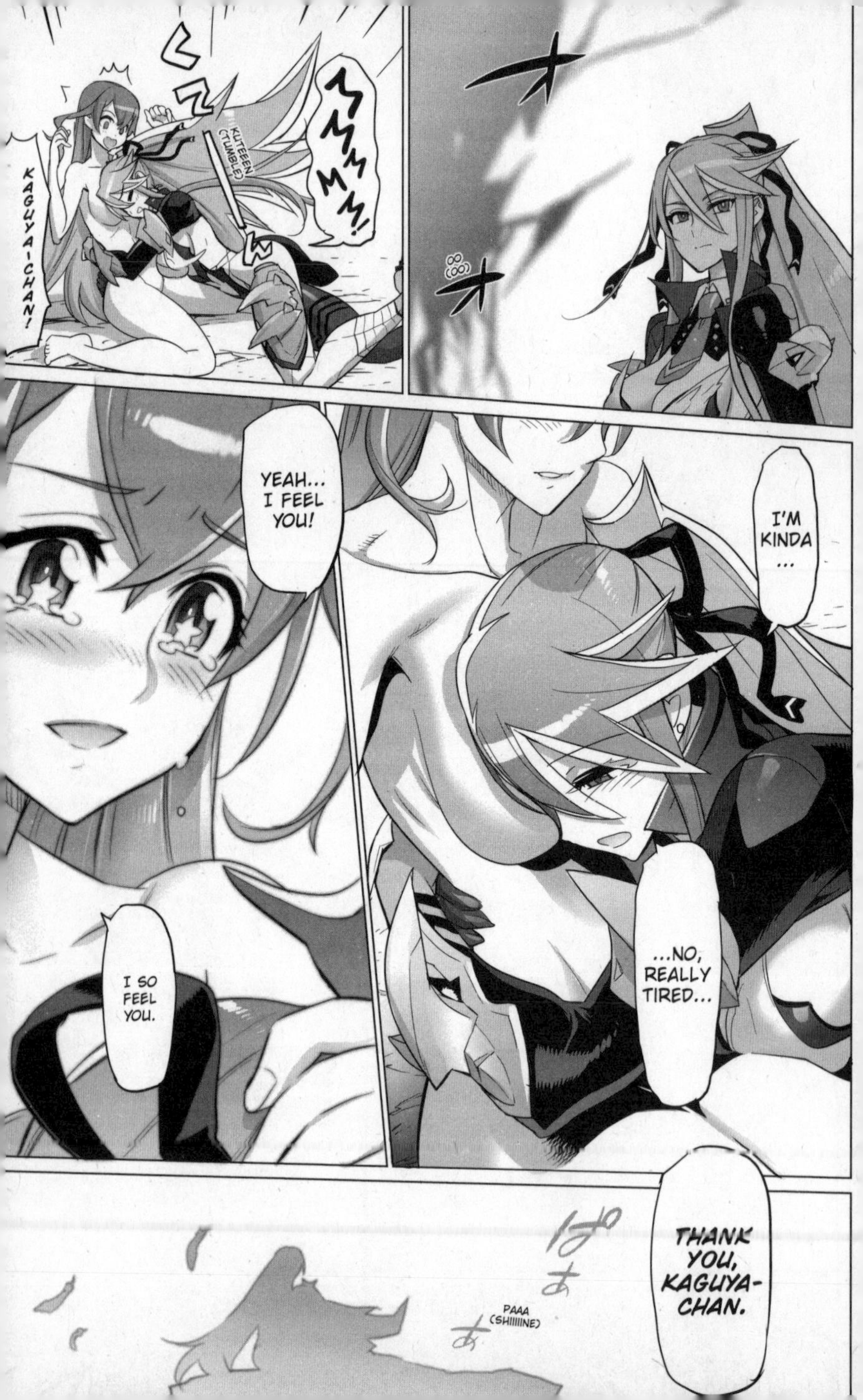
MMMMMM!
KUTEEEN (TUMBLE)
KAGUYA-CHAN!
I'M KINDA...
...NO, REALLY TIRED...
YEAH... I FEEL YOU!
I SO FEEL YOU.
THANK YOU, KAGUYA-CHAN.
PAAA (SHIIIIINE)

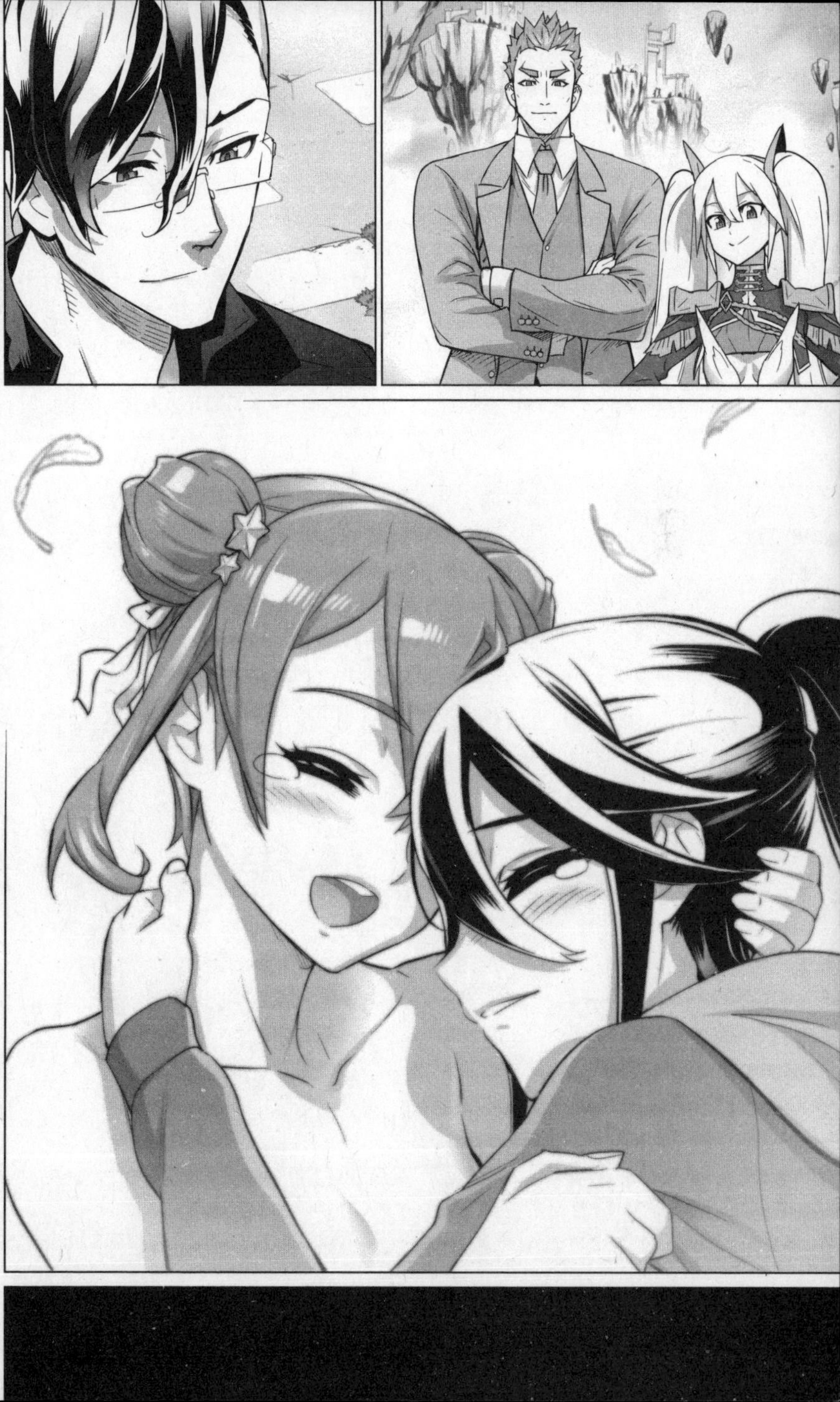

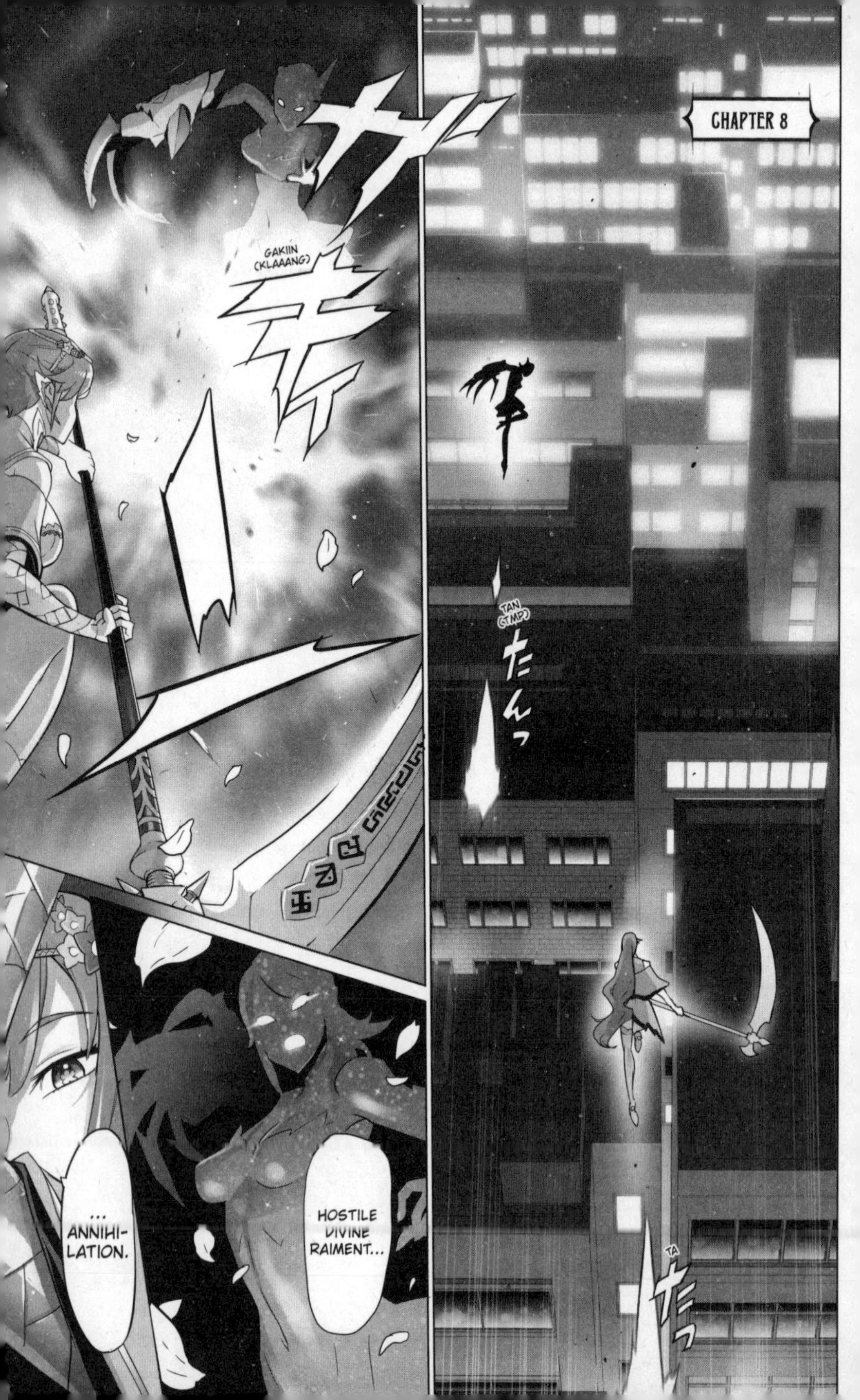
CHAPTER 8
TAN (TMP)
たんっ
TA
たっ
GAKIIN (KLAAANG)
HOSTILE DIVINE RAIMENT...
... ANNIHILATION.

CHAPTER 8 DIVINE DUSK PRINCESS DARK CELESTIA

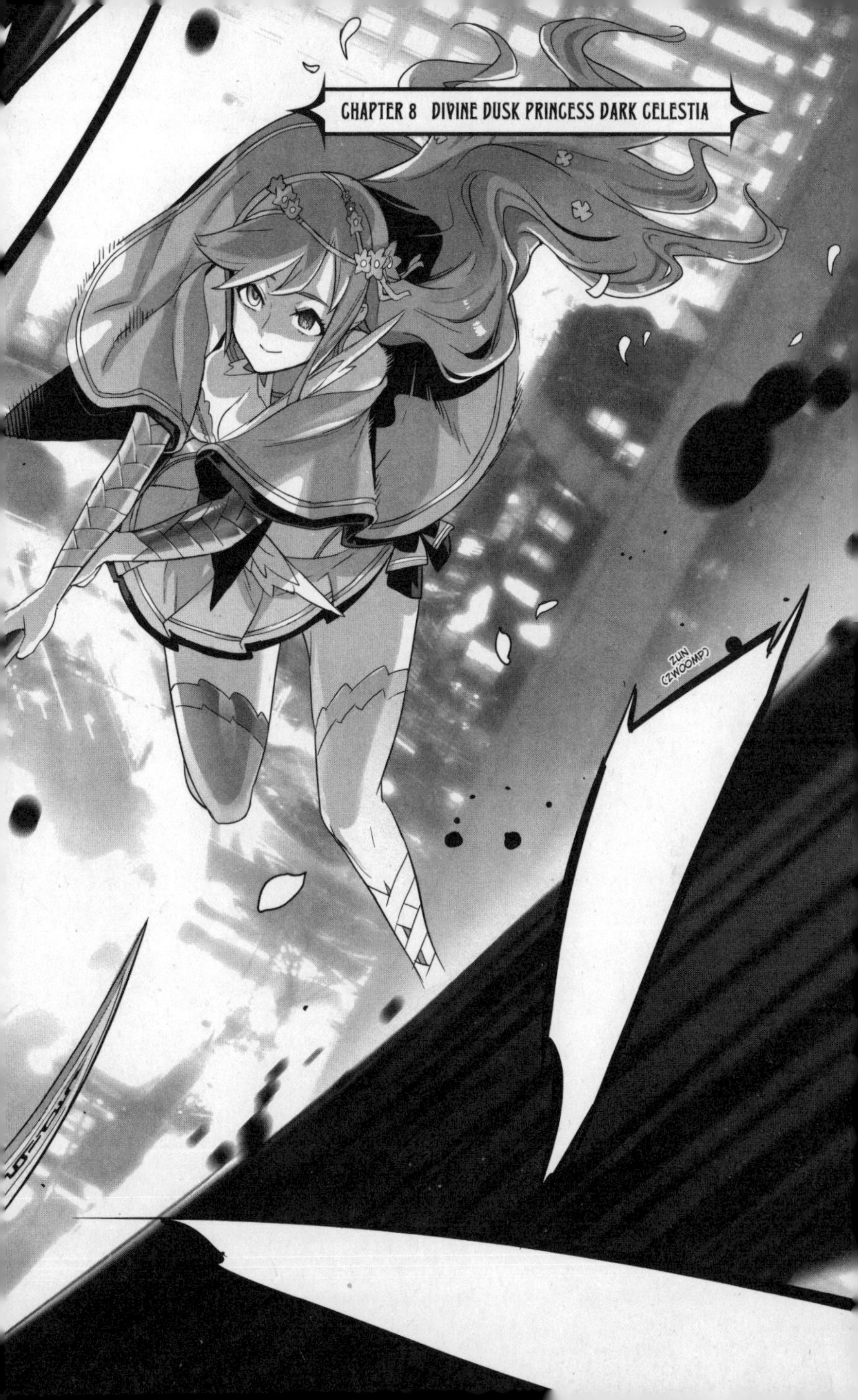
ZUN
(ZWOOMP)

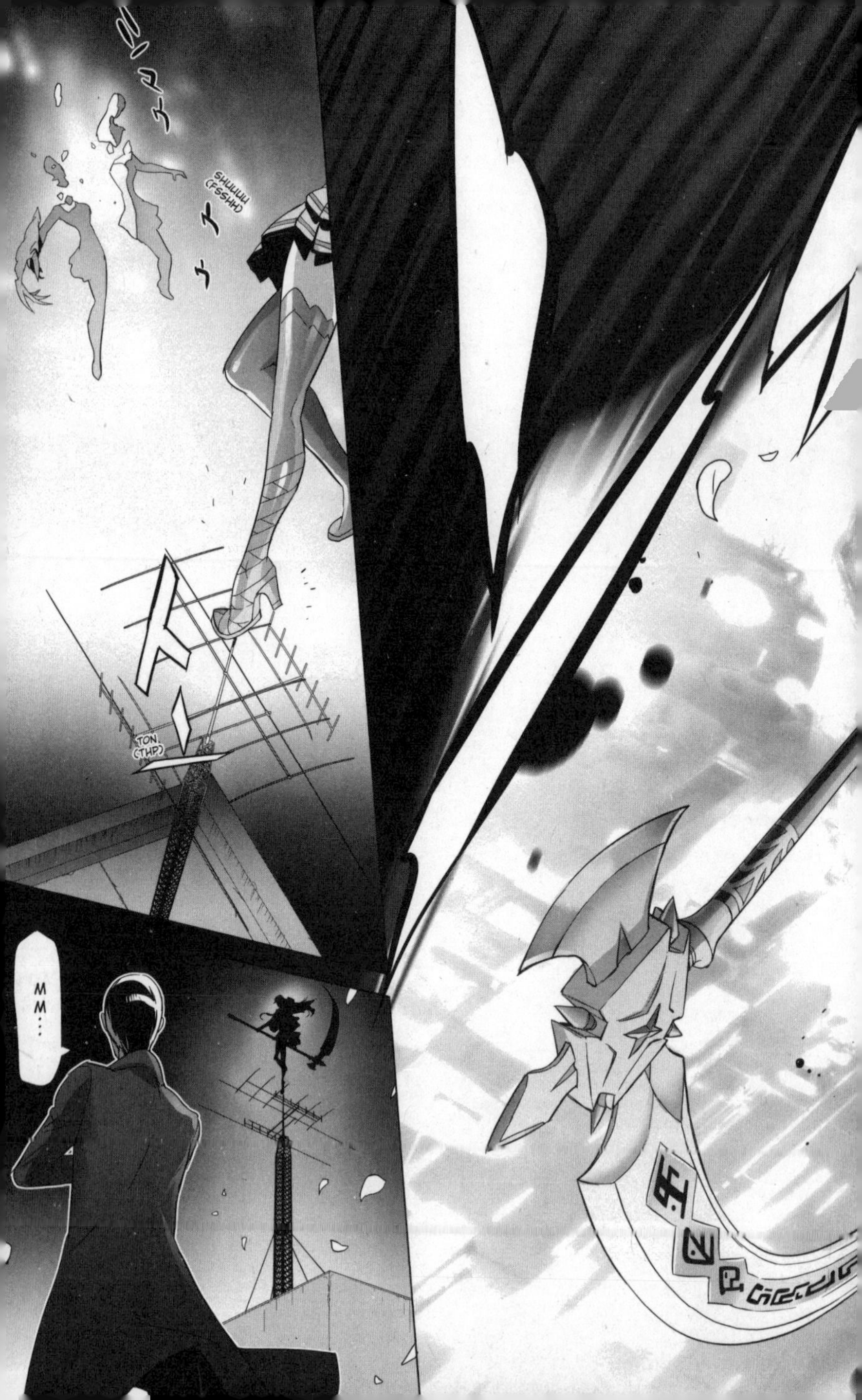
SHUUUUN (FSSHH)
TON (THP)
MM...

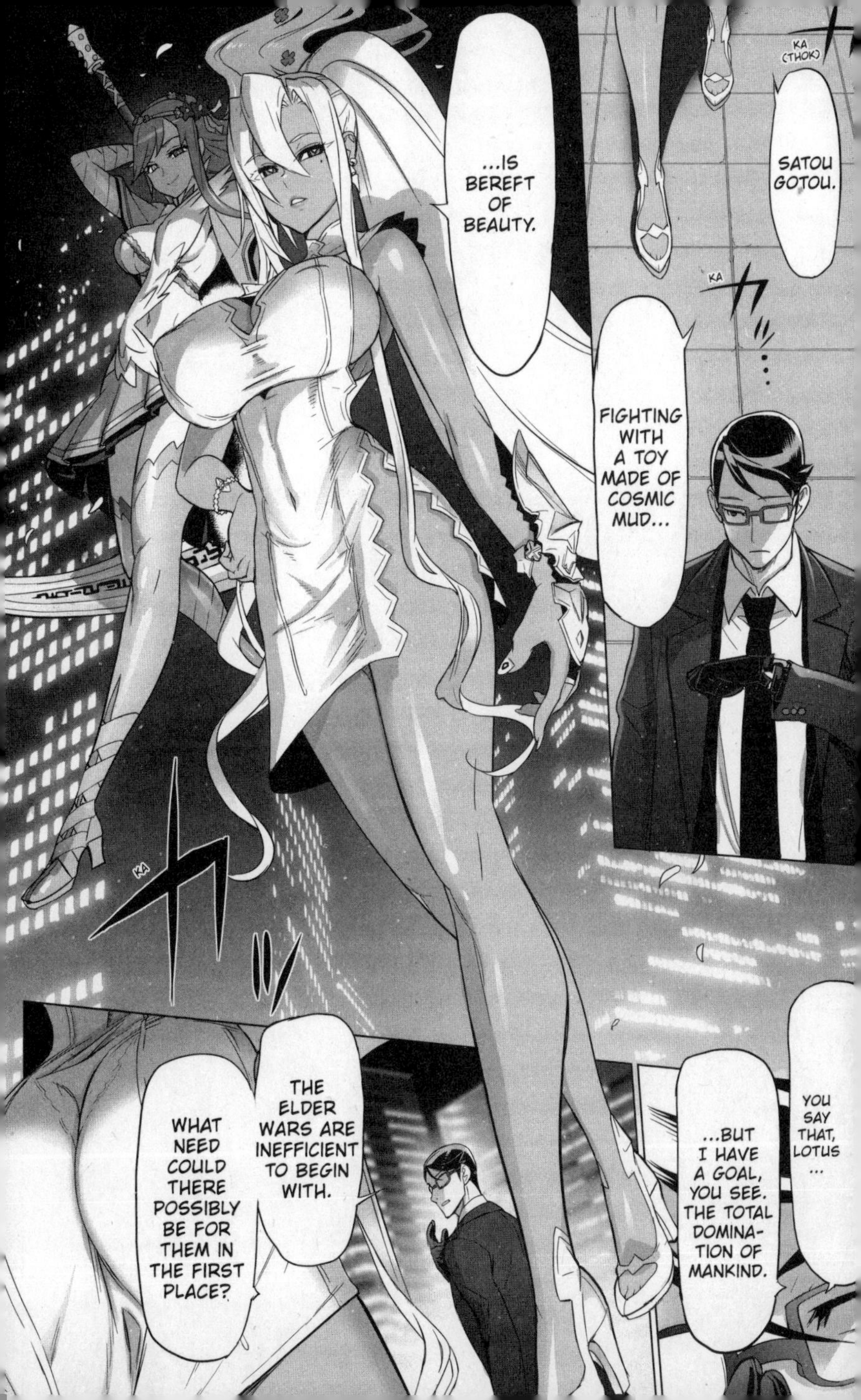
KA (THOK)
SATOU GOTOU.
KA
FIGHTING WITH A TOY MADE OF COSMIC MUD...
...IS BEREFT OF BEAUTY.
KA
YOU SAY THAT, LOTUS...
...BUT I HAVE A GOAL, YOU SEE. THE TOTAL DOMINATION OF MANKIND.
THE ELDER WARS ARE INEFFICIENT TO BEGIN WITH.
WHAT NEED COULD THERE POSSIBLY BE FOR THEM IN THE FIRST PLACE?

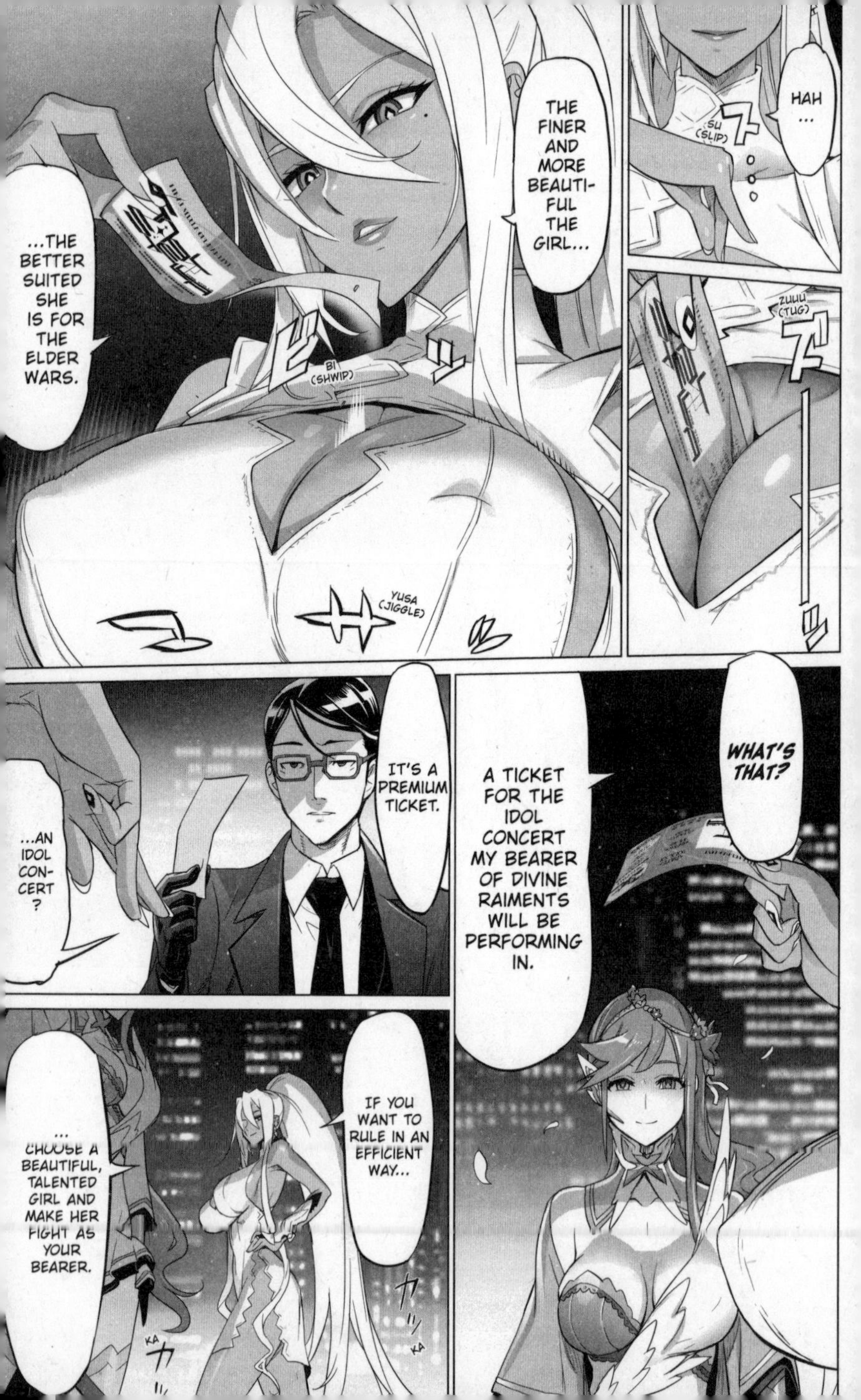
HAH ...
SU (SLIP)
ZUUU (TUG)
THE FINER AND MORE BEAUTI-FUL THE GIRL...
...THE BETTER SUITED SHE IS FOR THE ELDER WARS.
BI (SHWIP)
YUSA (JIGGLE)
WHAT'S THAT?
A TICKET FOR THE IDOL CONCERT MY BEARER OF DIVINE RAIMENTS WILL BE PERFORMING IN.
IT'S A PREMIUM TICKET.
...AN IDOL CON-CERT?
IF YOU WANT TO RULE IN AN EFFICIENT WAY...
... CHOOSE A BEAUTIFUL, TALENTED GIRL AND MAKE HER FIGHT AS YOUR BEARER.
KA
KA

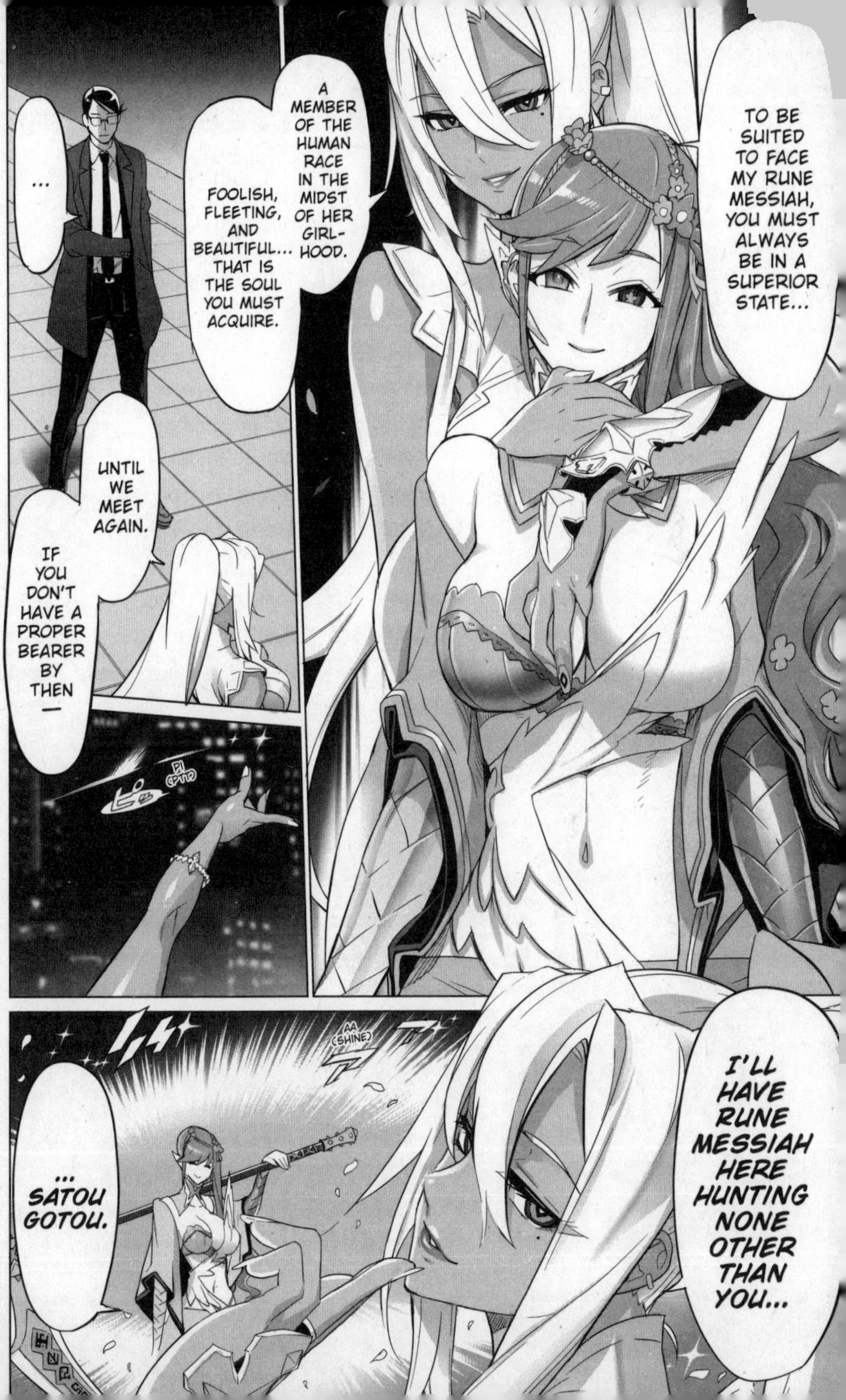
TO BE SUITED TO FACE MY RUNE MESSIAH, YOU MUST ALWAYS BE IN A SUPERIOR STATE...
A MEMBER OF THE HUMAN RACE IN THE MIDST OF HER GIRL-HOOD.
FOOLISH, FLEETING, AND BEAUTIFUL... THAT IS THE SOUL YOU MUST ACQUIRE.
...
UNTIL WE MEET AGAIN.
IF YOU DON'T HAVE A PROPER BEARER BY THEN —
PI (PTT)
I'LL HAVE RUNE MESSIAH HERE HUNTING NONE OTHER THAN YOU...
AA (SHINE)
... SATOU GOTOU.

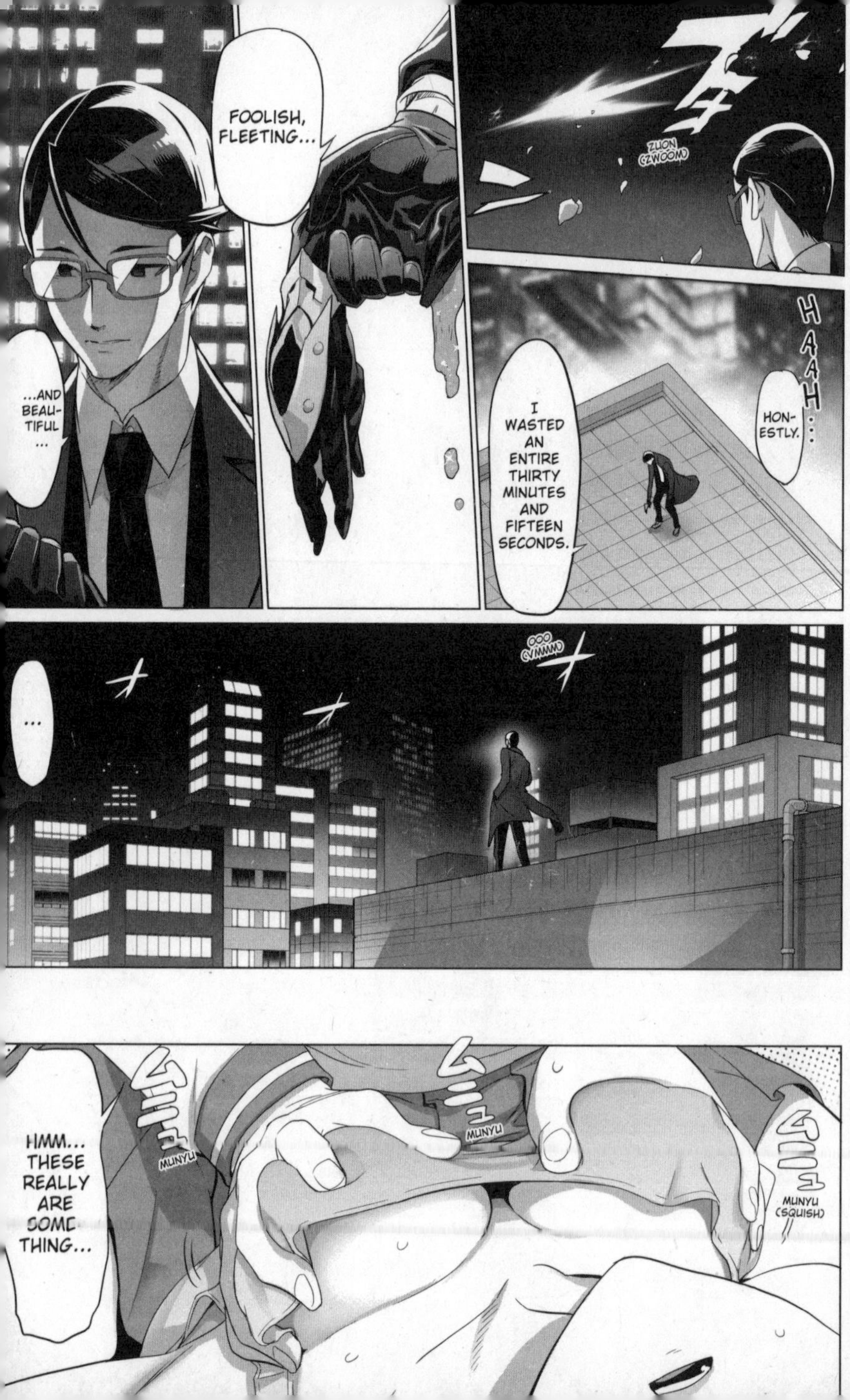
ZUON (ZWOOM)
HAAAH…
HON-ESTLY.
I WASTED AN ENTIRE THIRTY MINUTES AND FIFTEEN SECONDS.
FOOLISH, FLEETING…
…AND BEAU-TIFUL…
OOO (VMMM)
…
MUNYU (SQUISH)
MUNYU
MUNYU
HMM… THESE REALLY ARE SOMC THING…

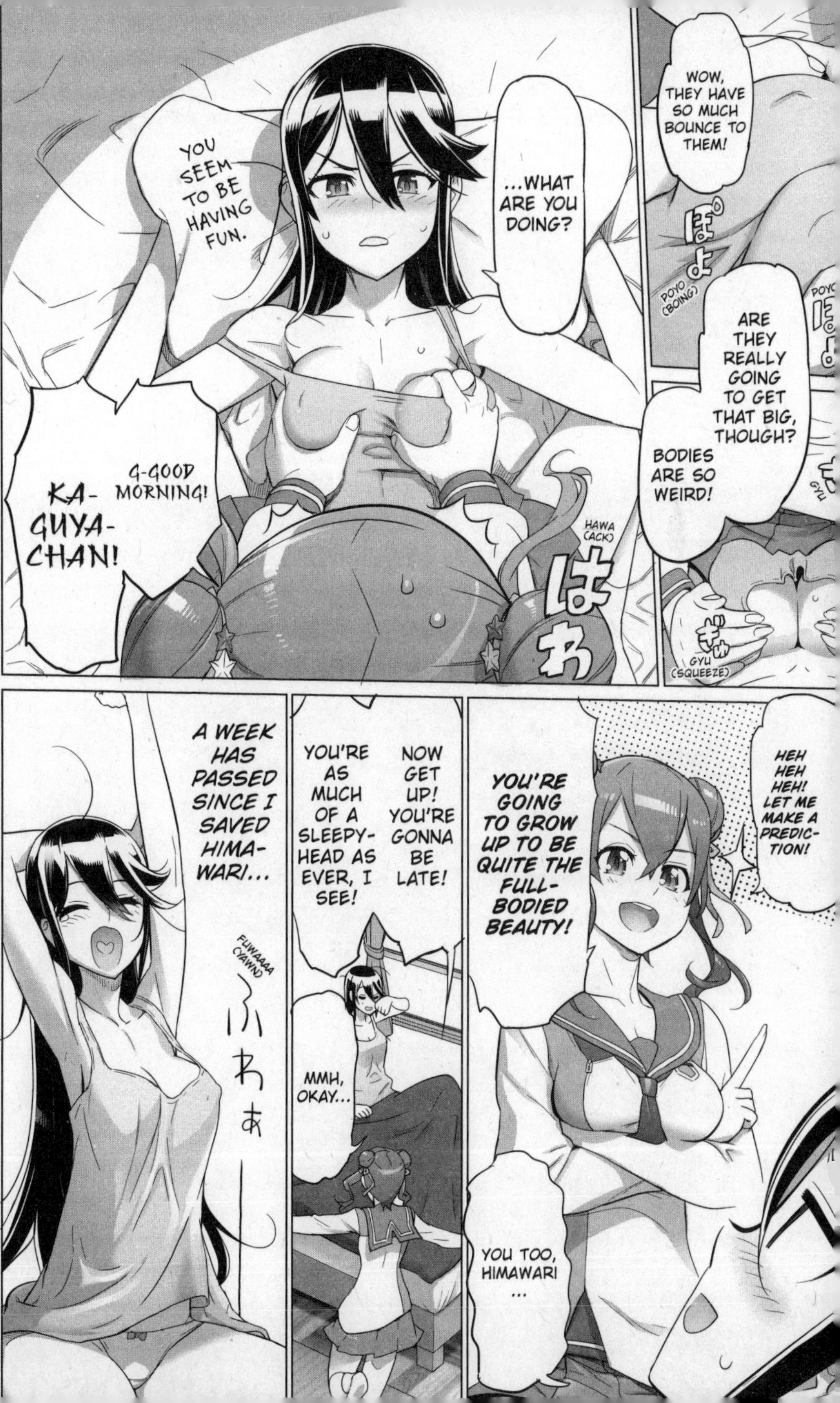
WOW, THEY HAVE SO MUCH BOUNCE TO THEM!
ぽよ
POYO (BOING)
POYO
ARE THEY REALLY GOING TO GET THAT BIG, THOUGH?
BODIES ARE SO WEIRD!
ぎゅ
GYU (SQUEEZE)
...WHAT ARE YOU DOING?
YOU SEEM TO BE HAVING FUN.
HAWA (ACK)
はわ
G-GOOD MORNING!
KA-GUYA-CHAN!
HEH HEH HEH! LET ME MAKE A PREDICTION!
YOU'RE GOING TO GROW UP TO BE QUITE THE FULL-BODIED BEAUTY!
YOU TOO, HIMAWARI...
NOW GET UP! YOU'RE GONNA BE LATE!
YOU'RE AS MUCH OF A SLEEPY-HEAD AS EVER, I SEE!
MMH, OKAY...
A WEEK HAS PASSED SINCE I SAVED HIMAWARI...
FUWAAAA (YAWN)
ふわぁ

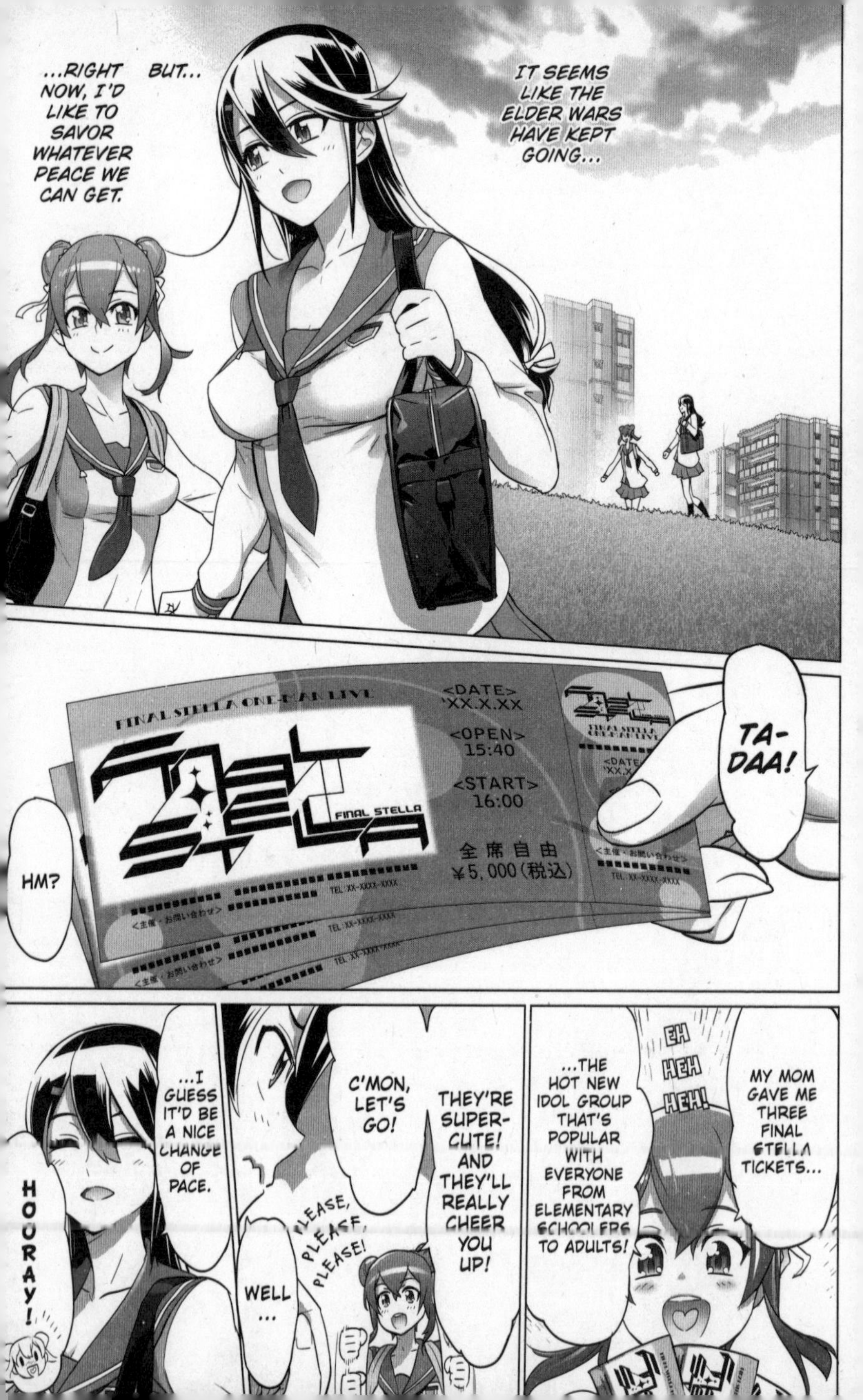
IT SEEMS LIKE THE ELDER WARS HAVE KEPT GOING...
BUT...
...RIGHT NOW, I'D LIKE TO SAVOR WHATEVER PEACE WE CAN GET.
TA-DAA!
FINAL STELLA ONE-MAN LIVE
FINAL STELLA
<DATE> 'XX.X.XX
<OPEN> 15:40
<START> 16:00
全席自由
¥5,000(税込)
<主催・お問い合わせ>
TEL XX-XXXX-XXXX
HM?
MY MOM GAVE ME THREE FINAL STELLA TICKETS...
EH HEH HEH!
...THE HOT NEW IDOL GROUP THAT'S POPULAR WITH EVERYONE FROM ELEMENTARY SCHOOLERS TO ADULTS!
THEY'RE SUPER-CUTE! AND THEY'LL REALLY CHEER YOU UP!
C'MON, LET'S GO!
PLEASE, PLEASE, PLEASE!
WELL...
...I GUESS IT'D BE A NICE CHANGE OF PACE.
HOORAY!

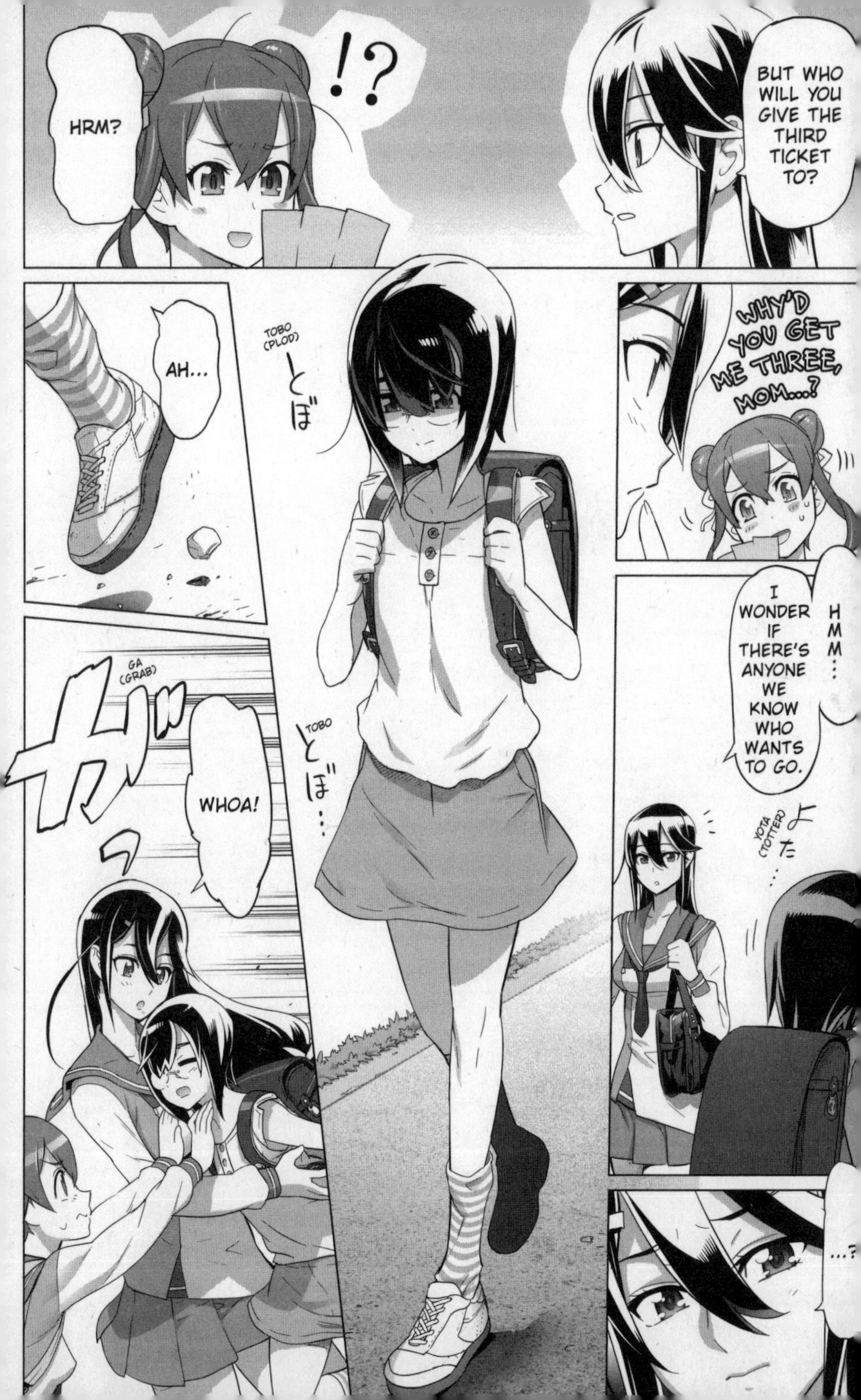
BUT WHO WILL YOU GIVE THE THIRD TICKET TO?
!?
HRM?
WHY'D YOU GET ME THREE, MOM...?
HMM...
I WONDER IF THERE'S ANYONE WE KNOW WHO WANTS TO GO.
YOTA (TOTTER)
よた…
…?
TOBO (PLOD)
とぼ
TOBO
とぼ…
AH...
GA (GRAB)
ガッ
WHOA!

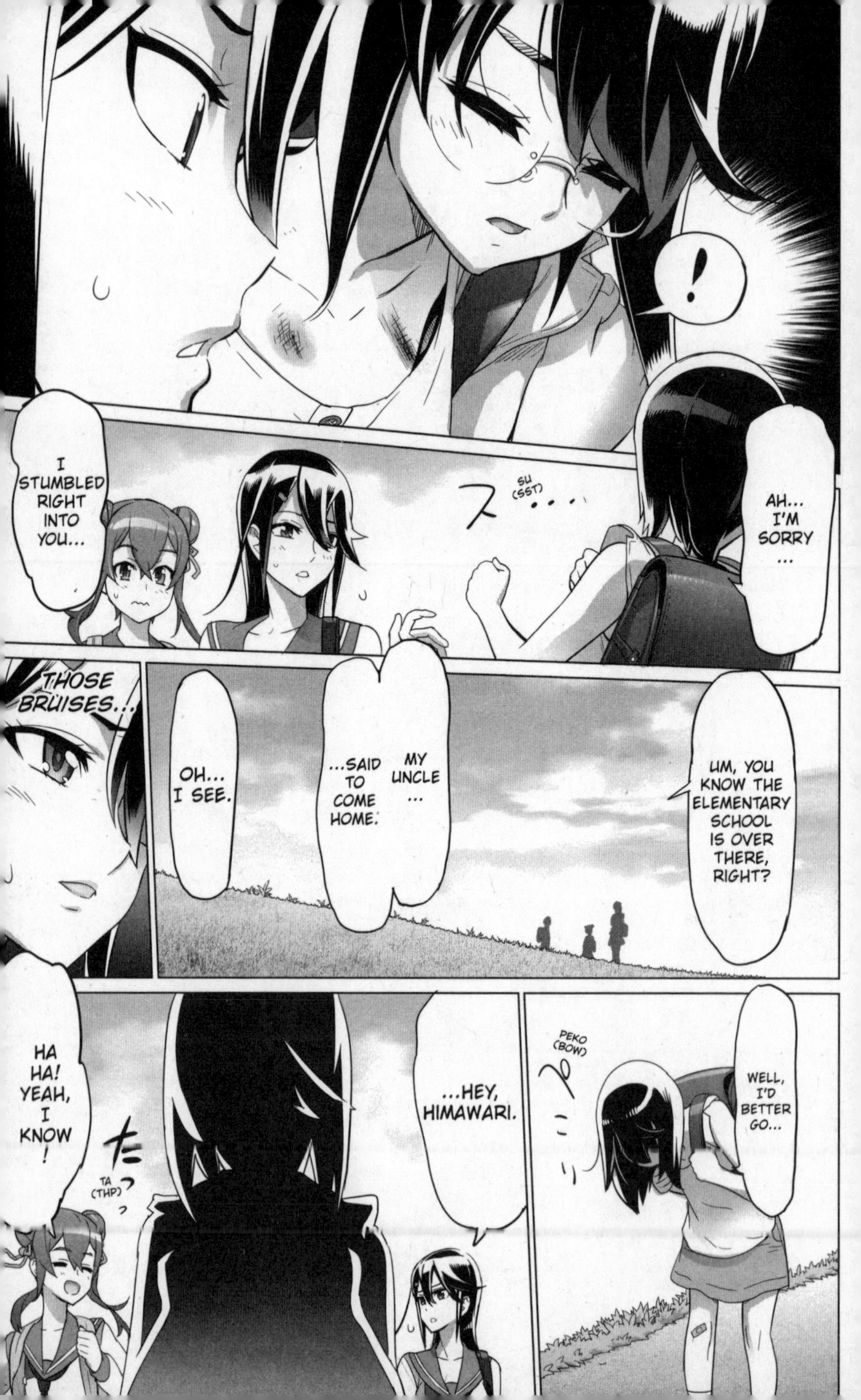
!
AH... I'M SORRY ...
SU (SST)
ス...
I STUMBLED RIGHT INTO YOU...
UM, YOU KNOW THE ELEMENTARY SCHOOL IS OVER THERE, RIGHT?
MY UNCLE ...
...SAID TO COME HOME.
OH... I SEE.
THOSE BRUISES...
PEKO (BOW)
WELL, I'D BETTER GO...
...HEY, HIMAWARI.
TA (THP)
HA HA! YEAH, I KNOW!

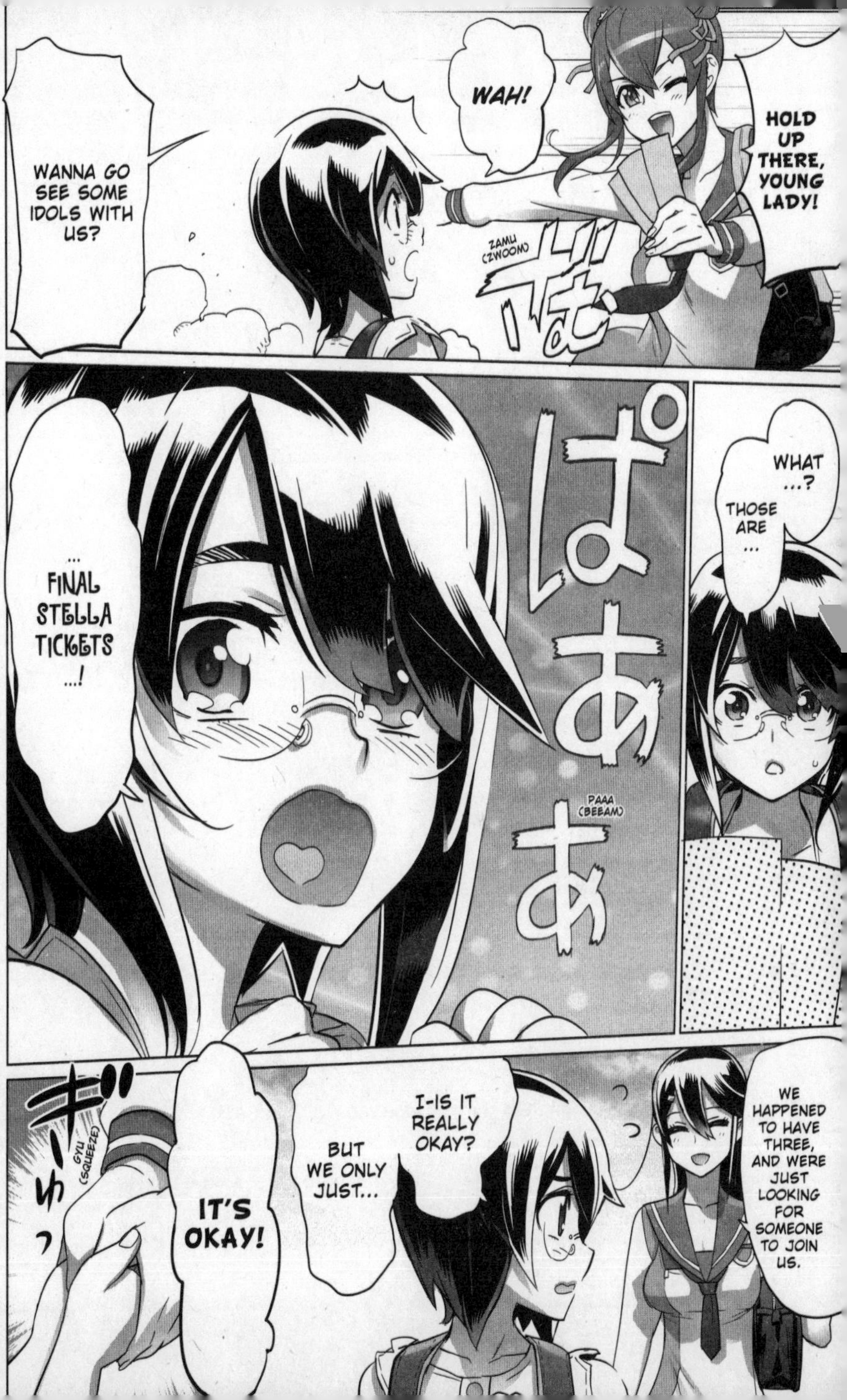
HOLD UP THERE, YOUNG LADY!
WAH!
ZAMU (ZWOOM)
WANNA GO SEE SOME IDOLS WITH US?
WHAT ...?
THOSE ARE ...
PAAA (BEEAM)
... FINAL STELLA TICKETS ...!
WE HAPPENED TO HAVE THREE, AND WERE JUST LOOKING FOR SOMEONE TO JOIN US.
I-IS IT REALLY OKAY?
BUT WE ONLY JUST...
IT'S OKAY!
GYU (SQUEEZE)

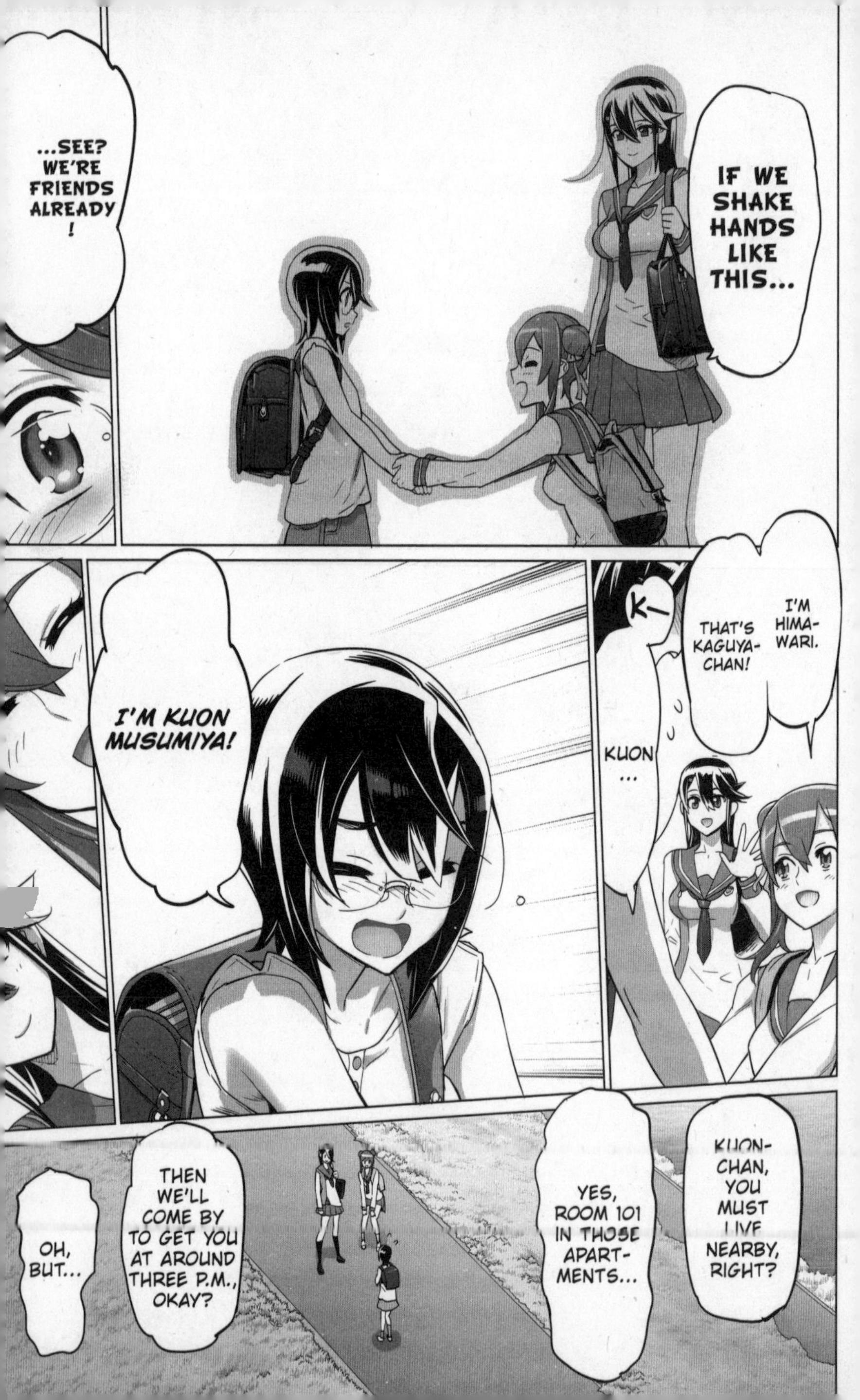
IF WE SHAKE HANDS LIKE THIS...
...SEE? WE'RE FRIENDS ALREADY!
I'M HIMAWARI.
THAT'S KAGUYA-CHAN!
K—
KUON...
I'M KUON MUSUMIYA!
KUON-CHAN, YOU MUST LIVE NEARBY, RIGHT?
YES, ROOM 101 IN THOSE APARTMENTS...
THEN WE'LL COME BY TO GET YOU AT AROUND THREE P.M., OKAY?
OH, BUT...

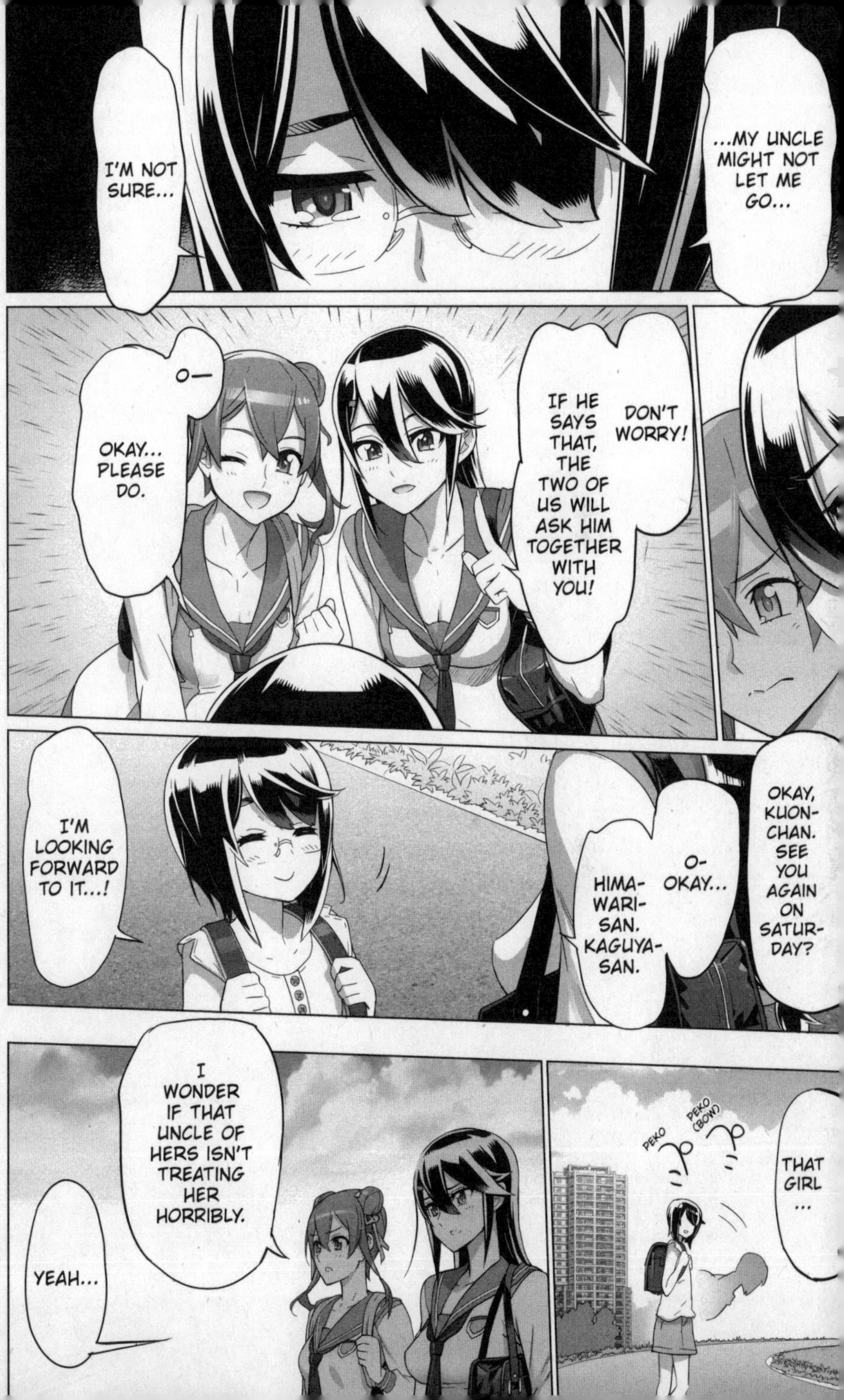
...MY UNCLE MIGHT NOT LET ME GO...
I'M NOT SURE...
DON'T WORRY!
IF HE SAYS THAT, THE TWO OF US WILL ASK HIM TOGETHER WITH YOU!
O—
OKAY... PLEASE DO.
OKAY, KUON-CHAN. SEE YOU AGAIN ON SATURDAY?
O-OKAY...
HIMAWARI-SAN. KAGUYA-SAN.
I'M LOOKING FORWARD TO IT...!
THAT GIRL ...
PEKO PEKO (BOW)
I WONDER IF THAT UNCLE OF HERS ISN'T TREATING HER HORRIBLY.
YEAH...

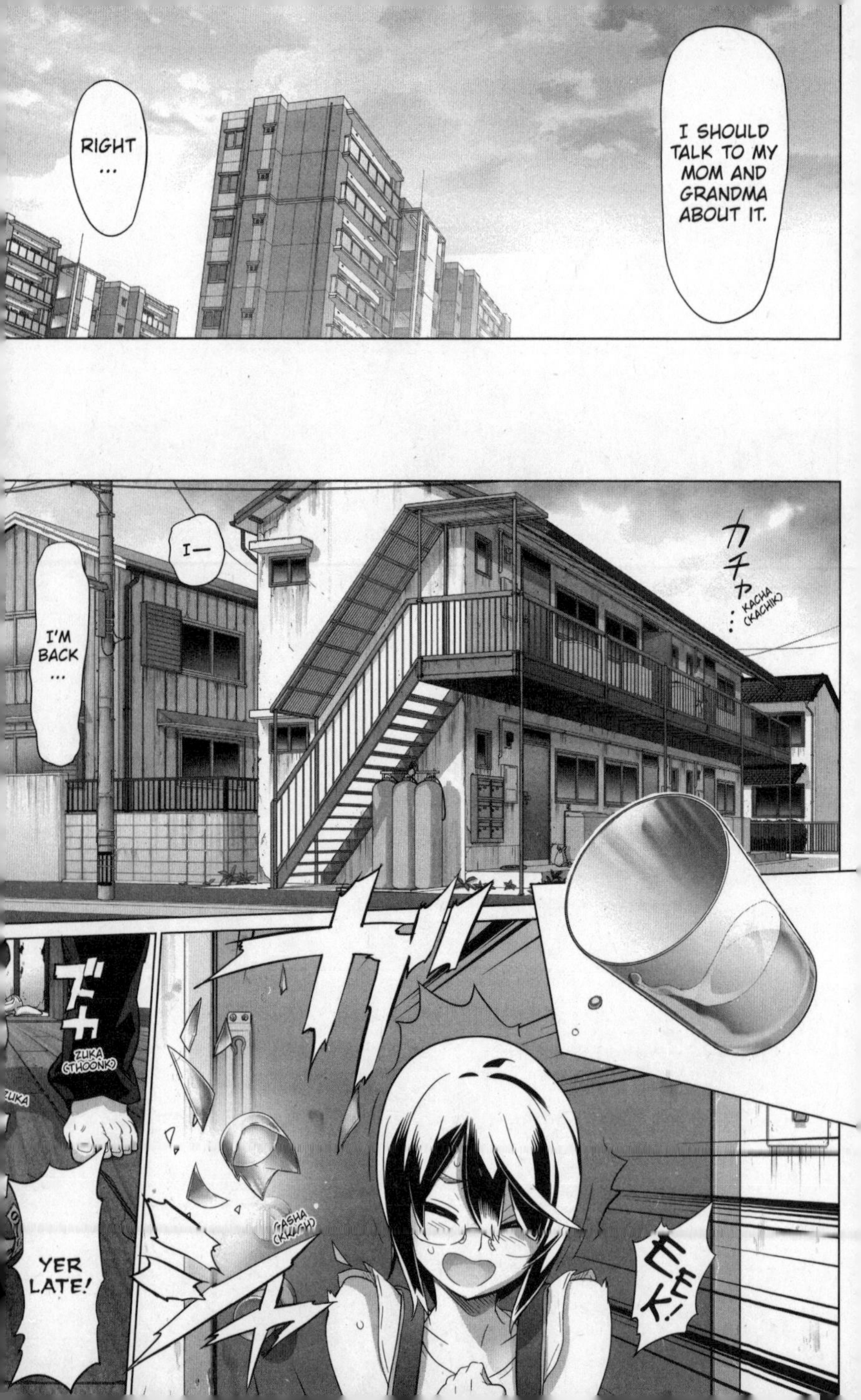
I SHOULD TALK TO MY MOM AND GRANDMA ABOUT IT.
RIGHT ...
カチカ
KACHA (KACHIK)
...
I—
I'M BACK ...
EEK!
ズカ
ZUKA (THOONK)
ZUKA
YER LATE!

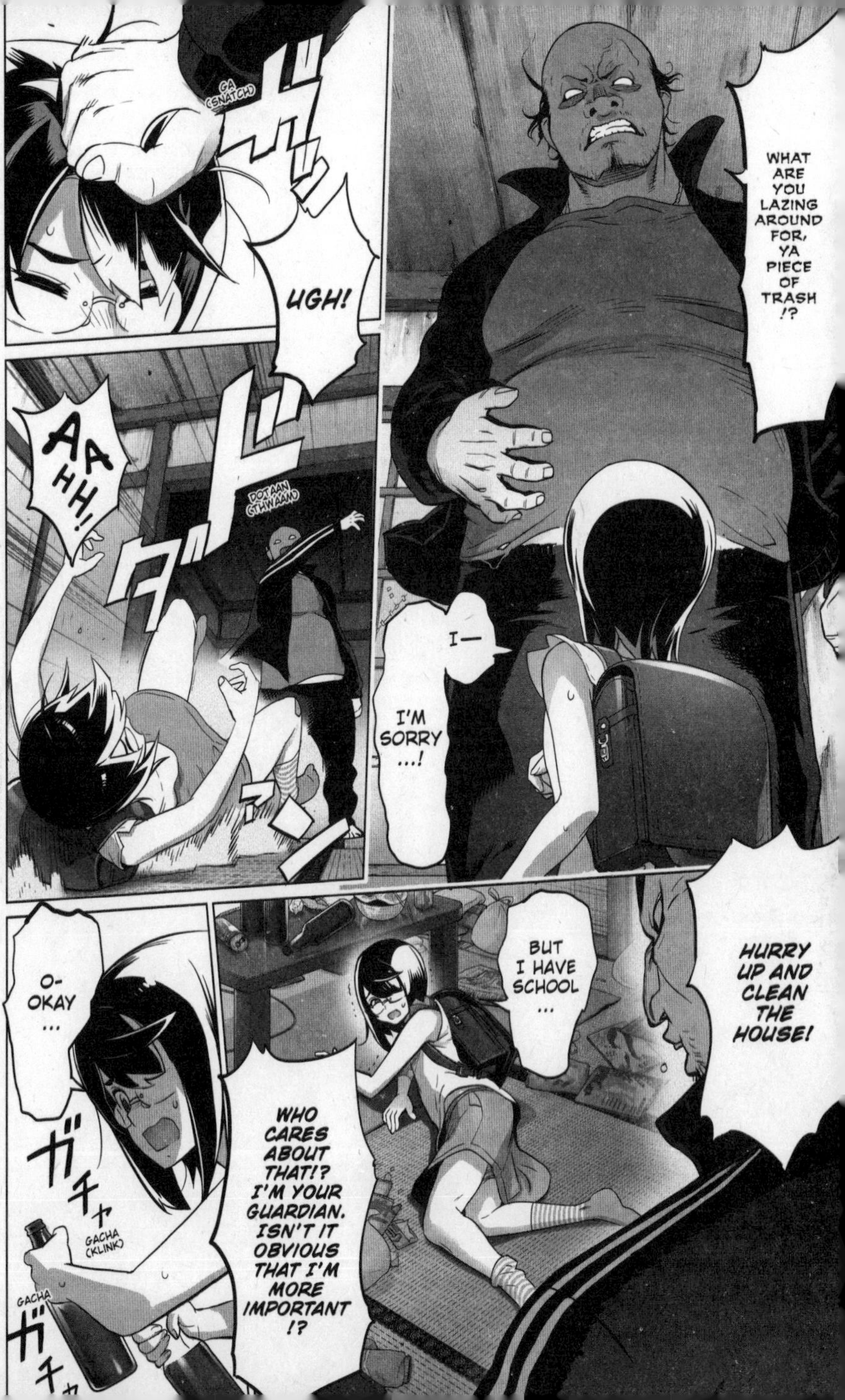
WHAT ARE YOU LAZING AROUND FOR, YA PIECE OF TRASH!?
I—
I'M SORRY...!
GA (SNATCH)
UGH!
AAHH!!
DOTAAN (THWAAM)
HURRY UP AND CLEAN THE HOUSE!
BUT I HAVE SCHOOL...
WHO CARES ABOUT THAT!? I'M YOUR GUARDIAN. ISN'T IT OBVIOUS THAT I'M MORE IMPORTANT!?
O-OKAY...
GACHA (KLINK)
GACHA

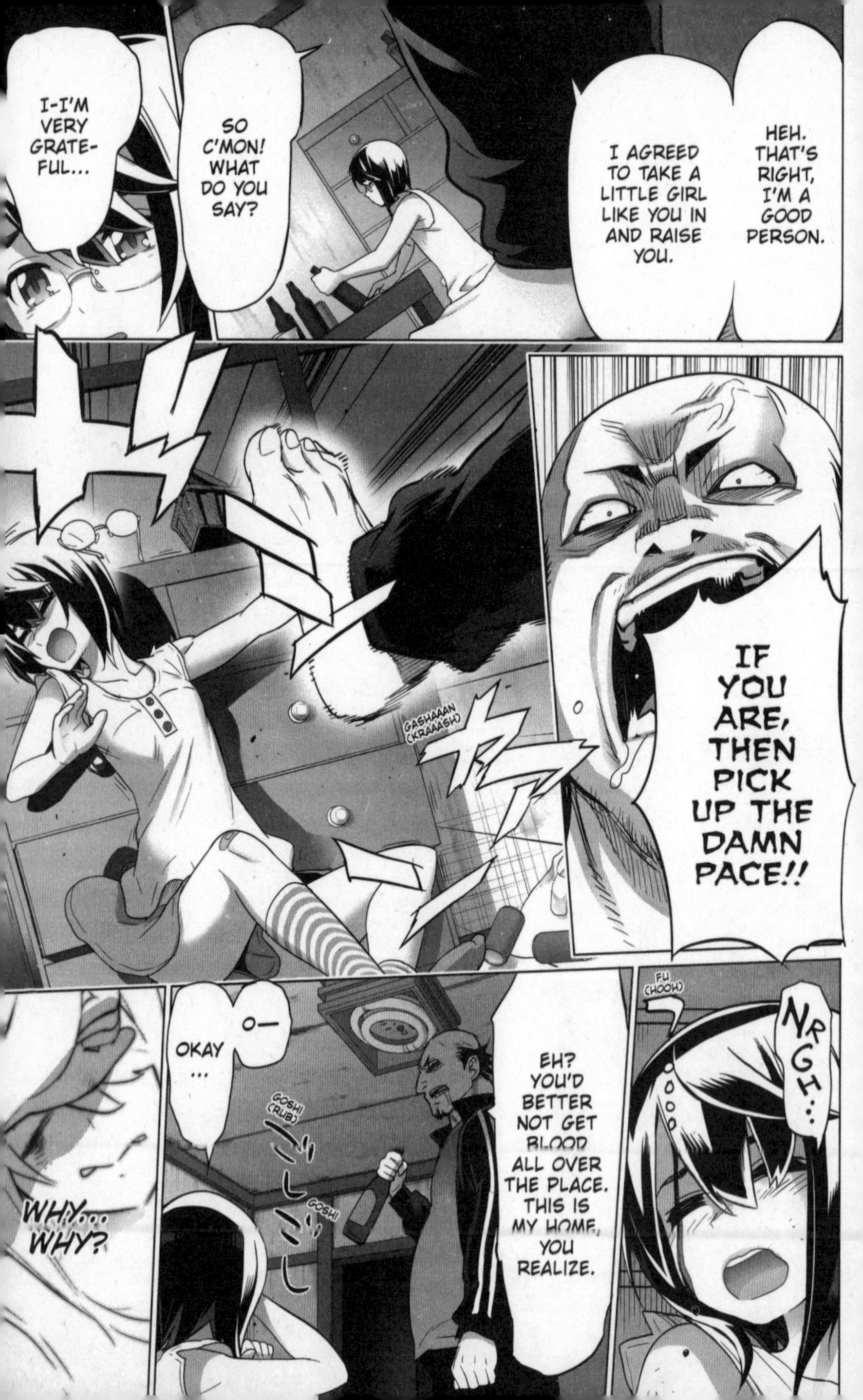
HEH. THAT'S RIGHT, I'M A GOOD PERSON.
I AGREED TO TAKE A LITTLE GIRL LIKE YOU IN AND RAISE YOU.
SO C'MON! WHAT DO YOU SAY?
I-I'M VERY GRATE-FUL...
IF YOU ARE, THEN PICK UP THE DAMN PACE!!
GASHAAAN (KRAAASH)
FU (HOOH)
NRGH...
EH? YOU'D BETTER NOT GET BLOOD ALL OVER THE PLACE. THIS IS MY HOME, YOU REALIZE.
GOSHI (RUB)
GOSHI
O— OKAY ...
WHY... WHY?

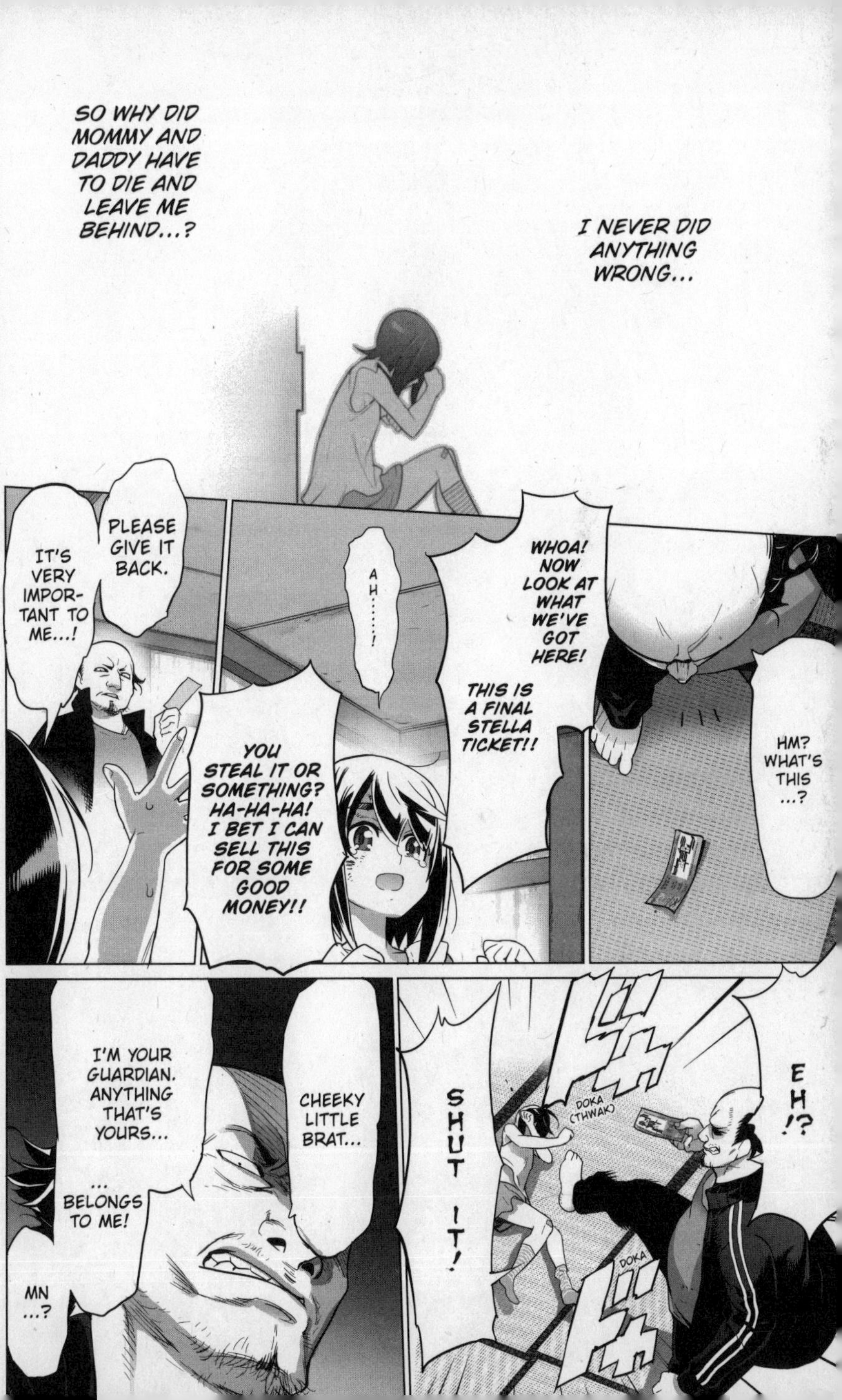
I NEVER DID ANYTHING WRONG...
SO WHY DID MOMMY AND DADDY HAVE TO DIE AND LEAVE ME BEHIND...?
HM? WHAT'S THIS ...?
WHOA! NOW LOOK AT WHAT WE'VE GOT HERE!
THIS IS A FINAL STELLA TICKET!!
AH......!
YOU STEAL IT OR SOMETHING? HA-HA-HA! I BET I CAN SELL THIS FOR SOME GOOD MONEY!!
PLEASE GIVE IT BACK.
IT'S VERY IMPOR-TANT TO ME...!
EH!?
SHUT IT!
DOKA (THWAK)
DOKA
CHEEKY LITTLE BRAT...
I'M YOUR GUARDIAN. ANYTHING THAT'S YOURS...
... BELONGS TO ME!
MN ...?

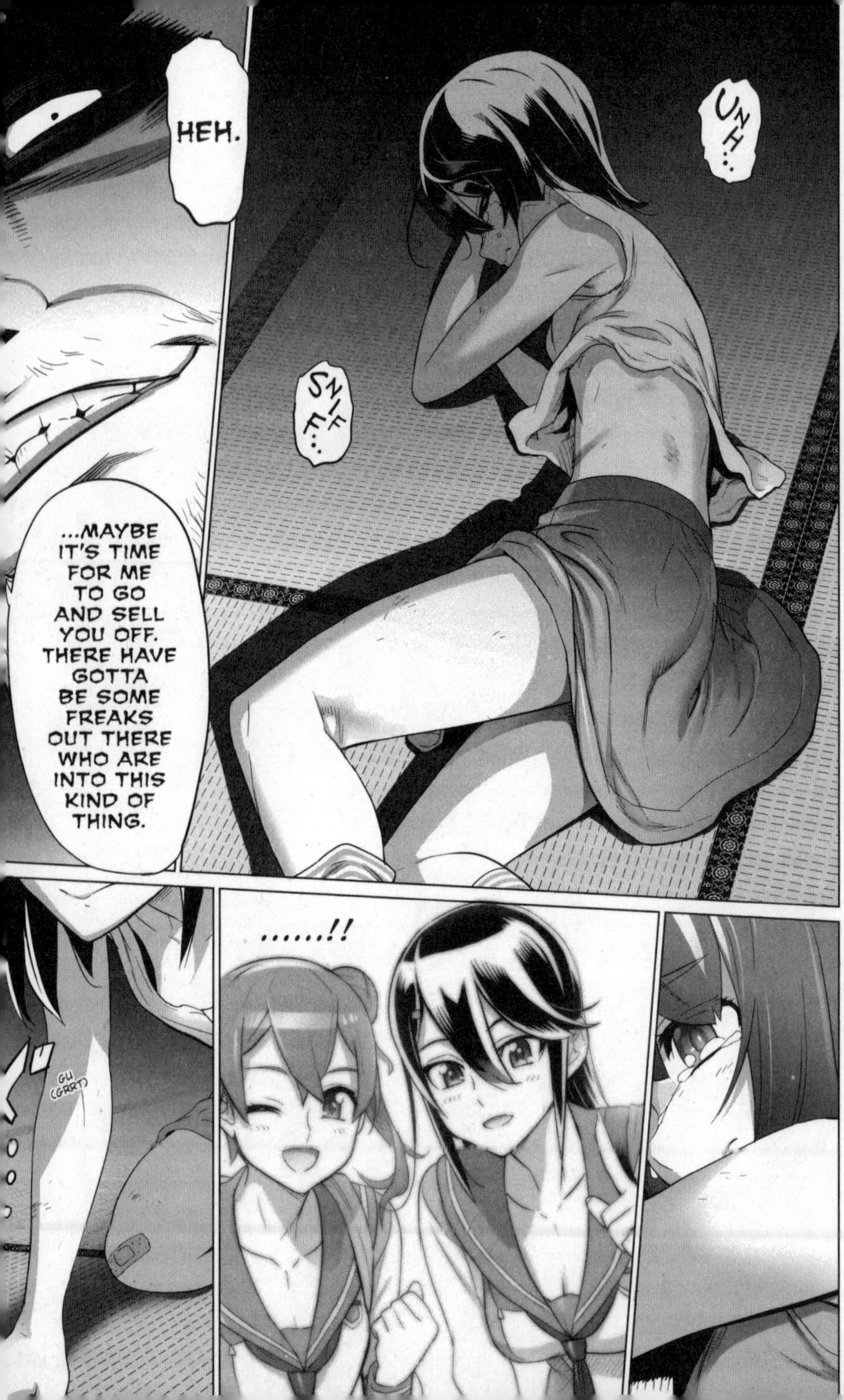
UNH...
SNIF...
HEH.
...MAYBE IT'S TIME FOR ME TO GO AND SELL YOU OFF. THERE HAVE GOTTA BE SOME FREAKS OUT THERE WHO ARE INTO THIS KIND OF THING.
......!!
GU (GRRT)

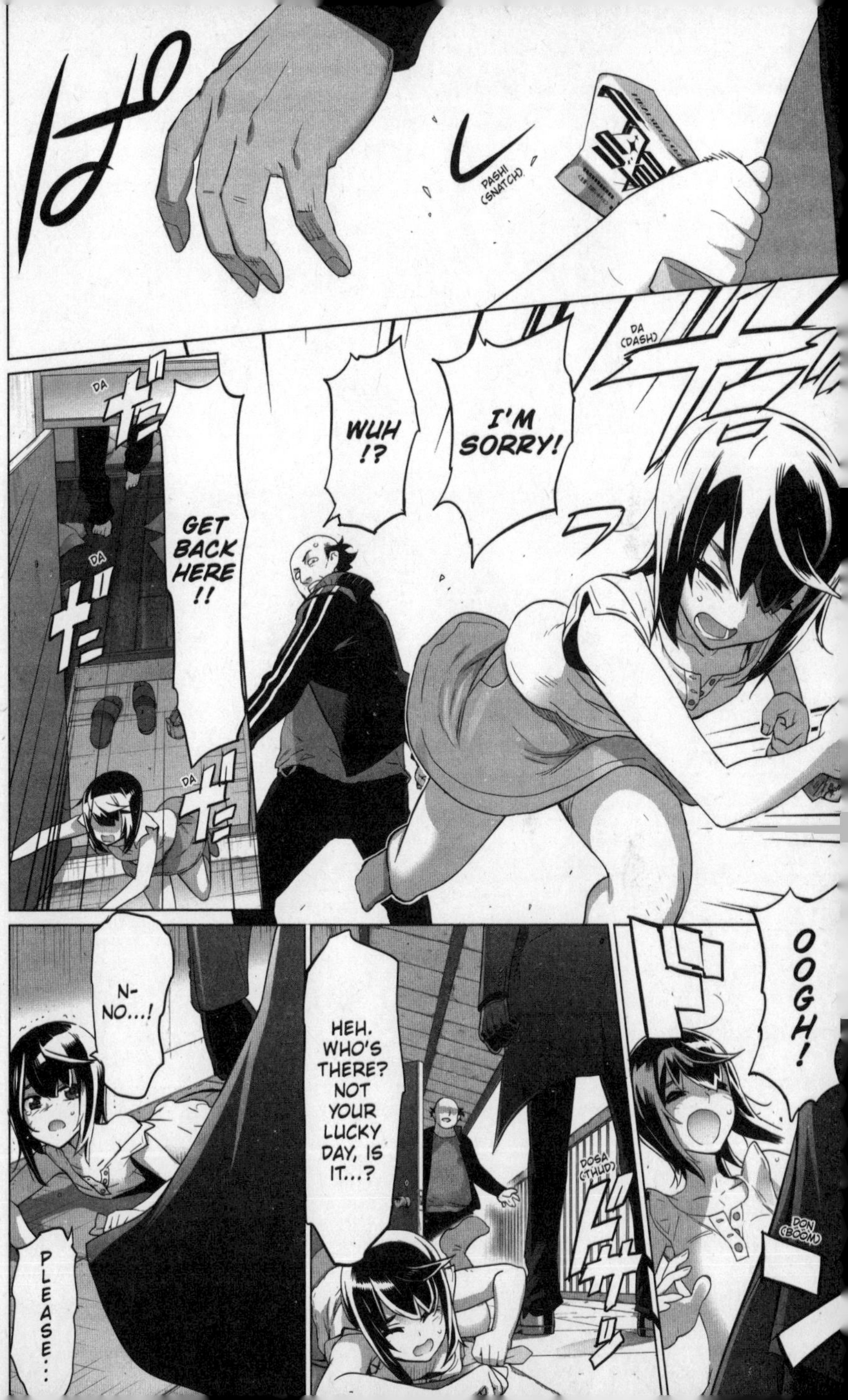
PASHI (SNATCH)
DA (DASH)
I'M SORRY!
WUH !?
GET BACK HERE !!
DA
DA
DA
OOGH!
DON (BOOM)
DOSA (THUD)
HEH. WHO'S THERE? NOT YOUR LUCKY DAY, IS IT...?
N- NO...!
PLEASE...

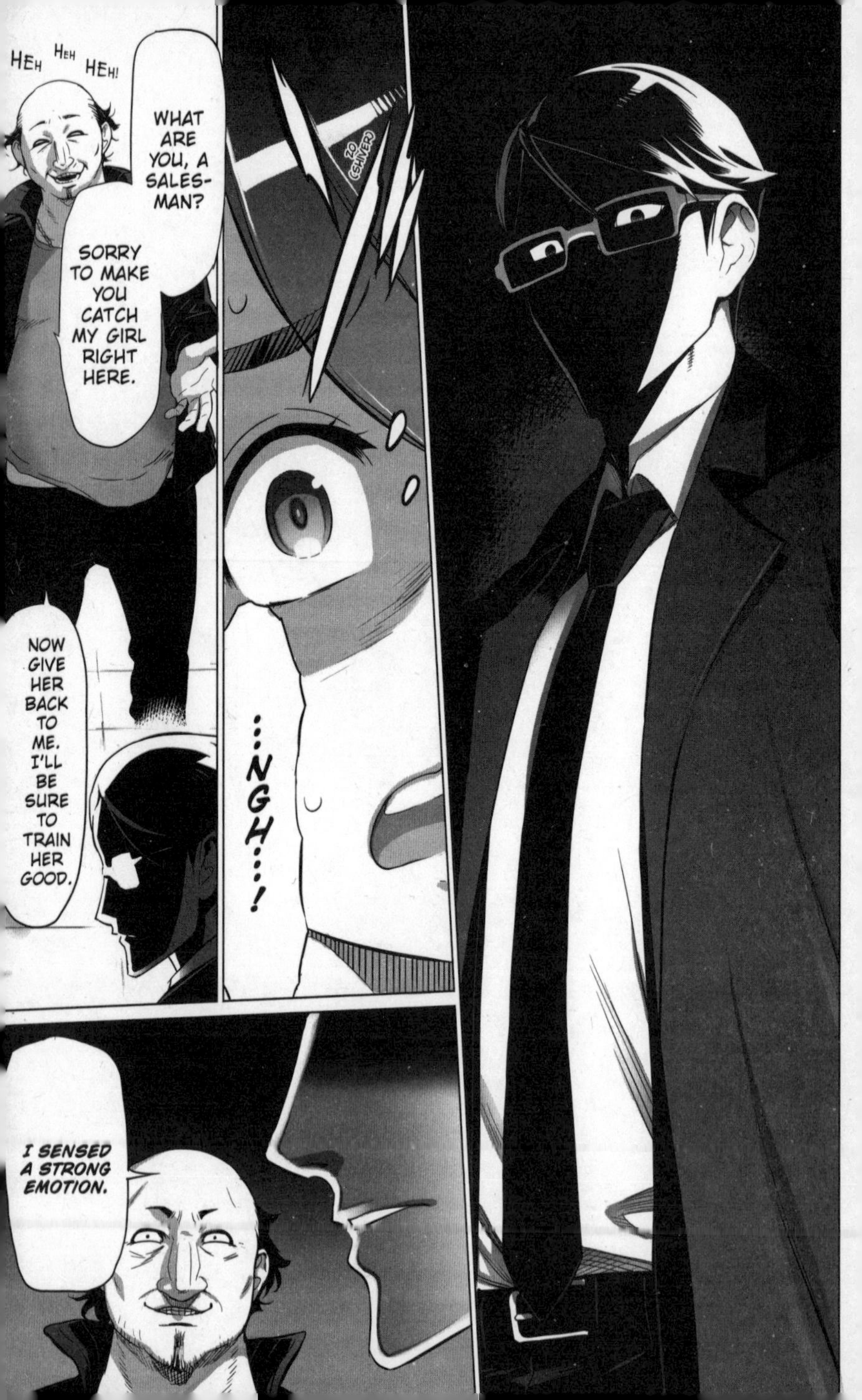
ZO (SHIVER)
...NGH...!
HEH HEH HEH!
WHAT ARE YOU, A SALES-MAN?
SORRY TO MAKE YOU CATCH MY GIRL RIGHT HERE.
NOW GIVE HER BACK TO ME. I'LL BE SURE TO TRAIN HER GOOD.
I SENSED A STRONG EMOTION.

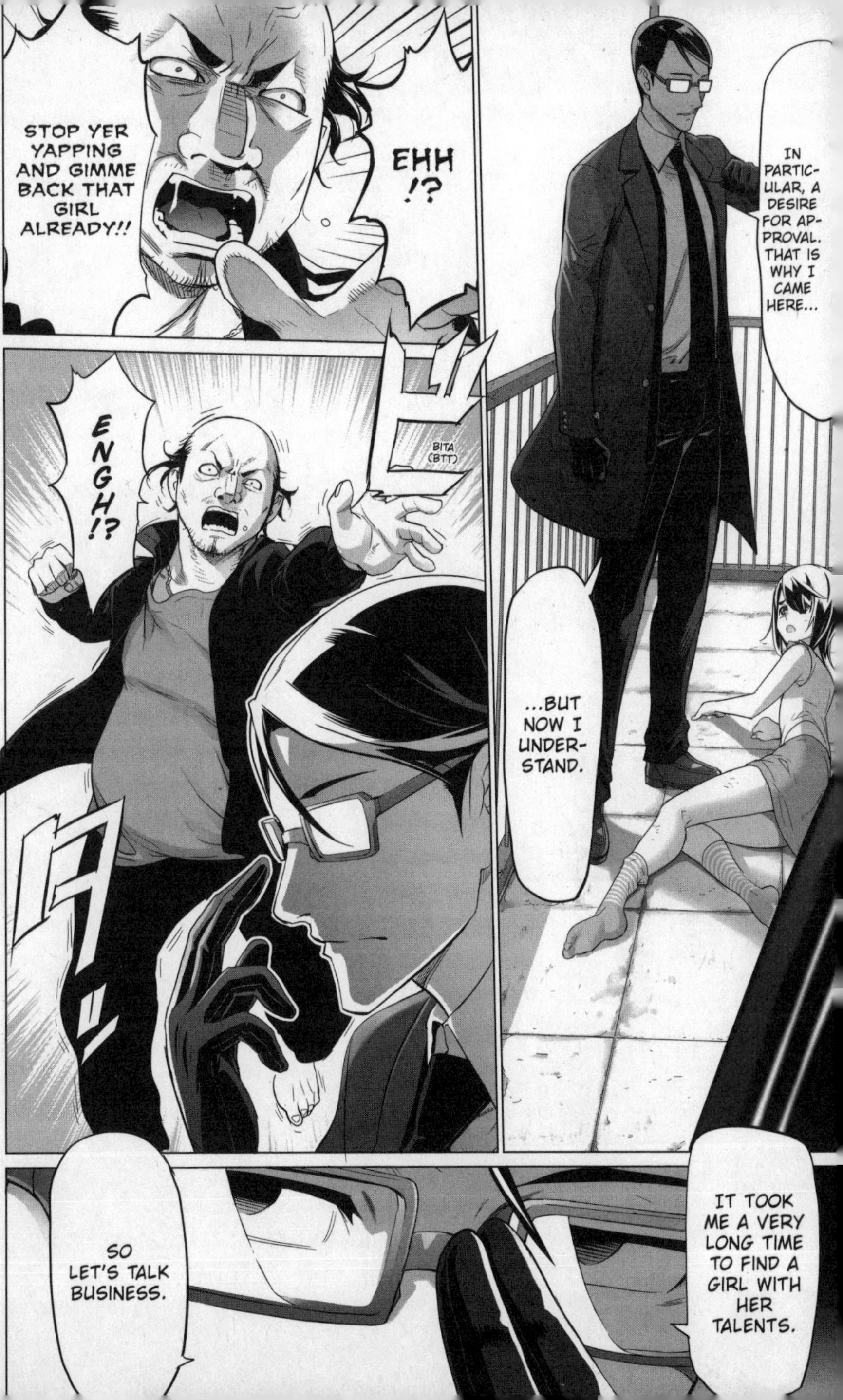
IN PARTICULAR, A DESIRE FOR APPROVAL. THAT IS WHY I CAME HERE...
...BUT NOW I UNDERSTAND.
STOP YER YAPPING AND GIMME BACK THAT GIRL ALREADY!!
EHH!?
ENGH!?
BITA (BTT)
IT TOOK ME A VERY LONG TIME TO FIND A GIRL WITH HER TALENTS.
SO LET'S TALK BUSINESS.

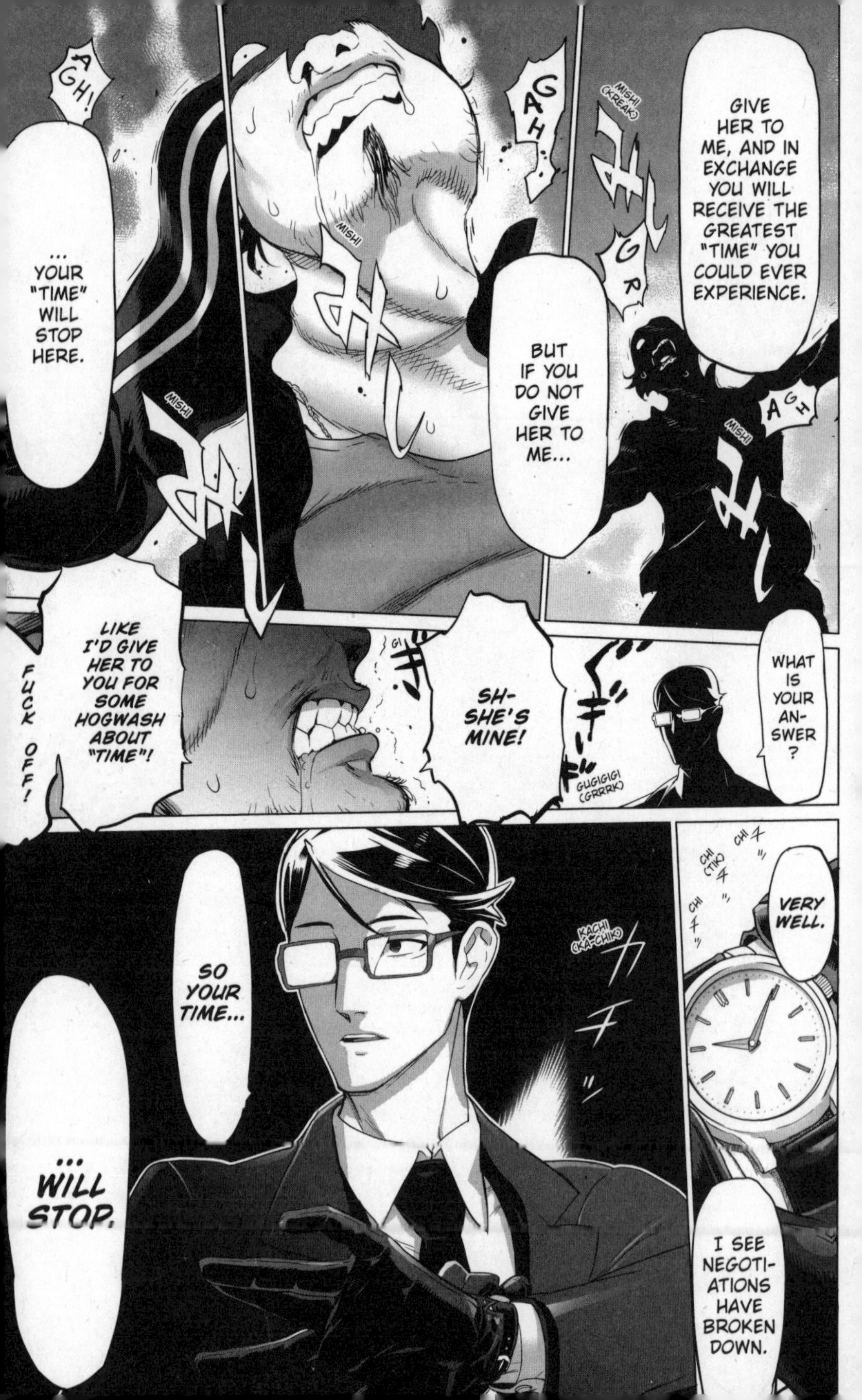
GIVE HER TO ME, AND IN EXCHANGE YOU WILL RECEIVE THE GREATEST "TIME" YOU COULD EVER EXPERIENCE.
MISHI (KREAK)
GAGH
GR
BUT IF YOU DO NOT GIVE HER TO ME...
AGH
MISHI
MISHI
AGH!
... YOUR "TIME" WILL STOP HERE.
MISHI
WHAT IS YOUR AN-SWER?
GUGIGIGI (GRRRK)
SH-SHE'S MINE!
GI
LIKE I'D GIVE HER TO YOU FOR SOME HOGWASH ABOUT "TIME"!
FUCK OFF!
CHI (TIK)
CHI
CHI
VERY WELL.
I SEE NEGOTI-ATIONS HAVE BROKEN DOWN.
KACHI (KA-CHIK)
SO YOUR TIME...
... WILL STOP.

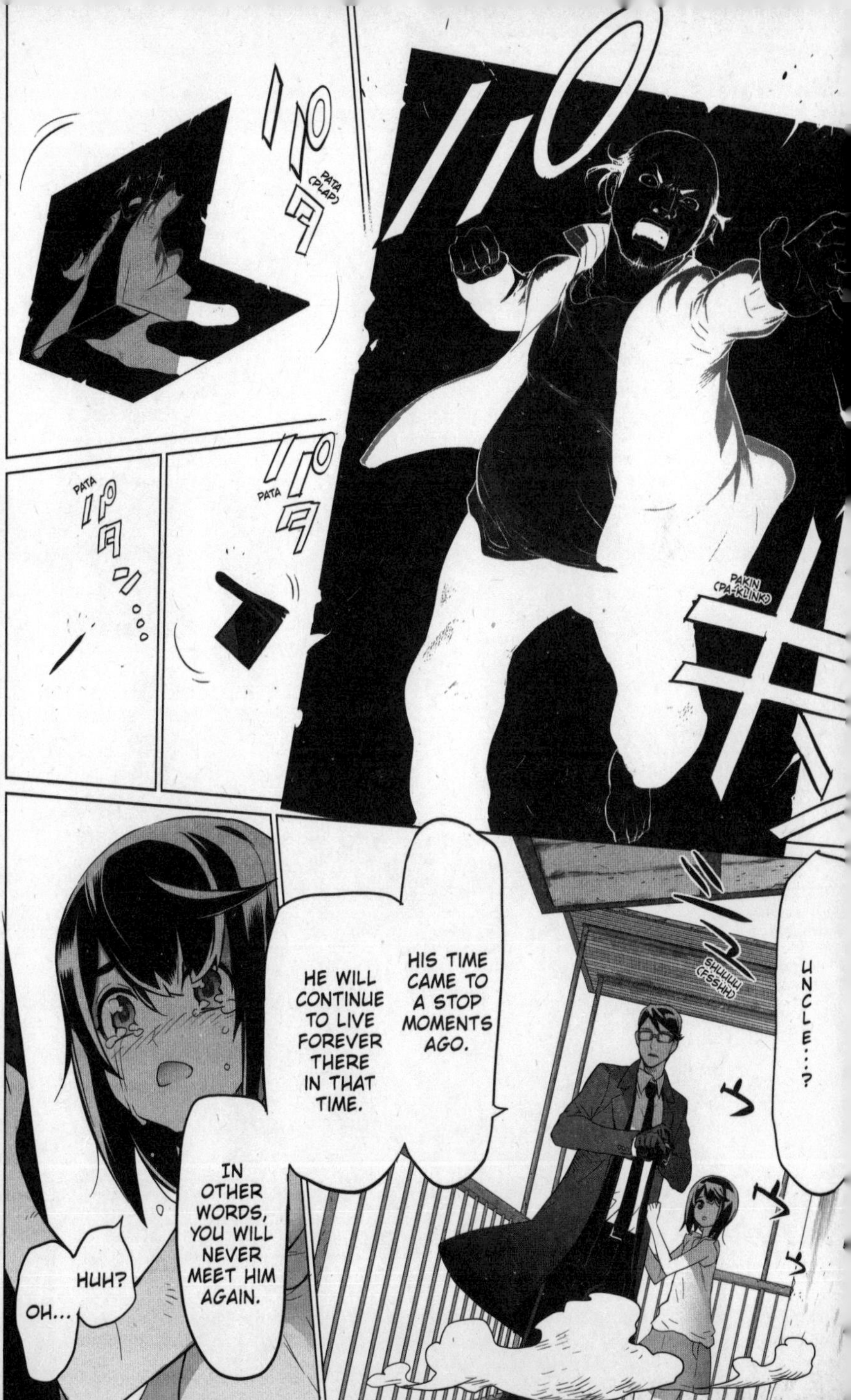
PAKIN (PA-KLINK)
PATA (PLAP)
PATA
PATA
UNCLE...?
SHUUUU (FSSH)
HIS TIME CAME TO A STOP MOMENTS AGO.
HE WILL CONTINUE TO LIVE FOREVER THERE IN THAT TIME.
IN OTHER WORDS, YOU WILL NEVER MEET HIM AGAIN.
HUH?
OH...

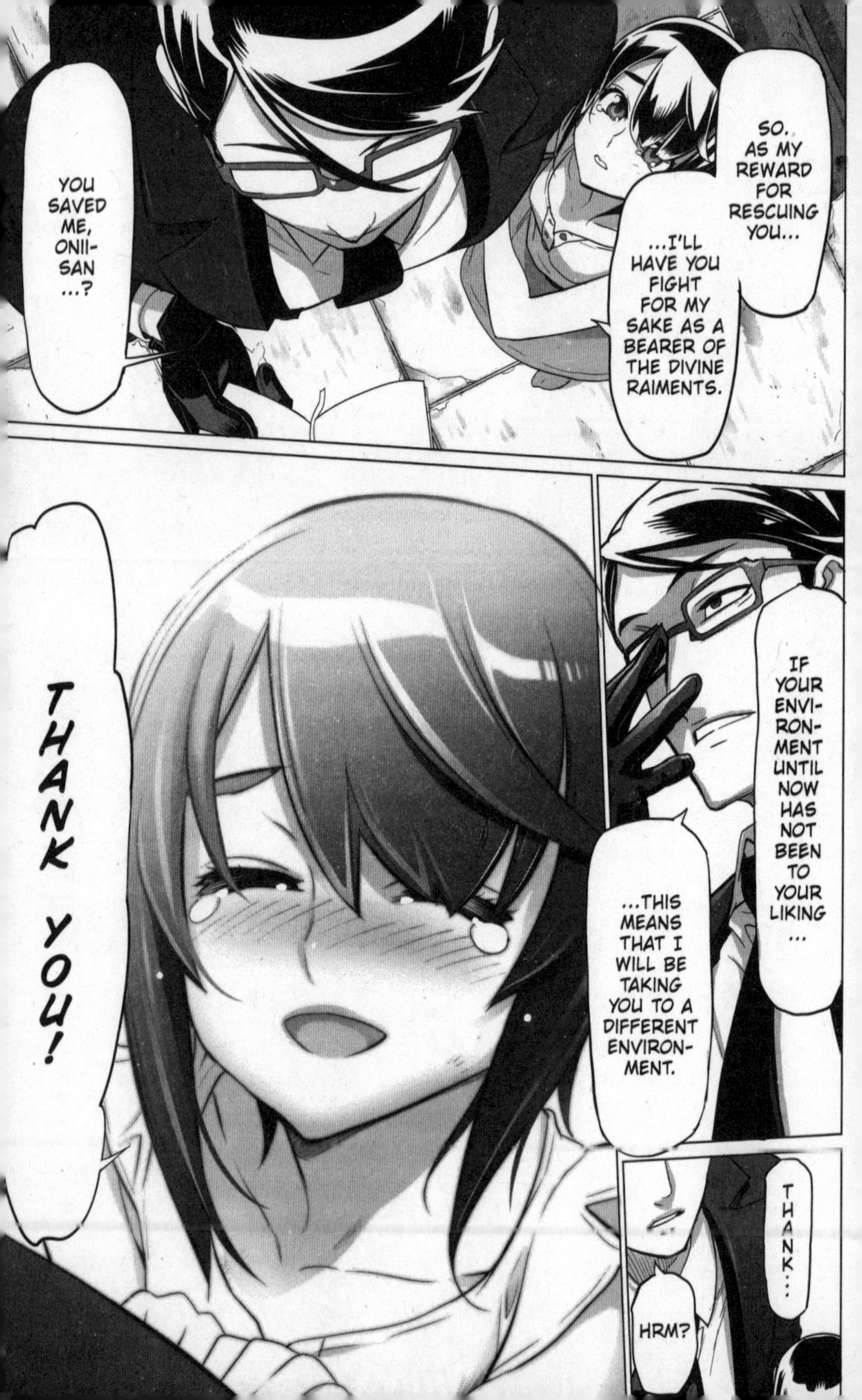
SO. AS MY REWARD FOR RESCUING YOU...
...I'LL HAVE YOU FIGHT FOR MY SAKE AS A BEARER OF THE DIVINE RAIMENTS.
YOU SAVED ME, ONII-SAN ...?
IF YOUR ENVIRONMENT UNTIL NOW HAS NOT BEEN TO YOUR LIKING...
...THIS MEANS THAT I WILL BE TAKING YOU TO A DIFFERENT ENVIRONMENT.
THANK...
HRM?
THANK YOU!

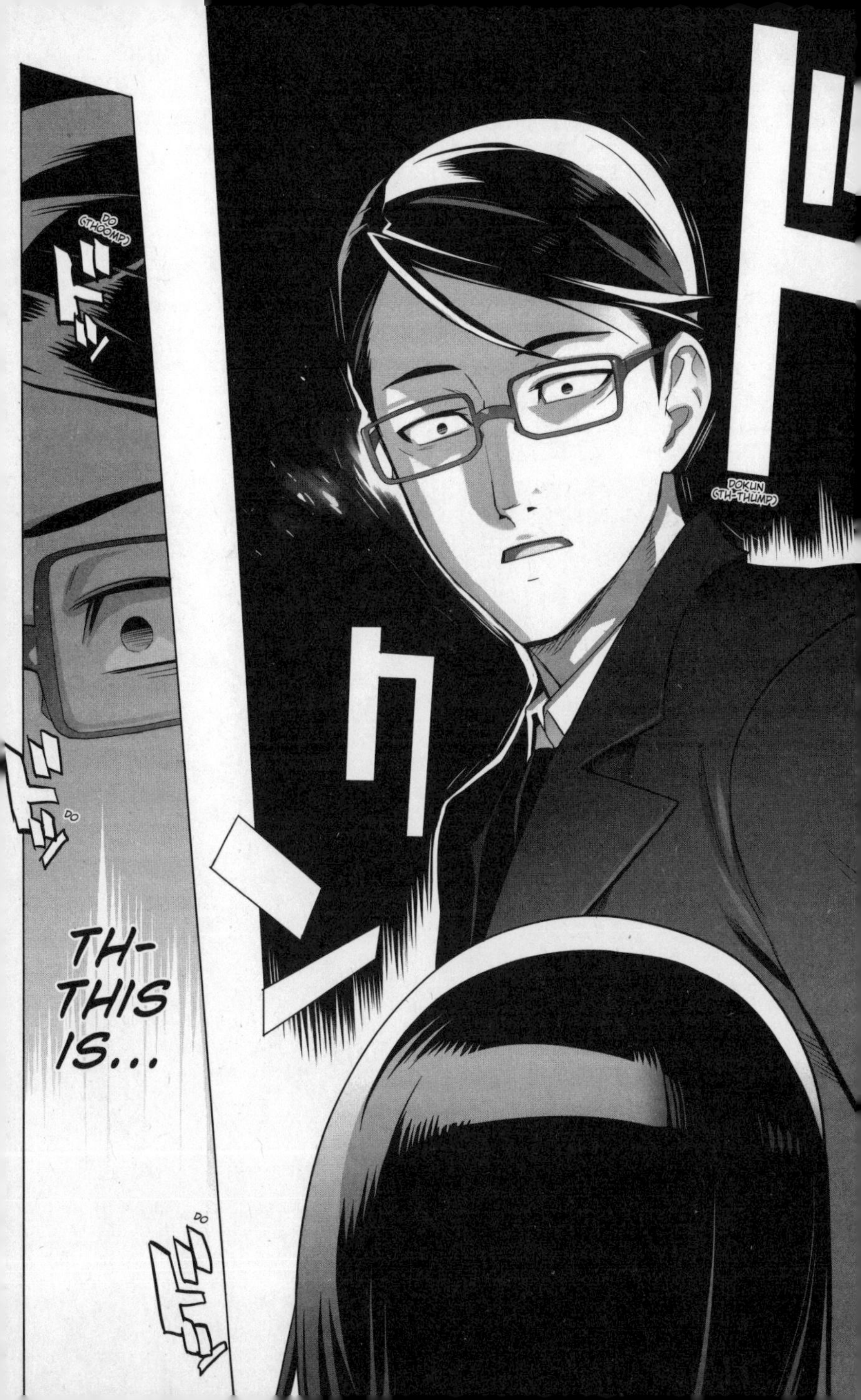
DOKUN (TH-THUMP)
DO (THOOMP)
DO
TH-THIS IS...
DO

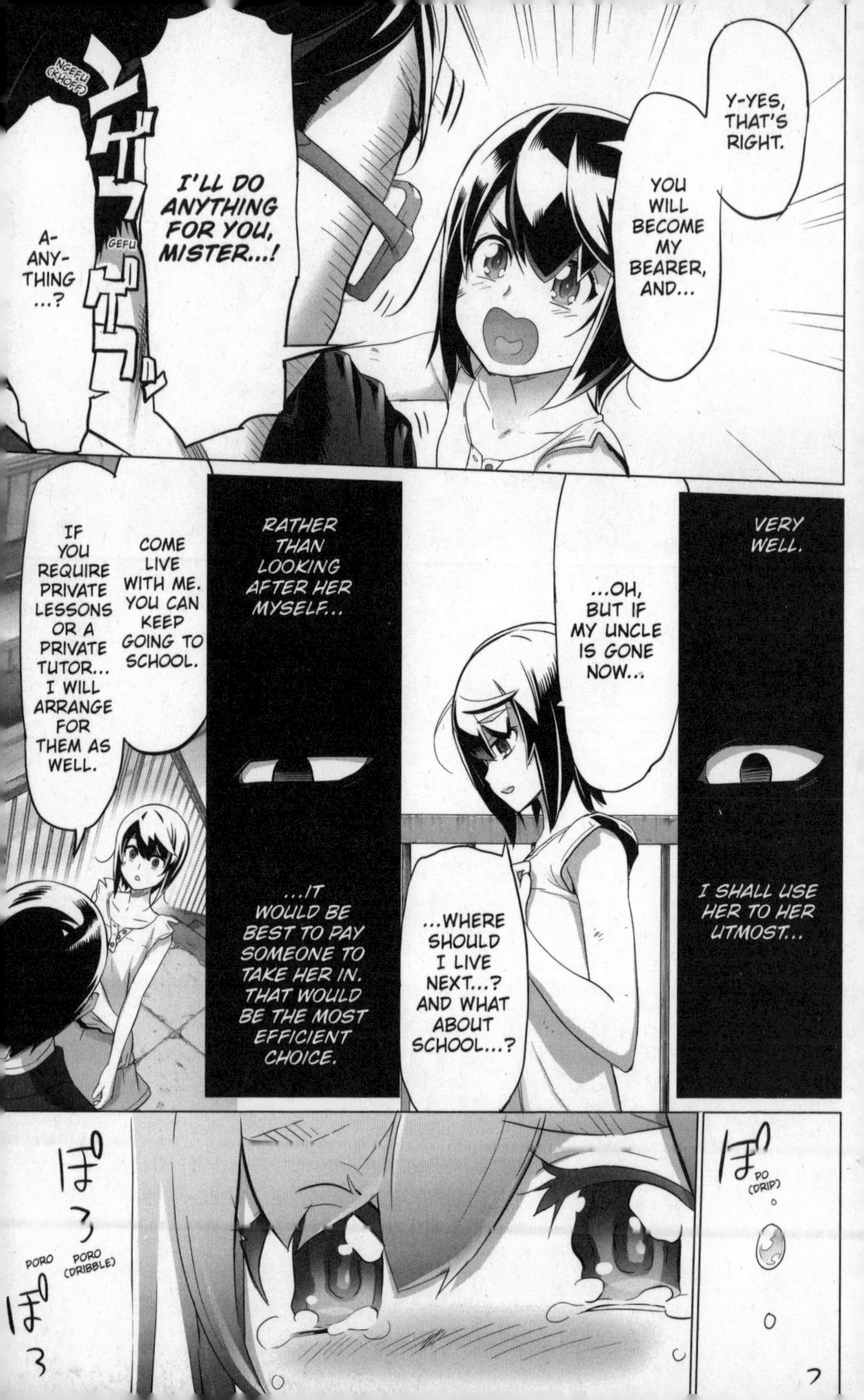
Y-YES, THAT'S RIGHT.
YOU WILL BECOME MY BEARER, AND...
I'LL DO ANYTHING FOR YOU, MISTER...!
A-ANYTHING...?
NGEFU (KHOFF)
GEFU
VERY WELL.
I SHALL USE HER TO HER UTMOST...
...OH, BUT IF MY UNCLE IS GONE NOW...
...WHERE SHOULD I LIVE NEXT...? AND WHAT ABOUT SCHOOL...?
RATHER THAN LOOKING AFTER HER MYSELF...
...IT WOULD BE BEST TO PAY SOMEONE TO TAKE HER IN. THAT WOULD BE THE MOST EFFICIENT CHOICE.
COME LIVE WITH ME. YOU CAN KEEP GOING TO SCHOOL.
IF YOU REQUIRE PRIVATE LESSONS OR A PRIVATE TUTOR... I WILL ARRANGE FOR THEM AS WELL.
PO (DRIP)
PORO PORO (DRIBBLE)

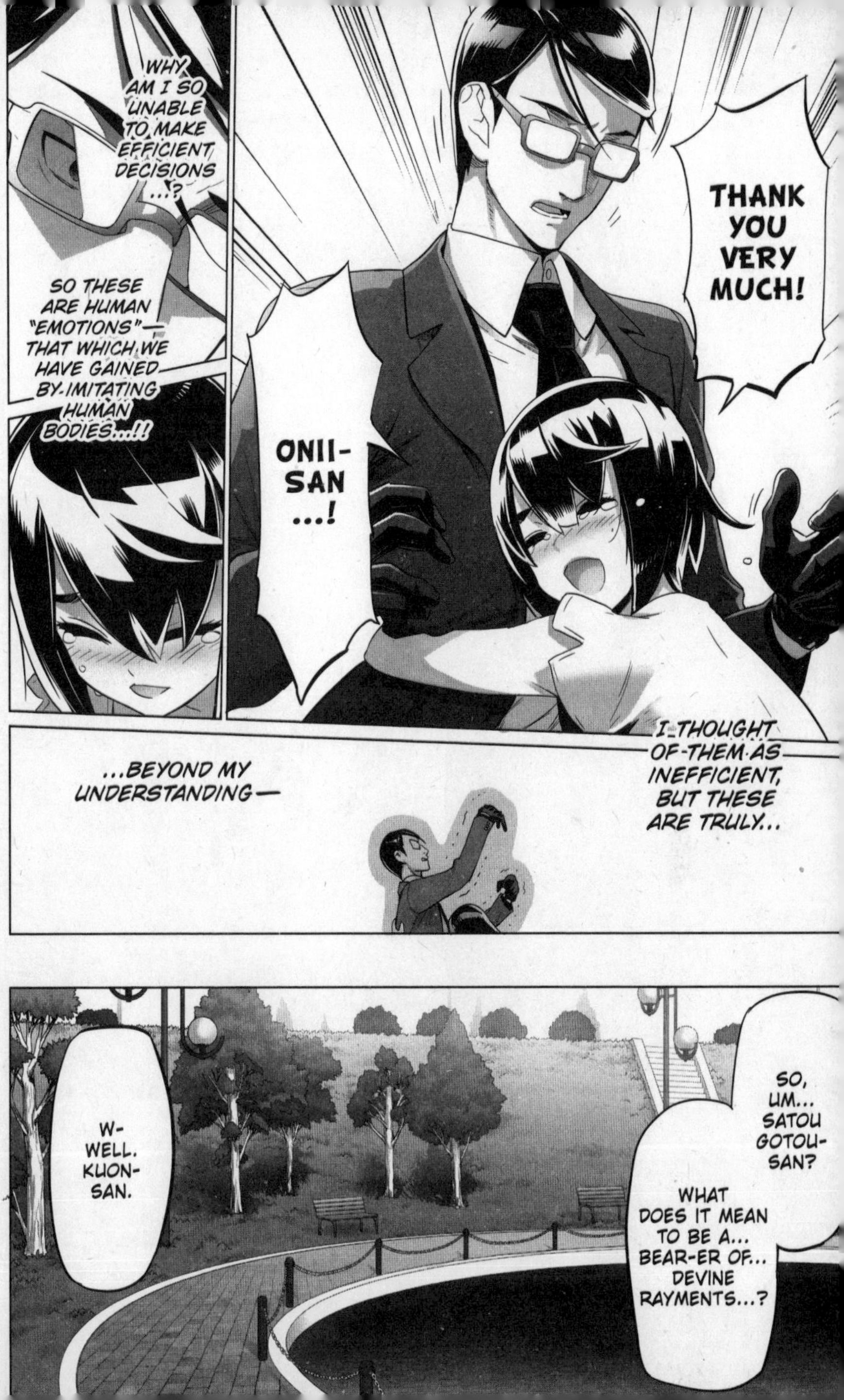
THANK YOU VERY MUCH!
ONII-SAN...!
WHY AM I SO UNABLE TO MAKE EFFICIENT DECISIONS...?
SO THESE ARE HUMAN "EMOTIONS"—THAT WHICH WE HAVE GAINED BY IMITATING HUMAN BODIES...!!
I THOUGHT OF THEM AS INEFFICIENT, BUT THESE ARE TRULY...
...BEYOND MY UNDERSTANDING—
SO, UM... SATOU GOTOU-SAN?
WHAT DOES IT MEAN TO BE A... BEAR-ER OF... DEVINE RAYMENTS...?
W-WELL. KUON-SAN.

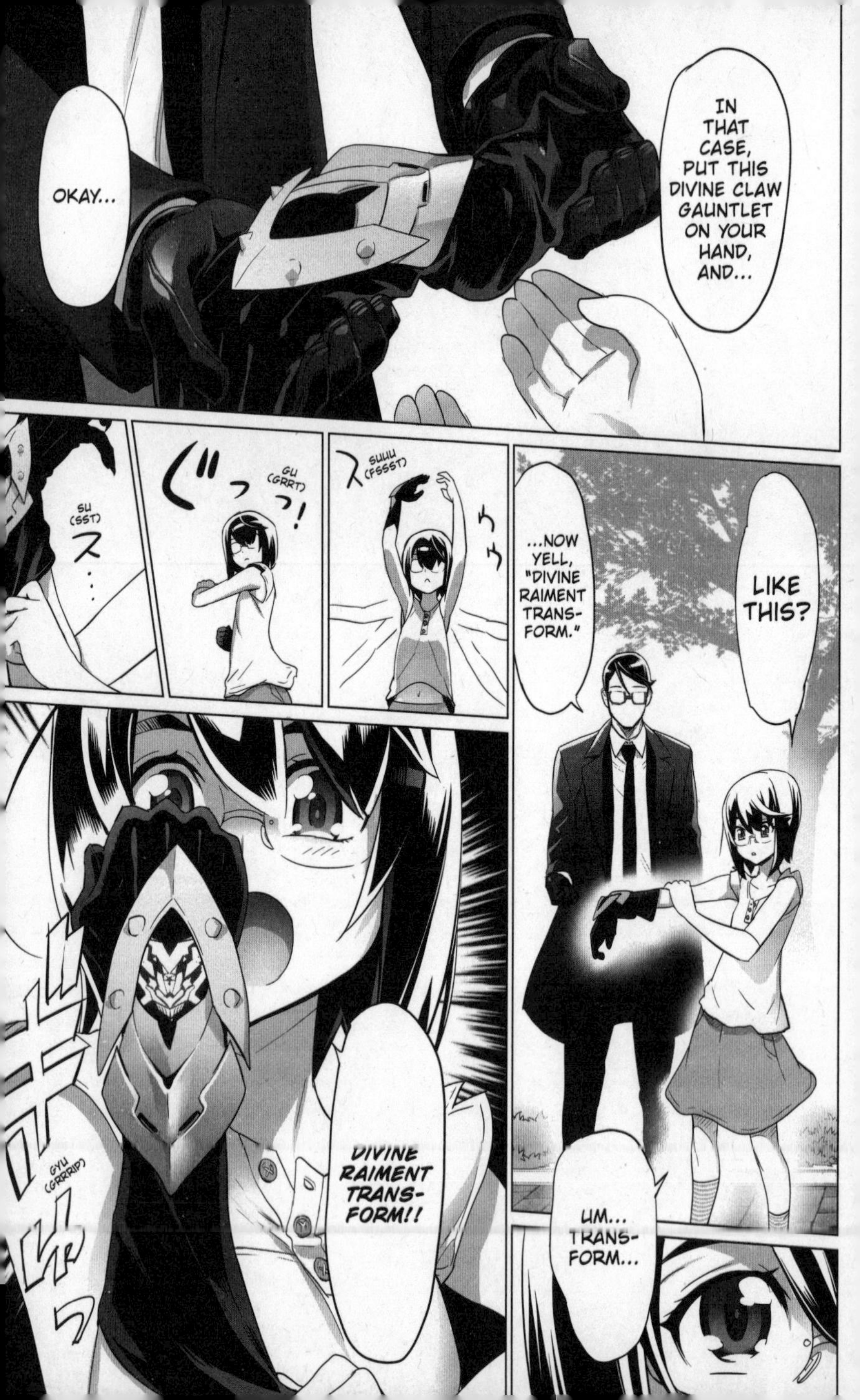
IN THAT CASE, PUT THIS DIVINE CLAW GAUNTLET ON YOUR HAND, AND...
OKAY...
LIKE THIS?
...NOW YELL, "DIVINE RAIMENT TRANS-FORM."
UM... TRANS-FORM...
ス SUUU (FSSST)
ぐっっ! GU (GRRT)
SU (SST) ス...
DIVINE RAIMENT TRANS-FORM!!
GYU (GRRRIP)

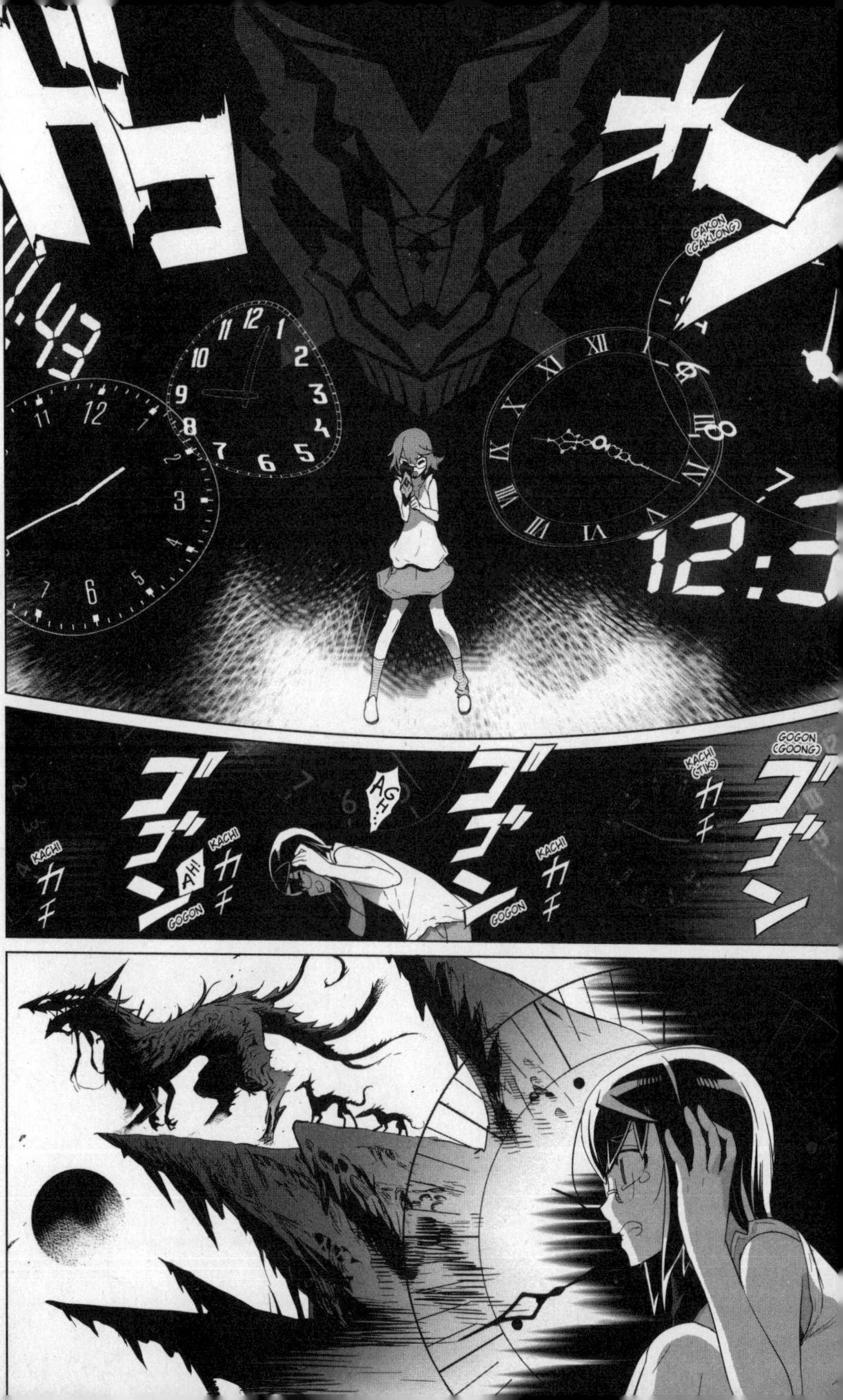
GAKON (GAKWONG)
GOGON (GOONG)
ゴゴン
KACHI (TIK)
カチ
KACHI
カチ
ゴゴン
GOGON
AGH...
KACHI
カチ
AH!
ゴゴン
GOGON
KACHI
カチ

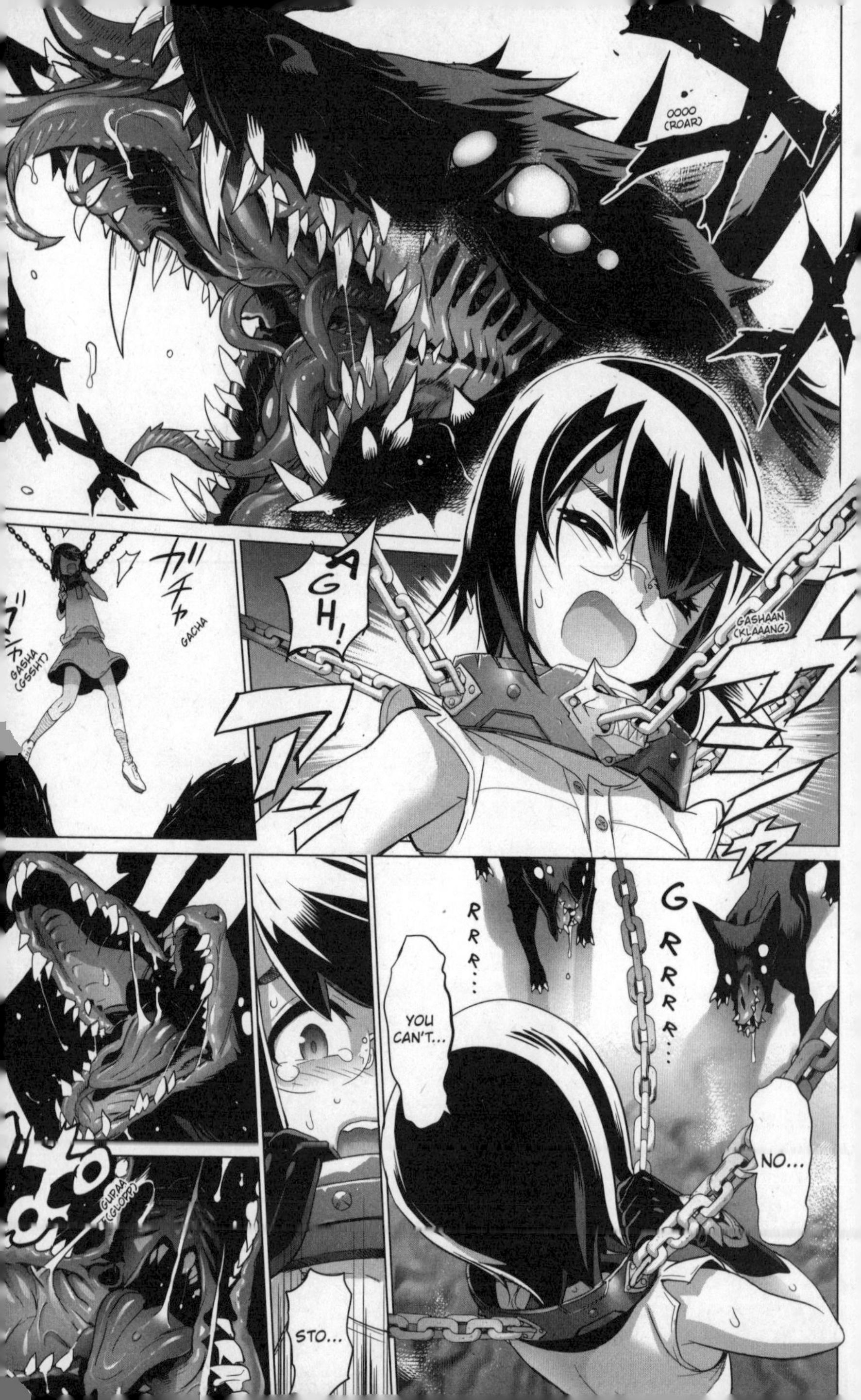
OOOO
(ROAR)
GASHAAN
(KLAAANG)
AGH!
ガチャ
GACHA
GASHA
(GSSHT)
GRRRR...
RRR...
YOU CAN'T...
NO...
STO...
GUPAA
(GLOPP)

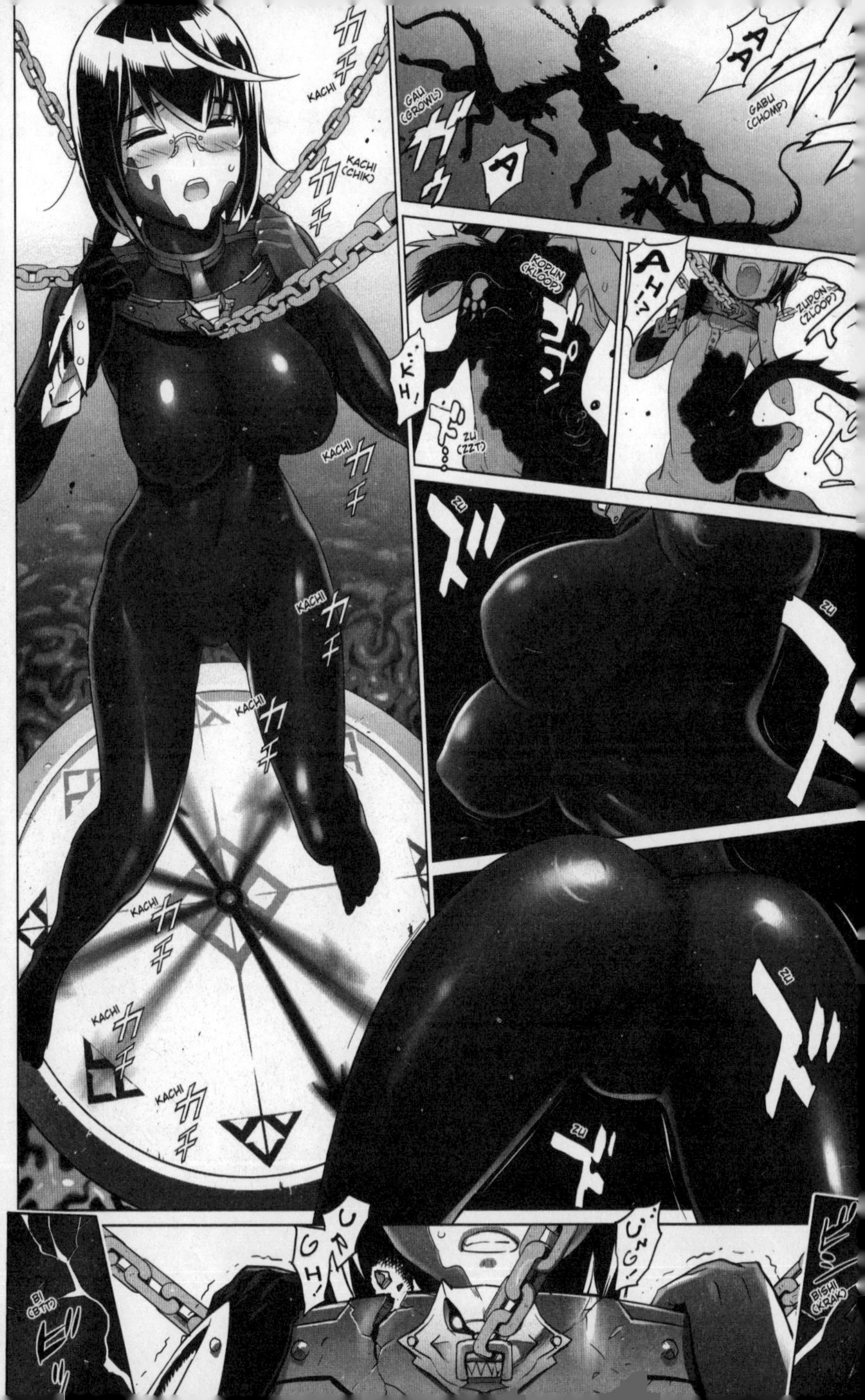
AAA
GABU (CHOMP)
A
GAU (GROWL)
AH!?
ZUPON (ZLOOP)
KOPUN (KLOOP)
...KH!
ZU (ZZZT)
ZU
ZU
ZU
ZU
KACHI
KACHI (CHIK)
KACHI
KACHI
KACHI
KACHI
KACHI
KACHI
BISHI (KRAK)
UNG!
URGH!
BI

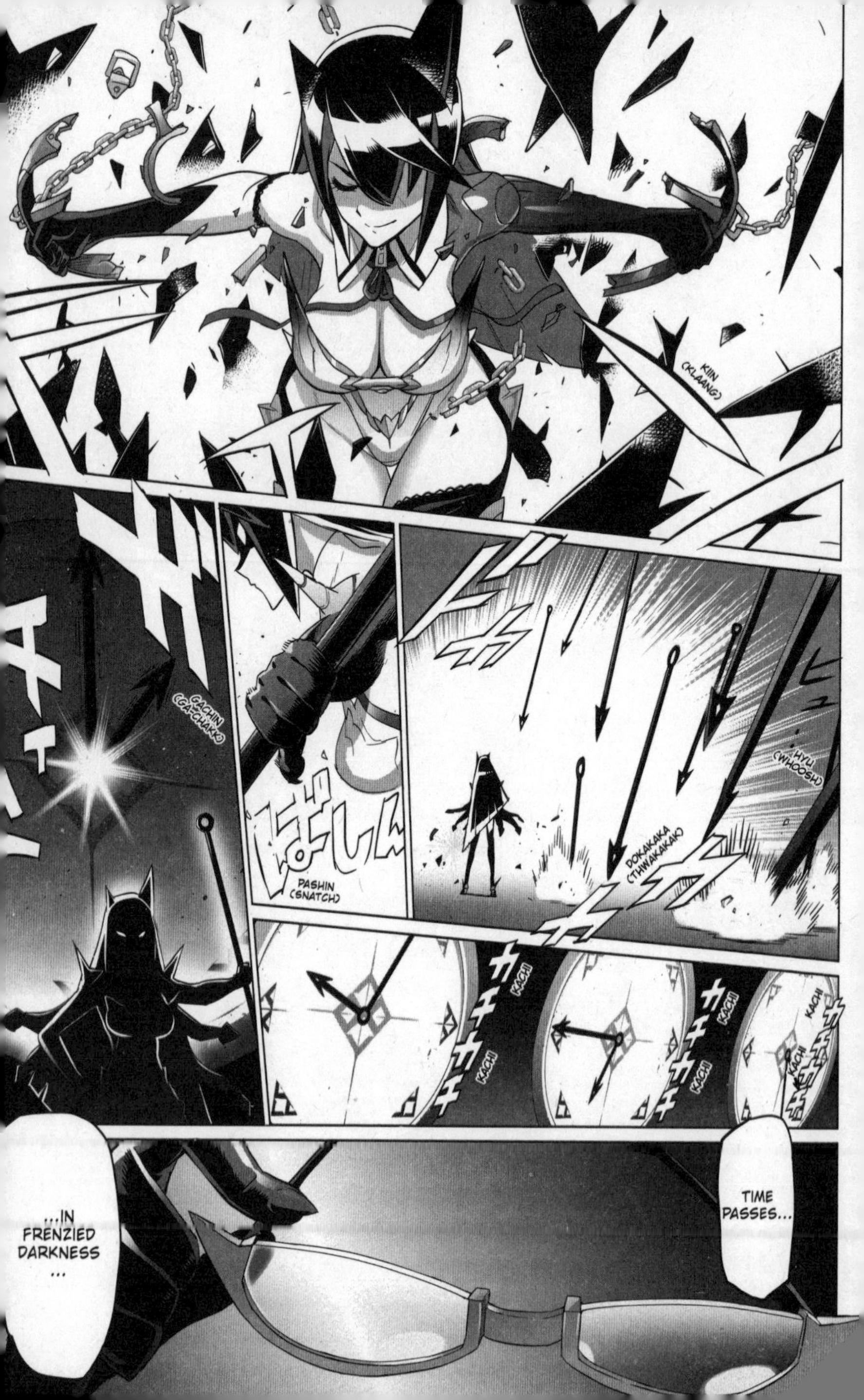
KIIN (KLAANG)
HYU (WHOOSH)
DOKAKAKA (THWAKAKAK)
ぱしん
PASHIN (SNATCH)
KACHI
KACHI
KACHI
KACHI
KACHI
KACHI
GACHIN (GACHAK)
TIME PASSES...
...IN FRENZIED DARKNESS...

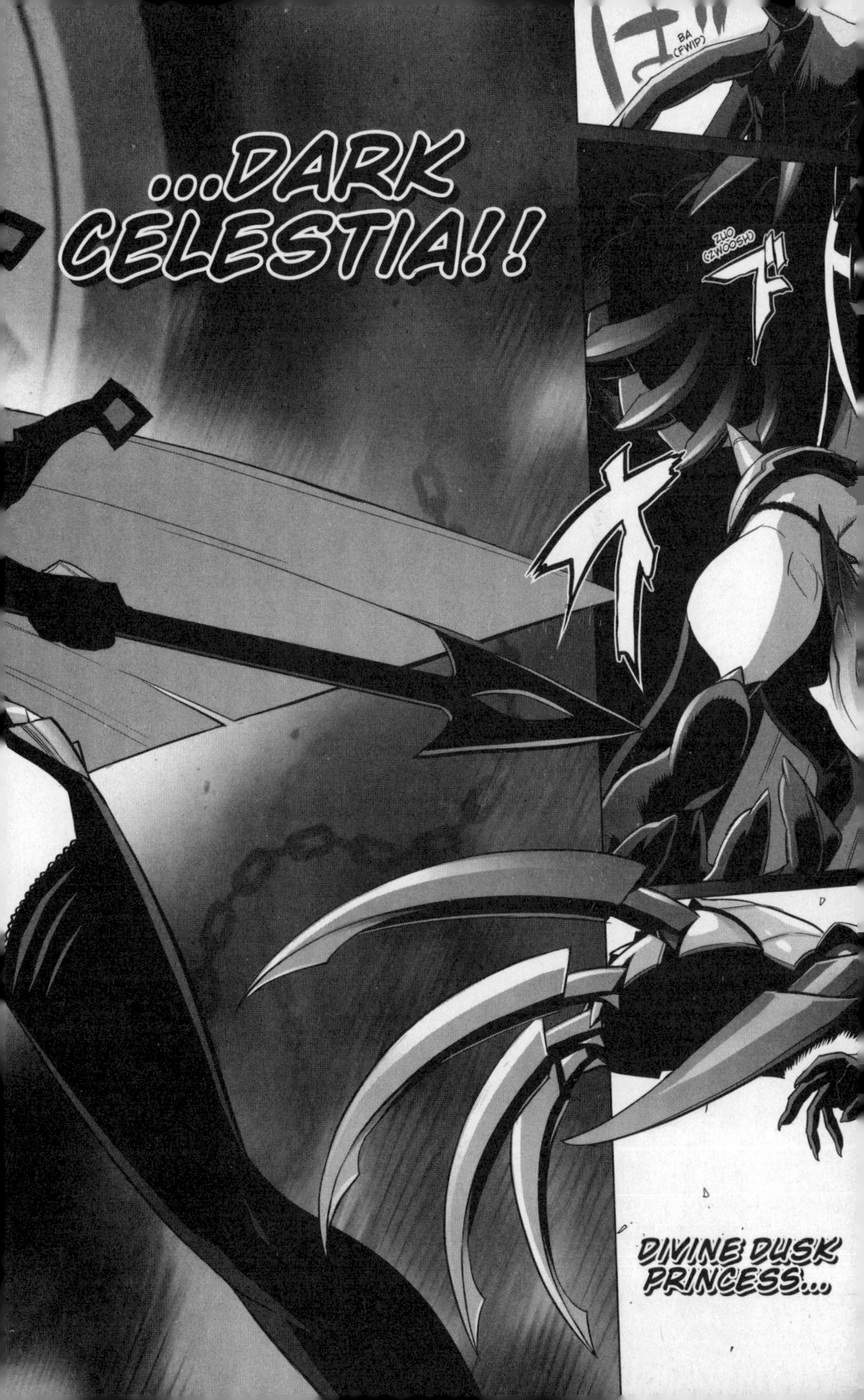
BA (FWIP)
ZUO (ZWOOSH)
DIVINE DUSK PRINCESS...
...DARK CELESTIA!!

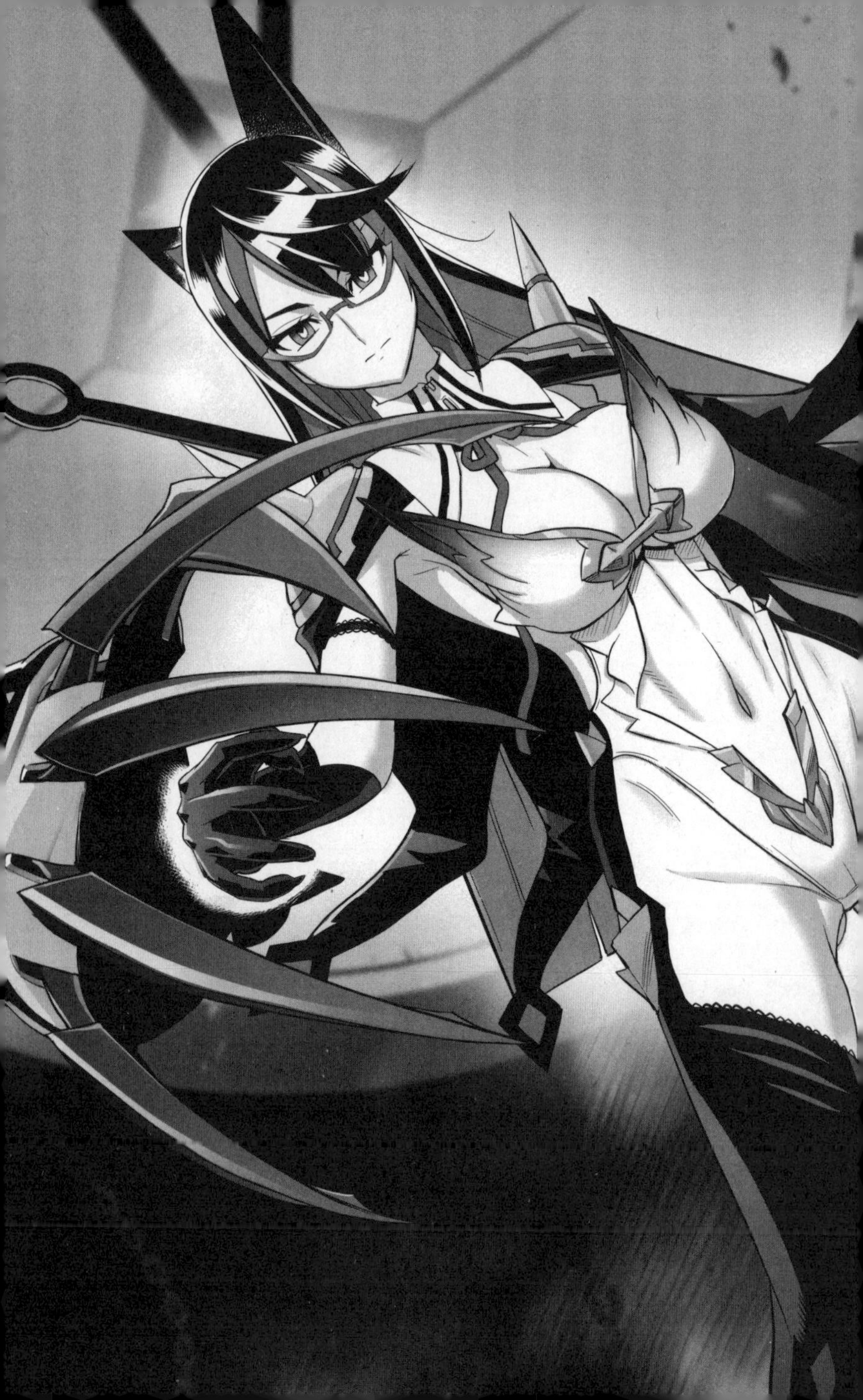

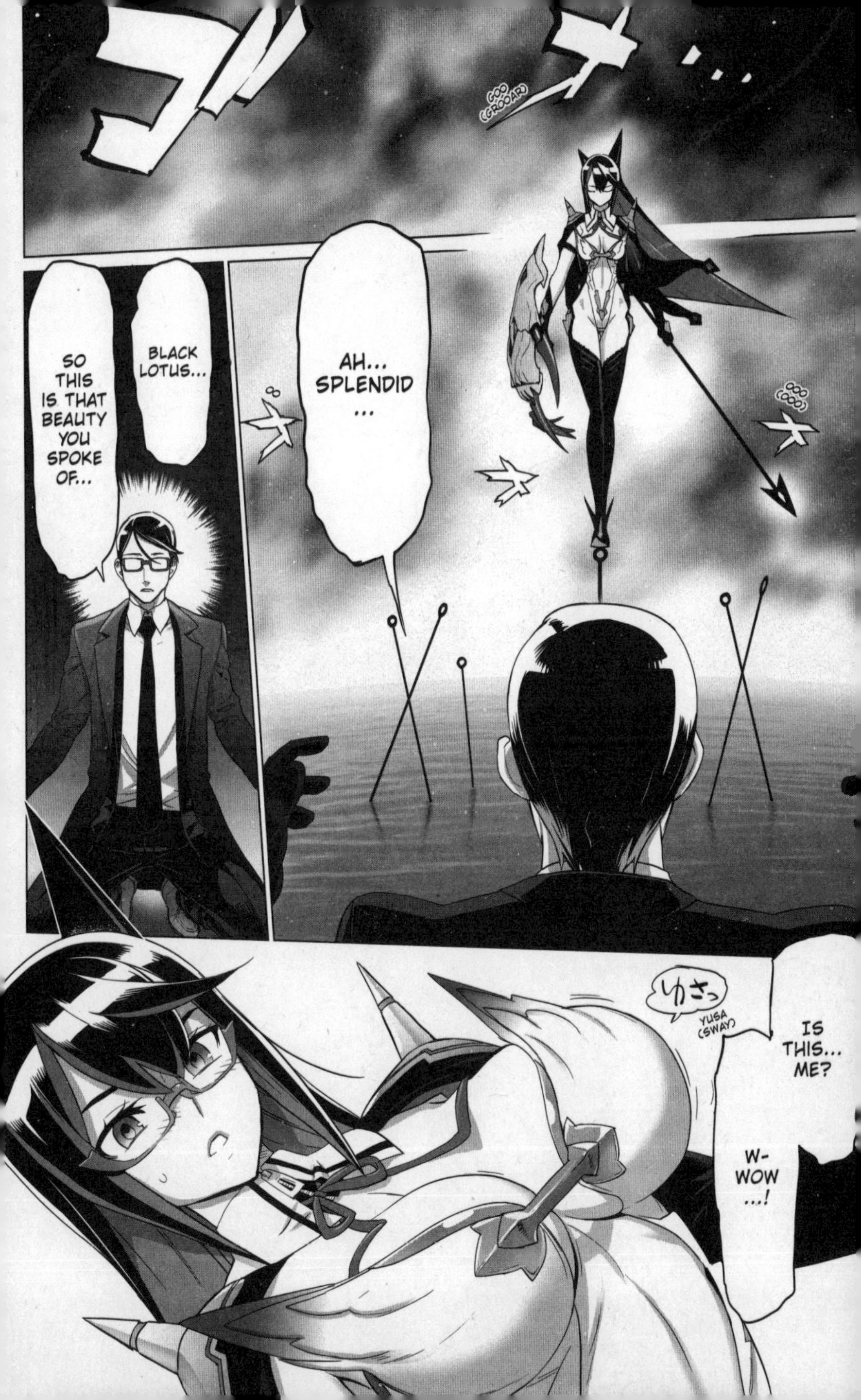
GOO (GROOAR)
GOO (GOO)
AH... SPLENDID ...
BLACK LOTUS...
SO THIS IS THAT BEAUTY YOU SPOKE OF...
ゆさっ
YUSA (SWAY)
IS THIS... ME?
W-WOW ...!

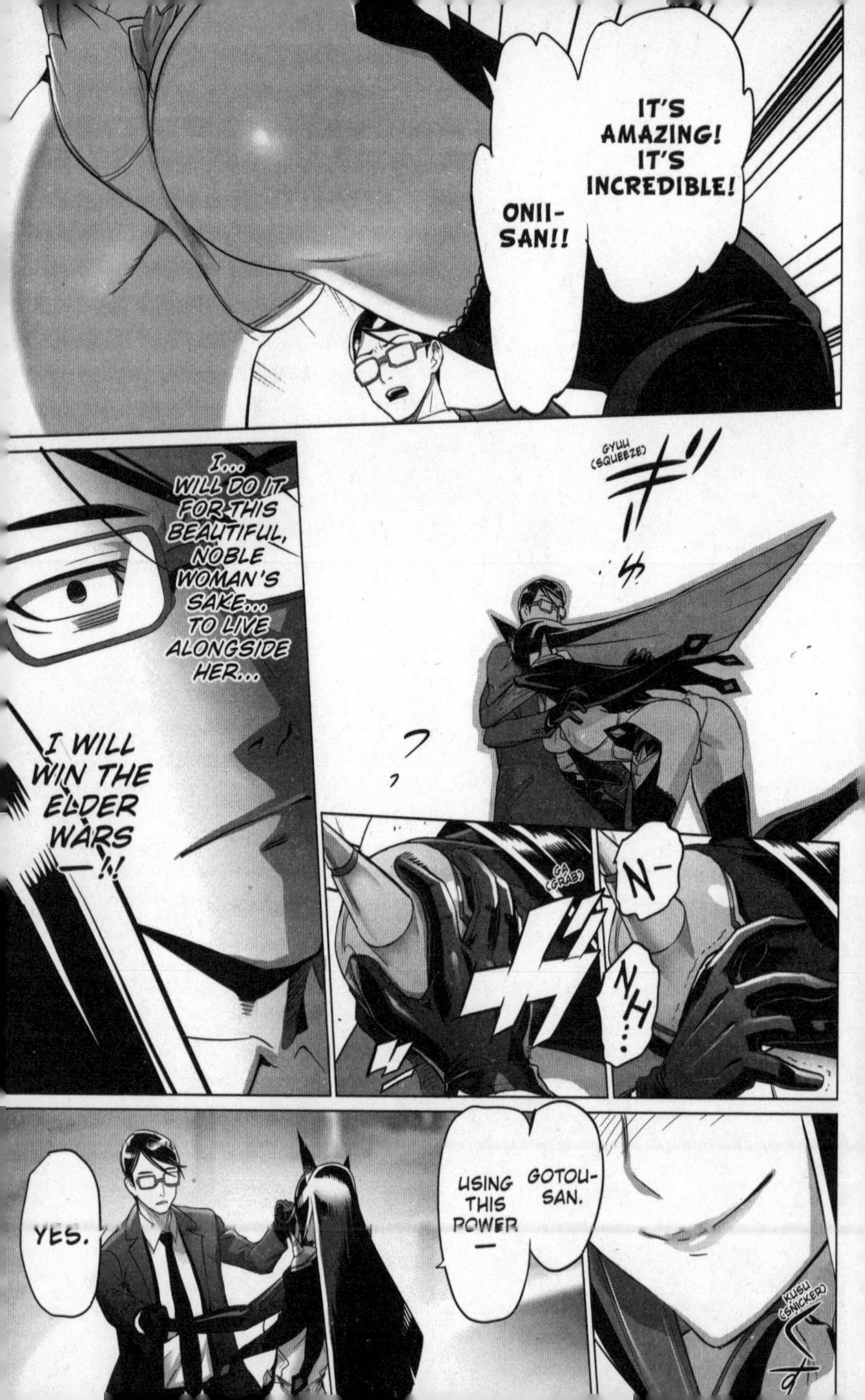
IT'S AMAZING! IT'S INCREDIBLE!
ONII-SAN!!
GYUU (SQUEEZE)
N-
NH...
GA (GRAB)
I... WILL DO IT FOR THIS BEAUTIFUL, NOBLE WOMAN'S SAKE... TO LIVE ALONGSIDE HER...
I WILL WIN THE ELDER WARS—!!
KUSU (SNICKER)
GOTOU-SAN.
USING THIS POWER—
YES.

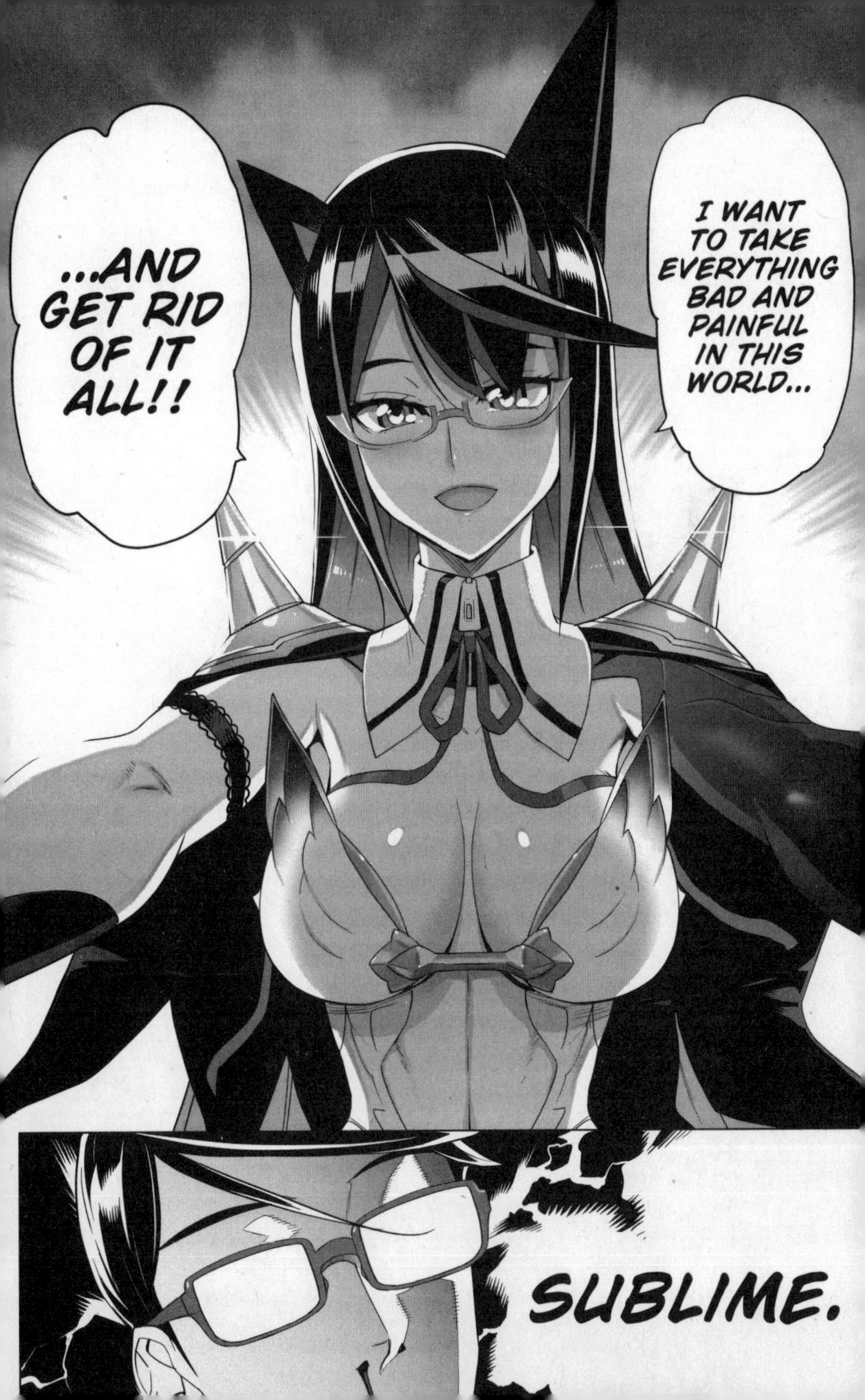
I WANT TO TAKE EVERYTHING BAD AND PAINFUL IN THIS WORLD...
...AND GET RID OF IT ALL!!
SUBLIME.